Praise for *Romans: Verse by Verse*

"Grant Osborne's commentary on Romans reflects everything we have come to expect from a scholar who is one of the deans of evangelical scholarship. Osborne's exegesis of Romans, which he rightly says is Paul's most important letter, is marked by clarity, exegetical rigor, and yet also has a pastoral tone. We can be grateful to receive the fruit of Osborne's scholarship, which reflects his many years of study, writing, and teaching. Students, pastors, and all those who desire to understand Romans will be helped by Osborne's contribution."

—**Thomas R. Schreiner**, professor of New Testament,
The Southern Baptist Theological Seminary

"Grant Osborne is one of my favorite expositors. In this commentary, he explains the meaning of every verse of the great book of Romans. Sometimes he introduces ongoing debates over some passages, but he never lets that detract from the task of getting his readers to grasp the meaning of the text. When necessary, Osborne rounds off his exposition by referring to other passages of Scripture, giving us a fuller biblical teaching on a theme. Throughout, he makes a conscientious effort to show how the teaching of Romans applies in daily life. These are the elements that make for great exposition, and here we see exposition at its best."

—**Ajith Fernando**, teaching director, Youth for Christ, Sri Lanka

"In this latest offering in the Osborne New Testament Commentaries, Grant Osborne tackles Paul's densest epistle with the clarity and insight that characterizes all of his scholarship. In an epistle where every passage is hotly debated, Osborne graciously presents differing opinions while also clearly articulating what he considers to be the best interpretation."

—**H. Daniel Zacharias**, assistant professor of New Testament studies,
Acadia Divinity College

T0366948

Praise for the Osborne New Testament Commentaries

"With this new series, readers will have before them what we—his students—experienced in all of Professor Osborne's classes: patient regard for every word in the text, exegetical finesse, a preference for an eclectic resolution to the options facing the interpreter, a sensitivity to theological questions, and most of all a reverence for God's word."

—**Scot McKnight**, Julius R. Mantey Chair of New Testament, Northern Seminary

"The Osborne New Testament Commentaries draw from the deep well of a lifetime of serious study and teaching. They present significant interpretive insights in a highly accessible, spiritually nurturing format. This is a tremendous resource that will serve a new generation of Bible readers well for years to come. Highly recommended!"

—**Andreas J. Köstenberger**, founder, Biblical Foundations; senior research professor of New Testament and biblical theology, Southeastern Baptist Theological Seminary

"Grant Osborne has spent his entire professional career teaching and writing about good principles for the interpretation of Scripture and then modeling them in his own scholarship, not least in commentaries on numerous New Testament books. The Osborne New Testament Commentaries, therefore, are a welcome new series by a veteran New Testament scholar determined to spend as much time as God gives him in his retirement years distilling the conclusions of the finest of scholarship without bogging down the reader in detailed interaction with all the various perspectives that have been suggested. If all the volumes are as good as this inaugural work on Revelation, the series will become a most welcome resource for the busy pastor or teacher."

—**Craig L. Blomberg**, distinguished professor of New Testament, Denver Seminary

"Like many others in the church and academy, I have greatly benefitted from the writings of Grant Osborne over the course of my professional career. Grant has a gift for summarizing the salient points in a passage and making clear what he thinks the text means—as well as making it relevant and applicable to believers at all levels of biblical maturity. I especially commend the usefulness of these verse by verse commentaries for pastors and lay leaders."

—**Stanley E. Porter**, president, dean, professor of New Testament, and Roy A. Hope Chair in Christian Worldview, McMaster Divinity College

"For years I have found Grant Osborne's commentaries to be reliable and thoughtful guides for those wanting to better understand the New Testament. Indeed, Osborne has mastered the art of writing sound, helpful, and readable commentaries and I am confident that this new series will continue the level of excellence that we have come to expect from him. How exciting to think that pastors, students, and laity will all be able to benefit for years to come from the wise and insightful interpretation provided by Professor Osborne in this new series. The Osborne New Testament Commentaries will be a great gift for the people of God."

—**David S. Dockery**, president, Trinity International University

"One of my most valued role models, Grant Osborne is a first-tier biblical scholar who brings to the text of Scripture a rich depth of insight that is both accessible and devotional. Grant loves Christ, loves the Word, and loves the church, and those loves are embodied in this wonderful new commentary series, which I cannot recommend highly enough."

—**George H. Guthrie**, Benjamin W. Perry Professor of Bible, Union University

"Grant Osborne is ideally suited to write a series of concise commentaries on the New Testament. His exegetical and hermeneutical skills are well known, and anyone who has had the privilege of being in his classes also knows his pastoral heart and wisdom."

—**Ray Van Neste**, professor of biblical studies, director of the R.C. Ryan Center for Biblical Studies, Union University

"Grant Osborne is an eminent New Testament scholar and warm-hearted professor who loves the Word of God. Through decades of effective teaching at Trinity Evangelical Divinity School and church ministry around the world, he has demonstrated an ability to guide his readers in a careful understanding of the Bible. The volumes in this accessible commentary series help readers understand the text clearly and accurately. But they also draw us to consider the implications of the text, providing key insights on faithful application and preaching that reflect a lifetime of ministry experience. This unique combination of scholarship and practical experience makes this series an invaluable resource for all students of God's Word, and especially those who are called to preach and teach."

—**H. Wayne Johnson**, associate academic dean and associate professor of pastoral theology, Trinity Evangelical Divinity School

ROMANS

Verse by Verse

ROMANS

Verse by Verse

GRANT R. OSBORNE

LEXHAM PRESS

Romans: Verse by Verse
Osborne New Testament Commentaries

Lexham Press, 1313 Commercial St., Bellingham, WA 98225
LexhamPress.com

Print ISBN 9781683590538
Digital ISBN 9781683590545

Lexham Editorial Team: Elliot Ritzema, Joel Wilcox
Cover Design: Christine Christopherson
Typesetting: ProjectLuz.com

Printed and bound by CPI Group (UK) Ltd, Croydon, CR0 4YY

24 iv / UK

CONTENTS

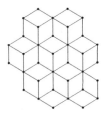

SERIES PREFACE

There are two authors of every biblical book: the human author who penned the words, and the divine Author who revealed and inspired every word. While God did not dictate the words to the biblical writers, he did guide their minds so that they wrote their own words under the influence of the Holy Spirit. If Christians really believed what they said when they called the Bible "the word of God," a lot more would be engaged in serious Bible study. As divine revelation, the Bible deserves, indeed demands, to be studied deeply.

This means that when we study the Bible, we should not be satisfied with a cursory reading in which we insert our own meanings into the text. Instead, we must always ask what God intended to say in every passage. But Bible study should not be a tedious duty we have to perform. It is a sacred privilege and a joy. The deep meaning of any text is a buried treasure; all the riches are waiting under the surface. If we learned there was gold deep under our backyard, nothing would stop us from getting the tools we needed to dig it out. Similarly, in serious Bible study all the treasures and riches of God are waiting to be dug up for our benefit.

This series of commentaries on the New Testament is intended to supply these tools and help the Christian understand more deeply the God-intended meaning of the Bible. Each volume walks the reader verse-by-verse through a book with the goal of opening up for us what God led Matthew or Paul or John to say to their readers. My goal in this series is to make sense of the historical and literary background of these ancient works, to supply the information that will enable the modern reader to understand exactly what the biblical writers were saying to their first-century audience. I want to remove the complexity of most modern commentaries and provide an easy-to-read explanation of the text. I have read nearly all the recent literature and have tried to supply a commentary that sums up the state of knowledge attained to date on the meaning and background for each biblical book.

But it is not enough to know what the books of the New Testament meant back then; we need help in determining how each text applies to our lives today. It is one thing to see what Paul was saying his readers in Rome or Philippi, and quite another thing to see the significance of his words for us. So at key points in the commentary, I will attempt to help the reader discover areas in our modern lives that the text is addressing.

I envision three main uses for this series:

1. **Devotional Scripture reading.** Many Christians read rapidly through the Bible for devotions in a one-year program. That is extremely helpful to gain a broad overview of the Bible's story. But I strongly encourage another kind of devotional reading—namely, to study deeply a single segment of the biblical text and try to understand it. These commentaries are designed to enable that. The commentary is based on the NIV and explains the meaning of the verses, enabling the modern reader to read a few pages at a time and pray over the message.

2. **Church Bible studies.** I have written these commentaries also to serve as guides for group Bible studies. Many Bible

studies today consist of people coming together and sharing what they think the text is saying. There are strengths in such an approach, but also weaknesses. The problem is that God inspired these scriptural passages so that the church would understand and obey *what he intended the text to say*. Without some guidance into the meaning of the text, we are prone to commit heresy. At the very least, the leaders of the Bible study need to have a commentary so they can guide the discussion in the direction God intended. In my own church Bible studies, I have often had the class read a simple exposition of the text so they can all discuss the God-given message, and that is what I hope to provide here.

3. **Sermon aids.** These commentaries are also intended to help pastors faithfully exposit the text in a sermon. Busy pastors often have too little time to study complex thousand-page commentaries on biblical passages. As a result, it is easy to spend little time in Bible study and thereby to have a shallow sermon on Sunday. As I write this series, I am drawing on my own experience as a pastor and interim pastor, asking myself what I would want to include in a sermon.

Overall, my goal in these commentaries is simple: I would like them to be interesting and exciting adventures into New Testament texts. My hope is that readers will discover the riches of God that lie behind every passage in his divine word. I hope every reader will fall in love with God's word as I have and begin a similar lifelong fascination with these eternal truths!

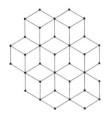

INTRODUCTION TO ROMANS

When we get to heaven I suspect we will learn that this supposition was exactly correct: In AD 57 in the city of Corinth, the Apostle Paul wrote the greatest book ever penned in human history: his letter to the Roman church. Martin Luther's study of this book fueled the Reformation, and since then many Romans commentaries have stood out as landmark works in their time, from John Calvin in 1540 to W. W. Sanday and A. C. Headlam in 1895 to Karl Barth in 1919 to C. E. B. Cranfield in 1975 to Douglas Moo in 1996. Each has had a profound effect on theological reflection and on the understanding of Scripture in general.

The issues discussed in this letter are at the core of what it means to be a Christian. I am in awe at the privilege I have had these months digging into the magnificent truths of Romans and sharing the results, hopefully with individual readers and Bible studies in many different places. At the end of this process, I echo the thoughts of John Calvin: "I fear, lest through my recommendations falling far short of what they ought to be, I should do nothing but obscure its merits. ... When anyone gains a knowledge of this

Epistle, he has an entrance opened to him to all the most hidden treasures of Scripture."[1]

AUTHOR AND DATE

Paul's authorship of this letter is universally accepted in the world of scholarship. The style, issues discussed, and origin of this letter clearly belong to Paul. There is general agreement regarding the date as well—about AD 57.

Here is how we arrive at this date. One of the assured events behind the dating of New Testament events is the appointment of Gallio as proconsul of Achaia (a Roman province in central and southern Greece whose capital was Corinth). A series of inscriptions discovered by archaeologists shows his time as proconsul to have occurred in AD 51-52. Paul was tried before him in August of that year (Acts 18:12), after which Paul stayed in Corinth awhile (Acts 18:18). From there he went to Jerusalem and then on to Antioch, from which he began his third missionary journey (Acts 18:22-23). On this journey he spent two and a half years in Ephesus and then traveled to Greece, where he stayed three months (Acts 20:1-3). While in Corinth during that time, he wrote Romans.

When we put these facts together, the likely date for the writing of Romans is AD 57-58. Paul's writing in the year or so leading up to Romans has to be one of the greatest single periods of creative activity ever in history. During the latter part of his time in Ephesus (Acts 19) he heard discouraging news about opposition against him in the Corinthian church and wrote three letters—a "previous letter" (1 Cor 5:9-11), 1 Corinthians, and a "severe letter" (2 Cor 2:6-9; 7:12)—and also visited Corinth once (the "painful visit," 2 Cor 2:1; 12:14, 21; 13:1-2). Then he wrote 2 Corinthians just a month or two before coming to Corinth and writing Romans.

Romans 16 seems to show an untroubled situation at Corinth for the first time in a long while. This may mean that the strong

---

1. Calvin, *Romans*, xxix.

admonitions of 2 Corinthians 10–13 had worked. It was a happy time in which he could plan for the future. While in Corinth, he stayed at the home of Gaius (see Rom 16:21–23), whom he had baptized on an earlier visit (1 Cor 1:14). He penned Romans by dictating it; he had bad eyesight and could not write a letter by his own hand (see Gal 4:15; 6:11). His **amanuensis,**[2] or secretary, was an associate named Tertius (Rom 16:22).

At the time of writing, he was returning to Jerusalem with a collection to give to the poor (see 1 Cor 16:1–4). In Romans 15:23–33 he relates his plans—deliver the collection, then visit Rome on the way to Spain. He intended the gift to represent the desire of all the Gentile churches he had founded on his missionary journeys to help the poverty-stricken Jewish Christians of Palestine. To make this evident he had delegates from various churches accompany him with the gift (Acts 20:4). These were from Galatia (first missionary journey), Macedonia (second missionary journey), and the Roman province of Asia (third missionary journey). His desire was to unite Jew and Gentile into one body of Christ and cement it with this collected gift.

While he wrote Romans at a relatively untroubled time, there are two sources of worry reflected in his prayer request of 15:31. He was concerned about serious opposition from the Jews when he reached Jerusalem, and did not know how the Jewish Christians of Jerusalem would receive the gift from the Gentile churches.

The second request went very well. All the indications are that the Jerusalem saints were appreciative and deeply gratified for the sacrificial gift. However, the first request (protection from the Jews) turned out quite badly from a human perspective. While Paul was protected from being killed, he was taken prisoner by the Romans (to save him from rioters in Jerusalem) and kept for two years in a jail in Caesarea and then two years under guard in an apartment in Rome while he faced a capital trial under Nero.

---

2. Terms in bold type are discussed in the glossary (page 521).

Yet we discover that God orchestrated it all in answer to prayer and so had actually said yes to the request of Romans 15:31, just not in the way Paul would have expected. God answers prayer his way rather than our way, but the result is always the same—it is for the best (Rom 8:28).

RECIPIENTS

Paul's writings and the book of Acts give us more data about him than they do about the Roman church. We know nothing about its origins and only a little about its history. Some have claimed that Peter founded it, but that is unlikely, as Acts tells us he spent the early years of the church near or around Jerusalem. It is even less likely that Peter and Paul founded it together.[3]

The most likely scenario is that it was founded by Jewish Christians, either pilgrims returning to Rome from the Pentecost of Acts 2 or traveling merchants who visited Rome on business. These would have acted like Paul on his missionary journeys and brought their Christianity into the local synagogues, which is only natural, for Jesus was indeed the Messiah the Jewish people were expecting. There were a significant number of Jews in Rome, with estimates as high as forty to fifty thousand (close to the population of Jerusalem itself!), so there would have been a great number of synagogues.

The preaching of Christ in these Roman synagogues would have led to the same result as Paul's ministry to the Jews—conflict with and opposition to the Christian preachers (as in Acts 13:50; 14:4–7, 19; 17:5–8, 13; 18:6; 19:9, 23–24). The church was predominantly Jewish in the early years, but other Jews' hatred of the

---

3. Irenaeus, *Against Heresies* 3.1.1. It is likely that Peter and Paul ended their careers and were martyred in Rome, but this would have been well after the church there was founded.

church led to rioting, and in AD 49 the emperor Claudius expelled the Jews and Jewish Christians from Rome because of it (Acts 18:2).[4]

As a result, the Gentile faction of the church that remained had to develop its own leadership. It also would have developed its own polity and style, including adopting the view that the injunctions of the law were no longer in effect in the new era of Christ. Many Gentiles had originally been attending synagogues but were not willing to undergo circumcision and become full converts to Judaism. These people were called "God-fearers" (Acts 10:2, 22; 13:16, 26). Many of the Gentile converts came from this group and would have evangelized their friends and neighbors. In this way, in the years after AD 49 the Roman church likely developed as a Gentile church with Gentile leadership.

When Claudius died in AD 54, many of the expelled Jewish Christians, like Priscilla and Aquila (Rom 16:3), returned to Rome. They returned to a Gentile-dominated church. Natural tensions developed over things like the observance of food laws and holy days, subjects Paul addresses in Romans 14:1–15:13. Those tensions were part of the reason why Paul wrote this letter. Only three years had passed since the Jewish believers had returned, and the tensions needed to be resolved.

PURPOSE

From the letter itself, we know that Paul was writing the Roman church with the intention of visiting them for the first time. His plan was to deliver the collection to the Jerusalem church and then proceed to Rome as the first step in his fourth missionary journey, in which he planned to take the gospel to Spain and the lands in between (15:23–29).

Paul believed his calling was to "preach the gospel where Christ was not known" so as not to build on anyone else's "foundation" (15:20). He had planted churches in Arabia (possibly, according to

---

4. See also Suetonius, *Life of Claudius* 25.4.

Gal 1:17–18), Cilicia (Tarsus, his hometown; Acts 11:25–26), Galatia (Pisidian Antioch, Iconium, Lystra, and Derbe; Acts 13:13–14:20), Mysia (Troas; Acts 16:8), Macedonia (Philippi, Thessalonica, Berea; Acts 16:11–17:15), and Achaia (Corinth and possibly Athens; Acts 17:16–18:17). He felt he had fulfilled God's will in the eastern half of the Roman Empire (Rom 15:23), so it was now time for local pastors like Apollos to take over and "water" the churches he had planted (1 Cor 3:6).

I believe Paul's main purpose for writing to the Romans was that he believed God was leading him to begin the second half of his life's work in the western half of the Roman Empire. He hoped the church at Rome would have the same place in his mission work in the west that Antioch had in his three missionary journeys to the east (Acts 13:1–3)—to be the sending church. Thus in part Romans is a letter of introduction to begin familiarizing the church of Rome with Paul and his gospel.

To that end, Paul planned a fairly lengthy stay in Rome to strengthen the church (1:11–12) and have a "harvest" of souls, proclaiming the gospel there (1:13, 15). To be his sponsor, Rome would need to know not only Paul but his theology as well. They must realize he was orthodox and had the same gospel they did. They would need to be able to trust both his mission strategy and the content of his gospel. In short, he must become one of them, a part of their church, so that they could send him and his team off to Spain.

Paul's second purpose in writing was to ask for prayer as he took the collection to Jerusalem. He needed protection from his enemies and also prayed that the churches in Palestine would accept the gift he was bringing from Gentile churches (15:31). To Paul the collection for the poor was more than a financial gift from Gentile churches for the poverty-stricken Jewish churches of Judea. It was to be the glue that united Jewish and Gentile churches throughout the nations.

Paul's third purpose was to bring unity to a church in conflict. While he had never visited Rome, friends would have kept him abreast of issues there (see the list in 16:3–15). Jews and Gentiles were fighting over the place of the law in the Christian life (14:1–15:13). Gentile Christians believed that Christ had fulfilled the place of the law and that they were therefore free from its demands. Jewish Christians thought the food laws and observance of holy days mandated by the law were still binding.

It is important to realize that these Jewish Christians were not the Judaizers who had replaced the cross with the law as the basis of salvation. Paul writes against this group in Galatians, Philippians, and Corinthians. Here it was not an issue of heresy, for the tone of 14:1–15:13 is one of tolerance rather than discipline. Both groups were orthodox believers. Paul himself at times observed Jewish sacrifices (Acts 21:24–26) and vows (Acts 18:18), but he agreed with the Gentile Christians that the demands of the Jewish Christians to keep the law showed they were weak in faith (Rom 14:1–2).

Still, the Gentiles were to accept the "weaker" Jewish Christians and not "put any stumbling block" in their way by trying to force them to eat meat that was offensive to them, for in doing so they could "destroy" the faith of the weaker Christians entirely (Rom 14:13–15). Both Gentiles and Jews were to understand that God accepted both sides as they were. From this the two sides were to forge a unity out of their differences and bring peace to the church as a whole (14:17, 19; 15:5–7). Peace is a critical theme, first between the sinner and God through forgiveness of sins and justification through the atoning sacrifice of Christ (1:18–3:20; 3:21–4:25), and then between groups in the church who are in conflict with one another (14:1–15:13).

This message of reconciliation is where Paul shows his fourth purpose for writing: Romans is a treatise—a study on the doctrine of salvation and an in-depth presentation of the gospel. The

Jew-Gentile troubles at Rome reflected such differences throughout the Christian world, and Paul wanted this letter read everywhere, not just in Rome. He wished churches everywhere to know
he was not opposed to the law (see 7:7, 12–14, 16; 8:4) and believed
it was valid for Jewish Christians to live as they did (14:5–7) as an
expression of the level of their faith (14:23). God honored their
conscience so long as their trust for salvation was anchored in the
cross, not the law. Observance of food laws, holy days, and so on
was viable so long as their true faith was in Christ, and such obser-
vances were an expression of their worship of him.

Romans provides an important model for Christians today who
may differ in their theological underpinnings (Reformed, Arminian, charismatic, dispensational, pacifist) and worship style (high,
low, liturgical, holiness, Pentecostal) but not in their adherence to
the cardinal doctrines of the faith. Unity and understanding are
needed as much in the church today as in Paul's day.

GENRE

Based on this last purpose for Paul's writing, some have thought
that Romans is not a letter addressing the Roman church at all but
perhaps a general treatise on the doctrine of salvation or the gospel—a compendium of Christian teaching for the whole church.
According to this argument, the opening introduction and closing
greetings were added later to turn it into a letter.

However, every point of the text can be shown to address issues
in the Roman church. Also, there are simply too many issues Paul
would have stressed more if this were a general treatise on the
gospel or salvation (like the "in Christ" motif he uses elsewhere,
or the church as a body or temple). Further, there are other parts
present in this letter that would not be here if it were only a treatise on salvation, like submission to government or the strong and
the weak factions in Rome.

At the same time, it is true that in 3:21–8:39 there are elements
of a treatise on the meaning of salvation. Therefore, most scholars

identify this as a letter with elements of a treatise, as Paul goes beyond the needs of the church at Rome to present a detailed look at his gospel, drawing the Roman readers into his vision for the salvation of the lost and for true Christian life and mission.

UNITY AND INTEGRITY

Virtually all scholars agree that Romans is a united whole, yet some have doubted the integrity of individual sections. "In Rome" in 1:7 and "to you who are at Rome" in 1:15 are missing in a few manuscripts but found intact in the vast majority. Probably these phrases were removed from a few in order to turn Romans into a general letter for the church as a whole.

Some think that either chapters 15–16 or 16 alone were added later. The reason is that 15:1–16:23 is missing in several ancient manuscripts.[5] According to this theory, Romans was a general letter for non-Pauline churches to which 1:7, 15, and 15:1–16:23 were added later to turn it into a letter for Rome. But there is material showing it was written for Rome elsewhere in the letter (1:8–13), and 14:23 is not a valid ending for a letter.

Some believe that chapter 16 was originally written for a letter to Ephesus, since Priscilla and Aquila seem to be back in Ephesus in 2 Timothy 4:19 and it is unlikely Paul would have known that many people in Rome. However, as above, it is unlikely that the first fifteen chapters ever existed without chapter 16, and there is also no reason why one of the major figures in the church would not have come to know that many people even in a place he had not visited. There was incredible mobility in the Roman world, and Christians in particular had a great deal of care and concern for one another. This is shown in the willingness of the church at Troas to stay up past midnight just to hear news about the other churches (Acts 20:7–12).

5. Some copies of the Latin Vulgate (1648, 1792, 2089) as well as this material in Marcion, Tertullian, Irenaeus, and Cyprian.

In short, Romans can be confidently affirmed as a well-integrated whole as we have it in the New Testament.

OUTLINE

I. Paul introduces himself and his gospel (1:1–17)
   A. Greeting and description of the mission (1:1–7)
      1. Salutation and Paul's calling (1:1)
      2. His gospel message about Christ (1:2–4)
      3. His mission task: reaching the Gentiles (1:5–6)
      4. Recipients and greeting (1:7)
   B. Thanksgiving and prayer regarding his visit (1:8–15)
      1. Thanksgiving for their faith (1:8)
      2. Prayer for them and his visit (1:9–10)
      3. His desire to visit them (1:11–13)
      4. His obligation to preach the gospel (1:14–15)
   C. Theme of the letter: righteousness from God (1:16–17)
II. The universality of human sinfulness (1:18–3:20)
   A. God's wrath against the Gentiles (1:18–32)
      1. Their rejection of God's revelation of himself (1:18–20)
      2. Divine retribution for deliberate sin (1:21–31)
      3. Conclusion: they both commit sin and approve of sinners (1:32)
   B. God's wrath against the Jews (2:1–3:8)
      1. The truth of God's judgment on the Jews (2:1–16)
      2. The Jewish failure to keep the law (2:17–29)
      3. God's faithfulness and Israel's failure (3:1–8)
   C. The sinfulness of all humanity (3:9–20)
      1. The universal nature of sin (3:9)
      2. The extent of human depravity: total (3:10–18)
      3. The universality of sin (3:19–20)
III. The righteousness of God in justification (3:21–4:25)
   A. Thesis: the righteousness of God and justification (3:21–26)

3. Exhortation to love (12:9-21)
4. Submission to government (13:1-7)
5. Love as the fulfillment of the law (13:8-10)
6. Living in light due to Christ's return (13:11-14)

B. Love and unity in the community (14:1-15:13)
1. The command to stop fighting (14:1-12)
2. The strong are not to cause the weak to stumble (14:13-23)
3. Bear the burdens of the weak (15:1-6)
4. Mutual acceptance of one another (15:7-13)

VII. Conclusion to the letter (15:14-16:27)
A. Paul's ministry plans (15:14-33)
1. Paul's past ministry to the Gentiles (15:14-21)
2. Future plans: Jerusalem, Rome, Spain (15:22-29)
3. Request for prayer (15:30-33)

B. Concluding greetings (16:1-27)
1. Greetings to the leaders in Rome (16:1-16)
2. Warning against false teachers (16:17-20)
3. Benediction (16:20b)
4. Greetings from Paul's coworkers in Corinth (16:21-23)
5. Concluding doxology (16:25-27)

THE THEOLOGY OF THE LETTER

While it is not a systematic theology, Romans has a great deal of theological teaching in it. It contains a deeper presentation of the doctrine of salvation than any other book in the Bible. This is so because Paul has two interdependent goals: to address certain issues in the church at Rome and to present his gospel to them and convince them of his orthodoxy.

It has been common among Protestants since Luther to think the central theme of Romans is justification by faith. However, this view has come under increasing scrutiny, and scholars now commonly understand this view to center on 1:18-4:25 and under-emphasize other themes throughout the letter. Renewed attention to Paul's discussion of the Spirit-filled life in chapters 5-8, election in chapters 9-11, ethics and the Christian walk in chapters 12-13, or the unity of Jew and Gentile in chapters 14-15 has forced a rethinking of the old axioms.

All these themes—sin and salvation, justification, the Spirit, election, the church, unity—are central components of the book but not unifying themes. The closest thing to a unifying theme would be the gospel in all its diverse elements, but personally I am not sure Paul's purpose was to draw everything around one single idea. That would fit a treatise but not a letter. It is best to see the gospel as the primary theme, but the needs of the church at Rome are at the core as well.

THE DOCTRINE OF GOD

Paul begins the letter in 1:1 by calling himself "set apart for the gospel of God." God is sovereign over and the source of all truth, especially the central truth of them all: the gospel. In Romans Paul presents God as Creator of this world and the controlling power over it. He decided to create this world in spite of knowing it would fall into sin. From before the creation of this world he decided to send his Son to redeem it, thereby solving the problem of sin. His grace and mercy are at center stage, for it is he who brought salvation to humankind and made eternal life possible.

God is not only Redeemer but also Judge. He is the one who justifies. He sits on his throne of judgment and examines penitent sinners who come by faith, applies the blood of Christ to their sins, and declares them forgiven and right before him (3:21-26). At the same time, he sits in judgment over those who choose sin and deliberately reject him (1:18-32). He sees their calculated refusal to repent and turns them over to their sins. At the final judgment, he casts them into punishment. He is the eternal Lord over all.

THE DOCTRINE OF CHRIST

The first three chapters of Romans center on the sinfulness of the Gentiles (1:18–32), the sinfulness of the Jews (2:1–3:8), and, in summation, the absolute sinfulness of all humanity (3:9–20). Through the "one man," Adam, all humans were "made sinners" and forced to endure condemnation, judgment, and death (5:12–14). Since "all have sinned and fall short of the glory of God" (3:23), there is no hope unless God makes salvation possible. We cannot save ourselves, for we could not pay the price for sin or purchase our salvation. Only Christ, the one perfect man, could do this.

The coming of this "one man," Christ, brought grace, justification, and reigning in life to those who accept him by faith (5:12–21). In 3:24–26, Paul explains that Christ became the "sacrifice of atonement" that brought about "redemption," the purchase of our forgiveness by the payment of his blood that atoned for our sins. On this basis, God applied that payment to our sins, forgave us, and declared us to be right in his sight.

With our salvation secured, Christ has become Lord of all and Savior of humankind. The meaning of this is symbolized in our baptism (6:3–4). As we go into the water, we are buried with Christ "into death," and as we come out of the water we are raised with him to "new life." As a result we are "in Christ" (or united with him) and part of the body of Christ (the church).

THE DOCTRINE OF THE HOLY SPIRIT

As the Father sent the Son, the Father and Son sent the Holy Spirit. According to Romans, the Spirit enters the scene at conversion. The Spirit enters believing, penitent sinners and leads them to be adopted as the children of God so that they cry "Abba, Father," in joy at the new family of which they have become an eternal part (8:14–17). The Christian life is a Spirit-filled walk in Christ, with the Spirit the empowering presence of the Godhead within us, making it possible to live the victorious Christian life.

The key is the Spirit-flesh dualism of Romans 7–8, introduced by the struggle of the flesh in chapter 7: "What I want to do I do not do, but what I hate I do" (7:15). The answer is to turn from the "flesh" (which for Paul primarily means not the physical body, but our tendency to sin) and embrace the indwelling Spirit (8:1–13). As long as the flesh is in control, spiritual defeat is the result. The answer is to reject the flesh and enter the new life of the Spirit. As we allow the Spirit to empower and guide our choices, we learn to live in him. We find assurance of our salvation as the Spirit "testifies with our Spirit" that we are heirs and "share in his glory" (8:16–17).

THE ELECTION OF THE BELIEVER

In Romans 9–11, Paul answers the question: Have God's covenant promises to Israel failed (9:6), and is God therefore unjust (9:14)? Paul's answer is threefold: (1) God is sovereign and has the right to elect or reject whomever he wishes, and his sovereign choices are always just (9:6–29). (2) Israel has itself chosen to reject God, and they have brought his judgment down on their own heads (9:30–10:21). (3) God has not cast away his covenant people, for his election has included a remnant—the believing Jews.

God chose to elect a new Israel for salvation before this world was created, and the choice is God's entirely. Yet at the same time his foreknowledge plays a critical role. Theologians intensely debate the interplay between God's choosing and foreknowledge, and there is no final answer, but my view is that the Spirit convicts all human beings of sin and gives them the opportunity to make a faith-decision. God knows this decision, and it plays a role in his divine choice to elect them to himself.

Another view, an equally viable interpretation of the text, is that of irresistible grace: that those God elects are overwhelmed by his grace and mercy and brought to their knees by the love of God in electing them to salvation. It is difficult to decide whether a faith-decision is a human choice made possible by the Spirit or entirely the work of God within the elect. I will discuss this in the commentary at 8:28 and at the end of chapter 10, and readers will have to decide for themselves.

THE CHRISTIAN WALK

The last chapters (12–16) are dedicated to living the Christian life at both the individual and corporate levels. Individually, we must yield our total selves as sacrifices to God by allowing the Spirit to transform us so as to live out his perfect will (12:1–2). Corporately, we live as members of his body, the church, and use our gifts to serve one another (12:4–8). The successful Christian life is lived in union with Christ and according to the Spirit's direction. This life is characterized by the battle against sin (ch. 6), which is won when we rely entirely on the empowering presence of the Spirit (ch. 8).

Love is to be the central feature of the Christian life. Our experience of God's love when we were still his enemies (5:8) enables us to experience his grace and mercy. His love must fill us as we interact with those around us, whether they are believers (12:9–13; 13:8–10) or unbelievers (12:14–21). Moreover, we must live in the light of Christ's return. This enables us to put on the armor of light and clothe ourselves with Christ (13:11–14) as we face the pressures of this world.

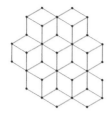

PAUL INTRODUCES HIMSELF
AND HIS GOSPEL
(1:1-17)

P aul usually begins his letters the same way, following ancient
Hellenistic and Jewish letter-writing practices and beginning
with the author and recipient. Normally he identifies himself and
moves on to his recipients fairly quickly. Here he makes a radical
departure—the identification of the author takes six verses. The
reason is that Paul is introducing himself to a church he does not
know. As 15:23-33 will make clear, Paul wants Rome to become
his sponsoring church for his future pioneer mission work to the
western half of the Roman Empire, just as Antioch had been in the
east.[1] But the Roman Christians did not know Paul, so this letter is
his opportunity to present himself and his gospel.

PAUL GREETS THE ROMAN CHRISTIANS
AND DESCRIBES HIS MISSION (1:1-7)
In the first seven verses of the letter Paul describes his calling (1:1),
recounts his gospel message (2-4), identifies his mission task (5-6),
and gives his greeting to the recipients (7).

---

1. See "Purpose" in the introduction.

SALUTATION AND PAUL'S CALLING (1:1)

Paul begins by providing a threefold description of his office, centering on his status, his calling, and his gospel purpose. First, the NIV "servant of Christ Jesus" could be better rendered "slave of Christ Jesus" (NLT, NET, LEB). Paul is following Old Testament precedent in which, after God liberated them from Egypt, the Israelites were called slaves of God as a title of honor indicating that they belonged to Yahweh (Lev 25:55). Leaders of Israel such as Moses (Josh 14:7), Joshua (Josh 24:29), Elijah (2 Kgs 10:10), and David (Ps 89:3, 20) were designated this way, pointing to their servanthood to God. In the first century, slaves became part of their owner's family, being protected by and often sharing the high social status of the owner. Paul is showing the source of his authority. It is not inherent in who he is but in the God to whom he belongs.

Second, he is "called to be an apostle," a reference to his conversion, told in Acts 9, when he was called to be the apostle to the Gentiles (Acts 9:15; 22:21; 26:16-18; Rom 11:13). The term *apostolos* comes from *apostellō* (to send), referring to a person sent with authority who bears an official message. It can refer to a church representative or missionary; the NIV translates it "representative" in 2 Corinthians 8:23 and "messenger" in Philippians 2:25. But here it refers to Paul's calling by Christ to be God's special agent and leader of the churches with a status equal to the Twelve (Mark 3:14), Barnabas (Acts 14:4), and James (1 Cor 15:7). In Acts 1:21-22, the apostles state that to be an apostle you had to have walked with the Lord and witnessed him risen; Paul held that office on the basis of having seen the risen Lord in his Damascus road vision (1 Cor 9:1; 15:8). This is a statement regarding the authority with which Paul will visit the Roman church.

Finally, he has been "set apart for the gospel of God," expanding his declaration of his calling. To be called is to be set apart for God, to be given a mission to perform. In Galatians 1:15 he declares he was "set apart from [his] mother's womb and called by his grace," alluding to Jeremiah 1:5. Paul was called, set apart, and has become a slave for the service of Christ and his gospel.

His Gospel Message about Christ (1:2-4)

After telling the Romans three things about himself, Paul proceeds to describe three things about the gospel, or good news, he has been sent to proclaim. The gospel is the core idea in this opening section (the noun and verb occur in vv. 1, 9, 15, 16). Paul uses the term to refer both to the message conveyed and the events that produced it—the death and resurrection of Christ.

Prophesied in Scripture (1:2)

God promised the gospel "beforehand through his prophets in the Holy Scriptures." Throughout this letter Paul anchors virtually every point in the Old Testament. He is using a technique called **typology**, in which Old Testament events and passages point forward to and are fulfilled in New Testament realities. God guided the ancient events (types) so that they promised or looked ahead to the greater event of Christ and the church (realities). The great events Jesus established in the new covenant were prefaced beforehand by the great redemptive acts of the old covenant, especially Abraham and the exodus from Egypt.

The prophets, including Moses (Acts 3:22) and David (Acts 2:30), proclaimed the early form of the gospel, establishing the promises that would come to fruition in the return of Israel from exile and the new exodus. Throughout his writings, Paul uses "promise" twenty-two times for the blessings of salvation (see 2 Cor 7:1; Gal 3:22), stressing the continuity of God's redemptive work in both covenant periods. The Bible as a whole, not just the New Testament, points to the gospel.

Davidic Messiah (1:3)

There are two thrusts in verse 3. First, it teaches Jesus' preexistence, seen in the opening "his Son, who as to his earthly life" (*tou genomenou*, "coming into being" or "birth"). Jesus is the Son whom God sent into this world through the incarnation. As in Philippians 2:6, Jesus was "in very nature God" and assumed human flesh. In John 1:14 we learn that "the Word became flesh and made his dwelling among us." In the incarnation, "very God of very God" (as the Nicene Creed says) assumed human flesh and walked among us. The very thought of this should make us tingle with wonder!

Second, this preexistent Son was "a descendant of David." This builds on 2 Samuel 7:12–16, in which David was promised an eternal throne. After David's time, there developed the idea of a Messiah descended from him who would deliver the nation and maintain this throne.[2] In calling Jesus a descendant of David, Paul is presenting him as the preexistent Son come to inherit the Davidic throne.

Appointed Son of God by His Resurrection (1:4)

The three aspects of Jesus progress forward in time. He was prophesied throughout the Old Testament, then at his birth was seen to be descended from David, and now at his resurrection he is appointed Son of God.

"Appointed" (*horizō*) means to "designate" or "determine," and pictures Jesus as assigned to his God-determined place in this world. Some have taken this to mean that Jesus was not Son of God until he was "adopted" at his resurrection, but that is hardly what this is saying. He was also designated "beloved Son" at his baptism (Mark 1:11), yet sonship defined his entire earthly life. Jesus is the preexistent Son, and there is never a moment in all eternity when he fails to be Son of God. Others take this appointment as the switch from his "earthly life" (v. 3) to his heavenly glory (v. 4).

---

2. This idea is present in the Old Testament (Ps 89:3–4; Isa 11:1; Jer 23:5–6; Ezek 34:23–24), intertestamental Judaism (Psalms of Solomon 17–18; Qumran's 4QFlorilegium 1:11–14), and is also a major emphasis in the New Testament (Matt 1:1; 20:30–31; 22:42; Mark 12:35–37; Luke 1:27, 32; 20:41–44; Acts 2:30; 13:22–23; 2 Tim 2:8).

This is not the emphasis either, for his preexistence is the thrust in verse 3 as well. The point here is that he was fully revealed as the Son by his resurrection. His essential being does not change, but his revelation to humankind has come in stages.

This verse describes Jesus' enthronement as messianic King and Lord of all. In Acts 13:33 Paul sees the resurrection as fulfilling Psalm 2:7: "You are my son; today I have become your father." Again, this does not mean that he was not Son of God before, but that a new stage was initiated—his glorious heavenly reign. The turning point of the ages comes through both the incarnation and the resurrection. Jesus lived his earthly life at the end of the old covenant period. With the resurrection, the new covenant period came into being.

Jesus is also Son of God "in power." This phrase should be understood as modifying the noun rather than the verb; it is not "powerfully appointed" but "designated Son-of-God-in-power." During his earthly life he was the lowly king, but at his resurrection he was exalted to the right hand of God and his divine power was revealed to all. He is now cosmic Lord with "all authority in heaven and on earth" (Matt 28:18). In verse 5 Paul will state that he participates in this authority in his apostolic mission to the Gentiles, and in verse 16 he will develop this point by stating that his gospel is "the power of God that brings salvation to everyone who believes."

The instrument of this divine appointment is "the Spirit of holiness," the Holy Spirit, who is the turning point from Jesus' earthly, messianic ministry to his lordship as Son of God in heaven. The resurrection is the turning point from the age of Jesus to the age of the Spirit (Luke 24:49; Acts 1:8), as symbolized on Pentecost fifty days after the resurrection. He is "the Spirit of holiness" in that he set Jesus apart (the meaning of holiness) as cosmic Lord of all.

The title "Jesus Christ our Lord" provides a fitting conclusion to this meaning-filled verse. In verses 3-4, Paul's words about

Jesus have moved him from descendant of David to Messiah to Son of God to Lord. The gospel Paul proclaims is all about Jesus and his remarkable being and work on our behalf. Jesus has become incarnate and been enthroned as Lord of the universe, who has come to provide salvation from sin and eternal life as a member of God's family. The title "Lord" culminates all of this, for it combines who Jesus is (the One who is Lord of all) with his function (the One who exercises that lordship on our behalf). This makes the gospel possible.

His Mission Task: Reaching the Gentiles (1:5–6)

The core of the gospel is Christ; the outworking of the gospel is mission. The **christological** underpinning for Paul's mission frames this verse, with Christ both the instrument ("through him") and the recipient ("for his name's sake") of his ministry. The Lord Christ is the means and the focus of Paul's gospel proclamation. He receives two things from the Lord—"grace and apostleship"—which can be combined to state that Paul's apostolic commission was an undeserved gift from Christ. Paul was always amazed that Christ would choose him, the worst of sinners (1 Tim 1:15–16), as his instrument to the Gentiles.

The focus of Paul's commission is "to call all the Gentiles" to Christ. This does not mean that he neglected his fellow Jews, as he will say in 1:16, "first to the Jew, then to the Gentile." Rather, his call from the Lord was to be the focal point for the new mission in fulfillment of God's covenant with Abraham (Gen 12:3, "all peoples on earth will be blessed through you").

The purpose of his mission is to call the Gentiles to "the obedience of faith" (the literal Greek). This phrase could be understood in several ways, but most interpreters understand it both as referring to the source ("the obedience that comes from faith") and as having parallel meaning ("the obedience that is faith"). Evangelism was at the heart of Paul's gospel, but evangelism always leads to discipleship—to a Godward lifestyle. A truly New

Testament church will be strong in both arenas—reaching the lost for Christ, and then enabling them to grow more deeply in their walk with Christ.

In verse 6 Paul includes the Roman Christians among the Gentile recipients of Paul's apostolic mission ("you also are among those Gentiles"). He may not have founded their church or been instrumental in their development, but he considers himself to be one with them. They are part of the Gentile world, and as such they too are "called to belong to Jesus Christ." Moreover, as Paul is the apostle to the Gentiles, they come under his sphere of ministry, and that in itself gives him the right to write this letter to them and to come visit them.

There is some debate about the phrase "among those Gentiles." Is Paul saying the Roman church was predominantly Gentile, or that they existed among the Gentile nations?[3] The first is more likely correct (see also 1:13 below), but it is difficult to know how much Paul is saying here. He does not heavily emphasize the makeup of the church elsewhere in the letter, so he is most likely saying that he considers their church to be part of those whom God had called him to serve.

RECIPIENTS AND GREETING (1:7)

As stated at the outset of this chapter, in nearly all Paul's letters he addresses the recipients right after he identifies himself as the author. Here there is an intervening paragraph that shows Paul's heart as well as his right to address this church with which he has never before had contact. Only now, in verse 7, does he address the church. His usual practice is to address his recipients as "the church in _____," but again he deviates and calls them "all in Rome," meaning all the house churches in the city and its environs.

---

3. See "Author and Date" in the introduction.

He calls them "loved by God" and "called to be his holy people" (literally "called to be saints"), defining the privilege and responsibility of Christians. These are major Old Testament designations of Israel as the people of God, and Paul is reminding these Roman Christians that they as Gentiles are also part of God's people—the new and true Israel. They have received and can experience God's love, leading to a security that will lift them above the problems of life and allow them to find joy even as they suffer the vagaries of human existence. The world may turn against them, but God will never leave or forsake them (Deut 31:6; Josh 1:5). Then they are responsible to fulfill their calling to be set apart for God, to be "the holy ones." Their calling is to be pulled out from this world to belong to him and to serve him.

Paul's greetings always consist of "grace and peace," which combines the Greek greeting (*charis*, "grace") and the Jewish greeting (*shalom*, "peace"). This combination creates an **eschatological** promise, saying in effect, "The things you have always longed for in your very greetings are now offered to you in reality by Christ." The source of this promise is the Godhead, stressing the intimate love of the Father and the authoritative power of Christ.

PAUL GIVES THANKS AND PRAYS REGARDING HIS VISIT (1:8–15)

After the greeting, another fixture of ancient letter openings was a brief thanksgiving and prayer-wish. Paul expands this as well, turning it into a virtual table of contents introducing the major issues he will discuss in the letter. His primary purpose, however, is to establish a close connection with his readers. Paul wants to show the Romans how deeply he cares for them. Yet there is also a certain formality; Paul is declaring that he is coming as an official emissary of Christ. Finally, Paul's tone in this passage is slightly hesitant, perhaps caused by his apprehension that many Jewish Christians in Rome suspected him of abandoning them and favoring the Gentiles.

THANKSGIVING FOR THEIR FAITH (1:8)

Paul begins, "first," but never gets around to a second. He may have meant "primarily," or "of first importance." He then thanks "my God" for all the Roman saints "through Jesus Christ." This phrase is unusual and not found in his other thanksgivings. Paul likely added it on the basis of verses 2–4; it is Christ who has made all this possible. Like Paul, we can pray to God for one another because Christ has saved us and brought us into the presence of God.

Paul is especially thankful because "your faith is being reported all over the world." Some think this relates to the extraordinary nature of the Roman Christians' faith, but probably it is meant to bring out the fact that the gospel had made inroads into the capital city of the world. (To Romans, their empire *was* the world.) The church in Rome became almost a microcosm of the world, and the gospel was growing there. People all over the Christian world were talking about it.

PRAYER FOR THEM AND HIS VISIT (1:9–10)

Paul's traditional prayer for his readers morphs in this letter into a prayer regarding his planned visit. The visit has been caused by two things, which he will discuss more deeply in 15:23–29. First, the situation in Rome needed his attention. There was tension between the Jewish and Gentile factions in the church there. Second, he felt God's call to take the gospel to the unreached people groups in the western half of the empire. As mentioned in the introduction, he was called to pioneer mission work, and the eastern half of the empire had now been evangelized (Rom 15:24, 28).[4]

Paul introduces his prayer with a solemn oath: "God ... is my witness." When he uses this affirmation, he is attesting the truth of his assertion (see 2 Cor 1:23; Gal 1:20; Phil 1:8). He wants the Romans to know that he regularly prays for them. He adds

---

4. See "Purpose" in the introduction.

that he "serves [God] in [his] spirit in preaching the gospel of his Son." This places his prayers for them in the larger sphere of his service to God. His prayers are part of his ministry to them, and "serve" (*latreuō*) indicates worshipful service to God. Paul's ministry of prayer on the Roman church's behalf is a worship response to the Lord. In fact, Paul views his intercessory prayers as an aspect of his proclaiming the gospel. Ministering in Rome includes both prayer at a distance (v. 9) and active mutual sharing (vv. 11–12). Both are an essential part of preaching the gospel, for Paul through these is enrolling the Roman believers in his own gospel ministry.

Paul provides two clarifications regarding what his service to God entails. First, it is "in [his] spirit," referring to the fact that every part of his being is involved in his ministry. His service to God is wholehearted, defining him and consuming him. Second, the sphere of his ministry is "preaching the gospel," and the gospel, as in verses 2–4, centers on Jesus Christ, Son of God. The particular aspect of his gospel ministry that he wants to emphasize for his Roman readers is his constant remembrance of them in prayer. This language appears in several of Paul's other letters (Eph 1:16; Phil 1:3; 1 Thess 1:2; 2 Tim 1:3; Phlm 4) and describes regular prayer on behalf of others. The hyperbolic language describing his regular prayer life ("constantly ... at all times") is not unusual for the time and would have been understood by his readers.

The content of those prayers is found in verse 10: "that now at last by God's will the way may be opened for me to come to you." He realizes that his trip will only come to pass if it is God's will. This does not mean Paul is hesitant or unsure of his plans but that he recognizes and trusts God's sovereignty. It is God, not Paul, who will "open a way" for him to come.

HIS DESIRE TO VISIT THEM (1:11–13)

Paul "longs to see" the Roman Christians in order to accomplish three ministry purposes.

To impart a spiritual gift (1:11)

First, he wishes to impart to the Romans "some spiritual gift to make you strong." It is difficult to know what he means here. Would this be one of the spiritual gifts he speaks about in 1 Corinthians 12 or Romans 12:4–8? Those are imparted by the Holy Spirit, not by Paul himself, so this is unlikely. Could this refer to Paul's apostolic gifts, perhaps his gospel preaching or doctrinal teaching? Or might this be a spiritual blessing or insight Paul would like to share with them? Based on the context it must in some way be related to the gospel, but it could encompass several of these possibilities. The primary thing is the divine nature of the gift and Paul's desire to benefit the church with it. Here the gift primarily has to do with internal ministry to the Christians rather than evangelization of the lost. It is an exciting way of speaking about ministry: "sharing a spiritual gift" with the recipients.

Paul's purpose, possibly stemming from the controversies that had divided the church and weakened it, is "to make [the Roman church] strong." In this case Paul would be introducing one of the primary goals of the letter, to enable the Roman Christians to solve their problems and make their church stronger. It could also be intended more generally: Paul simply wanted to see the spiritual fiber of their church strengthened.

To mutually encourage each other (1:12)

Second, Paul desires that he and the Roman saints "may be mutually encouraged by each other's faith." This clarifies verse 11: Paul wants them to minister to him as he is ministering to them. As he strengthens them, they will strengthen him. "Encouragement" is connected closely to "exhortation" (*parakaleō* has both meanings), and Paul likely includes both here. They will not only strengthen one another but challenge one another as well.

Still, most interpreters agree that the primary thrust is mutual comfort. Their mutual faith (the literal translation of the Greek is "faith, both yours and mine") produces this sharing. "Faith" here refers to the Christian faith they share, which means they each have differing gifts and ministry strengths that will enhance and complete each other. This is similar to the body-life theology of 1 Corinthians 12:12–26 or Romans 12:4–8. Sharing the same faith, Paul and the Roman believers are members of the body of Christ and so have differing gifts that enhance, complete, and comfort one another as they exercise those gifts in the body of the church.

To have a harvest among them (1:13)

Third, many of the Roman Christians may have wondered why Paul, the leader of the ministry to the Gentiles in the church, had never deigned to visit them, since Rome was the center of the Gentile world. Now Paul tells them, "I planned many times to come to you (but have been prevented from doing so until now)." He repeats this in 15:22 ("This is why I have often been hindered from coming to you"). There it seems his mission in the east "from Jerusalem to Illyricum" (15:19) was the reason for his absence. "Been prevented" here and in 15:22 is a divine passive, meaning God was the one who prevented Paul from coming. Paul didn't want them to think his failure to visit them meant a lack of concern.

Paul's purpose in coming then and now was "in order that I might have a harvest among you." This is probably meant two ways—an evangelistic harvest among the lost and a spiritual harvest in the churches as the believers grow in Christ. Paul was a pioneer missionary, taking the gospel to the unreached: "It has always been my ambition to preach the gospel where Christ was not known" (Rom 15:20). Yet his letters demonstrate an equally great concern that his converts grow spiritually. Paul states in Philippians 1:22 that if God spared his life at the end of his trial in Rome, it would mean "fruitful" (karpos, the same word as here) labor among the Philippian churches. The early church would not have understood the dichotomy in many of today's churches between reaching the lost and strengthening the believers. As the great commission itself says, "Go and *make disciples* [not just win the unsaved] of all nations" (Matt 28:19).

Paul adds, "just as I have had among the other Gentiles," which shows two things. First, while he cares about building up the church, evangelism among the Gentiles is uppermost in his mind. Second, Paul does consider Rome to be a predominantly Gentile church. He feels his ministry will not be complete until he ministers in the heart of the empire. He cannot go to the next step of his ministry objectives (from Rome to Spain; see 15:23–29) until he has culminated the first stage (from Jerusalem to Rome; 15:19).

HIS OBLIGATION TO PREACH THE GOSPEL (1:14–15)

God prevented Paul's planned trip to Rome earlier because he had ministry obligations to the larger Gentile world. He was "obligated both to Greeks and non-Greeks, both to the wise and the foolish." He divides the Gentile world into two pairs—Greeks and non-Greeks and the wise and foolish. Non-Greeks (Greek: *barbarous*) were not what we would call "barbarians" today but simply people groups who did not speak Greek as their native tongue (like the Jews!) and were considered uncultured. The "wise and foolish" were the same two groups looked at from the Roman point of view. Paul is saying the gospel is for everyone, whatever their national origin or status in society, no matter whether they are among the intelligentsia or the ignorant.

As a result, Paul is "eager to preach the gospel also to you who are in Rome." He cannot fulfill his obligation to God until he has ministered there as well. Since he did not found the church there, he is reluctant to be too aggressive, so he has been cautious in his language throughout verses 8–15. Moreover, since it is an established church, the proclamation of the gospel includes not only evangelistic preaching to the unsaved but also a teaching ministry in the churches.

PAUL PRESENTS THE THEME OF THE LETTER: RIGHTEOUSNESS FROM GOD (1:16-17)

In four short subordinate clauses Paul summarizes the main arguments of the letter, centering on the fact that salvation comes entirely from God and is a gift of grace. Each one explains the one before it in a series of *gar* (because) clauses, showing the string of acts that has made preaching the gospel possible.

(1) Paul preaches to all the Gentile world, first, because he is "not ashamed of the gospel." The negative "not ashamed" is a litotes, a literary device that stresses the positive by stating it negatively, as in "not too bad." Paul is confident in the power of the gospel to bring God's saving power to bear on sinful humanity. In spite of the difficult situation of the church in a world that opposes it, Paul is fearless in preaching gospel truths to sinners. The "shame" to be avoided is not only embarrassment at being a Christian but also fear of the repercussions of proclaiming God's truths to a world that does not want it (John 3:18-20). Jesus warned his disciples about being ashamed of him (Mark 8:38), and Paul elsewhere speaks of the "foolishness of the cross" (1 Cor 1:18, 23, 25). Timothy's timidity in confronting the false teachers led Paul to challenge him to not be "ashamed" of the Lord or of Paul himself (2 Tim 1:7-8).

(2) Paul is not ashamed because the gospel "is the power of God that brings salvation to everyone who believes." Paul need not worry about his own strength, for the gospel is not dependent on him. God's power is behind gospel proclamation, so it is always efficacious. No human being can avoid the convicting power of the Spirit behind the announcement of God's salvation. Elsewhere Paul writes that "to us who are being saved it [the message of the cross] is the power of God" stemming from "Christ the power of God" (1 Cor 1:18, 24). All three members of the Godhead are involved in this divine power that brings salvation. God the Father is sovereign in salvation; the sacrificial death of the Son on the cross

is the basis of salvation; and the Spirit enters the believer at the moment salvation comes (Rom 8:14–17).

There is also a present and a future dimension to salvation. At conversion the Godhead takes up residence in the new believer, and we are delivered from the power of sin and the cosmic powers. At the same time eternal life begins, and we are delivered from final judgment and reconciled eternally with God. This power and deliverance is given to "everyone who believes"—that is, each one who comes to God in faith and accepts his offer of salvation. Individuals do not save themselves but open their hearts to receive God's salvation (Eph 2:8–9). The call to faith and the act of salvation comes entirely from God; faith commitment is both active and passive. Our part is the surrender of the will, the open acceptance of what God has done. It is not a "work" (Eph 2:9), for it is the power of God alone that makes it possible. We produce nothing but our act of faith.

Paul defines "everyone" as "first to the Jew, then to the Gentile." On Paul's missionary journeys he always went to the synagogues first (Acts 13:5, 14; 14:1; 17:1, 10, 17). Since the Jewish people were the chosen people (see Rom 9) and still have a future with God (Rom 11:26–27), they must be given some priority in the gospel proclamation. It is not necessary to take "first" as indicating time; here it infers degree, that the gospel is meant for both but has special relevance for Jews. It is debated how binding this practice of preaching "first to the Jew" is for the church today, but I believe the reasoning still applies. This does not mean that every Christian is to be engaged directly in Jewish ministry, but there should always be a certain visibility in Jewish evangelism, and every Christian should pray for these covenant people.

(3) The reason for the universal proclamation of salvation to Gentile and Jew alike is that "in the gospel the righteousness of God is revealed," and this has universal relevance for all peoples. "Revealed," *apokalyptō*, is an important term, indicating the uncovering of God's hidden truths in these last days. Here it is God's plan

of salvation that is being uncovered, and its revelation is not just via prophetic proclamation but the events of world history. The meaning of "righteousness of God" is at the heart of this letter and quite debated. There are three primary interpretations:

1. It could be possessive: "God's righteousness." This would indicate that it is a divine attribute, either his justice (one meaning of *dikaiosynē*, the Greek word translated "righteousness") or his faithfulness.

2. It could be subjective, stressing God's actively making his people righteous. This would add a spiritual or moral dimension to the phrase, stressing God's power to bring people to himself and transform them so that they live rightly.

3. It could emphasize God as the source or origin, "righteousness from God," which brings out the forensic or legal ramifications. The thrust in this case would be God's judicial decision in declaring people to be right with him on the basis of Christ's sacrificial death on the cross as a substitute. Believers are given a new status as the children of God.

The third approach has been widely accepted since the days of Martin Luther and is Paul's main thrust. At the same time, many scholars agree that we don't have to choose one to the exclusion of the others, and an eclectic understanding is probably best. So while the subjective, forensic understanding is at the core, when believers are brought into a "right" relationship with God, a moral side also emerges as part of the meaning.

Paul uses "righteous/righteousness" in multiple ways in this verse. The verbal force in "one who is righteous" stresses God's legally declaring people innocent of their sins. The noun (righteousness) and the adjective (righteous) add the ethical aspect, in which God "makes us righteous" so that we "live rightly before him." This means there are three stages in which God works in our lives: (1) When we turn to Christ in faith, God declares us to be right in his eyes, forgiving our sins and justifying us (part of the meaning of the verb "make righteous"). (2) This begins the process of sanctification,[5] in which God begins to make us right as we grow in Christ. (3) Finally, we more and more begin to live rightly before him in righteous conduct.

This righteousness takes place "from faith to faith" (NIV "by faith from first to last"), a complex idea that probably modifies "righteousness" rather than "revealed," as most translations recognize. This has been interpreted in diverse ways, such as: from the faith of the Old Testament (the law) to the faith of the New Testament (the gospel), from Christ's faithfulness to our faith, from the preacher's faith to the hearer's faith, and from the faith of one believer to another. The best option is to see this as a metaphor calling for a high degree of faith, stressing that faith—and only faith—provides a sufficient basis for righteousness. The NIV and NLT get this right ("This is accomplished from start to finish by faith").

(4) Paul anchors the reception of "righteousness from God" in a quotation from Habakkuk 2:4. It is instructive to trace the translation from the Hebrew Old Testament to the **Septuagint** (the Greek Old Testament, commonly abbreviated LXX) to Paul. The Hebrew stresses the individual, "the righteous person will live by *his* faith." The LXX centers on God, "the righteous will live by *my* faithfulness." Here and in Galatians 3:11, Paul cites this verse in a more generic way, "the righteous will live by faith." By omitting both "he" and "my," he establishes a middle ground between the Hebrew and the LXX, emphasizing complete reliance on God rather than on self or the things of this world. Neither God nor Christ is the subject here; the individual person is in mind.

The question that remains is what "by faith" modifies. Is it the noun ("the one who is righteous by faith will live") or the verb ("the one who is righteous will live by faith")? In the context, the

---

5. Sanctification is a separate act resulting from justification, but this process *begins* at the moment when the believer is justified before God.

connection between "righteous" and "faith" seems so great that the first might be preferred. However, Paul may well be deliberately ambiguous and stress both aspects. Paul would then be saying that those whose righteousness is expressed in faith (absolute trust in God) will truly find life. There is also double meaning in "live": they truly live now and at the same time inherit eternal life—salvation now and for eternity.

———

Paul's description of himself, his calling, and the gospel he proclaims in Romans 1:1–7 provide a model for the church today. While none of us are apostles in the same sense he was, we are all privileged to be "slaves" of God who are sent with authority into the world to proclaim God's truths. We may not feel capable, but in reality God gives us his authority as we present him in the world. The anchor of our authority is the same as it was with Paul: in Christ. We need not worry about our worldly status, for our heavenly status means we have a power behind us that is more than sufficient. We too have the "Son-of-God-in-power" and the "Spirit of holiness" at work in our lives, and we need only to rely wholly on him.

Paul's mission, as defined in verses 8–15, shows that his vision encompassed not just the familiar (the eastern half of the Roman Empire) but the distant (the western half). Paul was a visionary, and he realized that the call of *world* evangelism meant just that. This was seen in the Twelve as well, for instance in Thomas and his mission to India.[6] Yet Paul was interested not only in evangelism but also in the spiritual growth of believers. He wanted to minister to the saints as well as reach the lost in Rome. This is an

---

6. For an excellent discussion of the evidence for an international missionary ministry on the part of the Twelve, see Eckhard Schnabel, *Early Christian Mission*, vol. 1, *Jesus and the Twelve* (Downers Grove, IL: IVP Academic, 2004), 527–32, 880–93.

important model for churches today, who often seem content to stress one to the diminution of the other in their ministry.

Finally, the opening section of Romans helps us to realize what gospel truth means and what the promise of salvation actually encompasses. God's righteousness is unobtainable by fallible humanity, so God sent his Son to bear our sins and suffer their penalty as our substitute. When we by faith accept Christ's payment on our behalf, God declares us innocent and in right standing with him. At that moment of justification, God begins the process of sanctification, and as we grow we begin to live rightly before him. This defines the gospel, and Paul will be expanding on these themes in the rest of his letter.

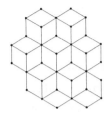

GOD'S WRATH AGAINST
THE GENTILES
(1:18-32)

Paul now sets forth in detail the first part of the gospel message: the utter depravity of sinful humankind. The "righteousness of God" first encounters human sinfulness. The ease with which national leaders plunge their nations into war and guarantee the death of thousands of our best and brightest leaves us aghast. Yet I am also distressed and disgusted at my own sinful tendencies and my constant struggle with pride and self-centeredness. This is Paul's subject matter in 1:18-3:20, moving from the utter depravity of the Gentiles (1:18-32) to the concomitant sinfulness of the Jews (2:1-3:8) and concluding with the universal sinfulness of all humankind (3:9-20).

In this section he explores the guilt of the Gentiles who face the wrath of God. Some, however, think this first section is about all humankind (including the Jews) rather than just the Gentiles. Paul calls them "people" rather than specifically Gentiles in verse 18, and the language could reflect the Adam story in Genesis 2-3. If this is correct, Paul would be moving from the general (the sinfulness of all humankind) to the specific (the sinfulness of the Jews). On the other hand, the wording and sins specified would be understood by any Jew reading this (including Paul) as a polemic against the Gentiles. That is the more likely scenario here.

There are three sections in this passage, covering first the Gentiles' rejection of God's self-revelation given through creation (vv. 18-20), then three examples of God's retribution against them for their depraved acts (vv. 21-31), and finally a conclusion showing how their deliberate sinning deserves death (v. 32). The message is that all human beings are alike in their complete inability to attain the righteousness of God. Only when they come to grips with this inability can they turn to God, open their hearts to his gracious gift in faith, and discover his saving power.

GENTILES HAVE REJECTED GOD'S REVELATION OF HIMSELF (1:18-20)

In verse 17 the righteousness of God was revealed, and now it is the negative side of the gospel, the wrath of God, that is revealed. The two exist side by side, connected to the two aspects of a holy God—his love and his justice. Divine righteousness and justice are both part of the meaning of dikaioō and its cognates, and his righteousness must react to human sinfulness with wrath. In both testaments the holiness of God demands wrath against the sinner and mercy to the repentant.

THE REASON FOR WRATH: SUPPRESSING THE TRUTH (1:18)

"Revealed" here could be seen in a final sense, the coming of God's righteous judgment at the end of history. But it is in the present tense here and probably refers to the ongoing wrath of God against sin in the world. God's righteous indignation is a present reality revealed "from heaven," a sovereign declaration of judgment from the very throne of God. The wrath of God now inaugurates and is a harbinger of final judgment to come.

The reason for the divine anger is "all the godlessness and wickedness of people." The first term refers generally to religious sin and the second to moral sins. Paul is possibly referring to the two tables of the Ten Commandments, where the first four are sins against God and the last six sins against other people. However, it is also possible to take the two terms as synonymous, both describing sins against God. I am drawn to the former interpretation, but either is possible.

The major point is that sinful people "suppress the truth in their wickedness." They know the truth about God (v. 19) and deliberately ignore it. The verb "suppress" means to hinder something by hiding or removing it from sight. The truths of God are buried under an avalanche of rationalization and wicked behavior. People surmise that their sinful behavior cannot be all that bad if they can engage in it over and over and get away with it. Nothing could be further from the truth!

Knowing God without Excuse: Revelation through Creation (1:19-20)

The sin of the Gentiles and their attempts to explain it away are deliberate. The Gentiles have always known the truth, so they are responsible for the divine reaction. God is justified in his wrath. God has given them knowledge of himself sufficient to be "plain" (phaneros) or "visible, clear" to them. Every person has been given a true understanding of God, both by conscience and by creation, but they have "suppressed" (v. 18) that knowledge and so are "without excuse" (v. 20). This is a judicial concept. They have no defense against their indictment from God.

There is an interesting relationship between "revealed" in verse 18 (special revelation) and "made plain" in verse 19 (natural revelation). Paul emphasizes God's revelation through nature in his messages to Gentiles at Lystra and Derbe (Acts 14:15-17) and at Athens (Acts 17:22-31). The Gentiles did not have revealed truth like the Jews had in their Scriptures, so God convicted them according to what they knew: nature.

The process of natural revelation is unpacked in verse 20. It has taken place "since the creation of the world." In the garden of

Eden God disclosed himself to Adam and Eve not only through his personal presence but also through the garden itself. In the same way the Gentiles, without God's word, have still been made aware of "God's invisible qualities," namely, his divine attributes, for God cannot be seen (John 1:18), is Spirit (John 4:24), and thus is invisible (Col 1:15; 1 Tim 1:17). Though God is invisible, all people can know of him through what he has revealed of himself in his creation (Ps 19:1; Isa 6:3). Look at the language used in verses 18-20: "revealed," "known," "seen," "understood." All these terms denote cognitive and not just emotional knowledge.

Creation demonstrates "his eternal power" in the very vastness of the universe. The power of a supernova, of stars colliding, the magnificent power of the sun itself—no one doubts the power of the Creator God. At the same time, creation demonstrates God's "divine nature," the necessity of a Being above his creation as seen in the very details of creation. The balance of the perfect vastness of the universe together with the perfect smallness of what makes up our world demands the existence of divinity behind it all. From this, all recognize the omnipotence of God and their own fallibility. This is not saving knowledge, but is meant to drive them to God and his word and be reconciled with him.

Since the perfect God has created, and since this created order has been seen and understood by all peoples, it follows that humankind is "without excuse." At the deepest level of their being, every person knows about God. If we still refuse to believe, it can only mean we have deliberately refused to allow the natural conclusion to affect our self-centered behavior. The conscious rejection of God's self-disclosure through nature proves our guilt and makes visible our hardened hearts.

Here we have the inherent weakness of natural revelation. It points to God, but it does not bring people to salvation. Instead, people invariably suppress its witness and turn to their own gods, primarily the self. Awareness of natural revelation alone brings people before God's throne of judgment without any way out. God has pronounced them guilty, and all that remains is the sentence to be given at the last judgment.

DIVINE RETRIBUTION IS THE CONSEQUENCE FOR DELIBERATE SIN (1:21-31)

The three "exchange" passages that follow (vv. 21-24, 25-26, 27-31) elaborate on why sinful humanity is "without excuse."

FIRST EXCHANGE: THE DEPRAVITY OF THEIR MINDS IN IDOLATRY (1:21-24)

Nature indeed reveals the power and divinity of its Creator, but the minds of these unsaved people have been darkened by sin. Yes, they knew God, but those truths were covered over by layer after layer of rationalization for the life of depravity they chose. True knowledge of God would lead to belief and surrender to him (1 Cor 1:21; Gal 4:9; Phil 3:7-10), but they refused to "glorify him as God" or "give thanks to him" for the gift of this world. Neither worship nor gratitude resulted.

Their futile minds and dark hearts (1:21)

How can we walk through the woods on a gorgeous spring day or ski down a beautiful slope without giving thanks to the God who gave us this magnificent creation? The only proper response is thanksgiving and worship as we realize anew our debt to a loving God who has given us so much beauty and joy in life, but the problem is that due to the depravity we have all inherited from Adam (Rom 5:12-13) our "thinking became futile and [our] foolish hearts were darkened." Our ability to think clearly and process what we perceive is perverted by sin. The "heart" in Scripture is not just the feelings but the mental processes as well. This means our thinking processes became "foolish," devoid of understanding (Mark 7:18; Rom 1:31; 10:19).

Exchange the glory of God for idolatrous images (1:22–23)

Despite this, the Gentiles "claimed to be wise," and we can see why. The Greeks developed a great concentration of philosophical and medical "wisdom," but their lifestyle and culture was incredibly depraved. Worldly wisdom is not the same as divine truth, so in the midst of all their knowledge they "became fools." Their pretension to worldly wisdom proved itself to be foolishness, because they worshipped, first, themselves, and second, false gods.

In so doing, they "exchanged the glory of the immortal god for images" (v. 23). "Exchange" (*ēllaxan*) means to substitute one thing for another. This explains the foolish nature of idolatry, for it substitutes false gods for the one true God. The "glory of the immortal God" refers to the grandeur and majesty of God on his throne as in Isaiah 6 and Revelation 4. The kings of ancient empires possessed merely temporary earthly splendor, but the Creator God is eternal and immortal. He alone is worthy of worship. Paul's phrase here alludes to Psalm 106:20 and Jeremiah 2:11, both of which have the nations "exchanging their glorious God for worthless idols." The glory spoken of here is the **Shekinah**, the glory of God dwelling in his sanctuary among his people (Exod 40:34–35; 1 Kgs 8:10–11; Ps 26:8).

Rejecting the immortal God, the depraved Gentiles preferred "images made to look like a mortal human being and birds and animals and reptiles." Two things in this phrase stress the inferiority and weakness of idolatrous images. First, "made to look like" stresses the artificial, fallible nature of these idols; second, "mortal human being" is in contrast with "immortal God," stressing the perishable nature of these idols. It is possible that the list is intended to mirror the fall of Adam and Eve, since the list parallels the creation of birds, the livestock, and the wild animals (Gen 1:20, 24). However, I think a more likely parallel is the prohibition of the images of human, animal, bird, reptile, and fish in Deuteronomy 4:15–18. Either way, the emphasis is on the worship of God alone, with idolatry representing sinful humankind's rejection of God and embrace of the earthly over the heavenly, the temporary over the eternal.

God gives them over to sexual impurity (1:24)

The divine **lex talionis** (the "law of retribution" that governed jurisprudence in the ancient world) led God to hand these Gentiles over to the results of their depravity. *Paredōken* (gave them over) refers to God's delivering them over to the life of impurity that they have chosen for themselves. In the **Septuagint**, it often has a military tone: Israel has sinned against God, so he has "handed them over" to their enemies. This is especially prominent in the book of Judges, which is organized according to cycles: Israel falls into sin and God delivers the people into the hands of other nations, who conquer and enslave them for a generation. Israel repents and God frees his people from the oppressing nation. The next generation falls once more into sin, and the cycle begins again.

God hands them over to "impurity" or "uncleanness" (*akatharsian*), a term often used in the New Testament of sexual immorality (2 Cor 2:21; Gal 3:19; Eph 4:19; 5:3). This does not mean God forced them to live immorally but rather that he allowed their sin to run its course, allowing "the sinful desires of their hearts" to lead them into "sexual impurity for the degrading of their bodies with one another." They refused to honor God in their minds, so he gave them over to dishonoring their bodies. Without God moral standards degenerate, and sex is degraded to animal behavior.

SECOND EXCHANGE: THE TRUTH OF GOD FOR A LIE (1:25–26)

There is a progressive development in the three exchanges. In the first, sinful Gentiles substituted idolatrous worship for the glory of God (v. 23). Here they exchange human lies for divine truths. The Greek "truth of God" does not refer to truths about God as proclaimed by his people. Rather, it is the truths about God he himself reveals to his people. In this context, it is knowledge that has come through natural revelation: his power and deity as stated in verses 20–21. Paul has now moved from idolatry to its root cause: false "truths" about God that are actually lies.

Served created things rather than the Creator (1:25)

Instead of divinely revealed truth, sinful Gentiles prefer "a lie," and as a result they have "worshiped and served created things rather than the Creator." Placing the creature above the Creator is the heart of sin. We worship and serve ourselves, the creature, and have removed God from the throne of our lives. Idolatry by definition is the elevation of created things—human, animal, or inanimate object—to the place of veneration in our lives that only God is meant to inhabit.

To stress this, Paul adds a formula of worship: "who is forever praised. Amen." This occurs only in three places in the New Testament (here; Rom 9:5; 2 Cor 11:31) and highlights the fact that God alone deserves our praise or blessing. Paul is horrified at the desecration of the name of God in pagan idolatry and thus adds a benediction affirming the One who alone is worthy of worship. Why venerate a mere *thing* that is soon to disappear when we have the "immortal God" (v. 23) to worship?

God gave them over to shameful lusts (1:26)

The same depravity that led Gentiles to prefer the created over the Creator also prefers degraded sexual activity over God-intended sexual expression. The "impurity" of verse 24 has now become "shameful lusts," referring both to internal illicit desire and the external sexual activity that results. These shameful lusts are doubly removed from God's true place for sex, as they are both outside of marriage and outside of the man-woman relationship that is the intent of creation itself. The primary example is homosexual activity, as "even their women exchanged natural sexual relations for unnatural ones."

The key terms are *physikēn* and *para physin*, "natural" and "unnatural" (or "against nature"). Paul is saying that homosexual practices are against God's created order. In the Old Testament and other ancient Jewish writings, "nature" is used for the created order. Paul is not just saying this behavior is against the natural way of having sexual relations but stressing that it is against what God intended in creation. It is interesting that Paul stresses female practices here, probably because in the ancient world this would have been more shocking. Male homosexual practice was common, almost expected in the Greco-Roman world, but female homosexual practice was rarer, probably because it was a male-dominated society.

The interpretation of "natural" I have just offered is commonly challenged today, because if correct it would mean homosexual practice is always a sin against God and his will for creation. Many argue that "natural" here should be seen as referring to a person's sexual orientation or the current custom in culture. If so, Paul would be saying homosexual practice is wrong only if an individual does not happen to have that sexual proclivity, or if culture currently prohibits it. According to this argument, since Greek culture accepted homosexual practice, Paul would here only be prohibiting it in Jewish circles. However, Paul is not writing from within a purely Jewish or Gentile perspective, and the Roman church contained both Jews and Gentiles. "Natural" here cannot be restricted to cultural preferences but refers to God's created order. For sexual sins to be "against nature" must mean they are against God's will, and the very phrase "shameful lusts" shows that Paul considers them a perversion of God's moral order. Paul is condemning homosexual practice for both Jew and Gentile.

Moreover, homosexual practices are condemned often in the Old Testament;[1] later Judaism likewise prohibited it (Wisdom of

---

1. Gen 19:5, 8; Lev 18:22; 20:13; Deut 23:17–18; Judg 19:22–24; 1 Kgs 14:24; 15:12; 2 Kgs 23:7; Isa 1:9; 3:9; Lam 4:6.

Solomon 14:26; 2 Enoch 10:1-5; 34:1-3; Testament of Naphtali 3:4-5); and so do other New Testament writings (1 Cor 6:9; 1 Tim 1:10; Jude 7). In short, Paul is writing from a context and tradition that for centuries categorically rejected homosexual practices, and he is in agreement with the tradition of which he is a part.

THIRD EXCHANGE: NATURAL SEXUAL RELATIONS FOR UNNATURAL (1:27-31)

Men lusting for other men (1:27)

The same "shameful lusts" that led women into homosexual practices led men to engage in three perversions: (1) They "abandoned natural relations with women," namely, God's will that sexual relations always take place between a man and a woman. This is an important statement for the issue of same-sex marriage, which Christians must see as going against the biblical model. (2) They were "inflamed with lust for one another," a strong metaphor describing them as burning up with sinful desires. (3) They have "committed shameful acts with other men," stressing the dishonorable and shameful nature of all such conduct.

The result is divine judgment, as they "received in themselves the due penalty for their error." As in verse 24, the *lex talionis* is at work. Since they have perverted the laws of sexuality God set before them, they will face his wrath. It is debated whether the "penalty" is homosexuality itself, with God abandoning them to their shame and allowing their depravity to come full circle, or whether it is eternal punishment as in 1 Corinthians 6:8-10. Since nothing is specified here, it is probably a combination of the two. God is allowing them to drown in the muck of their depravity, and they will pay eternally for what they are doing.

As with the previous verse, some try to explain this away as well, believing that Paul here is only condemning pederasty—that is, men having sex with small boys. Yet there is no evidence in the context that Paul is narrowing his field of vision. It is included, to be sure, but Paul's condemnation cannot be restricted to that one issue. He is speaking of men with men here and not only men with boys, so all types of homosexual encounters must be included. Another attempt to reinterpret this passage argues that the issue is not morality but purity. With this approach, Paul is not viewing homosexual behavior as sinful but rather as unclean from a Jewish perspective. However, this is very difficult to uphold, for the whole context of 1:18–32 (indeed, of 1:18–3:20) centers on moral depravity and not on ceremonial uncleanness. There is no emphasis in this material on purity issues; instead the focus is on issues of human sinfulness. Even verse 24 and its use of "impurity" is in the context of sexual sin. In short, those who wish to allow homosexual lifestyles should be honest and say the Bible disallows it, but that they disagree with Scripture and are determined to go another way.

God gave them over to a depraved mind (1:28)

This final judgment scene sums up the others. In all three, "they did not think it worthwhile to retain the knowledge of God." This recalls verses 18–20, where Paul says that God revealed knowledge of his power and deity through his creation, which would parallel knowledge of the created order and sexual issues. In all these areas, sinful humankind had knowledge of God but suppressed it and preferred to worship the creature (themselves) rather than the Creator. This establishes a correlation ("just as") between the sin and its consequences. Humans have tested God and dismissed him as unworthy of their attention.

Since their minds were bent on sin and willfully ignorant of God, God "gave them over to a depraved mind." In verses 24 and 26 this delivery took the form of immorality; they wanted sin, and God allowed them to wallow in it. Here the divine retribution is more basic. The word "depraved" (*adokimon*) means "worthless" or "disqualified" (by God). They had disqualified God as unworthy of their attention; now God has disqualified them as of no worth in terms of eternity. The folly of their sin has rendered them incapable of discerning truth or anything of value. All that is left for them is "to do what ought not to be done." They have been given over to their folly, which will be demonstrated in the list of one vice piled on top of another in the next three verses.

Their depravity explored: the vice list (1:29-31)

Greek philosophers, especially the Stoics, were consumed by "proper" conduct. The mindset described above is incapable of such behavior, so these depraved people are "filled with every kind of" sin seen in the list here. In these verses there are three categories of sins:

(1) The first four are general sins that introduce the others. Sinful people "have become filled with every kind of wickedness, evil, greed and depravity." The language pictures these people as cauldrons boiling over with filth. Three of the four are virtually synonymous, emphasizing the depths of their sin. The other characteristic, "greed," joins this list because it gets at the heart of sin. In Colossians 3:5 and Ephesians 5:5 Paul speaks of "greed, which is idolatry," because the demand to accumulate possessions is based on the worship of self above God.

(2) The next five begin similarly with "full of"; these are social sins stemming from the tendency to mistreat others. The first is the basic sin from which the others follow, as "murder, strife, deceit and malice" all proceed from "envy." Envy and greed tie the first two lists together. Greed produces envy, for the greedy want what others have and easily become envious. Then this desire to take what belongs to others leads to murder and strife, violently taking what belongs to another. In my experience, many church splits have taken place because of leaders who are envious of each other. I am amazed at the number of times I have seen churches or departments in a seminary refuse to hire someone because their extensive gifts threaten those already in power.

Deceit and malice, indicated by the willingness to trick others in order to take things from them or to get them to believe a lie, are basic sins. False teachers like those in Galatians, Philippians 3, the Pastoral Letters, or 1 John all used deceit to suborn people away from following Christ.

(3) The final twelve sins can be subdivided into sins of the tongue ("gossips, slanderers"), sins of pride ("God-haters, insolent, arrogant and boastful"), summary sins ("they invent ways of doing evil; they disobey their parents"), and negative sins ("no understanding, no fidelity, no love, no mercy"). The first two are closely related; the term for "gossiping" connotes a person whispering rumors and slander to others. Gossip may be even worse than slander because the gossiper turns slander into entertainment, carelessly playing with another person's reputation.

"God-haters" are those who have turned against God. It is possible that this could mean "hated by God," but in a vice list like this it more likely refers to those who are angry at God and oppose all he stands for, including his followers. The following three terms are all related: "insolent" is a strong term for pride that hints at violence against others, and the arrogant are so caught up with themselves that boasting is a natural outgrowth.

The two summary sins are grouped together not by subject matter but because they are phrases rather than single words. Those who "invent ways of doing evil" are so consumed with sin that they seek originality in their acts of depravity. They devise ways to hurt others and steal from them. Those who "disobey their parents" are not just children but also rebellious adults. They disregard the advice and challenges from their parents so as to commit evil acts; under the old covenant, cursing one's parents was punishable by death (Lev 20:9).

The final four are connected by the fact that in Greek they all begin with the negative particle a- and are used to summarize this section. Those who "have no understanding" point back to verses 18–20, where depraved humankind disregarded God's revelation of

himself through creation. Those with "no fidelity" break all promises to God or those around them and cannot be trusted to do anything except live for themselves (Jer 3:7-11). Those with "no love"
live only for themselves and show no care for others. The term
emphasizes a lack of love even for one's own family. Those with
"no mercy" trample over anyone who gets in their way.

Together, all of these depict the deep sin that leads people to
live only for themselves and care nothing for those around them.

THEY BOTH COMMIT SIN AND
APPROVE OF SINNERS (1:32)

In this last verse of the passage, those who commit the sins of
verses 29-31, namely, all humanity in its depravity, are declared
guilty. As in verses 18-20, they are without excuse because "they
know God's righteous decree," which includes the just condemnation of sin. The consciences of all people make them aware
of their guilt. They can rationalize their sins all they want, but
deep down they realize that "those who do such things deserve
death." Remember that Paul is describing the Gentiles here, so
he is not talking about the Jewish law. In 2:14-15 he describes how
the Gentiles "do by nature things required by the law" for they
have "the law ... written on their hearts, their consciences also
bearing witness."

However, in spite of their awareness of guilt, they "not only
continue to do these very things but also approve of those who
practice them." At first glance, this could be understood to say that
approving of and delighting in another person's evil deed is worse
than actually committing evil yourself. This is partially correct, for
encouraging sin in others spreads evil more widely than practicing
evil yourself. However, Paul is not saying that encouraging evil is
worse. Rather, he is saying that by both practicing evil and encouraging others to join them, they stand doubly guilty before God.
Total depravity is the only description that fits sinful humanity.

Romans 1:18–32 is not just a description of human sinfulness; it is final proof that it not only exists but also is in control of our world. At the same time, it is hard to ignore the perfection of our world and the evidence of the hand of God behind every detail of life. These two things—the perfection of creation and its opposite, the horror of evil in this world—demand the existence of the God of the Bible, who has revealed himself in the very details of creation.

Paul especially centers on sexual immorality as the proof of the total depravity of humankind. Sexual perversion of any kind is a form of idolatry, worshipping our own body and its pleasure above God. We need more sermons on idolatry today, for we in the West hold our idols as preciously as any nations ever have. Our idols include our overwhelming desire for pleasure, as well as our bank accounts and lists of our deeds and possessions. Our cathedrals are the brothel, the pornographic website, the mall, and the online store. Our pleasure, our possessions, and our status in society are our true gods.

Paul moves from general sexual sins to a specific example, homosexual practice. This is one of the most important passages in Scripture for the issue of homosexuality, for this is the clearest passage that the early church considered homosexual practice of any kind to be a sin. There is no way to water down what Paul is saying here. Homosexual sex is not worse than adultery, but it is another form of sexual sin, for God intended sexual pleasure to be exhibited only in marriage between a man and a woman.

The only conclusion one can draw from the powerful portrayal of depravity in this passage is that humankind is indeed consumed by sin and is therefore guilty before God. All of us commit the vices of verses 29–31, proving that we have no hope apart from Christ. But this folly, giving ourselves over more and more to evil practices even as we rationalize it away, is at the heart of the gospel.

The only answer for this sinful world is the atoning sacrifice of Christ, bearing our sin and guilt on the cross so that we could be forgiven of our sins and declared right with God at his judgment seat. This is the topic of the rest of Romans 1–8.

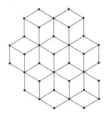

THE TRUTH OF GOD'S
JUDGMENT ON THE JEWS
(2:1–16)

In chapter 2 Paul turns from the sinful nature of the Gentiles to that of the Jews. He used the third person ("they") for the Gentiles in 1:18–32; now he switches to "you" as he speaks to his fellow Jews. Here he is even more forceful in his argumentation, for the Gentiles recognized their sinfulness while the Jews had rationalized away their depravity on the grounds that they were the covenant people. Paul uses a diatribe style in 2:1–3:8, turning the Jews into an imaginary opponent to whom he addresses rhetorical questions designed to expose their inconsistencies and presumptions. His message is that the Jewish people cannot escape God's condemnation. They are even more guilty than the Gentiles because they commit the same sins while "under the law" (2:12).

There are three parts to this section. First, in 2:1–16 Paul teaches the truthfulness of God's indictment of the Jews, showing that they commit the same sins as the Gentiles and are therefore without excuse. Then in 2:17–29 Paul shows that possessing the Torah (Hebrew for "law" or "instruction") and knowing its regulations are not enough because the Jews break the very laws they have been given by God. Even the covenant rite of circumcision condemns them, for breaking the law renders a person uncircumcised.

Finally, in 3:1–8 Paul contrasts God's faithfulness to his covenant people with their unfaithfulness; as a result, they stand guilty before God.

The Jews are thus the objects of the same wrath from God that they have heaped on the Gentiles, since they commit the same things they judged the Gentiles for doing (1–5). Then in verses 6–11 Paul switches back to a third-person style to declare that God is impartial and just in his judgments, pouring out wrath on the evil-doer and life on those who do good. Finally, in verses 12–16 he states that having the Torah provides no advantage, for it is not hearing the Mosaic law but obeying it that matters. Both Jew and Gentile are equally sinners before God and equally in need of divine grace.

GOD IS ANGRY WITH THOSE WHO PASS JUDGMENT ON OTHERS (2:1–5)

THE CONDEMNATION OF THEMSELVES (2:1)

Paul begins chapter 2 with a phrase that is literally translated as "You, O man, who. ..." This creates an imaginary opponent—a self-righteous critic who thinks the judgment of the Gentiles is the result of his own indictment. Paul does not name this foe until verse 17, but it is clear that this opponent stands for the Jewish people. Paul states at the outset that even while this so-called mor-ally upright opponent "passes judgment on someone else," he "has no excuse."

As in 1:20, "without excuse" means there is no legal defense against the divine indictment. To pass judgment on another when you are committing the same sins is the height of hypocrisy and renders you guilty in any court of law. Scripture tells us to admon-ish others when we see them caught up in sin, but this is done in love in order to help the person (Matt 18:15–18; Gal 6:1; Heb 3:13). Instead, judging is done in pride, looking down on the other. The Jews were smug in their condemnation and indicted themselves in their hypocrisy, for they "do the same things." This doesn't mean the Jews practiced the specific sins Paul mentioned in 1:18-32, but they had their own sins and so were just as guilty.

THE TRUTHFULNESS OF THE JUDGMENT (2:2)

To the self-condemnation of verse 1 God now adds his own condemnation, which takes place in the present and at the last judgment. This is the most critical comment of all, for divine judgment is "based on truth." When God judges sin, he does so justly and fairly. Moreover, "we know" this. In other words, the justice and fairness of God is a commonly held assumption (3:19; 7:14; 8:22, 28). God's judgment is true and just because it is always based on the facts of the matter, falling only on "those who do such things." The impartiality of this divine judgment will be the subject of verses 6-11.

RHETORICAL QUESTIONS SHOWING THEIR GUILT (2:3-4)

On the basis of God's just and impartial judgment, Jews stand before God guilty of the same sins as the Gentiles. At the same time, they are even more guilty because of their passing judgment on the Gentiles while practicing the same sins. There is an ABA pattern here, with Jewish guilt (vv. 1, 3) ratified by the impartial God (v. 2). This leads to Paul's first rhetorical question: "Do you think you will escape God's judgment?" The implied answer is, "Of course not."

The next verse (2:4) intensifies the challenge of verse 3. The rhetorical question here is a severe indictment, saying that in judging others "you show contempt for the riches of [God's] kindness, forbearance, and patience." The verb *kataphroneis* means to "despise or heap scorn" on a thing, to consider it valueless and beneath you. They are therefore scorning God's riches, a term Paul frequently uses for the incredible abundance of blessings from God, especially his mercy and grace (Rom 9:23; 11:12, 33; Eph 1:7, 18; Col 1:27; 2:2).

There are three areas of God's riches the judgmental person ignores. (1) His "kindness" or "goodness" (*chrēstotēs*) is a favorite term of Paul's (all ten New Testament uses are in his letters) that refers not just to God's mindset but also to specific acts of his benevolence experienced by people. The kindness of his character produces the goodness of his actions toward his created people, both the righteous and the unrighteous (1 Chr 16:34; Ps 25:7; 100:5). (2) His "forbearance" or "tolerance" (*anochē*) is seen when he postpones judgment and gives people time to repent (Rom 3:26; 2 Pet 3:9). (3) His "patience" or "longsuffering" (*makrothymia*) leads him to put up with the evil deeds of sinners since he "wants all people to be saved and to come to a knowledge of the truth" (1 Tim 2:4).

God's compassion for sinners (see Rom 5:8) here contrasts the Jewish condemnation of the Gentiles. When Paul adds that they "don't realize" God's true intention, he is not speaking of ignorance but deliberate rejection of the truth (as in 1:19, 21). They know that he had chosen the Jews to be the channel of blessing for the Gentiles (Gen 12:3; 18:18; 22:18). There is a double message in "God's kindness is intended to lead you to repentance," for it refers on one level to the repentance of the Gentiles (to whom the Jews show contempt) and on another level to the repentance of "you," the Jews.

Repentance means not just turning away from sin but also turning toward God. There must be both remorse for sin and commitment to God, or conversion will not take place. The Jewish people thought they were secure because they were the covenant people, but Paul, like Jesus before him (Mark 1:15; Luke 13:3), is showing them that they too must repent.

RESULT: STORING UP WRATH (2:5)

God's patience does not last forever. God gives sinners a long time to repent, but judgment must result when they spurn that opportunity (2 Pet 3:8–9). The Jews' need for repentance is due to their "stubbornness and unrepentant heart," and these become the basis (Greek *kata*, "because of") of God's wrath on them. This is strong language, stemming from the hardness-of-heart theme found often in Scripture (Exod 7:13; Deut 9:27; 10:16, 31:27), especially of Pharaoh's hardness exhibited also in the Pharisees (Mark 3:5) and the disciples (Mark 6:52; 8:17).

This refusal to repent causes the Jews to "store up wrath against" themselves, a commercial metaphor picturing them baling their depravity into God's silo, where it will accumulate not riches (they have already spurned that in verse 4) but wrath. Sin accumulates throughout their lifetime, ending at the final judgment, called in Scripture "the day of wrath" (Ps 110:5; Zeph 1:15; Rev 6:17).

This is not just a day of wrath but also the time "when his righteous judgment will be revealed." In 1:17 Paul says that God's righteousness was revealed, and in 1:18 that his wrath was revealed. There the time of revelation was the present, but here the judgment takes place at the end of history. God's wrath is part of his righteousness, based on the two aspects of God's holiness: his justice (wrath) and his love (righteousness). They are interdependent parts of his holy character. This prepares us for Romans 9–11, where Paul addresses in detail the issue of God's justice in removing the Jews from their place as his covenant people but placing believing Jews with believing Gentiles within his true family, the new Israel.

GOD'S JUDGMENT IS JUST (2:6–11)

In this section Paul proves that God judges both Jews and Gentiles without showing partiality. The emphasis is on what in the Roman Empire was labeled **lex talionis**, the "law of retribution," meaning that each person received a punishment that fitted the crime. Yet this is not only Roman justice. It also describes divine justice, with the difference that the Romans claim to do it while God truly does it. In fact, this is a summary of biblical ethics: What we do to others we are actually doing to God, for they are made in his image; and he will treat us in exactly the same way we have treated others. When we do good, God rewards us accordingly; when we do evil, God judges us accordingly.

This section is arranged as a **chiasm** to bring out these points:

A God judges fairly (2:6)
   B Those doing good are given eternal life (2:7)
      C Those doing evil receive wrath (2:8)
      C' Those doing evil receive trouble and distress (2:9)
   B' Those doing good gain glory (2:10)
A' God does not show favoritism (2:11)

The Absolute Fairness of His Judgment (2:6–10)

Eternal life for those who do good (2:6–7)

Paul begins with the theme of this section: "God 'will repay each person according to what they have done.'" This is a virtual quotation from Psalm 62:12, a psalm describing rest in God in the midst of attacks from enemies. The psalm stresses that God's power and love are on the side of the righteous. Paul intends it to be taken both positively and negatively.

"Repay" is a commercial metaphor meaning "return, render," referring to exact recompense for services rendered. What Paul is saying here does not contradict Ephesians 2:8–9; we are indeed saved by grace through faith, not by works. This relates not to our salvation but to living the Christian life. We are saved by grace, but we will also be judged by works.[1] All people will stand before God and give an account for their lives. We will be rewarded for

---

1. This is a major biblical theme, found often in the Old Testament (2 Chr 6:23; Job 34:11; Ps 28:4; 62:12; Prov 24:12; Eccl 12:14; Jer 17:10; Ezek 18:20; Hos 12:2), Jewish literature (1 Enoch 41:1–2; Psalms of Solomon 2:16; 17:8; 4 Ezra 7:35; 8:33; 2 Baruch 14:12), and the New Testament (Matt 16:27; Rom 2:6; 14:12; 1 Cor 3:12–15; 2 Cor 5:10, 11:15; 2 Tim 4:14; 1 Pet 1:17). In Revelation it refers to both believers (Rev 2:23; 11:18; 14:13; 20:12; 22:12) and unbelievers (18:6; 11:18; 20:13).

good and judged for evil, including sins of omission as described in James 4:17—those good things we should have done and did not do. This critical theological truth is often neglected in modern preaching and not understood by very many Christians.

The implications of this point are brought out in what follows, applied in verse 7 on the positive side and in verse 8 on the negative side. To those who "persist in doing good" God will "give eternal life." "Persist" means that good works will be the defining characteristic of a person's life and will become a regular occurrence. God is not satisfied by occasional goodness.

By doing good deeds the person seeks "glory, honor and immortality." These rewards (see also v. 10) are the gifts God will give to the faithful saints. On the surface this could sound self-serving, as if we are in it for the reward. But we don't do good for what we can get for it; we do it to serve the Lord. Here Paul is merely telling us what reward God will give us.

There have been many attempts to explain the seeming discrepancy between the works theology in verses 6–11 and Paul's statements elsewhere that people are saved by grace through faith and not by works. The solution is simple; Paul is addressing true believers here (those who have already been saved). He does not describe works as bringing about salvation but those works that result from salvation. After stating that we are saved by grace through faith and not by works in Ephesians 2:8-9, Paul states in verse 10 that we are "created in Christ Jesus to do good works, which God prepared in advance for us to do."

In short, we are not saved by our works, but good works must result from our salvation, and at the final judgment they will determine our reward from God. Jesus taught that the saints are to seek treasures in heaven rather than on earth (Matt 6:19-21), and Paul added that believers must seek after and think about heavenly rather than earthly things (Col 3:1-2). God's people are to work for eternal rather than temporary and earthly rewards.

Wrath for the Self-Seeking (2:8)

The opposite of eternal life is the punishment awaiting "those who
are self-seeking and who reject the truth and follow evil." This self-
seeking is the same word (*eritheia*) used for "selfish ambition" in
Philippians 2:3, and in James 3:14, 16, for Christian leaders who seek
their own glory rather than service to God. Here the term stresses
the self-centered attitudes of the secular person. This attitude is
linked to the rejection of truth in 1:18-20 and the pursuit of evil
in 1:21-31. As with the Gentiles, Jews who live for selfish pursuits
rather than for the will of God will face God's "wrath and anger."
Some have tried to separate the two terms, saying that wrath refers
to the inner disposition and anger the outward expression, but
they are more likely synonyms that stress the extent of God's anger
toward these depraved people.

This punishment refers to the wrath of the great white throne
judgment of Revelation 20:11-15, when sinners will be cast into
eternal punishment. There are two ultimate fates that every
person will face, and they depend on our relationship to God and
Christ. As stated in Daniel 12:2-3 and Matthew 13:40-43, 49-50, the
wise and the righteous will have everlasting life, while sinners will
be thrown into the blazing fires of eternal torment.

Trouble and distress for those who do evil (2:9)

Those who do evil (*katergazomai*, "produce" as a commercial product) will receive "trouble and distress." Paul is emphasizing that
every single person (the Greek is literally translated as "every soul
of a person") will receive from God exactly what they have earned
by the way they have lived their life (as seen in v. 6). Paul emphasizes the justice of God throughout this section. It is most likely
that the word "trouble" refers not to present difficulties and struggles in life but to the final judgment, with "trouble and distress"
the result of the divine "wrath and anger" of verse 8. As in verse
8, these synonyms stress the intensity of the judgment awaiting
those who choose evil over good.

In 1:16 Paul stated that the gospel was meant "first for the Jew, then for the Gentile." Now he states the mirror image of that. For those who reject the gospel and live in sin there will be eternal "trouble and distress," and this too will be "first for the Jew, then for the Gentile." As the Jews have had a certain priority in receiving the gospel (1:16), they will also have a certain priority in receiving judgment. As Jesus said in Luke 12:48, "From everyone who has been given much, much will be demanded; and from the one who has been entrusted with much, much more will be asked."

Glory for those who do good (2:10)

The three promises here for those who practice good works are similar to verse 7, changed slightly by substituting "peace" for "immortality." Peace in this context connotes eternal tranquility and bliss (see 1:7; 5:1). The point is the same as in verses 7–8. There are only two destinies for humankind: those who follow Christ and live for the good will have eternal glory and peace, while those who reject Christ and do evil will have eternal torment. All people will receive what they have earned by the way they have lived their lives—eternal reward for a Christ-centered life of good works, and eternal punishment for a Christ-negating life of sin.

THE BASIS: GOD DOES NOT SHOW FAVORITISM (2:11)

This verse repeats the sentiment of verse 6 and presents an important biblical concept. First Peter 1:17 states it well: "Since you call on a Father who judges each person's work impartially, live out your time as foreigners here in reverent fear." Paul uses an interesting term for impartiality here: *prosōpolēmpsia* (literally, "does not receive according to face"), which connotes that looks or social status will not dictate how the other is treated. Every human being is equally loved by God, and there will be no partiality at the last judgment.

There are numerous Old Testament passages against favoritism, building on God's impartiality (Deut 10:17; 2 Chr 19:7; Job 34:19) and extending the demand to his people (Lev 19:15; Job 13:8, 10; Prov 18:5; Mal 2:9). Both aspects are taught in the New Testament as well (Acts 10:34; Gal 2:6; Eph 6:9; Col 3:25). In fact, impartiality is a critical aspect of the justice of God—he will dispense both reward and judgment with fairness. This truth provides a fitting conclusion to this section and an important warning to all those who think God will dispense decisions on the basis of race, pedigree, or status. Unlike courtrooms today, the billionaire will have no advantage over the homeless person.

GOD'S JUDGMENT IS IMPARTIAL (2:12-16)

In this section Paul applies the theme of God's impartial judgment to Jew (with the law) and Gentile (without the law) alike. Every person will be judged by the same impartial criteria of divine justice. The Jews have the law of Moses; the Gentiles do not, but they have a law written on their hearts. All stand guilty before God, for all have *law*, either written in the Torah or written on their heart by God. He has revealed himself to both groups, and they must answer to him for their response to his revelation.

JUDGED ON THE BASIS OF OBEDIENCE RATHER THAN HAVING THE TORAH (2:12-13)

Paul now introduces the law of Moses for the first time in this letter. Paul provides the premise of this section in verse 12. Jews and Gentiles are differentiated as those "apart from the law" and those "under the law." The first half of the verse repeats a basic Jewish diatribe against the Gentiles: since the Gentiles were not the recipients of the Mosaic law, the Jews held them in contempt and believed God had rejected them.

The second half of the verse is Paul's rejoinder. Jew and Gentile are equally guilty before God, he says, for they have both sinned against God—one outside and the other inside the law. Since the

Gentiles have sinned apart from the law, they will be judged on the basis of their conscience: the law written on the heart (v. 15). The Jews do not get away scot-free, for they have sinned within the law and so will be judged by the law, just as the Gentiles will be judged apart from the law.

Because the sins of the two groups differ in their relation to the law but are alike in their relation to God, the penalty is the same— eternal torment (the second death of Rev 20:6, 11–15). This contains a warning for us today; many think their good deeds give them an advantage, but apart from Christ there is no salvation. Many who have been active in church or service organizations will hear the dreaded words of Matthew 7:23, "I never knew you. Away from me, you evildoers!"

In verse 13 Paul explains why (*gar*, "for") the Jews who have the law are condemned in their sin: "It is not those who hear the law who are righteous in God's sight, but it is those who obey the law who will be declared righteous." To make this clear he returns to the *dikaios* word group he introduced in 1:17: righteous, righteousness, justified. As mentioned in the comments on that verse, this concept describes how God declares us right from his throne of judgment. Paul's point here is that Jews cannot be accepted just because they know the law.

To be justified/declared righteous, they must "obey the law." This is nothing new, for the Old Testament says that one must not just hear but obey as well (Deut 28:58; Josh 1:8; Ps 119:1, 59, 67, 73). Paul seems to be saying that one can be justified by obeying the law, but in Romans 3:20 he rejects this concept: "No one will be declared righteous in God's sight by the works of the law." It is best to understand this as written from the standpoint of the Jew under the law, echoing the Old Testament teaching above. The point is that Jews who stand before God will be held accountable and "judged by the law" (v. 12).

THE ACTUAL SITUATION OF THE GENTILES (2:14–15)

A law unto themselves (2:14)

Paul now explains how the Gentiles can be judged. Although "they do not have the law," they "do by nature things required by the law"; as a result "they are a law for themselves." When looked at in the context of 1:18–3:20, these must be pagan Gentiles. Paul says here that while they do not have the law of Moses, they do indeed possess an internal "law," a conscience that enables them to know what is right and wrong. As a result, they inadvertently observe the basic laws of God.

Calvinists call this "common grace," and Greek philosophers like Plato or the Stoics also conceived of a moral law that all people understood by nature. Even those who do not know God have an internal barometer, a "law unto themselves," that allows them to follow God's basic moral requirements. Paul is saying that the Jews possess no true advantage from the law, for the Gentiles have been given their own form of it.

The law written on their heart (2:15)

The "law for themselves" that Gentiles live by Paul now clarifies as "the requirements of the law" (literally, "the work of the law") that are "written on their hearts." Paul is not saying that the Gentiles will be justified by obeying the law of Moses, for several times in Romans and Galatians he states that no one can be justified by the works of the law (Rom 3:27; 4:2–3; 9:32; 11:6; Gal 2:16; 3:2, 5, 10). The point here is that the Gentiles will stand with the Jews before God as equals. Their conscience gives them an inner awareness of God's demands, so they too are guilty. They don't have special revelation, but they have natural revelation and an innate knowledge of right and wrong.

Paul adds that this conscience is "bearing witness" to the Gentiles in such a way that their thoughts are "sometimes accusing them and at other times even defending them." Again he is using law-court imagery, with the Gentiles' consciences witnessing to them about how God is looking at their deeds. When they are acting rightly before God, their consciences defend the acceptability of their actions. When they are doing wrong, their consciences accuse them. The scene here is not taking place at the last judgment but in the present day.

THE DAY OF JUDGMENT (2:16)

The relationship of verse 16 to verses 12–15 is unclear. The best option is to see the present activity of the conscience (vv. 14–15) as preparing for and culminating in the final judgment. In this sense the paragraph is framed with verses 12 and 16, both referring to that final consummation when God "judges people's secrets." At that time God will bring to light all the hidden things (1 Sam 16:7; Ps 139:1–2; Matt 6:4, 6, 18; Mark 4:22; Luke 12:2–3). This refers to actions, including sins of omission (Jas 4:17), and thoughts. We can hide these things from ourselves and others, but we cannot hide them from God. God refuses to play favorites, in the present as well as at the last judgment.

This judgment will take place "through Jesus Christ," meaning that it will be initiated by the second coming of Christ (1 Thess 4:13–5:10; Rev 19:11–21) and that the saving work of Christ is the basis of that judgment. The closing "as my gospel declares" modifies the whole statement of verse 16. Paul is saying that the final judgment is an essential part of the gospel of Christ (Phil 1:27).

———

While the Jews are never named in Romans 2:1–16, they are the subject throughout. They have always considered themselves superior to the Gentiles. Yet their very self-righteous condemnation of the Gentiles made their own guilt even more clear, for they committed the same sins (vv. 1–5). This is critical for us to remember today, for we too have a tendency to smugly look down on others while failing to realize our own guilt. When we do this we indict ourselves before God.

According to verses 6–11, the just God will judge every person on the basis of what they have done. At the final judgment, Jew and Gentile (and each of us today) will receive from God what we have earned as a result of how we have lived our lives. This is not referring to salvation, which is based on faith in Christ, but judgment and rewards. God will repay us for what we have done, and Jew and Gentile (or rich and poor) will stand equally before God.

Verses 12–16 tell why the Jew will have no advantage over the Gentile—and why the wealthy, privileged Westerner will have no advantage over the impoverished person from the Majority World. Like the Jews, many churchgoers think we have an automatic "get out of jail free" card because of our status. Paul shows us the error of our thinking. It is not knowledge but action that matters. Are we truly living for Christ? In light of the future judgment, we must listen to our conscience and respond to make certain our thoughts and actions are in accordance with God's will.

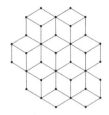

THE JEWISH FAILURE
TO KEEP THE LAW
(2:17–29)

I n this section Paul continues his criticism of the Jews for the
smug superiority they have shown over the Gentiles. In 2:1–16
he addressed their argument that God had given them the law, not
the Gentiles, showing that they were just as guilty as the Gentiles
before God. Here he addresses their claim that they had a better
pedigree and were the covenant people. The first cause for smug-
ness was their alignment with Moses and the law; this second is
their alignment with Abraham.

Paul begins by repeating his point that having the law brings
no advantage when you fail to obey it (vv. 17–24). The Jews thought
they were privileged because they had the law (vv. 17–18) and
believed that they were placed in this world to guide the blind
(vv. 19–20). However, they failed to keep it (vv. 21–22), and that
obviated their advantage of being the covenant people because
they dishonored God and the law by transgressing it (vv. 23–24).

Next he turns to the covenant and its sign, circumcision. He
argues that the advantage there, too, is nullified by the fact that
they are lawbreakers (vv. 25–29). Here Paul returns to the argu-
mentative style of 2:1–5, commanding "you Jews" to reflect seriously about their actual relationship to God and the law.

THE JEWS HAVE BROKEN THE LAW (2:17-24)

This has the form of a conditional sentence, beginning with a complex "if" clause (known as a protasis). In fact, all of verses 17–19 consists of a series of these "if" clauses building on the first. The "then" clause (apodosis) is assumed, but it is in effect, "you are wrong because. ..." This whole paragraph is a rhetorical indictment showing Jewish guilt. On the surface the statements of verses 17–20 are all valid claims, for the Old Testament states that these were indeed the covenant privileges of the Jewish people. But these advantages were also predicated on being a nation that followed God and kept his law, and that is where the Jewish people failed.

WHAT THE JEWS THOUGHT OF THEMSELVES (2:17-20)

There are two parts to this list, with verses 17–18 noting five Jewish strengths and verses 19–20 noting four ways the Jews related to Gentiles. The actual situation, however, will be seen in verses 21–23, where the guilt of the nation is proved.

Jewish strengths (2:17-18)

The section begins with five strengths of the Jewish people that they believed gave them special privileges with God. The list is positive, showing the value of the law in Jewish life. Still, Paul wants his readers to know the Jews ignore the importance of living out the law in their lives. The list is true on a national level, but individuals would have these privileges only if they were faithful.

1. They call themselves Jews, which means they have a special relationship with God as the covenant people. The title "Jew" was originally geographic and spoke of people who lived in the land of Judah, and it became the national name. As such it came to have religious status as representing the followers of Yahweh. When they call themselves Jews, they claim to be followers of God's law.

2. They are those who "rely on the law," meaning they depend on the law for their religious identity and claim to follow it. The problem was that they turned it almost into a magic formula for protecting themselves from harm or God's displeasure. This is one of the key problems Paul is addressing in this section. The law is not an automatic shield keeping them from wrath or harm. Their reliance should have been on their walk with God, not on the fact that he had given them the law.

3. They "boast in God," which again is a good thing on the surface, as Scripture makes evident (Ps 34:2, 44:8; Jer 9:23, 24; Rom 5:11; 1 Cor 1:31). But too often among the Jews there was a lack of humility that was not pride in God but pride in their status as God's people. Some wore their Jewishness as a status symbol, showing off their piety to all around.

4. They claimed to "know his will," and they did since they had his revealed law to guide them. God gave them his law to enable them to know what he demanded in daily conduct (Ps 40:8, 143:10; Heb 10:7, 9). Yet this too became a problem when they relied on their superior knowledge to make them right with God. Knowledge without obedience is insufficient and leads to hypocrisy and failure.

5. To "approve of what is superior" could mean either of two things. It could be "approve of things that matter," meaning the ability to distinguish between right and wrong; or it could be "approve of the things that are best" or truly excellent, meaning the ability to make higher moral choices. The second is preferred, for the Jews claimed to be superior to Gentiles in this area. This is also supported by the added "because you are instructed by the law," which is intended for all five but especially relates to the moral side of the law. The law of Moses was the sole criterion for moral decisions (as it should have been in the old covenant period).

From this list we learn that elevating the place of the law without living it in daily conduct leads to hypocrisy and guilt before God. The same is true for us today. We cannot experience the true value of being a Christian until we learn to walk the Christian walk.

Relationship with the Gentiles (2:19–20)

Paul now turns to another list, this time describing how the Jewish people related to the Gentiles. This is intended as positive, just like the five above. Think of these as indicating the way God wanted the Jews to be a blessing to the Gentiles, as the Abrahamic covenant commanded (Gen 12:3). It begins, "If you are convinced," showing that they believed these to be their divine calling as well as their personal prerogatives or rights. Since in the law they had special revelation from God that was "the embodiment of knowledge and truth" (v. 20), the Gentiles, who had only general revelation, were subordinate to them. Paul is saying that while this is in one sense correct, this gave the Jews greater responsibility.

1. They believed themselves to be "a guide for the blind," describing the Jewish mission to the Gentiles. In Isaiah 42:6–7 God told Israel he had called them to be "a light for the Gentiles, to open eyes that are blind," which according to Isaiah 35:5 would come when he restored the nation and returned the people to himself. However, in Matthew 15:14 Jesus declared that the Jewish people had failed in this because their leaders had themselves become "blind guides ... the blind leading the blind."

2. Similarly, the Jews claimed they were "a light for those who are in the dark." However, various groups within Judaism differed in their understanding of this mission. The community at Qumran who wrote and preserved the Dead Sea Scrolls considered the Gentiles destined for wrath and ignored them. There was some interest in winning converts in diaspora Judaism (those Jews who lived outside

Palestine), as seen for instance in 2 Esdras 6:26 ("the heart of the inhabitants shall be changed") and 1 Enoch 48:4 ("All who dwell on earth shall fall down and worship before him"). Still, such activity was sporadic at best. Pharisees did "travel over land and sea to win a single convert" (Matt 23:15), but in reality they only visited the synagogues and tried to talk the God-fearers (Gentiles who worshipped as Jews but were not willing to be circumcised) into becoming full converts.

3. The Jews considered themselves to be "an instructor of the foolish." In Galatians 3:24–4:2 Paul called the law itself a pedagogue or guardian, instructing Israel in the ways of God. The Jews applied it to their relationship with the Gentiles, who were "foolish" because they were ignorant and knew nothing about God or how to relate to him.

4. Finally, Jews thought themselves "a teacher of little children." These last two are virtual synonyms. The Jewish people looked on themselves as the repository of the knowledge of God and believed that they alone could teach the Gentile "babes" the eternal truths about God.

The basis for all these claims is that they have "in the law the embodiment of knowledge and truth." The Greeks and Romans may have had incredible philosophical schools (recognized in ancient times by a few Jews like Philo or Josephus), but they had no final truth, for they did not have God's law to guide them. Some truth may be found in earthly philosophy or medical and scientific knowledge, but all that has no final heavenly value. As a result, the Jewish people considered the Gentiles to be spiritual infants who could not grow into adulthood without the Jews to guide and teach them.

RHETORICAL QUESTIONS SHOWING THEIR TRUE GUILT (2:21–22)

Paul then turns to four rhetorical questions, using irony for the sake of his argument. Jesus used this approach to pronounce woes

against the Pharisees in Matthew 23 (see 23:2-3), exposing their
failure to practice what they preached.

Paul begins his searing questions by asking, "You, then, who
teach others, do you not teach yourself?" This parallels Matthew
23:15, where Jesus charged the Pharisees who traversed land and
sea to win converts with making them "twice as much a child of
hell as you are!" If teachers fail to live out what they are teaching,
they have forfeited the right to teach. The other three questions
all flow out of this one and provide examples from the Ten Commandments where the Jewish people have failed to teach themselves. The three here are stealing (the eighth commandment),
adultery (the seventh), and idolatry (the first two commandments),
found in Exodus 20:3-5, 14-15.

With the next two questions, Paul asks his readers if they are
guilty of stealing or adultery. It is doubtful whether many of the
readers had ever committed these sins. Some interpreters have
thought they should be understood in light of the antitheses of
Matthew 5:21-48, when murder is deepened to anger and adultery to lust. In that sense, stealing and adultery would apply to
every person, but there is no evidence Paul is intending this here.
Rather, they should be seen as general examples. The point is that
some Jews have broken the very commandments they teach. As
a people, their conduct obviated their right to teach, for they are
guilty of hypocrisy.

The fourth question is difficult to interpret: "You who abhor
idols, do you rob temples?" Jews in the first century AD would naturally have despised idols; the idolatry that had plagued the people
of Israel for much of their earlier history was virtually unknown
in the first century. But what would it mean to "rob temples"? Literal robbery of temples did occur occasionally in the ancient world,
because the gold and silver instruments in most temples would
be quite valuable. The word translated "rob" (*hierosyleis*) could
refer to committing sacrilege or irreverence toward a temple, so
some think this means that Jews were committing irreverent acts

against the Jerusalem temple, perhaps by believing themselves above the law. Others think it refers to actual stealing from the Jerusalem temple.

But these don't fit the question very well, so the majority view is that this speaks of literally robbing pagan temples or perhaps misusing or defrauding funds from such temples. This was not a widespread practice but, like stealing and adultery above, it would occasionally occur. Many Jews would argue that since these idols were blasphemous, stealing idols and instruments from pagan temples could constitute ridding the world of such idols. Paul would argue that such was still robbery and broke the commandments.

RESULT: GOD'S NAME DISHONORED AND BLASPHEMED (2:23–24)

Paul concludes 2:17–24 with the charge that in all these areas the Jewish people have dishonored the law. Many versions stand with the NIV in seeing verse 23 as a fifth rhetorical question concluding the four in verses 21–22 (KJV, NASB, NRSV, CSB, LEB, GNT). However, the grammar changes, and it is better to see this as a concluding condemnation, "You who boast in the law dishonor God through your transgression of the law" (with NLT, NET, ESV, NEB, JB). Paul uses *parabasei*, "transgression," or legal violation of the law. As lawbreakers they have lost the right to boast in the law.

As a result, they "dishonor God" because of their hypocrisy. The term translated "dishonor" also means to "insult" or "disgrace" another, and by their failure they have given Gentiles an excuse to heap scorn on God and on Judaism (v. 24). Paul quotes Isaiah 52:5 in this respect: "God's name is blasphemed among the Gentiles because of you." In the context of the quotation (Isaiah 40–66), the exile of Israel is the result of national sin, causing the name of God to be mocked by the nations. Here as well Gentile contempt results from Jewish transgression. The Jews are no better than the Gentiles, for both turned away from God and sinned against him. Yet in this the Jewish people were more guilty, for their sin caused the Gentiles to slander the name of God.

CIRCUMCISION ONLY HAS VALUE IF
YOU KEEP THE LAW (2:25-29)

Long before the giving of the law ratified the covenant at Mount
Sinai, the rite of circumcision ratified the Abrahamic covenant
(Gen 17:9-14). Now that Paul has demonstrated that the disobedience of the Jews has nullified the effects of the law (Rom 2:12-24),
he shows that their transgressions have also nullified the value
of circumcision.

TRUE CIRCUMCISION (2:25-26)

Verse 25 begins with *gar* ("for," not in the NIV translation), indicating Paul is anticipating the Jewish response: that they have under-
gone circumcision and therefore are the covenant community of
God. Paul counters that in the same way that their transgression
nullified the law by demonstrating their unfaithfulness to it, so
their transgression has also nullified the effects of circumcision
on their status as the covenant people.

One cannot state too strongly the importance of circumcision
to the Jewish people. In the intertestamental period the Syrian
king Antiochus Epiphanes banned circumcision in Palestine as
part of his attempt to outlaw Judaism (1 Maccabees 1:48-61). As
a result it became even more the definitive sign of Jewishness,
and by Paul's time it was the final step in making a Gentile a full
Jewish convert.

Paul is arguing that "circumcision has value [only] if you
observe the law," a point he made in verse 23 about the Torah. The
verb "has value" (*ōphelei*) means it "is of profit" to them in terms
of their relationship to God. He is saying that faithful observance
applies to the efficacy of both the law and circumcision. Disobedience to God's demands breaks all covenant relationships, so their
unfaithfulness to God means they "have become as though [they]
had not been circumcised." The larger context of this chapter
shows Paul has in mind not just their present relationship with
God but the final judgment as well. In light of their disobedience,

circumcision will no longer keep them from God's wrath and eternal fiery punishment.

A point must be made about Paul's demand to "observe" or "practice" the law. Most Jews understood observing the law as a sincere attempt to follow it faithfully, recognizing that no one could keep it perfectly. But that is exactly what Paul is demanding. In the old covenant the sacrificial system had been given so that when people broke the law they could find forgiveness. But Jesus the Messiah had come, and that system no longer sufficed. To find salvation, the law would have to be followed perfectly now (Gal 5:3, "obey the whole law").

Paul is saying that neither the law nor circumcision can bring salvation, for no one can obey it perfectly enough for that to happen. Faith in Christ is the only sufficient basis for salvation. Those who turn to circumcision negate their salvation by inevitably disobeying the law and thereby becoming as if they were uncircumcised. Paul will say in 3:20 that "no one will be declared righteous in God's sight by the works of the law" because they cannot keep it perfectly enough for that to happen.

In verse 26 Paul discusses the opposite issue. If the Gentiles ("those who are not circumcised") do practice the law and keep its commands, then they should be regarded as Jews ("as though they were circumcised") and as saved. If breaking the law turns the Jews into Gentiles, then obeying the law turns the Gentiles into Jews. Paul is not here advocating works righteousness; Gentiles cannot be saved by following the dictates of the law. He is saying only that Gentiles stand equally before God with the Jews because they too keep the law. In this new era of salvation history, Jew and Gentile stand before God in need of salvation on an equal footing.

Condemnation from the Uncircumcised (2:27)

For Jews under the old covenant, circumcision and having the law of God were an undeniable advantage that demonstrated the superiority of being a Jew over being a Gentile. In this new salvation-historical reality, that advantage has disappeared. Not only do Jew and Gentile stand equally before God as guilty, but also the Gentiles will condemn the Jews at the last judgment. This is unusual, as God is the final judge, yet several passages say the saints will participate in the judgment against sinners.[1] The difference is that the Jewish people thought they would judge the pagan world, not vice versa. This is in keeping with Matthew 12:41-42, where Jesus claims that the people of Nineveh and the queen of the South (the queen of Sheba from 1 Kgs 10) will rise in judgment against those Jews who had rejected Jesus their Messiah.

Many think the message here is hypothetical, describing Gentiles who inadvertently obey aspects of the law and in this way judge those Jews who disobey the law at those same points. I would follow others who believe this describes Christian Gentiles who keep the law and follow God and therefore will stand over unbelieving Jews at the final judgment. They are the true circumcision of verse 26, fulfilling "the righteous requirement of the law" (8:4) and paralleling the redeemed of Philippians 3:3—the new and true Israel.

This means having "the written code [literally, "letter"] and circumcision" will not suffice. The Jews cannot obey the law sufficiently and are all "lawbreakers." Only faith in Christ can bring about salvation. Both as guilty sinners and as recipients of Christ's salvific act, Jew and Gentile stand equally before God.

THE TRUE JEW: CIRCUMCISION OF THE HEART (2:28-29)

Paul closes this section on the Jewish failure to keep the law by showing why circumcision no longer makes one right with God. He does this by differentiating between a professing Jew and a true Jew. The professing Jew is described in verse 28 as a "Jew who is one only outwardly." One cannot be right with God merely by

---

1. This is so both in the New Testament and extrabiblical Jewish writings; see Matt 19:28; 1 Cor 6:2; Rev 3:21; Wisdom of Solomon 3:8; 1 Enoch 91:12.

possessing the covenant signs of law and circumcision. External realities are not enough. Note the several contrasts here—outwardly/inwardly, physical/of the heart, written code/Spirit, from other people/from God. Each designates what is essential for true salvation. The old covenant period, centering on circumcision and the law, has given way to the new covenant period, centering on faith in Christ and the coming of the Spirit.

The true Jew (v. 29) thus is "one inwardly," signified by "the circumcision of the heart," the spiritual reception of Christ. Since Christ has come and brought the true kingdom with him (Mark 1:15), it is the internal reality that matters. This was stated often under the old covenant (Deut 10:16; Jer 4:4, 9:25-26). For Paul, living in the new covenant era, this can only be fully realized in Christ in the age of the Spirit.

Those who have experienced this new covenant relationship are the recipients of the final contrast, receiving praise "not from other people but from God." In keeping with the rest of the chapter, there is an "already and not yet" thrust here as well, with the praise coming now and yet culminating in glory and praise at the last judgment (see 2:16).

———

This section has a great deal of relevance for us today. We too are prone to seek external praise from others more than from God. Since Christ has come and brought the true kingdom with him (Mark 1:15), it is the internal reality that matters. I ought to live to please God rather than those around me. In a larger sense I want to please both, but the ultimate criterion is God, looking forward to that final moment when I give account to him for my life.

Two points must be made about Paul's list in verses 17-20 of the positive ways the Jews' privilege and their responsibility related to the Gentiles. First, these privileges and responsibilities reflected God's intentions for Israel. This was how they could fulfill the Abrahamic covenant and God's intention in choosing them as his

covenant people. But that demanded both faithfulness in obeying
his covenant and laws and a willingness to be a source of blessing
to the Gentiles. The Jews failed in both. Second, these privileges
and responsibilities also apply to our relationships as Christians to
unbelievers. This demands humility and a desire to be used of God
as we take these truths to the world. Would Paul's assessment of
us be any better than that of his own people? We must continually
examine ourselves in terms of our witness and service to the lost.

Though they boasted in the law and in their relationship to
Yahweh, the Jewish people dishonored God by failing to honor his
law and covenant obligations. Therefore, they gave the Gentiles
reason to mock the kind of God who could not control his own
followers. This also continues today, as we frequently hear about
Christians who have brought dishonor on the church and the God
we follow.

The key, as we will see in every chapter of Romans, is the internal life of the believer. We fall into error when we are satisfied
with the external trappings of looking like a Christian and ignore
the internal realities of actually living like one. Since so many of
those around us are satisfied with external appearance, we too
easily forget that God looks on the heart. We must live at all times
to glorify him and not ourselves—something that is very hard to
do in our culture of appearances.

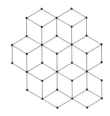

THE SINFULNESS OF THE JEWS
AND OF ALL HUMANITY
(3:1-20)

There are two parts to this passage. The first (3:1-8) is the third and final section dealing with the depravity of the Jewish people (2:1-3:8). It continues Paul's diatribe style of chapter 2 and consists of a series of rhetorical questions regarding two issues: the faithfulness of God in spite of the unfaithfulness of Israel (3:1-4) and the justice of his judgment in spite of claims that he is unjust (3:5-8). This is one of the most difficult passages in Romans because of Paul's dense logic. I will try to make that logic clear as we proceed. Paul's issue is this: If there is no advantage in being Jewish and God can reject members of his covenant people, then how can one claim that God is always faithful to his covenant promises?

The lengthier response to this question is in Romans 9-11, but Paul gives a beginning summary of that argument here. He argues that God's judgment of the Jews is actually part of his faithfulness to his covenant promises. There are blessings and curses in the covenant, and Israel's unbelief has led to a deserved divine response. The Jewish people have brought the situation down on their own heads, and God's righteousness is uppermost at every point.

The second part of the passage puts 1:18-3:8 together and sums up a basic truth: Since the Gentiles are consumed with depravity (1:18-32) and the Jews are as well (2:1-3:8), it must be concluded that all people are alike guilty of sin (3:9-20). This section contains three parts: the basic thesis on the universal nature of sin (v. 9), a series of Old Testament quotations demonstrating the total consuming power of this depravity (vv. 10-18), and a statement of the accountability of all people to God (vv. 19-20).

DIVINE FAITHFULNESS IS CONTRASTED WITH JEWISH FAILURE (3:1-4)

Throughout chapter 2 Paul argued that neither the law nor circumcision made the Jew superior to the Gentile. While Jews did have the law revealed to them, and circumcision did make them the covenant people, their disobedience negated their advantages and brought God's wrath down on them. Now Paul asks the basic question that would be on their lips as a result: "What advantage, then, is there in being a Jew?"

THE ADVANTAGES OF BEING JEWISH (3:1-2)

The Jews believed that since they had circumcision and the law, they were the chosen people, but Paul exploded that in chapter 2 and basically said they had no advantage over the Gentiles. If this is true, he asks, "what value is there in circumcision?" In the commentary on 2:25, we saw that "value" referred to "profit," so the question can be rephrased, "What profit is there in undergoing circumcision?"

The answer one would expect on the basis of chapter 2 is "none whatsoever," but Paul surprises us by saying, "Much in every way!" While circumcision and the law do not have salvific value, they do have religious value for the Jewish people. Paul never denied in chapter 2 that there was value in the law and in circumcision; his point was that they did not give the Jews special privileges over the Gentiles. Both groups would be judged at the *bēma*, or judgment seat, of God on the basis of *keeping* the law, not on the basis of *possessing* it.

In verse 2 Paul mentions "first of all" the primary advantage— they "have been entrusted with the very words of God"—but he does not mention any others. In 9:4–5 he provides a more detailed list (glory, covenant, temple worship, the promises), but here only one. This is the foremost of the advantages, the primary blessing God has poured out on his people. There is some question as to whether "the very words of God" signifies (1) the Mosaic law, (2) the promises of God to his people that anchored his faithfulness (v. 3), or (3) the Old Testament as a whole. This latter is likely the best and fits Paul's wide range of Old Testament quotations throughout Romans, by far the most extensive set of quotes in any of his writings.

The Greek may be translated "oracles of God," referring to his living pronouncements or utterances. When we read Scripture, we should picture God actually speaking these things to us directly! Paul is especially stressing here the promises of Scripture in which God has committed himself to working on behalf of his people, that we have a covenant God who cares for and works to better his people, and we can rely on those promises. One of the primary promise of Scripture is that God "never leaves nor forsakes" his children (Deut 31:6–8; Josh 1:5; 1 Chr 28:20).

This is an important perspective for us today. We call the Bible "the word of God," yet we don't act as if we believe it. Studies have shown that the level of Bible reading is going down as the years go by.[1] I have personally seen the amount of teaching in the average church lessening year by year. I would say that the number of preachers who give expository messages (Bible-based sermons) is going up somewhat, but there is less and less teaching in the

---

1. For one such report, see "The Bible in America: 6-Year Trends," *Barna*, June 15, 2016, https://www.barna.com/research/the-bible-in-america-6-year-trends/.

church apart from the pulpit. My constant prayer for the series of which this commentary is a part is that it might encourage more study of God's word in the years to come. If we truly believe the Bible is the Word of God, *how can we neglect it in our lives?*

THEIR UNFAITHFULNESS WILL NOT NULLIFY THE FAITHFULNESS OF GOD (3:3)

The primary difficulty with the promise of verse 2 regarding the advantage of being a Jew is that it hardly ever seems to have worked. Israel had a history of repeated failures in which God's promises seemed to have had little effect in helping his people to remain faithful to him. Paul now voices this objection: "What if some were unfaithful? Will their unfaithfulness nullify God's faithfulness?" What is Paul saying here? There are three options. Both questions could be objections to Paul's thesis, or they could both come from Paul (with an implied "What then?"), or the first could be an objection and the second Paul's response.

Given the context, the second option (that both come from Paul) makes best sense. The two questions here answer the implied question, What then do we do with the fact of God's blessings upon Israel (v. 2) in light of his judgment on them for unbelief (2:2–3, 5, 12, 16, 25–27)? Paul is responding that the unfaithfulness of Israel down through their history has not and cannot nullify the larger blessing of God's faithfulness to his covenant people. The verb "nullify" (*katargēsei*), literally meaning to "render powerless" or abolish a thing, is a favorite of Paul's (twenty-five times in his letters). Nothing Israel did in its checkered history could remove God's faithful actions on their behalf.

In the covenant ceremony of Genesis 15:1–21 God appeared in the form of a smoking firepot and blazing torch, walking between the parts of Abraham's sacrificed heifer, goat, and ram. This signified his taking a curse on himself. He was saying in effect, "May this happen to me if I do not keep my covenant with you," guaranteeing that he would always fulfill his covenant with Israel. It is important to realize that even God's punishing Israel for its wickedness was part of God's faithful activity toward the nation. The purpose of the repeated deliveries of the nation into the hands of the Philistines in Judges or of the exile in 2 Kings and 2 Chronicles was always redemptive, to wake up the nation to its folly and bring about repentance and restoration. In fact, it worked, and Israel did not fall into idolatry throughout the intertestamental period. As in 2 Peter 3:9, God never wants "anyone to perish, but everyone to come to repentance."

However, while God never fails, Israel has failed again and again. Ironically, the only time in its history Israel remained faithful for a prolonged period was after the return from exile, when for four hundred years Israel did not fall into idolatry and followed the Torah carefully, even developing an oral tradition of extra rules to help them stay faithful. However, when Jesus came, they rejected their Messiah. This act of unbelief became an even more serious time of faithlessness, so they were now more apostate than at any time in their history. Paul in Romans 11:17–21 will show that these unbelieving (= unfaithful) Jews have been removed from the olive tree (the true nation of Israel) and are no longer God's people.

God Proved Right (3:4)

Still, even this act of apostasy by an unbelieving nation cannot abolish God's faithfulness, so Paul responds to his two questions with "No way!" (*mē genoito*; NIV "Not at all!"). This is in effect a negative oath (KJV "God forbid"; NASB "May it never be"). It is the strongest possible denial. Jewish faithlessness can never cancel God's faithfulness, and the formula of verse 3 is restated in verse 4 as "Let God be true [= faithful], and every human being a liar [= unfaithful]." God is true to his promises even when his people are not, referring especially to the covenant promises of the Old Testament. God is faithful and true when he judges Israel

(Ps 45:4; Neh 9:32-33) even when others are liars (Ps 116:11, "In my alarm I said, 'Everyone is a liar'"). Paul is probably referring here to all humanity, with Israel in its unfaithfulness included.

Paul anchors this in a quotation from Psalm 51:4, "So that you may be proved right when you speak and prevail when you judge." The superscription of this lament psalm says David wrote it after being challenged by the prophet Nathan over his adultery with Bathsheba. In verse 4, he recognizes the righteousness of God and says any judgment God places on him will be just. Paul applies this confession to Israel's sin, saying that his judgment on his people is just. However, the difference between David and Israel was that Israel did not believe they had broken the covenant. Paul is a prosecuting attorney showing them that they are wrong. To be faithful to his covenant God must judge Israel for its unbelief/faithlessness. When he does so his is "proved right" in his judgment.

GOD IS JUST IN JUDGING ISRAEL (3:5-8)

In this second half of 3:1-8 Paul considers possible objections to verses 1-4, especially the faithfulness and truthfulness of God in the midst of his judging Israel.

IS GOD UNJUST IN HIS WRATH? (3:5)

The term translated "unrighteousness" here is *adikia*, "wickedness" (as in 1:29; 2:8). So we could translate the verse as, "If [Israel's] wickedness brings out God's righteousness." This would mean that the Jewish unrighteousness Paul talks about in verses 1-4 gave God the opportunity to demonstrate his righteousness more clearly. If this is so, Paul concludes, "[Should we say] that God is unjust in bringing his wrath on us?" Paul's logic is that if Jewish wickedness makes God's justice stand out more starkly, God should welcome it rather than be angry over it.

The wording anticipates the answer no, as if to say: "God is not unjust in pouring out his wrath on us, is he?" Paul's response is the same as we have seen in 2:1-3:4—when God judges his people, he is faithful to his covenant promises because wickedness demands judgment. The purpose of this judgment is redemptive; God wants to force his people to rethink their actions and repent.

Paul adds, "I am using a human argument." Even in raising the question of divine justice, he does so from a purely human point of view (compare 1 Cor 9:8; Gal 3:15). From a divine perspective, it could be no other way. Simple human logic will lead us to the same place a divine perspective would by proving the rightness of God's condemnation and judgment of evil.

No, for He Judges the World (3:6)

Paul's second emphatic "no way" (the same Greek phrase as in v. 4) makes it clear that God is not unjust when he directs his wrath at the unbelief of the Jewish people. He illustrates his position with a counterquestion: "If that were so, how could God judge the world?" There is some question whether this is present judgment (it is a present-tense verb) or future final judgment (the verb would then be seen as a "futuristic present," stressing the certainty of what is to come). There is frequently an inaugurated thrust in the New Testament ("already and not yet"), with present judgment the beginning of a process that will culminate in final judgment. This is a viable interpretation, but throughout chapter 2 the thrust was on final judgment, so the future is more likely in view here as well.

In Genesis 18:25, Abraham, beseeching God to spare Sodom, asks, "Will not the judge of all the earth do right?" This question of a just and righteous God echoes through the Old Testament (Deut 32:4; Job 8:3 2 Chr 19:7; Ezek 18:25) and is the point here as well. A righteous, just God must exercise judgment when faced with evil, and that is true for Jewish sin as well as Gentile sin.

We Should Not Do Evil So Good Might Result (3:7-8)

Paul here repeats the Jewish objection of verse 5 another way, building on the mention of falsehood/lies from verse 4: "If my falsehood enhances God's truthfulness and so increases his glory, why am I still condemned as a sinner?" Paul is saying that human sin would have to be lauded if it actually brought glory to God. The glory of God is the most important pursuit for every person, so if being a sinner makes his glory all the more visible, then it cannot be worthy of condemnation, can it?

In negating this false assertion (v. 8), Paul does not use "certainly not" (or "no way") like he does in verses 4 and 6, but the effect is the same when he shows the absurdity of such a premise. He states, "Why not say—as some slanderously claim that we say—'Let us do evil that good may result'?" The illogical nature of this is so obvious that he doesn't actually answer the charge; he thinks the ridiculous nature of the hypothesis is self-evident.

Still, apparently Paul's opponents were making this charge against him. If sin does indeed bring about the righteousness of God (v. 5) and increase his glory (v. 7), then it would be natural to want to sin all the more so that more and more good would result from it (as v. 8 would imply). Paul calls this charge "slanderous" (the Greek term also means "blasphemous"). Their charge impugns both the character of the righteous God and the gospel he has revealed to Paul, and its blasphemous nature demands that it be totally rejected.

Paul wants his readers to realize how wrong and dangerous such a premise is, so he adds, "Their condemnation is just!" It is not easy to identify who he is talking about; some think he means all the Jews in their sin and guilt, supposing that this is the conclusion to 2:1-3. Yet in the context of 3:7-8 this is unlikely. It probably refers to the opponents of verses 7-8 who stood against the gospel. These objectors deserve all the condemnation they are receiving, for blasphemy is the most heinous of sins. This comment provides a fitting end for this section, for the absolute justice of God is the core theme throughout 2:1-3:8. The covenant God must be seen in his righteousness and justice.

ALL HUMANITY IS SINFUL (3:9-20)

In 1:18-8:39 Paul presents his gospel to the church of Rome, and in this opening section (1:18-3:20) he demonstrates why we need God's salvation. To this point he has shown the total depravity of both Gentiles (1:18-32) and Jews (2:1-3:8); now he sums up by emphasizing the guilt of all humanity under sin. There are three sections in 3:9-20: another introductory rhetorical question and answer on the universal nature of sin (v. 9); a series of Old Testament quotations that prove the full extent of depravity (vv. 10-18); and a summary statement that the whole world is unrighteous and accountable to God (vv. 19-20).

THE UNIVERSAL NATURE OF SIN (3:9)

This section begins with the same "What then" of 3:1, a rhetorical question that calls for a conclusion to the material on the absolute sinfulness of Jew and Gentile. Paul wants his readers to make up their own minds about all the material he has presented on human depravity in 2:1-3:8.

The second question is a single word, *proechometha*, which can mean "make an excuse" or "surpass" or "have an advantage." It could be translated several ways: (1) "Should we [meaning Paul himself] make an excuse for the Jews?" (2) "Should we Jews make excuses for ourselves?" (3) "Are we Jews surpassed by them?" (i.e., inferior to the Gentiles). (4) "Do we Jews have an advantage over them?" The first two are unlikely because they force us to supply a direct object that is not in the text: "make an excuse (for something)." The third is based on a rare meaning of the verb and does not really fit the teaching of 2:1-3:8. The fourth, adopted by the NIV, is the most likely. This summarizes the emphasis of 2:1-3:8: the lack of any Jewish advantage over Gentiles.

Paul's negation of this—"Not at all!" (*ou pantōs*)—is slightly different but means the same as the "certainly not" of verses 4 and 6. In verse 2 Paul did say the Jews had one advantage (they were entrusted with "the very words of God"). However, there he was discussing religious benefits, but here he is speaking of salvation benefits. Both groups are equally answerable for their sins and equally in need of salvation through Christ.

Paul describes this very forcefully: "For we have already made the charge that Jews and Gentiles alike are all under the power of sin." He has made this charge throughout 1:18–3:8. The legal accusation and proof of guilt are certain—we are guilty before God. Paul pictures sin here and in chapter 6 as a malignant force invading Jew and Gentile alike and placing everyone under its control. The evil powers have conquered and enslaved all human beings.

THE EXTENT OF HUMAN DEPRAVITY: TOTAL (3:10-18)

This series of quotations is what the rabbis called a "pearl-stringing midrash," a sermon that strings together a series of "pearls" from Scripture on a single topic. Paul introduces it with the characteristic "as it is written," pointing to what God has inspired human authors to write down. He provides the basic thesis in verses 10-12: sin is universal throughout the human race. He follows this up with a list of specific kinds of sin, first of speech (13-14) and then sins of a violent nature (15-17) and finally the basic religious dimension, no fear of God (18).

None are righteous (3:10-12)

The list of quotations begins with Psalm 14:1-3 (also found in Ps 53:1-3). Paul here deviates from Psalm 14:1, which reads "there is no one who does good," in order to provide a summary of what he has just been saying: "There is no one righteous, not even one." No human being is right with God. Every single person stands before him stripped of all pretensions of righteousness (which Paul treats as a forensic or legal term; see 1:17, 32; 2:5, 13, 26; 3:4, 5).

Psalm 14 begins with the well-known "The fool says in his heart, 'There is no God,'" which in the ancient world would not have understood as atheism but rather a life that ignores God. The psalm defines this two ways: the complete inability to understand God and the failure to seek him (Rom 3:11). This is not just passive ignorance but also active rejection. The fool wants nothing to do with God (as in Rom 1:18–20). The refusal to seek God refers to a preference for the things of this world rather than the things of God (as in Matt 6:19–21; Mark 8:33; Col 3:1–2). Total depravity means that people worship themselves and want little to do with God, caring only for the temporary pleasures of this life.

Paul further describes this Godless life in Psalm 14:3 (Rom 3:12). These sin-obsessed individuals have deliberately "turned away" from anything having to do with God and thus have become absolutely "worthless." These people simply have no room for God in their lives and give him no time, with the result that "there is no one who does good, not even one." Paul, through the psalm, describes a self-centered, worldly person who does only that which benefits the self and ignores the things of God completely. However, this is not a denial that every human being is capable of good. Rather, it means that at the heart of every human being there lies a core of sin and self-centeredness that is in control. The actual golden rule of the world is, "Do unto others before they get the chance to do unto you."

Sins of speech: throats/tongues, lips, mouths (3:13–14)

This set of quotations combines three Old Testament passages connected to one another by centering on the organs of speech—the throat, the tongue, the lips, and the mouth. The first two stem from Psalm 5:9, the first picturing the throats of sinful humankind as "open graves." This graphic and apt metaphor depicts every word that comes out of a person as an unclean thing pouring out of a rotting corpse. The imagery includes both receiving and giving out. Like an open grave they take in death, and their open throats also bring forth death. The sins of the tongue follow in the psalm,

envisioning a form of deadly speech having especially to do with
the treacherous trickery that always accompanies evil deeds.

The third pictures "the poison of vipers ... on their lips"
(Ps 140:3). This describes the deadly effects of the tongue coming
from slander and gossip, the attempt to destroy another person by
spreading vicious lies about them. The final word picture stems
from Psalm 10:7 and depicts their mouths as "full of cursing and
bitterness." All of these sins of the tongue deal with death, deceit,
and the desire to hurt others. This final one is the human tendency
to yell and complain when we are thwarted. Everyone wants to get
their way or the whole world hears about it.

Sins of violence: shedding blood, producing misery (3:15-17)

This portion of quotations is taken from Isaiah 59:7-8, which is in
a section dealing with the effects of national sin. Because Israel's
hands were stained with blood, God had withdrawn his protection (Isa 59:1-8) and his justice (59:9-15) from them. Paul moves
the action from the mouth and lips in verses 13-14 to the feet and
pathways here. While Paul featured speech and communication
earlier, here he features the direction of their lives. Also, while
Isaiah speaks of the sins of Israel, Paul applies the passage to the
sins of all humanity.

First, they are "swift to shed blood," pointing to the propensity
of every nation to try to get ahead by means of war and the forceful takeover of other nations' property. In our time, the forty-year
period we have just passed through has included separate wars
on virtually every continent, and all of them due to the human
thirst for riches and land at any cost. The result, "ruin and misery,"
hardly needs to be developed. All you need to do is watch any news
program or pick up any newspaper to see the unbelievable ruin
we are making of our world.

The final comment, "the way of peace they do not know," is
also obvious. In Isaiah words for "way," "path, and "highway" are

found everywhere, and the contrast between the "paths of God" and the "paths of humanity" are a major theme in the book. The paths of God are peace and worship (11:16; 35:8; 40:3–5; 62:10), while the paths of wicked humanity are destruction and horror (33:8; 36:1–2; 59:8). Only in God via Christ can there be a lasting peace, but without the violence of the cross, that peace could never have been secured.

Summary: no fear of God (3:18)

This verse is a quotation from Psalm 36:1. In this psalm the sinfulness of wicked humanity is set in direct contrast to the righteousness of God, which is "like the highest mountains" (v. 6) in contrast to the depth of humankind's evil. In Proverbs the "fear of God" is the basis of wisdom (Prov 1:7; 9:10; 15:33), and "fear" throughout Scripture connotes both terror and reverence. The fear of God in this former sense is linked to his righteous judgment (Rom 14:12; 2 Cor 5:10; 1 Pet 1:17). We are responsible to God and will answer to him, but sinful humanity in its unbelievable hubris flaunts its sin before God and willingly ignores his warnings. To them God is powerless to do anything about it.

Here the psalm mentions another body part, the eyes, metaphorically referring to the outlook on life of those who are under the power of sin. In the midst of sin's enslaving power over their lives, these people ignore God, worship themselves, and have no fear of the repercussions this mindset will have on their future (or the absence of any future!). They care only about the here and now, and many of these "fools" (in Proverbs a fool is anyone who ignores God and his ways) in our time pretend there is no final judgment. In light of the certainty of a heavenly future it is illogical to spend so much time and effort preparing for retirement in the few years we will have left on earth and to be totally neglectful in preparing for eternity. To fail to give much thought to our eternity with God is the height of folly.

THE UNIVERSALITY OF SIN (3:19-20)

Paul is doing two things in these verses. First, this is a concluding summary, not just of verses 9-18 but of the whole of 1:18-3:18, describing the results of God's revelation of himself through the Mosaic law to the Jews and natural law to the Gentiles. The result is that "the whole world [is] held accountable to God" and the sin of all humanity is evident (v. 19). Second, Paul revisits the place of the law of Moses in God's new economy, saying that its purpose is relegated to making people "conscious of sin" rather than making them righteous before God (v. 20). I will take these issues one at a time.

The whole world accountable (3:19)

The world of humankind does not know God (3:11), but it does know certain things about the way he has made the world. As he did in 2:2, Paul begins with "we know" to make a point from a generally recognized truth. Here it is the way the law speaks to its practitioners. The "law" in this context is not just the Mosaic ordinances but the whole Old Testament. Paul has especially in mind the quotations of verses 10-18, which are not from the Torah but from the Psalms and Isaiah. "Those under the law" are the Jewish people under the old covenant.

The result of the law's speaking is that "every mouth [is] silenced," which expands the scene to cover all humanity, not just the Jews. This addresses the false security of the Jews, who believed that the condemnation of the Old Testament was addressed only to the Gentiles while they were safe. The actual teaching of the Old Testament was that all humanity came under judgment and thus that "the whole world," Jew as well as Gentile, is "held accountable to God." To continue the judicial metaphor Paul uses so often in these chapters, all humanity has no defense when they stand before the Judge of all the earth and give account for their sins. They are rendered silent in their guilt as they await their sentence at the great white throne judgment seat of Revelation 20:11-15.

No one is righteous (3:20)

There is some question whether Paul's use of "therefore" introduces a confirmation or a reason for what he has said in verse 19. Since the material in this verse restates the same point in slightly different form, it is best to see it as a confirmation or restatement of the truth regarding the sinfulness of all humankind. This verse also likely contains an echo of Psalm 143:2, "no one living is righteous before you." The message is that no one by keeping the requirements of the whole law can be made right with God. It is impossible to find salvation by works. As Romans 2 has said, no one can obey well enough to earn salvation. The use of "works of the law" here has special relevance for the Jewish situation, but it applies to Gentiles as well.

The "works of the law" is a major phrase in Galatians and Romans, and we must carefully determine its meaning. Interpreters have approached it from different vantage points. Some say that all who try to obey the law commit idolatry and sin because salvation comes only by grace.[2] But Paul does not say that keeping the law is sin in and of itself, so that goes too far. In fact, the truth is just the opposite: failing to keep the law is sin.

A more important option comes from what has been called the "new perspective on Paul." In his book *Paul and Palestinian Judaism*, E. P. Sanders developed the idea of "covenantal nomism," meaning that for the Jews keeping the law was not a means of getting into the covenant people but of staying among the covenant people. According to this interpretation, the "works of the law" described how God's covenant people maintained a proper relationship with

---

2. Ernst Käsemann, *Commentary on Romans*, trans. Geoffrey W. Bromiley (Grand Rapids: Eerdmans, 1980), 89.

God.[3] James D. G. Dunn modified this slightly by calling these works "boundary markers" that differentiated a Jew from a Gentile. God's people used them to mark their status under the covenant as distinct from the nations. This would mean Paul rejected the "works of the law" because they excluded the Gentiles and made it impossible to unify all peoples under Christ.[4]

The problem with this view is that there is too little evidence for seeing the works of the law as boundary markers, and Romans 2 as well as Galatians 3–4 clearly teach that God's people will be judged on the basis of their failure to obey the law of God. The problem for Paul is human inability to keep the law; the issue is not identity with the Gentiles but relationship with God. Sanders is largely correct about the use of the law as an instrument for staying in a covenant relationship, but it is that and much more. Moreover, Sanders is wrong to deny a basic legalistic bent in first-century Judaism. He is correct about the Old Testament but wrong about Judaism in first-century Palestine, for the "works of the law" had become a means of salvation for many in Jesus' and Paul's day.[5]

The central purpose of the law here in 3:20 is to make people conscious of their sin, and as such the works of the law play a key role in forcing people into a faith relationship with Christ. The law does not save, but it drives people into realizing their sin and their consequent need for salvation, for it makes them aware that their transgressions are indeed sin.

———

3. E. P. Sanders, *Paul and Palestinian Judaism: A Comparison of Patterns of Religion* (Philadelphia: Fortress Press, 1977).

4. J. D. G. Dunn, *Romans 1–8*, Word Biblical Commentary (Waco, TX: Word, 1988), 153–54.

5. See Douglas Moo, *The Epistle to the Romans*, New International Commentary on the New Testament (Grand Rapids: Eerdmans, 1996), 211–17.

In Romans 3:1–8 Paul shows that God's judgment of Israel is part of his righteousness and faithfulness to his covenant promises. God must judge sin, and the purpose of his wrath is redemptive. His goal is to bring the nation to repentance and return his people to himself. This is exactly how God operates in our lives as well. God often sends trials to bring us out of our spiritual stupor and force us back to himself. As in Joshua 1:5, God will "never leave or forsake" us, and that includes the times when he must judge us. We, like Israel in Joshua's time or Paul's, must respond in faith and repentance to the one who does not want "anyone to perish" (2 Pet 3:9). The absolute justice of God's wrath and judgment of human wickedness demonstrates the prevalence of evil in this world. Condemnation is the only viable response to human sinfulness, and it is needed today even more than in Paul's day.

We see in Romans 3:9–20 that the human ability to rationalize sin is extensive and amazing. Darkness likes to pretend it is just another valid and harmless lifestyle choice, as demonstrated in the red-light district of major cities. As our world descends deeper and deeper into the pit, it depicts itself as basically good at the core, and Hollywood buttresses it all with cinematic brilliance. We desperately need this section of Romans in our day, for we must face honestly the evil that exists at the core of our society and of our own hearts. We need revival, and that can never come until we acknowledge our sin and face up to it honestly.

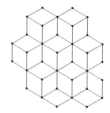

THE RIGHTEOUSNESS OF GOD
AT WORK IN JUSTIFICATION
(3:21–31)

O ur awareness of our need for salvation, our rescue from eternal death, begins with the realization of the extent of sin
in our world and our lives and the consequences of that sin: complete separation from God. Romans has been called the "systematic theology" of the New Testament, and Paul began by exploring
the total depravity of humankind in 1:18–3:20. This major section
concluded with the statement that the purpose of the law was to
make us "conscious of our sin" and thereby to turn us to God's
salvation in Christ. Now Paul turns to the meaning and process
of our salvation, and there is nowhere else in Scripture it is covered as thoroughly as here. There are two parts to Paul's presentation of the doctrine of salvation: 3:21–4:25, on the righteousness
of God in our salvation, and 5:1–8:39, on the new life in Christ and
the new hope provided in him. In these we learn that justification and sanctification are not two separate and only marginally
related experiences; they are closely related and interdependent
aspects of salvation. Justification is the first moment of the process of sanctification.

These first three chapters of Romans have proved the inability of Jew and Gentile to achieve salvation because of prevailing

sin. The universal depravity of humankind demands judgment (1:18–3:20). However, there is hope, and it is the result of the grace and righteousness of God (3:21), who provides salvation by sending his Son to be the atoning sacrifice and make justification for sins possible (3:24–26).

RIGHTEOUSNESS FROM GOD IS THE BASIS OF SALVATION (3:21–26)

The opening section of 3:21–31 is the core paragraph of Romans, expanding the purpose statement of 1:17, "In the gospel the righteousness of God is revealed." This righteousness is the basis of salvation, elaborated in the terms of 3:24–26: "justified," "redemption," "sacrifice of atonement," "faith," "righteousness." This is the gospel in embryo, the basis of the new life God has made available to humankind in its desperate need. The rest of Romans will build on this and unpack its meaning.

THE RIGHTEOUSNESS FROM GOD REVEALED (3:21)

The opening "But now" marks the end of Paul's discourse on the sinfulness of humankind and the movement to his next section, on the doctrine of salvation (what theologians call **soteriology**). This marks a return to the subject of 1:17, which stresses the source of our salvation: "the righteousness *from* God."[1] The change of topic and tone most likely is not logical; it does not build on the teaching of 1:18–3:20. Instead it is temporal, moving from the old era of Jews and Gentiles under the law and sin to the new age of salvation.

Paul is telling his readers that as a result of the incarnation and sacrificial death of Christ a new era has dawned. There has been a salvation-historical change, as God's final salvation has appeared concretely in history. This has taken place "apart from the law." On one level, "apart from the law" means this new truth cannot come merely by doing the works of the law as stated in 3:20. On

---

1. See comments on 1:17 for the reasoning behind this interpretation.

another, it refers to the new era initiated by Christ. This new age
of salvation comes separate from the law, and we enter it by faith
in the saving death of Christ. This is the primary meaning here.

In this new age of righteousness, God will justify sinners—
that is, declare them forgiven of their sins, acquitted of their guilt
in his eyes, and right with him—on the basis of Christ's atoning
death on the cross. This new age of righteousness/salvation is
"made known," a divine passive, meaning God is the one who has
revealed it.

THE RIGHTEOUSNESS FROM GOD RECEIVED (3:22-23)

Through faith to all who believe (3:22a)

Paul notes that this righteousness is "given" to the believer, further
clarifying that God is the source of this divine gift. Then Paul also
clarifies the means by which it is received: "through faith." Putting
verses 21–22 together, every person must be justified apart from
the law, which can only take place through faith.

Yet it is not really a passive act; we actively open up our hearts
to the Spirit's work, and salvation is actively received. Still, it is
God and the Spirit who justify and produce salvation in the heart.
The faith-decision is our human response to the Spirit's work. We
do not control the process; God does. It is the universal convicting
power of the Holy Spirit that allows the sinner to accept or reject
God's offer of salvation in Christ. Faith in the Pauline sense is both
a gift of God's grace and an active decision to accept that gift.

Historically, nearly all interpreters have understood the phrase
that the NIV translates "faith in Jesus Christ" to point objectively
to human faith ("faith in Jesus"). But an alternative understanding,
which has gained a great number of followers, says that this should
be understood subjectively ("the *faithfulness of* Jesus Christ"). This
latter understanding has some meaningful parallels in Romans,
such as "God's faithfulness" in 3:3 or the "faith of Abraham" in
4:12, 16.

Still, while this approach has merit, I would agree with those who hold to the classical interpretation here, that the emphasis is on our "faith in Christ." This objective sense is found often in the New Testament (Mark 11:22; Acts 3:16; Col 2:12; Jas 2:1; Rev 2:13; 14:12), and it is better in the context since throughout Romans 3:21–4:25 (seventeen times!) "faith" refers to belief in Christ. In these verses, Paul is establishing a contrast between being made right with God via the law and via faith in Christ. There is only one way by which anyone can experience God's saving righteousness—through faith not works—and it is only available to those who put their faith in Christ.

All have sinned (22b–23)

Paul now makes clear the basis of the universal availability of God's salvation: "There is no difference between Jew and Gentile." This was the subject of 1:18–3:20, the fact that Jew and Gentile are exactly alike in being sinners in need of God's grace. Whether they grow up under the law (Jews) or under natural revelation (Gentiles), both know they are sinners.

Paul sums it all up in his famous statement, "For all have sinned and fall short of the glory of God." The verb "sinned" is global in thrust, looking at all the sins of the human race as a whole. Whenever they try to approach God, they are like arrows that fail to reach their target and "fall short." This is a present-tense verb that stresses its continuous nature. In our own strength, we can never attain a right relationship with God because of the weight of sin that at all times forces us to fall short.

The "glory of God" is his majesty, splendor, and wondrous presence. Adam and Eve shared it in the garden but lost it when they fell into sin. Now it is an **eschatological** promise; believers experience it spiritually now (part of the "spiritual blessings" of Eph 1:3) but await its full realization. It will not be fully gained until the end of history, when evil is destroyed and eternity begins.

THE RIGHTEOUSNESS FROM GOD ACHIEVED (3:24-26)

Romans thus far has made clear that none of us could ever secure for ourselves a right relationship with God. In our sin we are doomed for eternity. But what we could not procure on our own God has in his grace provided for us via the sacrificial death of Christ. Every single term in these verses is significant.

Justified and Redeemed (3:24)

Verse 24 begins with a present participle, "being justified," which modifies the "all" in verse 23. It continues the theme of verses 21-22, that "all who believe" from among sinful humankind are justified before God. As in 1:17, "justified" means that on the basis of the atoning sacrifice of Christ God has declared repentant sinners righteous and acquitted them from the guilt and penalty for their sins.

God makes his judicial decision at the moment of faith-decision and does so "freely," meaning it is a grace-gift from him (as in Eph 2:9). The basis of this gift is "by his grace," a theme found ninety-seven times in Paul's writings to describe God's undeserved mercy. It is nothing we have done or earned on our own merit but entirely an act of his loving will, as in Ephesians 2:5, 8, "it is by grace you have been saved." We can never fully understand his gracious gift of salvation but simply accept it by faith. In the end, from God's perspective it is a matter of grace, and from our perspective it is a matter of faith.

The means by which salvation is accomplished is "through the redemption that came by Jesus Christ." Redemption is a concept that stems from the exodus, when God freed his people from slavery to Egypt. The term pictures the payment of a ransom that frees a person from bondage. The free grace-gift of salvation is effected by the payment of the blood of Christ. His sacrificial death has paid for our sins and purchased our forgiveness and freedom.

Writers in the ancient world used "redemption" and related terms for the freeing of a slave, a prisoner of war, or a debtor from bondage by paying off the debts. Jesus' death on the cross is therefore a ransom payment to free the repentant sinner from the bondage of sin. The recipient of the payment is not included in the metaphor. God is certainly not paying Satan, but the idea of God paying himself is not part of the image either. Redemption has taken place "in Jesus Christ," another major theme in Paul's writings (eighty-three times), referring both to our union with Christ and to the result of that union: membership in his body, the church. Our redemption "in Christ" means that we have been united with him in his death and made part of his family through faith (Rom 6:4–5).

The sacrifice of atonement received by faith (3:25)

To bring about the redemption of humankind God "presented Christ as a sacrifice of atonement." God is the initiating force who sent his Son to pay the price for sin. The verb means to "display publicly" (NASB) or openly so that atonement could be made directly on our behalf. As in John 1:9, "The true light that gives light to everyone was coming into the world."

The reason for the incarnation is the sacrifice that Christ was to make for each of us. The term *hilastērion* ("sacrifice") only occurs here and in Hebrews 9:15 but is an extremely important word for understanding the meaning of Christ's death. It is closely linked to the "mercy seat" in the holy of holies, the cover over the ark of the covenant, where the blood of the sacrifice was poured on the Day of Atonement (Lev 16:14). The mercy seat was the place where sins were covered by Yahweh. Christ here is the counterpart of the mercy seat, the means of atonement for all humanity who come in faith for forgiveness.

The exact meaning of *hilastērion* is controversial. The traditional understanding is "propitiation," which means that God's wrath was appeased as a result of Christ's sacrifice. Several have argued that this is too pagan an idea and have preferred "expiation," the idea that sin is wiped away or forgiven. The first centers on the idea that God is appeased and the second that sin is removed. I would side with those who recognize that God's wrath is inherent in the term, especially in Romans 1-3, where divine wrath over sin is paramount. Moreover, the idea of propitiation is not a pagan one but lies at the core of God's holy reaction to sin. Sin is antithetical to God and goodness, and it must be abolished. This is the only way God's justice can be satisfied.

We humans cannot pay for our own sinfulness. It is endemic to our very being, and the only just consequence for it is for God to send us into eternal damnation. The only solution is for God to pay the penalty on our behalf. That is why Christ came. The blood of Christ is the sacrifice for sin, the only means of atonement for fallen humanity. Through his atoning sacrifice the wrath of God was appeased, and sins were forgiven. As a result God looked at his death as our substitute and justified us at his judgment seat.

Paul next adds a series of phrases that define further the significance of this atoning sacrifice. First, it takes place "through the shedding of his blood," as Christ fulfills the imagery of the sacrificial system and becomes the once-for-all sacrifice for sin (Heb 7:27; 9:27; 10:10). Second, Christ's death as a sacrifice for us must be "received by faith." Faith is the defining theme of this section: the word occurs seventeen times in 3:21-4:25. It defines how the repentant sinner appropriates the effects of Christ's death for us (see also 3:22a).

Third, God's purpose was to "demonstrate his righteousness," to show the world his true character and love. He did so "because in his forbearance he had left the sins committed beforehand unpunished." This is a difficult sentence to understand. The key question is whether "righteousness" refers to God's saving activity or his judging activity.

Those who understand "righteousness" here in terms of God's saving work translate this, "In order to show his saving grace through his forgiving sins committed beforehand when he was patient." "Righteousness" here would then refer to God's saving faithfulness, and "passing over" or "left unpunished" refers to the forgiveness of sins. This makes a great deal of sense theologically and would certainly fit the context.

The problem is that it has several exegetical weaknesses: (1) it is difficult to read "righteousness" strictly as "saving grace," because God's justice is part of its meaning in Romans 1–3, especially in 3:25, where the idea is appeasing his justice. (2) The preposition *dia* can mean either "through" or "because of, on account of." Since it indicates cause here, the NIV is right to translate it "because." (3) While *paresin* could mean "forgive," it is better to read it here as "pass over" or "left unpunished" (see NIV) in a context like this. These are the sins committed under the old covenant, and God's failure to judge these former sins could call into question God's justice.

For these reasons, it is God's judging activity that is central here. Paul is explaining that God was postponing his judgment to demonstrate his "forbearance," or patience. God's self-restraint is part of his justice and shows his saving righteousness. God proves his justice in two ways: (1) He has made an eternal decree that Christ has become the atoning sacrifice for our sins and made justification possible. (2) In doing so, he has also made allowance for sins committed under the old covenant to go unpunished until Christ could become the ransom payment for them as well as us. In this way, God has made Christ the basis for the sufficiency of the sacrificial system, with the result that those who lived under the old covenant did not have to undergo the eternal punishment they deserved.

In other words, the effect of Christ's sacrificial death on the cross reached back to the old covenant as well as forward to the new covenant. All of human history, both before and after the central event of the cross, points to Jesus' atoning sacrifice as the basis of salvation. There is no greater proof of the absolute justice and righteousness of God, and at the same time no greater proof of the fact that Jesus is the only path to salvation (John 14:6; Acts 4:12).

The purpose: a present demonstration of his righteousness (3:26)

For the second time in two verses Paul asserts the purpose of God's saving and judging work—to demonstrate his righteousness. Here he adds that this demonstration has occurred "at the present time," a similar idea to "the fullness of time" in Galatians 4:4. The "present time" refers both to the life and death of Christ in the present era and the immediately present situation of the Roman church. This is the new covenant age of the Spirit, when God's salvation is being proclaimed to the world. God continues to prove his just and righteous character, showing that his justice from the old covenant continues in the new covenant (see also 8:18; 11:5; 13:11).

His purpose is to demonstrate to all that he is "just and the one who justifies those who have faith in Jesus." Paul says in verse 25 that he proved his justice by postponing the judgment deserved by those who sinned against him in the old covenant period, and in verse 26 he proves it by doing the same in the new covenant era. God's character is "righteous" and "just" (both connoted in *dikaios* here), and as a just God he is "the one who justifies" those who come to him in faith. His essential attributes (he is just) are also relational in nature (he is a justifier).

In verses 25-26, Paul is saying that God openly displayed Christ as the atoning sacrifice for our sins in order to demonstrate to all peoples his righteous character, first in postponing the judgment of sins committed under the old covenant and then in justifying those who come to him in faith under the new covenant. The effects of Christ's atoning sacrifice move backward and forward; Christ has become the Redeemer of all under both covenants who turn to God. In these verses we see the centrality of faith, as this will become the central theme of 3:17-4:25. God is sovereign over salvation, and God's salvation is only experienced by faith.

JUSTIFICATION COMES ONLY BY FAITH (3:27-31)

Paul builds on the centrality of faith in 3:22, 25-26, now focusing on the necessity of faith for justification. The term occurs four times in this section and ten more times in chapter 4. He says that faith as the only means of salvation removes any possibility of boasting in oneself (v. 27) because one can only be justified by faith and not by observing the law (v. 28). From this we realize that God is the God of the Gentiles as well as the Jews (demanding the inclusion of Gentiles in the people of God, vv. 29-30), and that the centrality of faith in salvation upholds rather than nullifies the law (v. 31).

BOASTING IS EXCLUDED (3:27)

In this verse Paul asks one of the basic questions that result from this: "Where, then, is boasting?" If salvation came from "the works of the law," then we would have room to boast in our piety. Instead, faith is the basis, so salvation is a gift from God and not anything we can control.

Paul's answer is succinct: "It is excluded." He discussed the boasting of the Jews in 2:17, 23, and that issue continues here. They were proud of their superiority to the Gentiles because they had the law. They were the covenant people (2:17-20), and they had the covenant of works that guaranteed their relationship with God (3:28). But Paul states unequivocally that this is no longer valid under the new covenant, so boasting is rendered null and void. The death of Christ removed any possibility of boasting of a right relationship with God.

Yet Paul is not saying that keeping the law is wrong. He himself observed the law on several occasions (Acts 18:18; 21:23-26), and in Romans 14:1-15:13 he argues for the validity of Jewish Christians keeping the law as part of their walk with Christ. It is when keeping the law becomes a basis of salvation (as it was for the Judaizers he argues against in Galatians) that Paul opposes it. That is his point here. We are saved by grace through faith and not works (Eph 2:8–9).

He states his message clearly, asking, "Because of what law? The law that requires works? No, because of the law that requires faith." It is common to see this as a contrast between the works of the Mosaic law and Christian faith. But it may be better to see the real contrast between the law of works and the principle of faith. This "law that requires works" actually refers to the Jewish misuse of the law as a system of works to attain righteousness through human achievement. This fits the context better. Paul is not looking at the Old Testament system of law but at the first-century Jewish misuse of the law.

Justification by Faith apart from the Law (3:28)

Paul's conclusion is important: "For we maintain that a person is justified by faith apart from the works of the law." Faith rather than works is the only basis of salvation and a right relationship with God. Faith, not works, predominates in the new covenant, and justification is entirely *by faith*, with righteousness attained *apart from the works of the law*. It is clear in both Galatians and Romans that works play no part in the process of justification.

God the God of Jews and Gentiles (3:29-30)

Since faith is the means by which we participate in God's salvation, that means that the Gentiles stand alongside the Jews not only in their sin and guilt before God (the subject of 1:18–3:8) but also in approaching Christ in faith. The form of Paul's question here expects the answer yes, as if to say: "He is the God of the Gentiles too, isn't he?" If the works of the law were indeed the basis of salvation, then God would be the God only of the Jews. But since that is not the case, and since Gentile and Jew alike come to God in faith, it stands to reason that both have the same God.

In verse 30 Paul anchors this promise in the Shema, the primary creed of Judaism, which begins, "The LORD our God, the LORD is one" (Deut 6:4). When he says, "since there is only one God," he means that God must be the God of the Gentiles as well as the Jews, since they must have a God too. If there is only one God, he has to be the God of everyone in this world—both Gentiles and Jews.

The belief in the one God (monotheism) was at the heart of Judaism, but the Jews thought he favored them and only had a true relationship with them. Gentiles could only have a part in the one God by accepting the law of Moses and circumcision. But in the Abrahamic covenant and in Isaiah, the Jews were especially chosen to be a source of God's blessing to the Gentiles (Gen 12:3; Exod 19:5-6; Isa 42:6; 49:6). Since Christ died for all, the Gentile is just as acceptable as the Jew for salvation.

Paul goes on to say that "God ... will justify the circumcised by faith and the uncircumcised through that same faith." In Romans 3:27-28 we saw that there is no longer any advantage in having the law to follow. Now we see that there is no advantage in the covenant rite of circumcision either. It is faith that is the means of salvation, and both Gentile and Jew have access to that. Circumcision is nothing but another "work" that fails to suffice. I agree with those who say that "will justify" refers to more than the immediate future and present salvation. Most likely it is eschatological, referring to final salvation at the last judgment. We will not stand before God as Jew or Gentile but as people, and we will be judged on an equal basis.

UPHOLD THE LAW BY FAITH (3:31)

What is the actual relation of faith to the law of Moses? Paul realizes that his readers would conclude from verses 27-30 that they are completely opposed to one another. Now he makes an important clarification, beginning with the natural question, "Do we, then, nullify the law by this faith?" We would expect the answer "yes," but he surprises us by answering, "Not at all," using his

characteristic *mē genoito* ("certainly not," "by no means"). His
answer is that in reality "we uphold the law."

Paul's meaning here is widely debated in light of his strong
claim that salvation comes by faith alone as a result of the grace
of God, and thus that salvation is experienced apart from works.
The two contrasting verbs are translated variously: overthrow/
uphold (ESV, NRSV), cancel/confirm (CEB), make void/establish
(KJV), nullify/establish (NASB), destroy/cause to be what the law
truly wants (NCV), forget about the law/truly fulfill the law (NLT).
The first verb (*katargeō*) is fairly common and means to render
powerless or destroy. The second (*histēmi*) means to establish or
validate. What does Paul mean when he says that faith-based salvation actually upholds or validates the law? There are three views
to choose from:

1. Many see Paul as saying that the law plays a testifying role
    with respect to faith; it witnesses to the validity of justifica-
    tion by faith. This is seen in 3:21 (the law and the prophets
    testifying), 27 (the law that requires faith), and 4:3 (Scrip-
    ture testifying to Abraham's faith). However, it is actually
    the whole of Scripture rather than the Mosaic law by itself
    that witnesses. The law of Moses is nowhere seen as wit-
    nessing to a faith-based salvation in Romans 3-4.

2. Others argue that the law is pictured as making people con-
    scious of sin (3:20) and thereby pointing the way to the
    necessity of faith, as in 3:19, where through the law "every
    mouth may be silenced and the whole world held account-
    able to God." This means that when the law judges and con-
    demns sinners, it prepares for the coming of Christ. This
    is viable but again does not fit the context of 3:27-31. The
    convicting power of the law is missing from this section,
    but verse 31 clearly emerges from this material.

3. The most likely view sees "the law" here referring to the
    law of Moses, since the "works of the law" are uppermost in
    verses 27-28. Paul clearly teaches that faith in Christ fulfills

the law in Romans 8:4; 13:8-10. This parallels Jesus' famous statement that he has not come to "abolish" the law but to "fulfill" it (Matt 5:17-20). Paul draws on this here and is saying that in Christ the law has not been nullified but fulfilled. Christ has completed the law in himself, and so when we turn to Christ in faith, we fulfill or keep the law in its entirety.

Paul here is countering a common Jewish objection that in the Christian system of salvation the law is destroyed. This is in keeping with Romans 10:4, where he states, "Christ is the culmination of the law," a much better translation than the traditional "Christ is the end of the law." Christ has not merely ended the law but completed its purpose. A salvation-historical switch has taken place; the law has completed its place in God's plan and been fulfilled in Christ.

———

In this passage we reach the theological center of Scripture, the very heart of the gospel message. Logically, we must begin with the total depravity of sinful humankind. There is no hope, for sin is in complete control, and in ourselves we cannot attain salvation. However, God in sending his Son has done for us what we cannot do ourselves. That is the message of Romans 3:21-26.

The gospel can be summed up in the three terms of verses 24-25, and in them we find the path to eternity. Christ provided salvation by becoming the antitype of the mercy seat and covering our sins by becoming the atoning sacrifice for us on the cross. His blood shed there became the ransom payment that purchased our freedom and led to God forgiving our sins. God placed that payment on our account and justified us—declared us acquitted and right with him.

Christ purchased our salvation, and it is our place to turn to him in faith (27-31) and accept his payment for us. It is impossible to overstate the importance of faith as the only basis for knowing

God. A me-oriented salvation centering on works will never be enough to produce salvation. We can never earn eternal life for ourselves. The necessity of faith will be the central theme of chapter 4 as well.

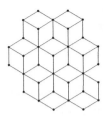

RIGHTEOUSNESS BY FAITH ALONE:
THE MODEL OF ABRAHAM, PART 1
(4:1-12)

The answer for sin in 3:21-31 is Christ's atoning death, the wondrous gift from God that made it possible for him to declare us sinners righteous. Our part in this is made clear in 3:27-31. God's salvation comes *sola gratia*, solely by grace, and we receive his gift *sola fidei*, solely by faith. Still, what is the relationship of justification through Christ to the old covenant era?

Paul answers by saying that this new era in salvation history is not a surprise or aberration. God planned for it all along: when he initiated his covenant people in Abraham, he did so through faith. Yet not only does Paul's argument establish faith as the means of salvation at the very beginning, but it also shows that the Gentiles were intended to have a part in it from the beginning, as seen in the Abrahamic covenant (Gen 12:3).

This chapter is basically a midrash, or rabbinic exposition, of Genesis 15:6, Abraham's belief "credited to him as righteousness." The primary terms, in fact, are "believed" (vv. 3, 5, 11, 17, 18, 24), its cognate term, "faith" (vv. 5, 9, 11, 12, 13, 14, 16, 19, 20), and "credited" (vv. 3, 4, 5, 6, 8, 9, 10, 11, 22, 13, 14). The message of the chapter is that God at all times (the old covenant as well as the new) centered his salvation on faith commitment to him.

IT IS FAITH, NOT WORKS, IN BOTH
ABRAHAM AND DAVID (4:1-8)

The opening "what then shall we say" points back to 3:27-28, in which Paul argues there can be no boasting since justification comes only by faith, not by the works of the law. Abraham becomes the model and illustrates point by point the assertions of 3:27-31.

ABRAHAM OUR MODEL: FAITH NOT WORKS (4:1-2)

This passage begins with another rhetorical question: "What then shall we say that Abraham, our forefather according to the flesh, discovered in this matter?" (the matter of justification by faith from 3:21-31). In chapter 3 Moses was the primary figure. Paul now goes behind Moses to ask, "What about Abraham?" Moses brought the law, but Abraham had even greater importance as the father of the nation. Abraham trumps Moses, and Abraham's faith trumps Moses' works of the law. Long before Moses, Abraham discovered key truths about God and his relationship with humanity—before there was any Jewish nation. At the very start of it all, he discovered (literally *heurēkenai*, "found" out) that justification is by faith alone!

Paul adds that he is "our forefather according to the flesh," a reference to 3:29-30, with "our" pointing to both Jew and Gentile. He is not only the earthly progenitor of the Jewish people but also the spiritual progenitor of Gentile believers, since salvation comes by faith and not by works. Abraham is father, not only of the Jewish nation, but also of the new Israel composed of all believers from all peoples.

Paul turns to the issue of works in verse 2, readdressing the problem of boasting from 3:27. The conditional sentence is rhetorical: "If, in fact, Abraham was justified by works [which he wasn't], he had something to boast about [which he didn't]." This isn't saying good works in and of themselves are wrong but only that they cannot lead to salvation. Neither Abraham nor we could have performed sufficient works to produce salvation. As a result, there is no basis for boasting before God. The Jewish people considered Abraham the primary exemplar of the pious Jew who kept the law even before it was given, so if they followed him vis-à-vis the law, they should follow him vis-à-vis faith. The conclusion— that he could not boast before God—is completely valid.

This is a message we need today as well. People in our time fail to understand that no one can earn their way into heaven by being a good person, for in reality none of us can be good enough to buy our way in. If Abraham could not achieve righteousness on the basis of merit, what makes us think we can?

Proof from Genesis 15:6: Belief Credited as Righteousness (4:3)

Paul introduces his proof for his premise with *gar*, "for" (not translated in the NIV), which presents Genesis 15:6 as the reason for denying that Abraham was justified by works. The introductory "What does the Scripture say" shows that it is the Scriptures that prove the inadequacy of works to make Abraham right in the sight of God and show the absolute necessity of faith for salvation. The singular "Scripture" points not just to a particular passage but to the whole of God's word as supporting the priority of faith over works. The faith mentioned here for the first time in the Old Testament becomes an ongoing theme in the rest of the history of Israel.

When Paul says God "credited" Abraham's faith as "righteousness," what does he mean? It goes a lot deeper than the idea that faith was a righteous act on his part and thereby produced righteousness as its natural result. Rather, his faith was a gift from God, a spiritual act that did not inherently belong to him, and so God credited righteousness to his account. This righteousness was not naturally his by virtue of his faith but itself was a grace-gift, in this way bringing Genesis and Romans together. Abraham, like us, did not possess any inherent righteousness.

Sin has marred the image of God in all of us, and we cannot gain salvation from it on our own. Only the grace of God can bring

it to us, and so Abraham is the model for the way it can take place—
through faith and the free gift of grace. This was not the way the
Jewish people understood Genesis 15:6. They linked it with Abraham's faithfully observing God's commandments in Genesis 22.
Therefore they considered faith a meritorious achievement in
keeping with observing the law. Paul, however, rightly saw it not
as a work but as trusting in God, not as something earned and
deserved but as something undeserved and given to us on the basis
of God's grace and mercy.

FAITH CONTRASTED WITH WORKS (4:4–5)

Paul now clearly presents the implications of the Abraham model
from Genesis 15:6. If Abraham was justified by faith, not works,
then salvation is a free gift from God rather than an obligation
on his part.

Using the metaphor of wages, Paul says that since wages are
earned by a person working for profit, they cannot be a "gift" (literally, "according to grace"). If this were the case, God would merely
be a shop owner under obligation to fulfill his contract with us,
his workers. Then God would be in debt to us and no longer sovereign. He would owe us an eternal reward, and we would control
our own salvation, earning it by our works. But due to God's mercy
the reverse is actually the truth. That is the heart of the gospel
and of Paul's teaching. Pelagius (c. AD 360–418) later espoused the
view that we could earn salvation by our works, which Augustine
(AD 354–430) and the church rightly deemed a heresy. If Pelagius
were right, the boasting of 3:27 and 4:1 would be valid, for our
merit would be the basis of our righteousness. However, Paul has
already shown that to be erroneous.

One of the keys to this passage is the verb "are credited," a
divine passive in the Genesis quotation and in verse 4, meaning
God puts it to our account. If works and earned wages were the
basis, then our eternal life as Christians would be owed to us by
God as a payment he is obligated to make. Verse 5 corrects this

erroneous viewpoint. The person "who does not work but trusts God who justifies the ungodly" is the true believer who does not count on works to earn their salvation but puts their trust entirely in the God who justifies. Since this is a person of faith rather than works, their "faith is credited as righteousness," a virtual definition of justification in Genesis 15:6.

The implications of this passage for a true doctrine of salvation are enormous. I cannot attain righteousness by my own merit or good works. It is a grace-based free gift from God, and it comes only through faith in Christ's blood sacrifice on the cross.

He is the "God who justifies the ungodly," a statement that does not at first glance seem right. We think it should read, "justifies the godly," the pious saints who deserve it. Yet the justification of the ungodly is the whole point. Paul will say in Romans 5:6, 8, that "while we were still sinners, Christ died for the ungodly."

Of course, Paul is not discounting good works in the Christian life. Paul's emphasis here is one side of the coin, that of justification, in which works-righteousness does not play a part. But the other side of the coin comes in Philippians 2:12, "continue to work out your salvation with fear and trembling" and in Ephesians 2:10, "For we are God's handiwork, created in Christ Jesus to do good works, which God prepared in advance for us to do." Works do not save us, but true salvation will result in good works and in working out the effects of our salvation.

FURTHER PROOF FROM PSALM 32:1-2: THE FORGIVENESS OF SINS (4:6-8)

Paul wants his readers to realize that Abraham is not the only example of faith-based salvation, so he introduces David. At the same time, he wants to show that the whole canon of Scripture supports his thesis by adding the poetic writings to the Pentateuch. When he states, "David says the same thing," he means David is in agreement regarding justification by faith "when he speaks of the blessedness of the one to whom God credits righteousness apart from works."

The connection between Genesis 15:6 and Psalm 32:1-2 is the verb "credited" (= "count" in the psalm), which is the reason why Paul chose this passage. This is a psalm of forgiveness, and so it was natural to associate the "credited to him as righteousness" from the Genesis quotation and "whose sin the Lord will never count against them" from the psalm. The two provide two aspects of justification, the negative "sins forgiven" and the positive "declared righteous." Note the process of justification: sins are forgiven or covered, then God credits our repentance and faith-decision as righteousness, and then we are in right relationship with him.

Paul's example of David as the second proclaimer (after Abraham) of justification by faith restates the thesis of 3:21-26. The total depravity of humankind erects an insurmountable barrier between us and God. We are helpless in our sin, for we cannot be good enough to enable ourselves to climb over the barrier or remove it. Christ's atoning work has "covered" our sins, so it is righteousness rather than sin that is put to our account.

ABRAHAM WAS JUSTIFIED BY FAITH, NOT CIRCUMCISION (4:9-12)

After using David to anchor his teaching on justification by faith, not by the works of the law, Paul turns to circumcision, the other great covenant rite. He discussed this earlier in 2:25-27 and 3:30, and his purpose here is to show that Abraham was justified *before* he was circumcised. This means that justification has priority over circumcision, and Abraham can thus be the father of the uncircumcised (the Gentiles) as well as the circumcised (the Jews).

THE CIRCUMSTANCES BEHIND ABRAHAM'S CIRCUMCISION (4:9-10)

Paul then asks, "Is this blessedness [declared by David in Psalm 32 above] only for the circumcised, or also for the uncircumcised?"

He is anticipating a question that his readers with a Jewish background would have asked, and they would have heard all their lives that the answer is "only for the circumcised." Paul is going to dispel that false teaching.

As stated above, this "blessedness" from Psalm 32 is the forgiveness of sins. Paul returns to Genesis 15:6, "We have been saying that Abraham's faith was credited to him as righteousness." First-century rabbis applied Psalm 32 and its message on forgiveness strictly to the Jewish people, but Paul widens its applicability by interpreting it through Genesis 15:6, thereby seeing its significance for Gentiles as well as Jews. Since the basis of forgiveness is faith rather than works or covenant membership via circumcision, it applies to Gentiles as well as Jews.

Paul drives this home by asking in verse 10, "Under what circumstances was it credited?" Then he makes the temporal nature of the question explicit: "Was it after he was circumcised, or before?" The issue has to do with priority. If before, circumcision was part of the justifying process; if after, it was not. If it came after, its origin was the law and its works, and the Jewish system was still in effect. If before, then Abraham's faith was the initiating force, and Christianity was correct. Paul's answer is clear: "It was not after, but before."

CIRCUMCISION AS THE SIGN AND SEAL OF HIS FAITH (4:11A)

There is still a question as to the relationship between Abraham's faith and the circumcision he received later. That question is answered in this verse, when Paul asserts that "he received circumcision as a sign, a seal of the righteousness that he had by faith while he was still uncircumcised." Genesis 17:11 explains this further, defining circumcision as "the sign of the covenant" between God and Abraham. Circumcision was the external symbol that pointed to the internal reality of the covenant. Jewish rabbis associated this with the Mosaic covenant, but Paul is correctly linking it with the Abrahamic covenant. It is the righteousness

attained by the faith of Abraham (Gen 15:6) to which circumcision refers, and it is Abraham's faith that links the old covenant
with the new covenant.

Paul further identifies the "sign" as "a seal" of this new righteousness. The sign signifies the covenant and the seal validates
it, a confirming act of God's covenant with his people. Both sign
and seal are external to the covenant. Paul's point is that faith precedes and supersedes the covenant. Abraham was already justified
when he was circumcised, so circumcision was not the essence of
the covenant but an external sign that it was in force.

ABRAHAM THE FATHER OF ALL WHO COME BY FAITH (4:11B-12)

Paul concludes this section with two interconnected purposes for
Abraham's faith: first, it shows Abraham is the father of those who
have faith but without circumcision (the Gentiles); and second, it
shows he is also the father of the circumcised, but only those who
follow in the steps of Abraham's faith (Jewish believers).[1]

This means that Gentiles who believe without being circumcised emulate Abraham, "in order that righteousness might be
credited to them" (v. 11b). Moreover, Abraham is their father as
well, for they have followed in the footsteps of his faith. In his faith
he is the father of believing Gentiles, and in his circumcision he is
the father of the Jewish nation. But this latter is not the point of
verses 11b-12. The Jews who follow only his circumcision are no
longer the people of the *new* covenant. It is only those Jews who
follow the more important element, "the footsteps of the faith that
our father Abraham had before he was circumcised." Circumcision

---

1. Some think that there are two groups here: the Jews (the circumcised) and
Jewish believers (who follow in the footsteps of Abraham's faith). But that is
not the natural reading of the text. There is only one group: Jewish believers.

has ceased to be the sign or seal of the new covenant. Faith is the new covenant sign.[2]

Jews claimed they were the chosen people, with Abraham the sole father of their nation. Gentiles joined them only by becoming proselytes and undergoing circumcision. Paul is making a radical claim: Since Abraham was justified by faith and not by circumcision, he is the father of believing Gentiles apart from circumcision and apart from the law. As a result, righteousness is credited to these believing Gentiles in the same way it was credited to Abraham, and they stand alongside believing Jews to make up the new and true Israel.

The second aspect of Abraham's heritage according to verse 12 is even more radical than the first: the Jewish people are no longer automatically included in God's family. As stated above, he is "the father of the circumcised" *only* if they "follow in the footsteps" of Abraham's faith when he too was uncircumcised. Covenant status is no longer linked to circumcision or the law. It is attained only be emulating Abraham's faith.

———

Abraham is not the central figure in Romans 4; God is. Every part of Abraham's story and our story is a grace-gift from God. He is sovereign and loving, and the result is Abraham's righteousness as well as ours. Many people today are just like the Jewish people of Paul's day, happy to be living their lives the way they like, certain they are okay with God on the basis of what they see as their basic goodness. This could not be more wrong. We cannot earn salvation or be right with God just because we come from a good family

---

2. Some have seen baptism as the sign of the new covenant, as in Colossians 2:12. But if you look at the discussion at 2:12 in my Colossians commentary in this series, you will see it is never presented that way in the New Testament. More likely, that new covenant sign would be the Holy Spirit, called the seal and deposit of our salvation in Ephesians 1:13–14.

and have grown up in a good national environment. We achieve rightness with God only by faith in the fact that Christ paid the price for our sin. Abraham could not claim righteousness except by faith; why should we be any better?

God is not the owner of a business obligated to pay us for work done. He is a loving ruler giving us a gift that we can only receive by faith. To receive this gift we must first realize the depth of our depravity and of our unworthiness and repent, pouring out our need to God. Then we turn in faith to Christ, whose atoning death covers our sins and brings forgiveness. This then leads to God accepting Christ's redemptive payment and acquitting us, declaring us right in his eyes.

Paul's addition of circumcision in verses 9–12 adds an essential point: Only faith, not outward observance, provides the basis and means of salvation. Circumcision was the covenant sign, and the works of the law defined the covenant activity. Since Abraham's faith (Genesis 15) preceded his receiving circumcision (Genesis 17), it alone is the basis of covenant relationship, not circumcision or the law. Faith has priority over works or community/church membership for us as well.

In verses 11–12 Paul clearly defines the messianic community of the new covenant age, the new Israel. The old covenant people was restricted to the Jews and Gentile proselytes, but that has radically changed. The Jewish people are no longer automatically the covenant community. Since membership is now based on faith in Christ, there is no national covenant sign like circumcision or the law, nor is Jewish ancestry any longer sufficient. The people of God are now composed of believing Gentiles and believing Jews. This means we may not look down on anyone, thinking them as beyond the reach of God's grace.

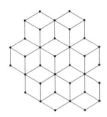

RIGHTEOUSNESS BY FAITH ALONE:
THE MODEL OF ABRAHAM, PART 2
(4:13-25)

I n this second half of the chapter on Abraham's model of righteousness by faith, Paul turns from circumcision back to the law
and argues that the Abrahamic promises did not come through the
law but through faith. The noun and verb for "promise" occur five
times in this section and center on faith as the anchor for these
divine promises. This means that those who come to God by faith
are the true seed of Abraham (vv. 13-17) and the heirs of the promises. Then Paul uses the birth of Isaac to demonstrate further the
centrality of faith for Abraham, since he trusted the power of God
entirely in that miraculous birth that anchored him as "the father
of many nations" (vv. 18-22). Finally, Paul concludes the entire
chapter by applying the Abrahamic faith and promises to those
of "us who believe" (vv. 23-25).

ABRAHAM RECEIVED THE PROMISE BY FAITH (4:13-17)

The movement of the chapter has been from the works of the law
in verses 1-8 to circumcision in verses 9-12 and now to the law
itself. The promises, Paul is saying, are Abrahamic in nature. This
means they are linked to Abraham's faith rather than to the law
of Moses and its works.

NOT THROUGH THE LAW BUT BY FAITH (4:13)

Paul has told his readers that Abraham is the father of both believing Gentiles and Jews, and now he tells why (the verse begins with *gar*, "for"). He says the fulfillment of the promise to Abraham cannot come "through law" but "through the righteousness that comes by faith." The Jews believed that the promise given to Abraham was mediated through the law, but Paul denies this, demanding that it was Abraham's faith, not Moses' works, that accounted for the realization of the promises. He will go on to cite the birth of Isaac (vv. 18–22) as proof of this.

But what exactly is this promise? Paul says that Abraham would be "heir of the world," using language not found in Genesis. There the promise is described variously: that he would have descendants (Gen 12:2; 13:16; 15:5; 17:5–6), be a source of blessing to the nations (Gen 12:3; 18:18; 22:18), and inherit the promised land (Gen 12:7; 13:15; 15:7; 17:8). "Heir of the world" sums these up from the viewpoint of the universal effects of the Messiah's coming. Abraham and his offspring would inherit the world through the victory of Christ over the world.

IF BY THE LAW, FAITH HAS NO VALUE (4:14-15)

With a second *gar* ("for"), Paul clarifies why the Abrahamic promise cannot come through the law. If the promise "depended on the law," that would nullify (Greek: *kenoō*; NIV "means nothing") faith's place in God's kingdom. If we could attain righteousness on the basis of our own effort through observing the law, there would be no need for faith. We, not God, would control our own destiny. The promise itself would become "worthless," robbed of its effectiveness. The tense of both verbs (perfect) refers to an ongoing state of affairs. We would be living in never-never land.

As Paul says in Galatians 3:18, "if the inheritance depends on the law, then it no longer depends on the promise." Law and promise are antithetical. His point in this chapter is that Abraham exemplifies the fact that the divine promise rather than the law is the sole basis of our salvation. It is faith rather than obedience that makes us the children of God, and this is as important today as it was in Paul's time. Too many Christians live their lives based on what they are doing rather than on the One in whom they are believing. All too often they lack commitment, going to church maybe once a month or spending their summer Sundays at the lake.

In verse 15 Paul turns his focus to why (the third *gar* in this paragraph) the law cannot fulfill the promise and produce the inheritance. The law "brings wrath" rather than the inheritance. At first glance this does not seem right. Why would God create a system that does not bring salvation but instead wrath upon his people? This is actually a wrongheaded question. God did not create the law for the express purpose of pouring his wrath upon humanity. The actual purpose of the law was to enable his people to have a proper relationship with him. However, because of prevailing sin they were not able to keep the law, and the resultant state of depravity caused his wrath to fall on them.

Sin produced the wrath, not the law, but Paul can still abbreviate the formula and say "the law brings wrath." The purpose of the law was to make God's people "conscious of … sin" (Rom 3:20), and that awareness led to more sin and brought about his wrath. Paul clarifies this point with a legal argument: "Where there is no law there is no transgression." This does not mean there was no sin committed before the law came. Paul will explain this in Romans 5:13-14. The issue here is awareness of sin, which forces us to confront the fact that sin is actually a legal transgression of God's laws.

If there were no law, we would not be able to identify what transgresses God's demands. But God did indeed give his law, so we are all aware of what we are doing, and our "transgressions" are spelled out in specific written decrees. This means God's "wrath" here is not just anger against sin but is judicial in scope, referring to the condemnation at his *bēma*, or judgment seat, as his law is transgressed.

THE PROMISE COMES BY FAITH TO ALL (4:16)

The basic premise of this section is that the promise came to Abraham (and us) not by the law but by faith (v. 13). The negative side is featured in verses 14-15: it did not come through the law. Now in verses 16-17 Paul develops the positive side: since the law is inadequate to produce the promised inheritance, this "promise comes by faith."

The purpose of this promise is that salvation "may be by grace," a concept introduced in the "grace-gift" of 4:4 (building on 1:5, 7; 3:24). God gives the gift by grace, and we receive the gift by faith. Salvation cannot be attained by human effort but is entirely the act of God on the basis of his grace and mercy. The point throughout this chapter is that the gift is not a matter of merit and wages earned; rather, God freely gives it by his grace, and we accept it by our faith.

Now we see the solution that reverses verse 14: not only is the promise not worthless; but it is also "guaranteed to all Abraham's offspring." God's grace leads not only to receiving the promised inheritance but also to seeing that promise "guaranteed" or "verified" (*bebaios*) as a reality. The promise is grounded in the grace of God. Further, it is certain to be fulfilled for all the offspring, not only "those who are of the law" (Jewish Christians) but also "those who have the faith of Abraham" (Gentile Christians). The seed of Abraham is Jew and Gentile alike, both groups coming to God in faith. He has become "the father of us all" (of all believers), a point that Paul will elaborate in verse 17.

ABRAHAM THE FATHER OF US ALL (4:17)

The basis of the universal fatherhood of Abraham is a citation from Genesis 17:5, "I have made you a father of many nations." This is a prooftext for Paul's point in verse 16, that Abraham by being father of believing Gentiles as well as believing Jews has become "the father of us all." Genesis 17 is another passage on the Abrahamic covenant and is also the place where circumcision is introduced. The "many nations" in Genesis are another reference to Abraham's descendants (17:6, "I will make you very fruitful"). Paul alters the emphasis from Genesis and instead is speaking of Jewish and Gentile "nations," especially the converts to Christianity who stem from many nations.

The flow of thought from the Genesis quotation to the phrase after it ("He is our father in the sight of God, in whom he believed") is difficult and debated. Of several options, the two primary possibilities are: (1) The two parts are consecutive, with the Genesis quotation confirming "the father of us all" at the end of verse 16, and 17b developing the Genesis quotation (NIV, TEV, REB, NLT). (2) Verse 17a is parenthetical, elaborating on "the father of us all" from verse 16b (KJV, NASB, NET, LEB, NRSV). I think the two parts of verse 17 belong together, and it seems best to see the second half as developing the first half rather than skipping past it to verse 16. I believe the NIV has it right. This means that Abraham, "the father of many nations," is clarified as "*our* father in the sight of God, in whom he believed." He thus becomes the father not of the Jewish nation but of believing Jews who join believing Gentiles as a new nation, a new Israel.

In the final portion of verse 17, Paul describes the God in whom Abraham believed. By that description, he builds a bridge from the patriarchal era to the Christian era. First, he is "the God who gives life to the dead," referring both to the life he placed in Sarah's "dead" womb in spite of Abraham's "dead" body (as in v. 19 below) and also to God's power to raise the dead, especially demonstrated in the raising of Christ from the dead.[1] The promise to Abraham

---

1. This is also emphasized in Jewish writings of the time such as Tobit 13:2; Wisdom of Solomon 16:13; and the Eighteen Benedictions.

is closely linked to the basic Christian story and the promise of eternal life for those who believe.

Second, God is the one who "calls into being things that were not" (literally, "things that are not as though they were"). In one sense this means that in the covenant with Abraham God called the nations that did not yet exist as if they did. Yet most interpreters correctly recognize there is more to it than this. Some think it a reference to God's creating the world out of nothing, but that would not make a lot of sense here in terms of the phrase "as though they existed." Most likely it means God has the power to treat those who do not exist (the dead) as if they did (by giving them life). Paul may have in mind spiritual life (= conversion) as well as physical life (= raising the dead).

ABRAHAM EXERCISED FAITH AT THE BIRTH OF ISAAC (4:18-25)

ABRAHAM THE FATHER OF MANY NATIONS (4:18)

This is a transition verse, both concluding 13-17 and leading into the theme of the next section. The key words "faith," "hope," and "promise" unite the two. Abraham as "the father of many nations" fulfills the promise of verses 16-17, while at the same time the emphasis on his faith and hope leads readers into the birth of Isaac in verses 19-22.

It begins strangely with "Against all hope, Abraham in hope believed." The first phrase, "against all hope," refers to human hope, particularly the hope that he and Sarah in their old age could conceive and bear an heir. The added note that he still "in hope believed" refers to a hope centered on God and resulting from faith. This is particularly his hope in the divine promise of Genesis 15:5 cited below (also 12:2; 17:2, 4; 18:18; 22:17)—that God would give him an heir from whom would come innumerable offspring.

Abraham's hope was the outgrowth of God's promise of an heir, a promise that enabled him to ignore his and Sarah's advanced age and the human impossibility of its ever coming to pass. In truth, his faith became hope, realized in the fact that he not only produced an heir but also became "the father of many nations," physically through Isaac and spiritually through the new covenant established by Christ. The two are intertwined in this paragraph.

This promise is anchored in God's promise to Abraham, cited by Paul here, in Genesis 15:5, the verse that immediately precedes the one quoted in Romans 4:3. In this part of the covenant God asks Abraham to count the stars, telling him, "So shall your offspring be." The "many nations" in Genesis are the innumerable descendants of Abraham that constituted not just Israel but also "many [future] nations," and in Romans these are the numerous converts who have come to Christ from "many nations" through a faith like Abraham's.

FACING IN FAITH THEIR INABILITY TO HAVE CHILDREN (4:19)

In light of this uncommon faith in God, Abraham faced the dilemma "that his body was as good as dead" and that "Sarah's womb was also dead," and he did so "without weakening in his faith." The connection between God's raising people to life from the dead (v. 17b) and his giving life to Abraham's dead loins (as well as bringing life out of Sarah's dead womb) is a remarkable **typological** leap (the birth of Isaac as a type of Christ).

Paul states that not only Abraham (ninety-nine) but also Sarah (ninety, see Gen 17:1, 17) made just such a leap of faith. The *Guinness Book of Records* tells us that the oldest woman on record to bear a child was a woman from India who was seventy, but the Guinness people obviously had not considered Genesis 17:17. Both Abraham and Sarah had laughed at the absurdity of the promise (Gen 17:17; 18:12), but when they realized God was serious, their laughter turned to faith.

ABSOLUTE FAITH IN THE PROMISE OF GOD (4:20-21)

In verse 19 Paul elaborates on Abraham's strong faith, saying he "did not waver through unbelief" but instead "was strengthened in his faith and gave glory to God." Paul emphasizes the basis of that remarkably triumphant faith was "the promise of God." In Genesis 17:17–18 Abraham had an initial moment of unbelief (how could he not?), but after that he displayed an ongoing trust in God. Paul centers on the long-term and deep-seated faith he exhibited until Isaac was born, a faith that provides a model for us.

"Strengthened" could be a divine passive meaning "God strengthened his faith," but more likely it parallels "without weakening" in verse 19 and means Abraham grew stronger and stronger in his faith throughout that period. It is not Abraham who grew stronger but his faith. This provides another model for us. As we pass through adversity and the trials of our faith, we must depend all the more on God (Jas 1:2–4; 1 Pet 1:6–7). Life's difficulties are like weights in a gym. The more we struggle against them, the more we are strengthened in our faith.

In verses 20b–21 there are two results of Abraham's growing strength in trusting God: (1) he "gave glory to God," refusing to depend on his own resources or ability but instead throwing himself entirely into God's hands and rejoicing that he could do so.

(2) Abraham was "fully persuaded that God had power to do what he had promised" (v. 21). As his faith grew stronger, so did his certitude that "he who promised is faithful" (Heb 10:23). He was completely assured that the covenant God "never leaves or forsakes" his followers (Deut 31:6; Josh 1:5), and thus he fulfilled Hebrews 11:1 with a faith that is "confidence in what we hope for and assurance about what we do not see."

RESULT: FAITH CREDITED AS RIGHTEOUSNESS (4:22)

This section ends with the very statement with which it began—Genesis 15:5 and faith credited to Abraham as righteousness—thereby framing it all with the necessity of faith (4:3, 22). This is also the last use of *pistis*, "faith," of the seventeen times it occurs in 3:21–4:25. Faith provided Abraham's entrance into the old covenant promises, and it provides our entrance into the new covenant promises. Furthermore, faith characterized Abraham throughout his earthly existence and is the criterion for life in God's family in every age. Paul's argument on justification by faith has come full circle.

ABRAHAM IS OUR MODEL (4:23–25)

Paul contextualizes the Abraham story for his readers. Everything he has been saying flows out of this point, with the Abraham story not merely a historical event but also a paradigm for faith-people in every age.

FAITH CREDITED AS RIGHTEOUSNESS FOR US AS WELL (4:23–24)

The key phrase from Genesis 15:6 is "credited to him," since it is the idea behind the theology of justification by faith: God takes our faith in Christ and on that basis credits it to our account, enabling him to declare us righteous. Thereby Abraham's faith and God's justifying activity in him becomes the primary Old Testament model for the new covenant established by the atoning sacrifice of Christ.

Redemption thereby requires not the "works of the law" stemming from Moses but the "faith credited as righteousness" stemming from Abraham. There is no merit theology in Christianity. When we exercise the same faith Abraham did, then for us as well this faith is "counted as righteousness." Paul adds here that this very faith "credited to him" on the part of Abraham was never intended "for him alone, but for us," namely, "for our sake."

In verse 24 Paul describes the Christian in two ways in light of justification by faith. First, believers are those "to whom God will credit righteousness," the very point Paul has developed throughout 3:21–4:25. Some take this as a reference to the last judgment more than to conversion on the grounds of the Greek "about to credit" (NIV "will credit"), which might convey the future act of God at the consummation of history when he provides the final "justifying" act for his people. However, the emphasis throughout

3:21–5:11 is on the present justification of sinners. Present conversion seems the better understanding, as there is no hint of future judgment in chapter 4 (it will come up in 5:9). It is possible that both aspects are intended here, but if so the primary stress by far is on the present aspect.

Second, we are those "who believe in him who raised Jesus our Lord from the dead." Paul here is emphasizing on the phrase "believe in him who," with God as the focus of our faith. Once again, God is the focus of this chapter, for it is he who makes faith possible and who justifies those who believe. This is slightly unusual, as Paul normally emphasizes faith in Jesus, but the parallel with Abraham's faith in God is behind this thrust.

The stress here flows out of verse 17, where Paul emphasized Abraham's faith in "the God who gives life to the dead." There Paul was referring mainly to Abraham's "dead" body given "life" through the promised son, Isaac. The promise to Abraham is a foretaste of the greater promise that is ours through Christ, with his resurrection the firstfruits for us (1 Cor 15:20, 23). Jesus the Messiah, who delivered us through his death, is also the elevated "Lord," sovereign over us and giver of eternal life.

BASIS: DIED FOR OUR SINS AND RAISED FOR OUR JUSTIFICATION (4:25)

Paul concludes with an amazingly apt summary of all he has said regarding the Christ who became the atoning sacrifice so we could be saved. In fact, this could be called a summary of the gospel itself, indeed of Scripture as a whole. Its form is quite creedal, and Paul may be quoting one of the major creeds of the early church. It is quite balanced, with passive verbs leading into causal statements. These are divine passives and as such should be translated:

> God handed him over because of our trespasses
> God raised him because of our justification.

The first clause echoes Isaiah 53:12 in the **Septuagint** (Greek Old Testament), "He was handed over because of their sins." In

Isaiah 53 "delivered" or "handed over" are found in verses 6 and 12, detailing how "the LORD has laid on him [the servant of Yahweh] the iniquity of us all" (Isa 53:6; see also 53:5, 10, 11). Paul is saying that both Isaiah and the Gospels depict God delivering Jesus his Servant to atone for our sins.

The preposition "for" here is Greek *dia* and means "on account of," teaching that Christ died because our sins could be forgiven in no other way. Sinful humanity could never atone for their own sins; without Jesus as the substitute for our sins, all humanity would be condemned to eternal damnation. If the suffering servant had not died for us, there could have been no forgiveness of sins.

It is strange that Paul states that Jesus was raised "because of" (the same *dia* as in the first clause) our justification, for elsewhere the thrust goes the other direction, with Jesus' death and resurrection the basis for justification. Here justification becomes the basis for the resurrection. In that light many, like the NIV translators, translate it "for" or "for the sake of." However, that is highly unusual for *dia*, and it is better to see God having his Son die and be raised because it is the only way justification could take place. Christ's death, as seen in the Letters, provides the theological basis for our salvation; and the resurrection, as seen in Acts (2:31–36; 13:32–39), is the apologetic basis of salvation.

The two lines fit together perfectly. The death and resurrection are a single, divinely appointed event, and it is our sins that are forgiven when justification is declared by the eternal Judge of all. This is the gospel in embryo, and it perfectly culminates the teaching in chapters 1–4 on the meaning of the salvation God has provided for the forgiveness of our sins.

In this paragraph Paul brings to a conclusion his great treatise explaining the gospel and the movement from sin to salvation by the redemptive act of Christ the Son as willed by God the Father. Justification by faith alone, apart from works, is now complete, and the redemptive results are fully known.

In Romans 4, Paul has turned to Abraham as the model proving
the centrality of faith for becoming a member of God's covenant
community. As the father of the nation, Abraham has priority over
Moses, and his faith has priority over the works of the law. Faith
then is the means by which God's people are saved. The purpose
of the law is to make us conscious of sin (3:20) as transgressing
God's legal demands, and as such it brings God's wrath down upon
sinners (4:15). There is no hope apart from the grace of God, and
through faith we encounter his salvation.

The result of this grace of God and the salvation it brings is the
union of Jew and Gentile into one people. Unity and true broth-
erhood are finally achieved through the cross, as believers from
all nations now form a new people, citizens of heaven (Phil 3:20)
and a "new humanity" (Eph 2:15). Abraham is now truly "the
father of us all" (4:16), and racial division can now end for those
in Christ! Finally, hope has become real (4:19) and a true gift of
God to redeemed humanity.

In verses 20-21 Paul lays a great deal of emphasis on the growth
of Abraham's faith through the crisis attending the birth of Isaac.
Through the great uncertainty and seeming impossibility of that
birth, Abraham's faith was greatly strengthened and grew expo-
nentially. That is the case with us as well. In the crises of life we
are forced to depend all the more on God, and as we experience his
presence and guidance we too grow in our trust in him (see 5:2-4).

Paul presents the "model for us" aspect in verses 23-25. As God
reckoned Abraham's faith to him as righteousness, so our faith
allows us to appropriate the sacrificial death of Christ for us and
to be declared by the Judge of all to be right before him. So as in
verse 25 our legal trespasses caused God to deliver Christ to death
so we could be forgiven, and our desperate need for justification
caused God to raise Jesus from the dead so we too could be raised
to eternal life.

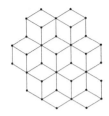

THE BLESSINGS OF
JUSTIFICATION:
A NEW PEACE AND HOPE IN CHRIST
(5:1-11)

We have finished the major section on sin and salvation (1:18-4:25) and established the centrality of justification by faith for the era of the new covenant and the new age of the Spirit. This final era of salvation history was inaugurated by the coming and death of Christ for us. Paul is giving the Roman Christians a logical presentation of his gospel, proceeding from sin (1:18-3:20) to salvation (3:21-4:25) and now to the Christian life (5:1-8:39). This next section (5:1-8:39) centers on the new life in Christ, as justification moves into sanctification, which describes the work of the Holy Spirit "making us holy" as we live our new life in Christ. These chapters tell how we can live out the effects of our justification.

There is considerable difference of opinion as to whether chapter 5 belongs with what comes before (chapters 1-5, 6-8) or what follows (chapters 1-4, 5-8). Those who see it as part of the discussion on justification argue that it continues the discussion of justification, centering on its effects. Those who see it beginning the discussion on sanctification see chapter 5 summarizing chapters 3-4 and moving into the new topic of life in Christ. While some of the same terms are used (faith, righteous[ness], boast, wrath, blood), they are utilized far less frequently, and the subject matter is quite different. Primarily, when we place chapter 5 with what follows, a **chiastic** arrangement[1] emerges that makes a great deal of sense:

> A The assurance of hope in future glory (5:1-11)
>> B The basis for this hope—the work of Christ (5:12-21)
>>> C The problem: the enslaving power of sin (6:1-23)
>>> C' The problem: sin and the law (7:1-25)
>> B' The basis for victory—the work of Christ through the Spirit (8:1-17)
> A' Assurance of future glory in the midst of groaning (8:18-39)

While some think the central theme in these chapters is hope, it is pretty much restricted to 5:2-5 and 8:24-25, so it is better to see the core theme being the new life in Christ. This combines the ideas of future hope and right living that define what it means to be a follower of Christ, one who has been justified by faith.

In 5:1-11 Paul turns from the process of justification to the consequences of justification: peace/reconciliation (1, 10, 11), hope (2, 4, 5), boast/joy (2, 3), and the love of God (5, 8). These are the four central themes in this passage, and they cluster in the following sequence: the love of God is poured out in the gift of God's Son, who brings peace and reconciliation through his blood, leading to hope and joy in our salvation and in the Spirit.

---

1. Chiasm is used hundreds of times in the Bible and takes place when the order of the thought development in the first half is reversed in the second half to emphasize in a stylistic way the points being made.

WE HAVE PEACE AND HOPE IN CHRIST (5:1–5)

PEACE RESULTING FROM FAITH IN HIS GRACE (5:1–2A)

Paul begins by summarizing the central message of the first four chapters, "since we have been justified through faith." We who were at one time sinners destined for final judgment and eternal condemnation (3:23) have been redeemed through the blood of Christ and declared right with God on the basis of Christ's dying as our substitute and our faith-decision (3:21–31).

The first blessing resulting from salvation is "peace with God." Paul is alluding here to the Hebrew *shalom*, which refers to that sense of well-being and tranquility that is the outgrowth of faith in the God who is faithful to his covenant people and guides their destinies. In both testaments it is closely aligned and almost synonymous with God's salvation. In the New Testament *shalom* is the explicit result of the reconciliation of verses 10–11 below. There is also an **eschatological** dimension, relating to the peace God would bring with his kingdom in the last days (Isa 9:6–7; 32:17; 48:20–22; 52:7; 53:5; Jer 37:26; Ezek 34:25; Zech 8:12).

This peace comes "through our Lord Jesus Christ," reintroducing the lordship of Christ from 4:25, highlighting his exaltation to cosmic Lord as a result of his death and resurrection. Jesus is both the means of our salvation and the Lord of our life. This peace is both objective (given by God to us) and subjective (the result of our faith in the Lord Jesus).

The second blessing is also a gift of God, "access by faith into this grace in which we now stand." The term "access" could indicate our entrance into the presence of God in his sanctuary (Eph 2:18; Heb 9:11, 24; 10:19–20). However, it more likely connotes our ongoing entrance into the presence of royalty, picturing our going into the audience chamber of the King of kings, not only in prayer but also in worship. The basis for this privilege is both the death of Christ (5:6–8) and faith ("by faith").

Paul's emphasis here is on the realm of God's grace that we experience in Christ, that is, "this grace in which we now stand." The two verbs are in the perfect tense, "have gained" and "now stand," expressing the force of a state of affairs to which we belong. We now have not only gained access but actually "stand" or have our being in God's kingdom. We are the royal children of God, for he "has made us to be a kingdom and priests" (Rev 1:6; 5:10; cf. 1 Pet 2:5).

The Four Steps from Suffering to Hope (5:2b–4)

This era of grace centered on a new time of hope, and thus we "boast in the hope of the glory of God." However, hope in the New Testament does not have the ephemeral, uncertain aura of hope in the secular world. It is a "living hope" (1 Pet 1:3), with an entirely new confidence and certainty. There is no "maybe" in this but a "yes it will" thrust that brings a smile rather than a grimace. The only uncertainty is when it will happen, not whether it will happen.

In 3:27 Paul said "boasting" in the law is excluded on the basis of the principle of faith (also 2:17, 23), and in 4:2–3 he argued that Abraham had nothing to boast about "before God" because he believed God rather than depended on his works. The word itself is variously translated, some as "rejoice" (NIV 1984) or "confidence" on the grounds that it is excluded in 3:27. However, boasting in God is different, and Paul can now "boast," but entirely in "the hope of the glory of God." Pride is sin when it centers on self but a spiritual blessing when it centers on God (and on others like our children).

This "glory of God" is not the present glory that the believer shares (as in John 17:22; Rom 8:30; 1 Cor 11:7; Heb 2:10; 1 Pet 4:14) but the future glory that will be ours at the end of the age (Rom 8:17, 18, 21; Eph 1:18; Col 1:27). Our "hope," as in 5:4, 5; 8:20, 24, is a glorious trust in and anticipation of the promises God has given for the future. The same idea is found in Colossians 3:4, "When Christ, who is your life, appears, then you also will appear with him in glory." Paul here relates four steps in the process of this hope-filled Christian life:

(1) *Sufferings:* In the rest of this section, Paul applies this glorious hope to the primary challenge to the joy of our salvation, the command to "glory in our sufferings" and afflictions. This applies both to trials of the faith in general and to persecution in particular (Rom 8:35; 12:12; 2 Cor 2:4; 7:4; Phil 1:17). It is common to understand these as the eschatological sufferings of the end time (Mark 13:19, 24), but while this is certainly part of the thrust here, the term most likely applies to difficulties in general, as in 1 Peter 1:6–7; also James 1:2–4, where we are told to rejoice or exult in our trials.

The reason we can glory or rejoice in our sufferings is "because we know" how the process functions in our lives. Paul here provides a chain of qualities similar to the "golden chain" of Romans 8:29–30 and especially to the chain attached to trials in James 1:3–4. It is likely that this passage along with the James and 1 Peter passage noted above belong to the same catechetical tradition of teaching in the early church.

(2) *Suffering produces perseverance:* This next step is the very same quality produced in James 1:3, "because you know that the testing of your faith produces perseverance." This is virtually a definition of trials—they test your faith and yield a by-product, perseverance. Perseverance is often connected with faith in God during hard times (2 Thess 1:4; 3:5; 1 Tim 6:11; 2 Tim 3:10) and is one of the primary themes in Revelation (1:9; 2:2, 3, 19; 3:10; 13:10; 14:12).

Our goal is to run the race of life in the way God "marked out for us" (Heb 12:1). We are all called to be marathoners in the race of life and to grow strong in Christ, to attain "the measure of the stature of the fullness of Christ" (Eph 4:13 ESV).

(3) *Perseverance, character:* This is also found in James 1:3 and 1 Peter 1:7, connoting a proven character produced by "testing," and *dokimēn,* "character," here is in the same word group as "testing" in these other passages. The word was associated with the

process of testing or purifying gold, as stated above. In the process gold recently mined is placed in a crucible and brought to the boiling point, forcing the lighter metals (gold is one of the heaviest of metals) to rise to the surface so the goldsmith can skim them off, resulting in pure gold. In 1 Peter 1:7 faith is refined and purified by the trials, the crucible of life, rendering the believer pure. In Romans 5:3-4 Paul states that trials "test" the believer and produce a pure, proven, and tested character.

(4) *Character, hope*: Paul introduced hope in 4:18, where it describes how Abraham "in hope believed" and thereby became "the father of many nations" through Isaac. Note the circularity in Paul's reasoning: in verse 2 hope turns suffering into endurance, and now here it is the final stage produced by the proven character forged in the fiery trials.

In conclusion, the interrelated experiences of sufferings, perseverance, godly character, and hope produce the Christian approach to the new life in Christ. Neither faith nor hope are passive actions. Both are active and powerful, enabling God's people to live victoriously in this world of suffering and difficulty, as we will see further in Romans 8:18-39.

HOPE THROUGH THE HOLY SPIRIT (5:5)

Paul, continuing on the topic of the place of hope in the Christian life, frames the section with the living hope we have in Christ (vv. 2, 5). Many have translated the first phrase of verse 5 as "hope does not disappoint," but the NIV's "does not put us to shame" is better. Paul's point is not that hope always fulfills and satisfies our needs but that hope brings us close to God, with the result that judgment and the shame of spiritual defeat do not overtake us. This is a frequent Old Testament emphasis (Ps 22:6; 25:3; 31:1; 71:1; Isa 28:16; 54:4) and is linked with verse 9 below, "saved from God's wrath," and so looks to the final judgment. When we live in the light of God's future, we will share his glory and avoid his wrath at the great white throne (Rev 20:11-15).

The reason we need not fear shame at the last judgment is because the love of God "has been poured out into our hearts." The "love of God" probably does not refer to our love for God (as Augustine thought) but his love for us (so Calvin and most Protestants today). This is the first time "love" has been mentioned in Romans, but it will become a major theme in the book.

Paul makes two further points here. First, this love is poured out "into our hearts," meaning we experience it as an inner, spiritual reality flooding us. Second, this takes place "through the Holy Spirit, who has been given to us." The Spirit is often described as poured out into us (Ezek 36:25-27; Joel 2:28; Zech 12:10; Acts 2:17-18, 33; Titus 3:6), but here the Spirit is the means by which God's love engulfs our lives. The Spirit is the supreme gift that makes it possible for us to experience the depths of God's love.

WE ARE RECONCILED WITH CHRIST (5:6–11)

CHRIST'S DEATH FOR THE UNGODLY (5:6–8)

Paul here builds on the emphasis in verse 5 regarding God's love poured out into our lives by plumbing the depth of this love and explaining that its true meaning is exemplified in the sacrificial death of Christ for us. These verses have an ABA pattern in which Christ's death for sinners (vv. 6, 8) is set in bold contrast with the deepest example of human love, dying for a good person (v. 7). While we may give our lives for someone we like and consider good, Jesus died for us when we were ungodly sinners, so he demonstrates the greater and deeper love of God. In the Greek, all three verses end with *apethanen* (died), making Christ's death for us the central idea.

His death for us when we were powerless (5:6)

Both clauses of this verse contain *eti*, "still": "at *just* [*eti*] the right time" and "while we were *still* [*eti*] powerless." The two combine to mean that Jesus' death occurred at the exact moment while we were "yet" in a state of sin. It was exactly the perfect moment—as Paul said in Galatians 4:4, "when the set time had fully come."

The meaning of "at just the right time" is debated. It could refer to the perfect moment in world history, such as when the Roman roads had united the nations as never before and made the world mission of the church relatively easy. That could be part of it, but most likely Paul has salvation history in mind. This was the moment God had chosen, that perfect time when God's salvation was meant to erupt into this world.

Two terms describe the human condition at that point. Because we were immersed in sin, we were "weak" or "powerless," completely unable to defeat sin and attain salvation on our own. We were helpless and hopeless. The term denotes the complete inability of sinful humanity to get right with God or to accomplish anything of eternal significance on our own.

The second term is "ungodly," a stronger term that describes a life lived without consciousness or concern for the things of God. In 4:5 it was used of those whom God justified, and here those for whom Christ died. The language of Christ "dying for" us is quite common (four times in 5:6-8; 14:15; John 11:50, 51; 1 Cor 15:3; 2 Cor 5:15) and connotes substitutionary atonement, Jesus' vicarious death as the suffering servant "for" (hyper) sinners (2 Cor 5:14, 21; Gal 3:13; 1 Tim 2:6).

God's love proven by Christ's death for us (5:7-8)

This verse is meant to contrast human love with divine love. The best humanity can accomplish is a willingness to die for a good person. We are willing to die for a cause or person we love, like our country or a child in trouble. In contrast, God sent his Son to die for us when we were ungodly sinners, enemies of Christ. He states this simple truth in a strange way with an ascending pair[2]

---

2. Some think these are synonymous, with "good" explaining a righteous person further. But it is better to see some development, as explained here.

of statements. The "righteous" person would be morally upright, a religious person but not someone we know well. We would respect them but not particularly know them well or love them. A "good" person is likely one we are closer to and know somewhat better, perhaps a Roman patron (financial supporter) or a relative who has been good to us. This is the best we can do on the earthly plane.

Christ in verse 8 does immensely better, dying for us when we were still ungodly and under the power of sin. Paul is emphatic here, saying that "God demonstrates his own love for us," meaning that he provides concrete proof of his love in the deepest possible way. This is a justly well-known verse, on everyone's memorization list, for it is at the apex of passages on the depth of divine love.

Moreover, he did so "while we were still sinners." If you discovered that a person who has ignored you all their life, constantly insulted you and did you wrong, and didn't really want your help had a need for financial aid or some such thing, would you be likely to help them? Christ didn't just offer his help; he died for us while we were his enemies, godless sinners who wanted little to do with him.

We deserve nothing but condemnation, the wrath of God, and eternal punishment; but Christ paid the price for our deep sins and procured redemption and forgiveness on our behalf (3:21–26). The best-known verse in Scripture says it so well: "God so loved the world that he gave his one and only Son, that whoever believes in him shall not perish but have eternal life" (John 3:16).

THE RESULTS OF JUSTIFICATION (5:9–11)

Saved from God's Wrath (5:9)

The conclusion for this section (5:9–11), stating the results of this incredible act of divine love, begins with a particle indicating result, *oun* (therefore), omitted by the NIV. Paul states that "since we have now been justified by his blood" (the message of 3:21–4:25), several spiritual realities have taken place. Note the various ways Paul has described the means of justification—"by his grace" in 3:24; "in his blood" in 3:25 and 5:9; "by faith" in 3:28; his resurrection in 4:25; "through his life" in 5:10. In this verse it is his blood that effects our salvation, stressing the sacrificial, atoning aspect of his death for us, especially the ransom price paid for our "redemption" (3:24). With the addition of "now," this redemptive gift is a present reality and force in our lives.

The results of our justification via the sacrificial death of Christ are even greater ("how much more"). This is rather shocking. How can anything be greater than the cross! Paul is using a Jewish hermeneutical technique called "from the weightier to the lighter." The idea is that since God has already done the more difficult thing (justifying the ungodly), how much more can he accomplish the less difficult aspect (delivering those he has declared innocent from his wrath). The result is that we have been "saved from his wrath"—Romans 1:18; 3:5; 4:15; 9:22; 12:19 describe his present wrath; and 2:5, 8, his final wrath.

"Saved" here means that we are delivered from God's wrath at the last judgment. As Revelation 20:6 puts it, "the second death has no power over" us. There is also a present aspect, as the forces of evil also have no power over us, and we have been given authority over these cosmic powers (Mark 3:15; 6:7).

Reconciliation and salvation (5:10)

This verse is a near repeat of verse 9, covering the same bases: our justification/reconciliation with God, the means by which it is accomplished (blood sacrifice on the cross), and the salvation that results. Paul's emphasis here is on reconciliation. It is the natural result of justification and the fourth of the terms for salvation from 3:24–24—justification, redemption, sacrifice of atonement, reconciliation. This is the social side of salvation, depicting the new relationship of God with humankind. After God has declared us righteous on the basis of Christ's atoning death, he has established a new relationship with us, as we have now joined his family (Rom 8:14–17) and become citizens of heaven (Phil 3:20). The language moves from the legal to the personal.

Those who were sinners and "God's enemies" have been redeemed and reconciled, and both were accomplished "through the death of his Son." The very meaning of reconciliation is to bring former enemies into proper relationship with each other. As a result of Christ's death, our hostility toward God (because of sin) and his hostility toward us (because of his judgment on sin) have been removed, and a new relationship has been forged.

When this more difficult aspect has taken place (the removal of sin by the death of Christ), "how much more" easily and powerfully can God "save [us] through his life." "Saved" here takes on a slightly deeper thrust from verse 9, connoting not only deliverance from his wrath but also deliverance to a new and ever richer life in Christ. "Through his life" refers to the resurrection of Christ as the means of our justification and reconciliation (4:25; 8:34). Paul's stress here is on the process by which our new life in Christ proceeds from the moment of our conversion to its culmination at the return of Christ.

Rejoicing in our reconciliation (5:11)

The concluding verse of this section reintroduces the idea of boasting/rejoicing from verse 2. We could say this section is framed by our pride and joy in what God has done in sending his Son to die for us. The "not only, but also" framework reaches back to verse 3, which stated that we "not only" boast of our hope in God "but also" boast or glory in our sufferings. This culminates the whole section: we rejoice not only in our reconciliation but also in all God has done for us. We now "boast in God through our Lord Jesus Christ." He is Lord over all, and our joy is because the Lord of the universe undergirds and strengthens us as we face all the vicissitudes of life.

God through Christ not only saved us from his future wrath but also has given us the joy of knowing that through him "we have now received reconciliation" in the present. Through the love and grace of God we have both future hope (2:2, 5, 9–10) and present salvation. Our trials and afflictions (5:2–4) now have new meaning as we contemplate our reconciliation with him and the new Father-Son-child-of-God relationship we enjoy as a sacred gift "received" from him.

———

This section sums up the doctrine of justification by faith and transitions into the new life in Christ that results from that conversion experience. The two primary results are peace and hope, and both relate to life's difficulties as we endure them. The new life in Christ turns the pain of our suffering into joy, for as we pass from one affliction to the next we learn to endure and depend on God, thus growing in hope and in the ability to persevere. Hope turns crisis into opportunity, for each one becomes a chance to rely on God and watch the Spirit work. As we pass through "the valley of the shadow of death" (Psalm 23), the light of Christ turns night into day and sorrow into joy (Jas 1:2).

In verses 6–11 we have the next result of our justification, reconciliation with God, beginning with its basis in the death of Christ. We human beings can barely comprehend the depths of the love of God, for Christ did not die for us because we were good people. Far from it; we were ungodly sinners and enemies of God. Yet he died as the substitutionary sacrifice for us so that his blood could cleanse our sins. That is a depth of love so magnificent that we can only accept it by faith and rejoice.

Out of that divine love anchored in the cross flows our reconciliation with God. We who were in a state of enmity with God have now been made his children and part of the messianic community of Christ, in a whole new relationship with the Triune

Godhead. God is our Father, Christ our joint heir and Lord, and the Spirit is the empowering and guiding presence of the Godhead in our lives. So adversity itself has been transformed into an opportunity to watch the Spirit work and to feel even more deeply the hand of God in our lives.

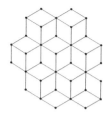

NEW LIFE AS CHRIST
OVERCOMES ADAM'S SIN
(5:12–21)

W e now arrive at another of the justly well-known and
important sections of Romans, the major theological passage behind the doctrine of the imputation of sin—God's act of
attributing or crediting sin to our account. Paul returns to the
issue of sin, but this is not sin and the unbeliever, as in 1:18–3:20.
This is sin in the life of the believer; 5:12–21 serves as a transition
to this issue, which will be developed further in chapters 6 (freedom over the enslaving power of sin) and 7 (sin and the law). As
such this passage is closely linked to the universality of sin passage
in 1:18–3:20, with 5:12–21 introducing 6:1–8:39 in the same way that
1:18–3:20 introduced 3:21–5:11. Paul begins with the cosmic effects
of sin in this world and the way Christ overcame those effects,
which serves as a precursor to his discussion in chapters 6 and 7
of the battle against sin. The basic theme in these three treatises
is victory over sin as found in Christ.

This opening section looks at the entrance of sin from the
perspective of its defeat by Christ. It continues the theme of the
results of justification from 5:1–11, describing God's salvation in
Christ overcoming the power of sin. Paul here introduces the primary barrier between people and God—the sin and guilt inherited

from Adam. His thesis is that Christ has overcome the power of sin and death in this world by becoming the victor over these evil forces and overturning the terrible effects of Adam's defeat in the garden.

In this passage, humanity under sin is personified in Adam and the victory over sin is personified in Christ. Adam's actions determined the victory of sin in this world, and Christ's actions determined the overcoming of Adam's defeat and the cosmic victory over sin. With Adam came the reign of death and its condemnation by God; with Christ came the grace of God and new life, conquering the effects of Adam's sin. The primary theme is not sin but the overcoming of sin by Christ.

SIN ENTERED THE WORLD THROUGH ADAM (5:12)

"Therefore" or "because of this" (*dia touto*) points back to the justification and salvation God has provided through Christ in 5:1–11. Paul wants us to understand how, due to this new life in Christ, sin can be nullified. He thereby draws a conclusion from the previous section: since Christ has justified us and reconciled us to God, we can unite with him and overturn the disastrous effects of Adam's sin on the human race.

Paul starts at the very beginning, when "sin entered the world through one man," Adam, with "the world" referring to all humanity. Paul here is drawing on the Jewish concept of corporate solidarity, according to which all humankind is found in Adam, who therefore represents humanity as a whole. As Christ provides the means of salvation (5:1, 6, 8, 9–11), so Adam is the means by which the human race entered this world. At the same time, Adam also is the means by which sin entered this world, gaining total control over humankind. Throughout 5:12–6:23 sin is pictured as an invading, malignant army trying to conquer the world.

Moreover, with sin came death, and "in this way," through Adam, "death came to all people." The progression is clear—from Adam to sin to death—and its force is universal; none can escape.

Throughout Romans, Paul often personifies sin and death as living powers ruling this world: "sin/death reigned" (Rom 5:14, 17, 21; 6:9), "died to sin" (6:3), "slaves of sin" (6:6, 16-17).

The most debated portion is the last brief clause, "because all sinned." The debates on the imputation of sin (see below) all flow out of the four Greek words behind this (*eph' hō pantes hēmarton*). The introductory particle *eph' hō* ("in whom," "because") has produced differing understandings:

1. It could be translated "in whom all sinned" and refer to "the one man," meaning that all humankind sinned in Adam. This was Augustine's view, called natural headship, meaning that sin passed down the generations and was inherited from Adam in every generation through natural birth. However, this reads too much into these few words and does not fit the larger context.

2. It might mean "because all sinned," taking the "sinned" to be every person sinning after the example of Adam, with sin and salvation controlled by each individual. Every person is born innocent with no link to Adam; it is merely an example here. This was the view of Pelagius, but it was rightly labeled as heretical and is contradicted by the context.

3. We could take *eph' hō* as sequential ("on the basis of which") with death being the antecedent, thus "on the basis of this death all sinned."

4. We might also take it as sequential ("in whom") or causal ("because") and understand "sinned" in a corporate sense, so that "all sin" by virtue of their solidarity with Adam, the representative head of the human race. This is called the "federal headship" view because sin is thereby imputed spiritually via the fact that all humanity is linked with Adam.

5. We may also take it as consecutive ("with the result that") or causal ("because all sinned"), referring to all the sins of humankind as a whole, thus meaning that all people inherit corruption from Adam and then participate in

that sin. This is called "mediate imputation" and is linked with Arminian theology, which seeks to affirm that sin is imputed/inherited but at the same time is also a matter of choice.

These last three views are the most likely, and it is difficult to choose between them. The federal view rightly sees all of verse 12 as corporate, but it has to take "all sinned" with verses 18–19 as corporate while Paul does not explicitly say that here. Mediate imputation reads "all sinned" in a more natural way as individual but then has to place the individual ("every person" who sins) in a context that is primarily corporate, which seems a bit contradictory. Still, this is more the natural meaning of "all sinned," which usually refers to the individual sins of people.

On the whole, I believe that the mediate imputation view (no. 5) is best. All people have inherited corruption from Adam (the first part of v. 12) and then have chosen to participate in that sin (here). So "all sinned" means that every person has willfully chosen to follow their inherited disposition to sin and commit sins. Therefore, they are guilty from two directions—the sin nature inherited from Adam (passive sin) and their personal participation in that via their own sins (active sin).

SIN AND DEATH CAME BEFORE THE LAW (5:13–14)

When did sin come into this world? Many would say that it arrived with the law and not earlier, so Paul breaks his thought (note the dash in the NIV) and addresses the presence of sin before the law. He has stated in verse 12 that "all have sinned" and that therefore death came "through sin." Many Jews would believe that this should mean that people did not sin or die before Moses, because "where there is no law there is no transgression" (4:15). Paul responds that this takes place through corporate identity with Adam—we have all sinned in Adam—and so this connection meant there was still sin among those who lived between Adam and Moses and thus that sin existed from Adam's transgression on.

SIN IN THE WORLD BEFORE THE LAW (5:13)

The universal reign of death is grounded in *gar* (for), telling us that "sin was in the world before the law was given" even though it was "not charged to anyone's account" *because* there was "no law." Since sin existed before the law of Moses arrived, people could see the effects of the fall even though it had not yet been explained that such sins transgressed God's demands. In other words, sin was present before there was legislative evidence for it.

"Charged to [an] account" is a commercial metaphor, indicating that sin would be registered in God's official law book as a transgression, as in Revelation 20:12, which states that at the last judgment "the dead were judged according to what they had done as recorded in the books." This means there was sin in spite of the fact that it was not officially known as such. The Mosaic law made sin a deliberate trespass against God, but people were guilty before that law came.

THE REIGN OF DEATH BEFORE THE LAW CAME (5:14)

This is Paul's second argument for the presence of sin between Adam and Moses: "Nevertheless, death reigned from the time of Adam to the time of Moses." There may not have been law to proclaim it as transgression, but still the universal rule of death over humankind proved the universal presence of sin. There was moral sin even if there was no official legislative declaration to identify it as such. Moreover, since death is God's legal punishment on sin, the reality of the problem was already on display. Death is personified here as a cosmic power reigning over humankind, so no one in that era could pretend that they lived in the "age of innocence." Sin was still punished, so guilt was proved to be present.

Now Paul returns to the argument of verse 12. While they were not "breaking a [legal] command," they did sin in the same way "as did Adam." Their sins were still moral failures in the same way Adam's was. Adam in fact was "a pattern of the one to come"; Paul here uses the term *typos*, "type," which was a mark or impression left by a sharp blow—for instance a stamp made by a die or a molded figure. For the church a type in this sense denoted an Old Testament person or event that prefigured Christ or a New Testament reality. Adam was a type of Christ in the sense that the universal effects of his actions prefigured the universal effects of Christ. Those effects will be presented in verses 15–19.

ADAM IS THE TYPE OF CHRIST (5:15–19)

Paul has established his thesis in verse 14b—Adam is a type of "the one to come." Now he sets forth that typology in detail. Adam was the representative person, the head of the race of humanity. He failed in that duty through sin, but now Christ has come, the true Head of humanity, and he has overturned Adam's terrible legacy point by point. The result is the absolute supremacy of Jesus as the last Adam. Through Adam the image of God was marred, but Christ is returning the fullness of that image to his followers. This means now humanity comprises two groups: those who live under and are controlled by the effects of Adam's sin, and those who live under and are controlled by the effects of Christ's sacrificial gift. The corporate solidarity is complete, with Adam the head of his race and Christ the head now of his race, the true humanity under God.

MANY DIED VERSUS THE GIFT OF GRACE (5:15)

The first antithesis is described in a peculiar fashion, literally "not as the transgress, so also the grace." The NLT translates this well, "But there is a great difference between Adam's sin and God's gracious gift." This is a different term than "transgression" in verse 14, a legal term that refers to breaking a written law. "Trespass" (*paraptōma*) here goes back to the meaning of "sin" (*hamartia*) in verse 12, a moral lapse. The trespass of Adam is countered by the gift of Christ; so the grace-gift of God in Christ is greater than Adam's sin.

Paul explains this by proceeding from the lesser to the greater, using the contrast "if ... how much more"[1] to demonstrate the superiority of Christ's victorious action over Adam's failure. In this first contrast Adam's trespass produced death while the grace-gift of Christ has brought abundance, "overflowing to the many." The contrast is not between the one and the many but between "the one" (Adam) and "the one man, Jesus Christ."

Note how Paul frames the contrast with "the many," first the many sinners who will die in Adam and second the many whose faith will allow them to participate in "the grace of God and the gift that came by the grace of the one man, Jesus Christ." The many who follow Adam have no future, while the many who follow Christ will experience "overflowing" grace, a flood of God's mercy and love that will overwhelm the effects of Adam's sin.

Here we have the two groups that comprise humanity, the only two groups that matter. It is irrelevant to think of Jew and Gentile or the racial and ethnic divides that are so crucial to the earthly scene. The fact is that these differences no longer matter. We who are black or yellow or red or white are all united in one of these two groups for eternity, and that alone is what counts. The most important questions we will ever face in this life are, "Which group do you belong to?" and, "Is your destiny death or life?"

The "many" are the recipients of God's grace (charis) and Christ's grace-gift (dōrea); divine grace alone has overturned the sin of Adam and the death it introduced into this world. "Gift" is a strong **Hellenistic** term for the highest-quality gifts possible and is chosen for the incredible gift of Christ's sacrificial death for us.

This gift will "overflow" or abound to their benefit and consists of justification and eternal life. This overwhelming gift is the true meaning of Christmas. The Christmas grace-gift of God

---

1. For more on this kind of argument, see the introduction to this chapter.

is the life of his Son given to pay the price for our sins so we could have life everlasting!

JUDGMENT AND CONDEMNATION VERSUS JUSTIFICATION (5:16)

The second contrast here centers on the results of the first. Paul begins with, "Nor can the gift of God be compared with the result of one man's [Adam's] sin." Obviously, that result is the condemnation and judgment stressed in the second half of the verse. Paul's point is that there is no comparison, so why would any person in their right mind choose to live their life under Adam's sin and forsake the gift of God in Christ? That is an insane way to go through the few years we have on earth.

There are two contrasts in this verse, the results and the scope of the sins affected. (1) The result of Adam's sin for everyone who chooses it is "the judgment ... [that] brought condemnation." The term for "condemnation" (*katakrima*) is found three times in the New Testament (Rom 15:16, 18; 8:1) and denotes both the sentence handed down and the execution of that sentence on the criminal. This is another reference to final judgment and eternal punishment, but this terrible result is nullified by the "free gift of grace" (*charisma*) from God and Christ, which "followed many trespasses and brought justification."

(2) The contrast regarding the scope of the issue is even more powerful. Paul emphasizes "many trespasses" and moves from the one to the many. Only "one sin," Adam's, was needed to bring universal condemnation and judgment. But the death of Christ covered "many trespasses"—*every* sin committed by those who come to him in faith. The sacrifice of Christ is all the more powerful and comprehensive than Adam's sin and covers the sins of all humanity.

DEATH VERSUS REIGNING IN LIFE (5:17)

This verse culminates the contrasts of verses 15–16 between the first Adam and the last Adam, between the condemnation that

led to death and the grace-gift of God and Christ that led to justification and life.

The universal reign of sin and death in verses 12–14 is solved
and overturned by the incredible grace of God. The idea of death
reigning is global in scope, incorporating the age of Adam into a
single comprehensive whole, with sin and death ruling the world
of humankind due to "the trespass of the one man," Adam. Yet
once more, that power was nullified when the grace of God in
"the one man, Jesus Christ" provided the all-powerful gift of life.

The act of the greater "one man" overturns the act of the lesser,
and Paul's language virtually stumbles over itself as he demonstrates "how much more" God's gift has accomplished. "Grace"
from verse 15 becomes "God's abundant provision of grace," stressing the overwhelming bountifulness and excess of life-giving
grace that is poured out into our lives. The "gift" becomes "the
gift of righteousness," emphasizing not only the act of declaring
us right with God but also the new status we attain and the new
life of living rightly for him that ensues.

Paul envisages three stages of salvation history, moving from
(1) the event on the cross, when Christ's atoning sacrifice overturned Adam's sin, to (2) the church age, as the proclamation of
the gospel and the lives of the saints put this new salvation into
practice, and (3) finally to that final event, the **eschaton**, which
ends this age and begins eternity. The overturning of death's reign
is a future event, but for the believer the new life in Christ reigns,
and our present life is lived in future hope.

Condemnation versus Justification that Brings Life (5:18)

Verses 18–19 in one way are meant to be taken together as a concluding summary of the three in verses 15–17 and actually of this
whole section from verses 12–17. Yet still, there are two contrasts
in these verses, so I will separate them. This returns to the language of verse 12 (just as … so also) and completes the thought

begun there. With the introductory "consequently" it also culminates the discussion in verses 15–17 and the one/many contrast
between Adam and Christ. There are actually three final contrasts,
not only verses 18 and 19 but also verses 20–21.

In the first contrast, here in verse 18, Paul not only consummates what was begun in verse 12 (yet not completed) but also
restates verses 16–17. As there, here he highlights the results of
the deeds. The "one trespass" of the NIV (and NASB, ESV, NET) is
better "one man's trespass" (NRSV, NLT, literally "the trespass
through the one"). This produces "condemnation for all people"
(as in verse 16) in contrast with "the one righteous act" of the
Last Adam that produces "justification and life for all people" (as
in vv. 16 and 17). In this section Paul presents justification as a
grace-gift given by God to those who believe, and it results not
only in forgiveness but also in the further gift of life. There is
some debate whether Paul's emphasis is on human sinning in
Adam or personal sin, but as in verse 12 he likely intended both
aspects intended here.

The "righteous act" could be the act of justifying repentant
sinners but more likely refers to Jesus' sacrificial death. The two
uses of the phrase "for all people" do not refer to all humanity but
to all those who follow Adam on the one hand and all who follow
Christ on the other hand.

Putting all this together, Adam's trespass brought condemnation from God to all humanity, but in contrast the righteous act of
Christ's sacrificial death overturned Adam's sin and brought justification of sins and the righteous life that ensues, leading to the
ultimate gift of eternal life for those who in faith choose Christ
over Adam.

MADE SINNERS VERSUS MADE RIGHTEOUS (5:19)

For emphasis, in verse 19 Paul in one sense restates the contrast of
verse 18 using a related set of terms. However, I agree with those

who think verse 19 is the basis, and verse 18 the results. A chart
will help us visualize the point:

BASIS (v. 19)	RESULTS (v. 18)
Adam's disobedience → made sinners →	condemnation
Christ's obedience → made righteous →	justification and life

Once again, Paul's stress is on the one and the many, as both
Adam and Christ affect the many who are corporately identified
with them. The emphasis in this contrast is upon their relationship
with God and his demands, with Adam in the garden disobeying
God's mandate and Christ, "being found in appearance as a man
[= the "one man" here] ... humbled himself by becoming obedient
to death—even death on a cross" (Phil 2:8).

The translation "were made" needs to be strengthened, for
kathistēmi in both clauses is a legal term meaning to "appoint"
someone to an office or duty. Adam failed in his commission while
Christ succeeded. The results deal with a state of affairs in which
people are categorically placed by God, either constituted as a class
to be "sinners" or "righteous." The latter category combines the
meanings of *dikaios*: they move from being declared righteous by
the divine Judge to being made righteous by the Spirit to a spiritual ethic of living righteously for God.

PAUL CONTRASTS SIN AND GRACE (5:20-21)

This concluding section returns to the question of the law from
verses 13-14, responding to those Jewish Christians who say that
the law still has an important role to play in the Christian life.
Their argument would be that Paul cannot sum up all of salvation
history by simplifying the two eras under the figures of Adam and
Christ, who began the old and new covenant epochs. Rather, the
Mosaic law was equally critical and was essential to the salvation
of Jew and Gentile alike.

WHERE SIN INCREASED, GRACE INCREASED MORE (5:20)

In light of this, Paul feels he has to set the record straight about the law, so he repeats his point from 3:20—the law could not solve the sin problem. Its purpose was to make people conscious about sin and its dangers. In this he elaborates his teaching regarding the purpose of the law in the new age of Christ and the Spirit. In verse 13 that purpose was to show that sin is a legal transgression against God's standards, while here he states that "the law was brought in so that the trespass might increase." The verb "was brought in" or "added" likely refers to the "entrance" of the law into salvation history, perhaps with a slightly negative thrust that it was added to a world dominated by sin and had no power to change the situation. It is subordinated to the grace of God at work in this world, but it still had a positive purpose in pointing out sin.

The added purpose that it was given "so that the trespass might increase" is somewhat surprising. This does not mean God wanted there to be more sin in the world or, as some have said, that the law might make sin more attractive by highlighting it. In this case the point would be that the law increased people's desire to sin by prohibiting it. While possible, this view does not really fit the language here. The goal was not to increase the number of sins but to increase the awareness of the seriousness of sin. The intended role of the law was not to solve the sin problem but actually to make sin more visible, so that people would know that sins transgress the laws of God and realize more powerfully the prevalence of sin in their lives and in the world.

The next antithesis asserts the solution to the sin problem. The true contrast is not between Adam and Christ but between the sin of Adam and the grace of Christ. Literally, Paul exclaims, "Where sin abounded, grace superabounded." Several say Paul's concern here is entirely with the place of Israel under the law. However, I stand with those who believe this sums up the exalted language of the entire section (see "much more" and "increase" in vv. 15, 17) and so culminates the message about the overwhelming grace and love of God for all humankind. Paul is also highlighting the extent this grace leads to the redemptive grace of Christ in covering sin. Paul here includes Israel under the law and both Gentile and Jew under grace, with grace triumphing over sin and the law.

Sin seems to be winning as evil abounds more and more in this world. In my seven decades things certainly seem to have got worse decade by decade. There really is only one answer—"Even so, Lord, quickly come"—and I often despair, feeling so helpless in the face of such abounding wickedness everywhere I look. Still, in individual instances I have experienced that superabundant grace and have seen it turn lives around. There has been an incredible worldwide explosion of the gospel in recent years, and the locus of world Christianity is shifting to Asia and Africa, where the grace of God has produced miraculous results. Truly God's grace is "increasing all the more."

Sin Reigns in Death, Grace in Righteousness and Life (5:21)

Paul now further explains the purpose of the superabounding grace of God, and this culminates the whole section. This climax states that "just as sin reigned in death [the point of v. 12], so also grace might reign through righteousness [the point of 3:21-4:25] to bring eternal life through Jesus Christ our Lord [the point of all of Romans]." Sin first enslaves us (the message of chapter 6 below) and then kills us.

However, as in verse 20, as all-embracing as sin seems to be, grace is far greater. Sin rules over its own empire of fallen humankind and in this world seems all-powerful, but there is a higher power, and he rules through grace, mercy, and love. The instrument of grace in this world (dia rather than en, "through righteousness") is a greater realm, the dominion of "righteousness" that has entered this world "through Jesus Christ our Lord." Two points stand out here. First, "righteousness" again is comprehensive, denoting God declaring us to be right with him (justification), the Spirit making us more and more righteous (sanctification), and our living rightly before him (ethics). Second, the lordship of Christ is the means through which the victory is won, and we are empowered to live according to his will.

———

Paul's brilliant essay in Romans 5:12–21 on how sin entered the world and then is imputed or credited to our account by God is the flip side of salvation history. It tells the historical progression of sin in this world and how it is defeated only in Christ. We see the origins in verse 12, in which Paul tells how sin entered this world through the act of one man, Adam, and then is inherited by every person who is born in Adam and therefore is in sin. At the same time, every person willfully decides to participate in that sin and from both perspectives, the corporate and the individual, becomes a sinner. We are all the children of Adam and so willingly give ourselves over to sin. We are overpowered by our flesh and without Christ have no hope of overcoming its power.

The universal effects of sin were critical for Paul's argument, so he had to show that sin was present in the world even during the time between Adam and Moses before the law had been given that proved sin transgressed God's laws (vv. 13–14). The presence of guilt and its punishment, death, proved sin reigned over humankind from Adam on.

The set of contrasts between Adam's disobedient response to God and Christ's obedience dominates this section (vv. 15–19). The basic premise is that every sad effect of Adam's trespass on sinful humanity has been nullified and overturned by Christ's righteous sacrificial deed on the cross. The grace of God is overwhelmingly more powerful than the sin and death resulting from Adam's sin. Adam's disobedience caused sin to enter the world accompanied by death, and these two evil forces reign over sinful humankind and have made them sinners, judged and condemned by God, ending in their eternal destruction. Here is the answer to the power of

Adam's sin, but we have to consciously turn our lives over to Christ to gain that strength for ourselves. In our own strength we fail every time.

Christ's obedience to God's command to yield his life on the cross has ended the reign of sin and death, rendering them powerless over those who have come to Christ in faith. Through his righteous sacrificial deed the grace of God has become supreme and brought justification to the many who turn to Christ. As a result believers receive life throughout their earthly existence in the sense that they live a righteous life and experience the richness of God now, and eternal life both now and in the future. Each of us must surrender our lives to Christ and experience his righteousness in us. Then we can overcome the power of Adam in us.

The glorious reality is that the powerful reign of sin and death in this world is actually not in control and has been rendered null and void by the far greater power of the grace of God (vv. 20-21). As sin gains a foothold and increases as this world goes on, God's grace in Christ and his sacrificial gift to humankind is superabundant and brings righteousness and life to those among humankind who will believe and turn their lives over to Christ.

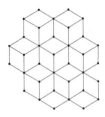

DYING TO SIN THROUGH THE NEW LIFE IN CHRIST

(6:1-14)

In the first major section (Rom 1:18-5:12), Paul developed the part of the gospel that centers on sin and salvation, showing that while the depravity of humankind is total (1:18-3:20), the power and grace of God are more powerful. God gave his Son to be the atoning sacrifice on the cross for sins, and this has allowed God the Judge to justify and forgive sins (3:21-5:11).

The previous material on redemption and sanctification dealt with the legal side of the salvation process, describing how Christ paid the price so that sin could be forgiven and salvation procured. Now we turn to the Christian life that results, looking at how sin is defeated within the life of the believer. Sin is an invading army trying to enslave us, but Christ through the Spirit liberates us from its attempt to take over our lives.

As converted followers of Christ, we have begun a new life. We are in the process of throwing off old habits and ways of thinking. We have changed our residence and become citizens of the new commonwealth of heaven (Phil 3:20; Eph 2:19). Sanctification is learning how to be the children of God, with a new career of being a "kingdom and priests to serve [our] God and Father" (Rev 1:6).

Justification is the first moment of sanctification, that moment when we are initiated into the new life of righteousness. This chapter tells how that process works itself out in us. We have left the dominion of darkness and entered the dominion of the light of God, and this mandates the triumph of the believer over sin through the empowering presence of the Spirit in our lives.

There are two sections in this chapter on sanctification, flowing from rhetorical questions in verses 1 and 15. The first (vv. 1-14) describes how the saints have died to sin and are now alive to God in Christ. The second (vv. 15-23) shows that God's people have been liberated from enslavement to sin and are now slaves to righteousness. Yet the believer is not totally free from sin. It is no longer our master, but it is still an active force trying to regain power over us. Through the power of Christ and the Spirit we learn to live more and more in the new life Christ has made possible.

SHOULD WE CONTINUE IN SIN OR NOT? (6:1)

The rhetorical question here grows out of the theme from 5:20-21, which states that as sin increases, grace increases all the more. Out of this one could make the mistaken inference that for grace to become greater, we should commit more and more sins. There is no evidence that anyone had actually voiced this opinion. It may be a theoretical query Paul used to make a point. On the other hand, it could be that Paul had encountered Jewish opponents who tried to impugn his logic on this. We cannot know for sure.

The introductory "What shall we say then?" is found in 3:5; 4:1; 7:7; 8:31; and 9:14, always to forestall a potential false conclusion. In 3:20 Paul noted the tremendous abundance of grace available to the sinner through Christ. It was possible for some to misunderstand the implications of this joyous promise and think they could receive more and more grace if they just could keep sinning (literally, "remain in sin"). The danger is that sin would reign all the more in their lives. You cannot live in both realms (good and evil) at the same time.

WE HAVE DIED TO SIN (6:2–5)

Paul responds, "By no means!" (see 3:4, 6, 31; 6:15; 7:1, 13; 9:14; 11:1, 11). There is no way that committing more sins is the way to gain more grace from God. It would do just the opposite, driving us further and further from God. The truth is that "we are those who have died to sin," so the question is, "how can we live in it any longer?" It is not just that we should not want to continue sinning. We who are truly in Christ have died with him with respect to sin, so we *cannot* live in it any longer. We are constitutionally incapable of doing so, because we live in the family of God.

WE CAN NO LONGER LIVE IN SIN (6:2)

When Paul says we "have died to sin," he is referring to our conversion, when death was defeated in Christ (as in vv. 15–19). We have ceased to be under the power of sin, as Paul will state again in verses 6 (sin is "done away with"), 11 ("dead to sin but alive to God"), and 14 ("sin shall no longer your master"). This does not mean sin has stopped affecting believers. Christians are indeed tempted by sin and often yield to it, but sin is no longer an internal force. It is an external force trying to regain control by luring us away from Christ, as stated in the old self/new self of verses 5–7 below (also Eph 4:22–24; Col 3:9–10).

In light of this, "how can we live in it any longer?" The all-embracing power of God took over when Christ performed his atoning work on the cross, and when we turned to him in faith, his blood price was put to our account by God and we were forgiven, declared right at his judgment seat. At that moment we "died to sin" and it lost its power over us. Yet at the same time it did continue its war against us. Christ is the inner power at work in us, yet still sin is operating from outside through temptation.

BAPTISM—SHARING CHRIST'S LIFE AND DEATH (6:3–4)

A second rhetorical question leads us into the key analogy of our victory in Christ: "Or don't you know that all of us who were baptized into Christ Jesus were baptized into his death?" The opening "Or don't you know" shows that in the early church baptism as dying and rising with Christ was common knowledge. The verb *baptizō* means to be immersed in water,[1] so the image of being "buried with" Christ flows out of the idea of going under the water.

Paul is using this analogy to help his readers understand more deeply what it means to "die to sin." Conversion means being "baptized into Christ Jesus," along the lines of the Great Commission (Matt 28:19; see also Acts 8:16; 19:3, 5; Gal 3:27). While some see a referential sense here ("baptized with respect to Christ"), it is better to see this in Matthew and here as designating union with or incorporation into Christ ("baptized into [union with] Christ").

Since baptism signifies our complete union with Christ, we are united with him in dying to sin. Therefore, we no longer live under the power of sin (v. 2) because when we were baptized, we signified that we have been united with Christ's death and entered the new realm of the redeemed and the justified. We have power to defeat sin due to the presence of Christ and his Spirit in our lives. God has given us "a way to escape" (NIV "a way out") so that we can "endure" and defeat sin (1 Cor 10:13).

Paul clarifies this further in verse 4, saying that "we were therefore buried with him through baptism into death." When we were immersed under the water, we united with not only Jesus' death but also his burial. Some see the sacramental aspect of baptism here, with the actual presence of Jesus in the rite, but the emphasis in the word picture is not upon baptism per se but on the union with Christ it is portraying. Paul is not telling *how* we are buried with Christ but what it means to be buried with Christ.

---

1. Paul is not contributing to the debate as to whether Christian baptism should involve immersion, pouring, or sprinkling; his use here is metaphorical.

Also, it goes too far to consider Christ's death and resurrection as timeless events that are repeated in every act of baptism; that goes beyond the text here.

There are further questions regarding the meaning of "buried with him through baptism." On one level it signifies the transfer of the eons, as we make a decisive break with the old self and way of life and begin the new life with Christ. Baptism becomes the instrument "through" (*dia*) which burial with Christ is mediated. Through it we at our conversion participate in Christ's death and burial to this world.

An important passage in this discussion is 1 Peter 3:21, that difficult passage which says "baptism ... now saves you." Conversion and baptism are in both passages part of a unified experience, with baptism not the basis of salvation (the means is Christ's atoning sacrifice) or the way we appropriate salvation (that is faith in Christ). Rather, it seals the salvation experience and signifies our death to sin. Baptism is not necessary for salvation but is a necessary part of the salvation experience.

As the second part of verse 4 makes clear, baptism is a participation not only in Jesus' death and burial but also in his resurrection: "just as Christ was raised from the dead through the glory of the Father, we too may live a new life." Christ was raised "through the glory of the Father," and he in turn will draw us into that same glory. We are glorified in him now, and our future state will be even more glorious.

In 1 Corinthians 15:20, 23 Christ was raised as the "firstfruits" of our own resurrection in him (the subject of vv. 5, 6 below), that is, as a sacrifice that makes the fruit of our own new life in him possible. There are two stages to this resurrection experience, first the resurrection life that we enjoy in the present, and second our final resurrection when he returns at the end of history to launch eternity.

The result (*hina*, "in order that") is that we may participate in his resurrection experience from the moment of our conversion and "live a new life" in him (literally, "walk in newness of life"). This means that the conduct of our daily lives must reflect the new priorities and lifestyle we have been given as we become more and more Christlike. As Paul will say in Romans 8, we must begin to live in the Spirit rather than in the flesh.

CONCLUSION: UNITED IN HIS DEATH AND RESURRECTION (6:5)

Paul now draws together what he has been saying about sharing in Christ's death and resurrection and makes it clear: "If we have been united with him in a death like his, we will certainly also be united with him in a resurrection like his." The "if" (*ei*) assumes the reality of the premise, but there is a question about the meaning of "united with him in the likeness of his death" (the literal translation). "Likeness" could mean a copy or image of something, but if that were the case it would denote baptism as the image of Jesus' death and resurrection, and that is doubtful. The point is our union with Christ rather than baptism, and the analogy itself centers on the meaning of this union.

I think it is better to take "likeness" as connoting the "form" Jesus' death takes rather than the image behind it. In several passages in Romans it refers to form, as in 1:23 (idols made in the likeness of mortals), 5:14 (sin in the likeness of Adam), and 8:3 (God sending his Son "in the likeness of sinful flesh"). Here it means we have experienced "a death like his" (NIV)—a spiritual death. We begin our new life through participation in his death; this is how we die to the age of sin and the old way of life that came along with it.

If we have been united with him in his death, then "we will certainly also be united with him in a resurrection like his." The question here is whether "will ... be" relates to the present experience of newness of life or to final resurrection with Christ. I don't think it has to be an either-or. It should be interpreted as inaugurated **eschatology**, with the perspective of the already (our present newness, v. 4) and the not yet (our future new life to come, vv. 8–10).

This truth is desperately needed today. Many members of our churches are more secular than they are godly and care more about their present pleasures than the things of Christ. The true meaning of Christianity has become obscured because of a this-worldly perspective in which self rather than Christ is on the throne of our lives. Followers of Christ must begin to think clearly about the material in this chapter and what is really important in our lives.

OUR OLD SELF IS CRUCIFIED WITH CHRIST (6:6–7)

It is common to think that verse 6 continues the thought of death with Christ from verse 5 and uses a different image to restate the same point. This is seen in a few translations like the NASB, which translates this as subordinate to verse 5, "knowing this, that our old self" (also KJV, NKJV, LEB). However, I agree with those who see this beginning a new paragraph (vv. 6–10) that expands the meaning of dying and rising with Christ). This opening portion (vv. 6–7) centers on the consequences of our union with Christ in his death with respect to sin (returning to the theme of v. 2). Paul first repeats the idea of verse 3, "For we know," referring to important material the Roman Christians had been taught.

Paul restates the meaning of dying with Christ in a metaphor, "our old self was crucified with him." This verse is commonly interpreted as referring to our individual death to self and the new life we each have in Christ after conversion. While this may be part of it, it is better to see this as corporate and salvation-historical. It refers to the new era Christ has brought into this world with his incarnation and death for us.

The old self is humanity in Adam, under the control of sin. This former way of life was "crucified with Christ" when we turned to Christ in faith and died to sin with him. Christ bore our sins on the cross, meaning that spiritually we were on the cross with Christ.

In that sense we were crucified with Christ when we died to sin in union with him, and the old eon also ceased to exist.

As a result, sin is no longer in control of our lives, yet it now tempts us through the "flesh" (Rom 7:5; 8:3-8, 12-13). Believers are in Christ rather than in Adam and so belong to the "new self" (Eph 4:24; Col 3:10). In Ephesians 4:22 Paul says that we must put off the old self, "which is being corrupted by its deceitful desires."

While we are no longer under the dominion of sin, we are still drawn into it and must resist it at all times. There are two purposes (hina, "so that") to our being crucified with Christ: The first purpose is so that "the body ruled by sin might be done away with" or, more accurately, "rendered powerless." When the old self was "crucified with him," it lost its power over us and was nullified (katargeō). The verb can mean "annihilated, destroyed," but here it probably means "rendered ineffective," nullified as a force that controls us. The "body of sin" is not the physical body but the whole person as "ruled by sin."

If we are no longer ruled by sin, why do Christians so readily fall into it? The key is the flesh (7:5, 25; 8:3-8), the proclivity to sin within us. Sin can no longer overpower us, but it can deceive us. Satan does not overpower but lives entirely by deception (Rev 12:9; 20:3, 8, 10). He in one sense is "the god of this age" (2 Cor 4:4), but he is only the god of the people of this age, not of believers. He can only defeat followers of Christ when they yield to his blandishments.

The second purpose is "that we should no longer be slaves to sin." This is the true identity of those in Adam, enslaved by those sins that control their lives. They are chained to the passions described in 1:18-32. Once sinners turn to Christ in faith and are crucified and buried with him to sin, they are liberated. We are no longer in Adam but in Christ (5:12-21), and the sin of Adam has been nullified so that we can start life anew.

Verse 7 tells why this incredible promise is true, "because anyone who has died has been set free from sin." We now see how being crucified with Christ ("died") relates to its result ("set free from sin"). The verb "set free" is *dedikaiōtai*, the same verb used for "justify" in 3:20, 24, and several take this to mean that the one who dies in Christ is "acquitted" from sin. However, that does not easily fit this context, and it is better to say with the NIV that it means that the one who is crucified with Christ is "set free" or liberated from the power of sin.[2] Of course, the two fit together well, as the justification of sinners leads to forgiveness and frees them from enslavement to sin.

DYING WITH CHRIST MEANS LIVING WITH HIM (6:8-10)

THE CERTAINTY OF THE RESURRECTION LIFE (6:8)

Having explored the contours of dying with Christ, Paul now develops the significance of living with him. The "if" here in verse 8 is a condition of fact and can be translated, "since we died with Christ," assuming the reality of the conversion experience. Since we have truly died with Christ to the old self (v. 6), "we believe that we will also live with him." As in verses 3-4, participation in the death of Christ leads to participation in his resurrection and in his resurrection life.

The question, as in verse 5, is whether this means our present life with him in this world or the final resurrection life that will characterize eternity. Both aspects flow out of the "new life" in verse 4, and I could argue for an already/not yet thrust here. Still, I think it best to see present experience more in verses 4-5 and the final sense here. To borrow language from verse 5, the same glory that raised Christ from the dead will attend our final resurrection as well, and our future life will be truly glorious.

---

2. It is a perfect tense and a divine passive ("has been set free" by God), describing a new state of being that defines our new life in Christ.

CHRIST'S EXAMPLE: DEATH NO LONGER HAS MASTERY (6:9–10)

The strength to overcome the world of sin stems from the knowledge that Christ has won the final victory over evil and death, and this makes our future absolutely secure in him. For the fifth time (with 2:2; 3:19; 5:3; 6:6), Paul states that "we know" a central truth: Christ is Lord of all (5:1, 11, 21), and death "no longer has lordship" (my translation of *ouketi kyrieuei*) over him. The old era (old self, 6:6) has ended, and the new era in which life rules in Christ has begun.

He was raised as the "firstfruits" of our resurrection (1 Cor 15:20, 23), and death no longer lords it over us either. Jesus "cannot die again," and our death will be merely physical and not even temporary, for the moment we die we are in the Lord's presence (2 Cor 5:1–10). The legends that after we die we loiter for a while in our death chamber are wrong; we are "absent from the body … present with the Lord" (2 Cor 5:8 KJV; see also Phil 1:21–23). We know "we will also live with him" (v. 8) because his resurrection guarantees our own. We too will conquer death because at our conversion we participate in his resurrection spiritually, and at his return we will participate in it comprehensively, entering eternal life.

Paul explores this glorious promise further in verse 10, telling us the next great truth: "The death he died, he died to sin once for all; but the life he lives, he lives to God." This verse tells why we can know death has lost its "mastery" over Christ (v. 9). The logic of this thought goes back to 5:12–21, to the fact that with Adam's trespass sin and death entered the world and conquered it. That remained the case until Christ came into this world, with his death conquering sin and his resurrection conquering death. This is the means by which we "died to sin" (v. 2)

The important point of the first part of this verse is the great truth that he not only conquered death in his resurrection but also conquered sin on the cross, and he did so "once for all." This critical particle is at the core of Hebrews (7:27; 9:12; 10:10) and means that Jesus' death ended the reign of sin and death once and for all. Sin and death are still evil forces in this world, and in John in Revelation pictures them as demonic figures (Rev 6:8; 20:14), but they are already defeated powers, and the victory has been "once for all" won for us by Christ.

Paul sets up a deliberate antithesis here between sin and God. Sin is a defeated foe, and it is "the glory of the Father" (v. 4) that raised Christ to life. Because sin and death have lost their power, there is new depth and meaning to "life," as seen in Christ, who was raised as the "firstfruits" and "lives to God," guaranteeing that we have joined him in this new life. No longer under the dominion of sin and death, he can devote eternity to living *for* God (better than "to God"). When he breathed his last and gave his soul up to God on the cross, he returned to his preexistent glory, and he paved the way for us to share in this glorious new realm of reality.

THIS HAS IMPLICATIONS FOR THE LIFE OF THE BELIEVER (6:11-14)

In verses 8-10 the attention was on Christ's monumental victory over sin and death, providing the basis for new life entering this world. Now Paul explores what this means for those who find faith in Christ. He shifts his focus from third-person singular (him) to second-person plural (you) and defines the results of Christ's death and resurrection for God's people. He switches from the didactic (teaching) to the imperative (commanding).

With the introductory "in the same way" Paul compares Jesus' great salvific deed to the life of the believer. The message exhorts the Roman believers to continue walking the walk. There are four steps to living a life of victory: consider yourselves dead to sin but alive to God (11); do not allow sin to rule in your mortal body (12); do not offer the parts of your body to sin (13a); yield every area of your life to God (13b). The result of this life is victory over sin, which Paul proclaims in verse 14.

Dead to Sin but Alive to God (6:11)

In the first command Paul builds on verse 2 and the fact that in Christ we have "died to sin." In light of this, Paul says, you should "consider yourselves dead to sin." The verb "consider" (*logizomai*, NIV "count") is the same verb as in 4:3-4, where Abraham's faith was "credited" or "reckoned" to him as righteousness. We reckon ourselves as dead to sin on the grounds that we are united with Christ in his death. He is more than just the model for our own victory over sin; we overcome it because we are one with him (v. 5).

"Consider" is a present-tense command, and it means that even though we are dead to sin, we must continually reckon ourselves dead to the power of sin in our lives. While it has been "done away with" (v. 6), it is still an invading army trying to regain control and enslave us, so we must as an act of will consider ourselves at every instance of temptation to be dead to it.

The means by which this defeat of sin is accomplished for us is our being "in Christ Jesus." The "in Christ" motif occurs more than 150 times in Paul, and there are generally two aspects of it, primarily our union with Christ and secondarily our membership in his body, the church. Every aspect of chapter 6 thus far—buried, crucified, dying, and living—take place only "in Christ," our complete union with him.

Sin Cannot Reign over Us (6:12)

Once we are dead to sin and on a regular basis consider ourselves to be so (vv. 2, 11), we control our fleshly impulses and refuse to allow sin to "reign in [our] mortal body so that [we] obey its evil desires." "Body" here does not mean just our physical bodies but our whole person. We must control every area of our life so that sin cannot "lord it over" us. "Mortal" simply stresses our finite human condition.

Our fallen condition renders us susceptible to our flesh or sinful impulses, so we must all the more depend completely on the strength Christ provides. This verse contains a present prohibition meaning either "stop letting it reign" or "at no time let it reign," but in this context the emphasis is on the regular decisions of the Christian life, so the latter is more likely.

The background to this verse is 5:12-14, where Paul says that sin and death "reigned" over humankind due to Adam's trespass. In 6:2-10 we learn that believers in Christ have left that realm, uniting with Christ and his victory. The promise in this section is that "sin shall no longer be your master" (v. 14), and this takes place when we put the "incomparably great power" (Eph 1:19) God has made available in Christ to use in our lives. Then we will have the strength to turn our backs on temptation and refuse to "obey its evil desires." These are not just bodily lusts (as some have said) but all self-centered desires of the flesh (see also 1:24; 7:7-8). These desires are antithetical to God's will and must be avoided and rejected.

Refuse to Offer Self in Service to Evil (6:13a)

Since we refuse to allow sin to reign in us (v. 12), it makes perfect sense to go the extra mile and refuse to "offer any part of yourself to sin." "Yourselves" is literally "members [of your body]," but as in verses 6 and 12 "members" refers not to the physical parts of our body but to our various faculties or capacities. Paul means that we must restrict all our abilities and actions for the glory of God and never allow anything in our life to have an evil outcome.

The idea behind "offering" something as an "instrument of wickedness" could be a military image of offering our weapons in service to a tyrant or perhaps our services to a ruler or tools to a master craftsman. The military metaphor fits the language best and also fits the prevalence of military images in Paul's writings. We are not spiritual mercenaries who use our weapons to serve evil. The rule of the tyrant has been broken on the cross, and Satan cannot draft us into his army, for we have been freed by the greater power.

Yet we can still be defeated when we yield to temptation. We cannot defeat sin in our own strength; we must rely on Christ and the Spirit to give us the power we need to achieve victory.

YIELD EVERY AREA OF YOUR LIFE TO GOD (6:13B)

This is the positive counterpart to the refusal to use your life in the service of evil in verse 13a. Instead, Paul instructs, "offer yourselves to God … as an instrument of righteousness." We have refused to be drafted into Satan's army but instead have volunteered to become part of heaven's armies. The title "Lord of hosts" (1 Sam 1:3, 11; 2 Kgs 19:31) in the Old Testament means "Lord of heaven's armies" (the NLT translation), and in Revelation 17:14 and 19:14 the saints join those armies at the final battle that ends history. We are in a spiritual war that will determine the contours of eternity, and as in Ephesians 6:10–18 we are mustered by God into battle against the "spiritual forces of darkness." We are citizens of heaven and belong to God, and as with the armies of Israel all citizens are part of the armies of the new Israel, the church.

We have been "brought from death to life," which means we have transferred from the realm of sin into the realm of righteousness. Our realm henceforth is the kingdom of light, and we serve the good rather than the wicked. We need to work at good spiritual sight so that we can recognize what belongs to light and what stems from darkness, then make sure we walk only in the light.

As a result, Paul says, "offer every part of yourself to him as an instrument of righteousness." "Every part" means every single area of ourselves, our abilities and capacities to serve God rather than self. "Righteousness" is one of the central terms in Romans and here could be legal (the status of being declared right with God) or moral (upright behavior that pleases God). I have gone back and forth on this, preferring the legal in my earlier

Romans commentary,[3] but the moral in recent times. In the end, both thrusts are interdependent here. The righteousness of God imputed to our account must lead us to live righteously before him.

Too many people in our churches give the Lord lip service while largely living for themselves and their earthly pleasures. They are serving the wrong master and inadvertently using their resources or "instruments" for the wrong things. That is a great and tragic mistake. A key part of the ministry of every church should be not just winning the lost but waking up the sleeping saints who are wasting their lives on the wrong things. As Paul says in Ephesians 5:14, "Wake up, sleeper, rise from the dead, and Christ will shine on you."

Result: Sin Cannot Be Your Master (6:14)

Paul demands that his readers offer themselves to God because (gar, "for") "sin shall no longer be your master." Throughout this section, sin is personified as a hostile power trying to conquer and enslave the people of God. In this sense, this sentence is primarily a promise, "sin will not lord it over you," but also borrows some imperatival force from verses 11–13, "sin must not be allowed to master you." The power of sin over God's people ended at the cross, and we now have a new Master, "the Lord Jesus Christ" (5:1, 11, 21).

As I have also said above, this does not mean sin cannot gain some control and defeat us. But it never has to be that way, for God always gives us a "way to escape" and the strength to do so (1 Cor 10:13, my translation). We are "more than conquerors" (Rom 8:37) and can always resist should we turn to Christ and the Spirit for strength.

This promise is grounded in the second half of the verse, "because you are not under the law, but under grace." Paul is

---

3. *Romans*, IVP New Testament Commentary (Downers Grove, IL: InterVarsity Press, 2004).

returning to the issue of the law (5:13, 20) as an instrument of sin (3:20; 4:15). This was the case in the old era; the law was a power that caused sin to increase (5:20). This era ended with Christ; the grace of God has broken the power of sin through his sacrificial death. This clause summarizes the salvation-historical switch from the old era of law, characterized by enslavement and condemnation (Gal 3:23-29), to the new era of grace, characterized by redemption and freedom from sin.

In this section, Paul says we will continue to be defeated in our spiritual walk until we realize the reality of our conversion as a union with Christ in his death and resurrection. If we know Jesus as Savior we must know him also as Lord, and if we are part of the family of God we must live like it. Union with Christ's death means that we must "die to sin." His death on the cross paid for our sins, but it also drew us into his victory over sin and gave us the strength to be free from sin's power.

There are two metaphors behind this. Baptism (vv. 3-4) pictures us dying and being buried with respect to sin (going under the water) and then rising in a spiritual resurrection to newness of life (coming out of the water). Then the image of old self and new self (vv. 6-7) depicts the abolishing of sin's control that we inherited from Adam and then the new life of victory over sin that results. In Christ sin has been rendered powerless and is no longer a force within us. It is an external force invading our lives and trying to defeat us and regain control. But when we allow our union with Christ to guide our choices, we are then "set free" from sin's controlling power (v. 7) and can rise above the temptations of life in this world.

The second half of this passage (vv. 8-14) centers on the other side of this wondrous truth: in Christ we share not only in his death (to sin) but also in his resurrection (to life). Sin has lost its hold, and death has been defeated in Christ. Our future is entirely centered on life. Death is indeed the last "sting" (1 Cor 15:55–56), but it is a defeated foe, and our own coming death is mainly a step upward to glorious life with him.

To enjoy fully the new life we have in Christ, we must defeat sin in our lives and yield ourselves fully to Christ. Then we can begin to live. The way we do so is to stop "offering" ourselves to the self-centered desires that try to master us and to "offer" every area of ourselves to living rightly for God (v. 13). When we allow the grace of God that has saved us to guide us in our choices, we end the mastery of sin and enter the life centered on the lordship of Christ. Then we finally start to live.

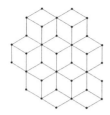

FREEDOM FROM SIN'S ENSLAVING POWER
(6:15-23)

As I wrote in the introduction to the previous chapter, the theme of Romans 6 is the process by which we in Christ are liberated from the power of sin. In verse 1 Paul asked whether we should continue sinning so God's grace can increase. This led to the teaching that the new life in Christ means dying to sin. Now in verse 15 the question looks at the same problem from the grace side of the issue. We are liberated from enslavement to sin because by God's grace we have become slaves of him and of righteousness. In this section Paul offers four responses to the issue of yielding to sin: He begins by telling them that everyone is enslaved to something because surrendering to anything is to become its slave (15-16). He then reminds them that they have been emancipated from slavery to sin so that they can become slaves of righteousness (17-18), concluding that in this light they must become slaves of righteousness that leads to holiness (19). Finally, the two destinies mandate this move, for being slaves to sin results in death (20-21) while being slaves to God results in holiness and eternal life (22-23).

TO SURRENDER TO A THING IS TO
BECOME ITS SLAVE (6:15–16)

As in verse 1, Paul introduces the paragraph with a rhetorical question, "Shall we sin because we are not under the law but under grace?" The focus shifts from the negative side in verses 1–14, that we should not continue sinning because we have died to sin. Now he switches to the positive side, that we should defeat sin because we are freed from it to become slaves of God and of righteousness.

Paul is anticipating a misunderstanding of his statement in verse 14, that "we are not under law but under grace." This could be interpreted by some Jewish Christians to say that given the absence of Moses' law they are free to do whatever they want since there are no longer any legal regulations prohibiting those actions. The presence of grace then would mean God would understand and forgive whatever they decided to do. People in our day are often guilty of a similar dangerous denigration of the problem of sin, holding to a form of free grace that says God will automatically forgive and overlook whatever sins we commit.

Paul responds with his famous *mē genoito*, "By no means!" (see also 3:4, 6, 31; 6:2; 7:7, 13; 9:14; 11:1, 11). Such an assumption will bring the wrath of God down on the sinner. The solution comes in verse 16 via realizing anew a commonly known truth in the ancient world.[1] It has been estimated that as high as 85–90 percent of the population of Rome either had been or were slaves, nearly all of them due to debt.[2] Few were lifelong slaves, for most would work off that debt in ten to twenty years and return to their lives. This was a powerful metaphor for the Roman church.

---

1. "Don't you know" in vv. 3, 6, 9, referred to what they had been taught in the church. Here it is an axiom that lay behind everyday experiences in the Roman world.

2. See Arthur A, Rupprecht, "Slaves, Slavery," in *Dictionary of Paul and His Letters*, ed. Gerald F. Hawthorne, Ralph Martin, and Daniel G. Reid (Downers Grove, IL: InterVarsity Press, 1993), 881.

Paul says if you "offer yourselves to someone as obedient slaves, you are slaves of the one you obey." The present-tense "offer" and "obey" refer to a life of continual obedience and would have the force of "so long as you do so." The mark of enslavement, Paul is saying, is continual obedience to the dictates of a thing. Prevailing sin is a type of slavery, so Christians must never give in to it. Paul uses the same verb for the opposite effect in 12:1, "offer your bodies a living sacrifice." Sin must never be allowed to control our life.

Paul challenges his readers to carefully choose their slavery. Everyone will be a slave to something, so we must be discriminating in our choices. The sign that reveals our choice is obedience, whether we allow sin or God to guide us. We have to sign one contract or the other. To try to be neutral is to choose sin, for that constitutes a refusal to serve God. Jesus in Matthew 6:24 says it well: "No one can serve two masters. Either you will hate the one and love the other, or you will be devoted to the one and despise the other. You cannot serve both God and money."

The consequences of that choice are serious, for eternity is at stake. To choose sin "leads to death," and to choose obedience (to God) "leads to righteousness" and then to eternal life (v. 22). The "death" here probably includes physical death that ends one's earthly life, but in the context the major thrust is spiritual or eternal death, the "second death" of Revelation 2:11; 20:6. It is our eternal destiny that is uppermost in Paul's mind.

The "righteousness" here is more difficult to interpret, for it could refer to final righteousness (eternal life), but it could also mean believers' present status as justified or the right living that will characterize those who obey God and Christ. It is best to see this as a comprehensive reference embracing all three ideas. Those who turn to God are the redeemed, who are declared right with God, then live in order to please him, and then finally will receive the reward of eternal life given to the righteous.

WE MUST BE LIBERATED FROM SIN (6:17–18)

Paul is not discouraged about the Roman Christians' situation. He begins positively, saying "thanks be to God" that they are indeed following God with all their hearts and defeating sin in their lives. At the same time, by giving thanks to God he is stating that it is the grace of God, not their own ability to live the Christian life, that has enabled them to depart from a life of sin and choose to live rightly for him.

God deserves all the credit for the fact that they "used to be slaves to sin" and are now liberated from bondage. As verse 16 said, they have obeyed God and submitted to his salvific work in their lives. Their days in chains to the powers of darkness are over, and they have made a "wholehearted" (NIV "from your heart") faith commitment to Christ, meaning they were radically converted and yielded themselves completely to God.

The result of this conversion is that they have obeyed "the pattern of teaching that has now claimed [their] allegiance." God has transferred them from the realm of sin, from the lies they had been taught by the world, to the realm where they are taught and learn to obey his truths.

The "pattern of teaching" refers to the doctrinal pattern these truths take but even more to the way that Christian teaching shapes or molds the believer. Christians are no longer under the law but still have their own doctrinal teachings to follow. Many have designated the Sermon on the Mount as a Christian Torah, the new "pattern" of kingdom laws. These new forms mold believers and guide them in the new life in Christ.

I have devoted my life to upholding this "pattern of teaching," to making serious Bible study available to churches. I am alarmed by the lack of deep Bible study I observe in churches. We claim to believe the Bible is the word of God, yet we marginalize it in our lives. There are some great exceptions like Bible Study Fellowship, but far too few. What I am praying I can accomplish in this commentary series is to make the exciting treasures of God's word and its "pattern of teaching" accessible and desirable to pastor and layperson alike.

Verse 18 restates what Paul has just said and summarizes the chapter by saying, "You have been set free from sin and have become slaves to righteousness." The two verbs are divine passives, emphasizing God as the driving force in transferring the new convert from the realm of sin to that of righteousness. This verse revisits the theme of liberation or freedom from the bondage of sin, first introduced in 6:7 ("set free from sin").

When we give in to sin, we are overwhelmed by the seductive power of evil. When we respond to Christ, we choose to become "slaves to righteousness." It is God who enables us to do so, and it is Christ's blood sacrifice that makes it possible. God has called us into a new relationship with himself and transferred us from the realm of sin into the kingdom of righteousness, enabling us to rise above sin and live rightly for him in our lives. "Righteousness," as in verse 16, primarily has an ethical thrust, dealing with the results of justification (declared right with God) and sanctification (made righteous and holy [v. 19] by the Spirit): we live out this new status and spiritual reality in our daily conduct.

WE MUST BECOME SLAVES TO RIGHTEOUSNESS (6:19)

Paul is aware that his slavery metaphor only goes so far, so he says, "I am using an example from everyday life because of your human limitations." This transition statement relates to what comes before as well as to what comes after, that is, to all of verses 15–23. "Human limitations" is literally "the weakness of your flesh," and can be understood several different ways. Paul could be referring negatively to the tendencies to sin and self-deception or perhaps apologizing for such a negative image, but it is more likely that he is speaking simply of the human inability to understand such deep truths without an analogy to help them picture the spiritual truth. An earthly metaphor like slavery is not completely sufficient for such a task, but we finite creatures need word pictures to enable us to grasp theological realities that would be over our heads otherwise.

He then restates the basic point of this chapter. In the past the Roman saints "used to offer yourselves as slaves to impurity and to ever-increasing wickedness." They were foot soldiers in the evil army, serving the demonic officers in the areas of "impurity" or "uncleanness," a term that often has a sexual connotation in Paul, and also of "wickedness" or "lawlessness" (sin as countering the laws of God) in general.

All this describes a life of pleasure-seeking and self-centeredness. "Ever-increasing wickedness" is literally "wickedness to wickedness." Applying this phrase to the slavery metaphor, people are willingly throwing themselves into sin with deeper and deeper addiction to its destructive powers. It is not a hostile takeover but a willing plunge into "reckless, wild living" (1 Pet 4:4), ignoring the fact that they are plunging to their deaths.

However, for God's people this is not the case. They have rejected the muster for Satan's army and have willingly joined God's army (v. 13b) to become "slaves to righteousness leading to holiness." As I have said (vv. 13, 16, 18), "righteousness" includes both the new status (justification) and the righteous lifestyle (ethics) that results. This lifestyle is part of the theme in chapters 5–8 centering on sanctification, or the process by which we are set apart for God and live a holy life. Paul contrasts "wickedness [leading] to wickedness" and "righteousness leading to holiness." Christians make decisions that determine whether their lives will be characterized by more and more evil or more and more holiness. Those choices will determine their destiny.

WHY WE SHOULD CHOOSE A LIFE OF RIGHTEOUSNESS (6:20–23)

The introductory *gar* (for), omitted by the NIV, tells us the reasons why we must obey the mandate of verse 19 to turn from wickedness to righteousness. The basis for choosing a life of righteousness and holiness is seen in the contrast between enslavement to sin (vv. 20-21) and enslavement to God (v. 22). The first results in death, and the second results in holiness and life. The choice could not be simpler or more obvious. So why it is always so difficult? Because it is at the heart of the great battle between good and evil, between God and Satan, for the souls of those who were made in the image of God. We who are the object of that war are bombarded with the subtle and not-so-subtle temptations to self-centered desires and sin. We are deceived by self and Satan and so fail to recognize the true consequences of our choices.

Being Slaves to Sin Results in Death (6:20-21)

Paul next reminds his readers once more what it was like before their conversion. "When you were slaves to sin," that is, before the Roman Christians met Christ and were liberated, "you were free from the control of righteousness." Note the irony of Paul's wording. They were "free" and yet had to be liberated from it. All they were actually free from was "the control of righteousness."

This is the basic delusion of unbelievers who think they are free because they *seemingly* have no one controlling their choices. In truth they are not even free to choose sin, for sin has enslaved them and they cannot help but live for themselves. They think they can do whatever they want, unlike the poor Christians who have all these terrible restrictions forced on them by the Bible and the church.

The unsaved make this assumption because they are ignorant of the true meaning of sin and its control over their minds and hearts. The only thing they are really free from is the ability to do that which pleases God and is right in his sight. However, this does not mean non-Christians are incapable of doing good. Calvin's doctrine of "common grace" points out that sinners are able to perform good deeds and think good thoughts. What non-Christians cannot do is overcome sin and find God. Jesus points out that "no one can serve two masters" (Matt 6:24). Every person is either under sin or under grace. You cannot serve both.

The real tragedy is not the enslaving power of sin but its results (v. 21). Paul asks: "What benefit did you reap at that time from the things you are now ashamed of?" There are two images here: wages for work accomplished, and the fruit that grows from what is planted. When people plant sin, they harvest shame. When they work at attaining pleasure, the payback is not worth the effort. Moreover, shame is far more than the embarrassment of having committed wrong. Shame in Scripture is shame before God and connotes divine judgment. Every person will stand before God at the last judgment and account for their deeds. To stand in shame is to stand condemned by God. One only has to look at the state of things on the average university campus (binge drinking, frat parties) or at a typical New Year's celebration or Mardi Gras to realize the depravity of our way of life. I have had non-Christian friends who throughout the week (every week!) talked only about getting drunk the next weekend. Clearly it never satisfied and could only be repeated week after week! Paul is saying that a life of debauchery pays no benefits, and later that time of pleasure means only shame at what fools we were.

The final judgment arising from these shameful deeds is severe: "Those things result in death!" This is the second death of Revelation, the eternal punishment of the lake of fire (Rev 20:13–15). All humankind must choose God or sin, and there are only two destinies that result from that choice—eternal life or everlasting punishment. This is by far the most important decision any of us will ever make, for eternity itself is at stake!

Being Slaves of God Results in Holiness and Life (6:22)

"But now" moves from the past life to the present reality for these Roman believers. The false freedom of the unsaved past is now replaced by true freedom in Christ. They have transferred from the realm of sin and entered the realm of grace by faith in Jesus.

When we respond to Christ, the past shame (v. 21) is replaced by
the present path of holiness, and death is replaced by life. Shameful deeds result in death, and holiness results in eternal life. The
wicked empire of sin was "rendered powerless" (v. 6; NIV "done
away with") by the cross, and we were liberated to become slaves
of God and righteousness (v. 18).

Sanctification is defined first as freedom from the dominance
of sin and second as a process of being made more like Christ.
The former is the path to the latter. Here Paul describes this process in terms of its fruit, and in contrast to the process of sin in
verse 21, shame is replaced by holiness. We plant righteousness
and harvest holiness, that is, sanctification, and this has its own
harvest, eternal life. As Christ becomes increasingly the Lord of
our life, we become more and more God-directed and Spirit-led.
As in Matthew 6:19-21, "treasures in heaven" increasingly replaces
"treasures on earth," and we start to seek and think about "things
above" (Col 3:1-2).

THE WAGES OF SIN VERSUS THE GIFT OF GOD (6:23)

This justly well-known verse puts everything in chapter 6 together.
Paul returns to the metaphor in verse 21 of wages paid for work
done: "the wages of sin is death." We earn judgment by works,
while justification and life come only by faith and are a gift from
God. There is also a military connotation, for those who sin are
part of the armies of darkness. As soldiers are paid by the powers
behind them, they will be paid by God according to what they have
earned from their military missions and the evil they have done.

In contrast, the saints have a "gift of God," something they
could not earn by their merits—"eternal life." The greatest contrast is here, eternal life versus eternal death. The first is the greatest gift ever given, life in heaven, and the second is the most terrible pay ever received, everlasting punishment in the lake of fire.

All of this is possible "in Christ Jesus our Lord." The sinner
has *turned down* Christ and lived a life apart from him, while the

saints have *turned to* him in faith. As John 3:16 has said, those who believe "in him shall not perish but have eternal life." The full title "Christ Jesus our Lord" occurs also in 1:4, 7; 5:1, 11, 21; 7:25; 8:39; 13:14; 15:6, 30. It is the key **christological** title in this letter, and here it reinforces that the gift of eternal life is only possible "in Christ." It is his lordship that will put it to work and produce our eternity in heaven.

———

All of us want to think we are free to do as we wish, and that in the end we make our own choices. In reality the opposite is true. As Paul says in verses 15–16, everyone is a slave of something. We do get to choose, but only that to which we will surrender as our master. There are ultimately only two that matter, sin or righteousness, what is opposed to God or what is of God. That choice will determine our eternal destiny.

In verses 17–19 we see what the choices we make will accomplish in our lives. Freedom from the enslaving control of sin comes about when by faith we choose Christ over the world and accept the gift of salvation from God. At this point we experience two things that at first glance seem paradoxical: we are liberated from the realm and power of sin, and we become slaves of righteousness and of God. In the past we chose "ever-increasing wickedness," but when we turn to Christ we reject that sad and destructive lifestyle and dedicate our lives to "righteousness leading to holiness" (v. 19). Our lives finally attain a meaning and purpose that can ultimately be worthwhile.

In verses 20–23 we are shown the reasons for making the only proper choice. The sinners think they are free, but in reality they are brainwashed and spoon-fed the great lie that a life of sin produces joy and true pleasure. A life of self-centered seeking results first in shame for a wasted life and ultimately in eternal torment for the God-rejection that sin represents. On the other hand, a life of living for God produces satisfaction and true happiness in

our earthly life and eternal glory and joy in the next. We receive
the gift of salvation now and the gift of life everlasting in heaven.
Our choice is to depend on the wages we earn with our works, or
by faith to accept the gift we did not earn, eternal life with Christ
Jesus our Lord.

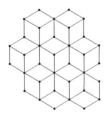

FREEDOM FROM CONDEMNATION
UNDER THE LAW, PART 1:
THE UNBELIEVER AND THE LAW
(7:1–12)

The two most prolific themes thus far in Romans have been the twin problems of sin and the law, specifically the law of Moses. These come together in chapter 7, and we see more clearly how they relate to each other. The primary emphasis in this chapter is that sin not only reigns over fallen humankind but also rules specifically over those who are living under the law.

In Romans 7 we see that those who are under grace have been freed from bondage under the law. None can be justified by observing the law (3:21, 27–28), and righteousness is attained only by faith, not the law (4:13–16). The law's purpose was not to bring salvation but to identify sin. Under the law sin actually increased rather than decreased (5:20), and death reigned through sin and the law (5:14, 21). In chapter 7 the one who has come to Christ in faith is not under the condemnation of the law but must live a life of freedom from it and from sin.

The transition from 6:15–23 and its emphasis on the liberation of God's people from the enslavement of sin takes place via 7:1–6. This paragraph provides further detail regarding the fact that Christ has broken the bondage of the law. Death has actually

provided the means of severing the chains of the law (for this
image, see Gal 3:23; 4:2, 7). Paul illustrates this by saying that, as
a marriage ends with death (vv. 2-3), so when believers die to the
law and embrace freedom in Christ, they are free (vv. 4-6). The
saints are the bride of Christ and live a life of freedom rather than
of bondage to the legal demands of the law.

The primary focus of the chapter is 7:7-25, which continues the
dichotomy initiated in verse 6, the old way of the law (vv. 7-12) and
the new way of the Spirit (vv. 13-25). In verse 7 Paul begins to speak
in the first person ("I"); one of the great debates about Romans is
over whether Paul is writing about himself, the unbeliever under
the law, or the Christian under the power of sin and temptation. I
will deal with that issue in the introduction of verses 7-12 below.

THE BELIEVER IS LIBERATED FROM
THE LAW TO JOIN CHRIST (7:1-6)

THE AUTHORITY OF THE LAW: ONLY FOR THE EARTHLY LIFE (7:1)

Two interrelated ideas dominate this verse: lifelong bondage to
the law, and liberation from it only through death. Paul's concern
over this issue as it relates to the Roman Christians is heightened
by calling them "brothers and sisters" (also in v. 4), which pictures
him putting his arm around them to show how much he cares. He
is drawing them close to him in order to stress that, since they
are justified by God, they are freed from their bondage to the law.

He assures them that he writes to them as people who "know
the law," that is, are acquainted with its intricacies and the difference that Christ has made. As in 6:3, 6, 9 (also 1 Cor 6:2, 9, 16, 19), he
appeals to their previous teaching about the law and seeks to correct a possible misunderstanding regarding its place in the Christian life. As those who understand the law, they should realize the
truth about God's people who are "not under law" according to 6:14.
Many in the church were Gentile in background (see ch. 1), but still
they were knowledgeable of the Jewish law, especially since many

were God-fearers—Gentiles who worshipped in synagogues and accepted Jewish traditions (see Acts 10:2; 13:16, 26).

So he is speaking of the law of Moses when he clarifies that "the law has authority over someone only as long as that person lives." This is something that all the members of the congregation should know. "Has authority over" is the same verb used in 6:9, 14, for the "lordship" or "mastery" of death and sin over humanity. The law of sin and death rules over this world, and the central teaching of 5:12–7:25 is that there is only one solution—faith in Christ. As a result of Christ's atoning sacrifice on our behalf, the saints in Christ have been transferred from the domain of darkness to the domain of light. Faith in him constitutes dying to the domain of sin and death.

The Metaphor of Marriage: Released When the Husband Dies (7:2–3)

Paul turns to the imagery of marriage to illustrate the lifelong commitment of God's people to the law. In Jewish law only the husband could break a marriage (Deut 24:1), while in Roman law either partner could break the bond. The term for "married" here is unusual, *hypandros*, "under [the power of] a man." This same idea is seen in the phrase "released from the law," meaning "from the law of the husband." While Jesus expanded the Jewish law to cover a wife as well as a husband (Mark 10:11–12), Paul is reflecting the Torah requirement that God's intention was release from the marriage bond only upon the husband's death.

He elaborates the Deuteronomic injunction in verse 3 by stating that if divorce had taken place, any attempt to remarry while the husband was still alive would constitute adultery, while marriage after his death would not. Note also that it says "released from the law" rather than from her husband, further emphasizing the legal rather than marital aspect. The actual point is not freedom from marriage but freedom from the law.

We must be careful to realize this is an illustration, not an allegory. If we envisage the wife as a believer and the husband as the law, then we could say that the law died so that we would be free to become the bride of Christ (which was the interpretation of church fathers like Origen, Augustine, or Chrysostom). However, that would clash with the wording of verse 4, which says it was believers who "died to the law" so they could "belong" to Christ. Others take the husband as the old self and the wife as the new self. None of this fits the context here. When we recognize there is no spiritual meaning of husband and wife here, this illustration takes its rightful place as demonstrating the fact that when Christ came, God's people died to the law and entered a new realm of faith in him.

THE CHRISTIAN: RELEASED FROM THE LAW TO JOIN CHRIST (7:4)

Paul now asserts that the Roman believers have "died to the law through the body of Christ." This verse, in light of what I have just discussed, does not provide the allegorical significance of 2–3 but rather shows the significance of verse 1, namely, that the Christian has "died to sin" and been united with Christ.

It is not that the law has been put to death but that Christians have died to the law. According to the traditional understanding believers have died with respect to condemnation by the law. While this is correct, it does not go far enough. As in 5:12–6:23 (especially 5:13, 20; 6:14), the reign of the law has been abolished and God has transferred us from that kingdom to the kingdom of Christ. We have died to the law *as a whole.*

This also goes against the Reformed or Calvinistic separation of the legal aspect of the law (the office of the law with its regulations) from the ethical aspect (the law as a rule for life). In Reformed theology we have been freed from the first but not the second. I disagree. Paul is not talking about the Jewish perversion of the Mosaic law into an instrument of justification but the failure to realize the inability of the law to solve the sin problem. It is a salvation-historical issue; the era of the law (as a whole) has ended and the believer has been transferred to the new realm of Christ.

Yet this also does not mean that the law no longer has any place at all in God's plan. The law teaches how God deals with his people and what holiness means. The law of Moses has been "fulfilled" or brought to completion in Christ (Matt 5:17–20; Rom 10:4), and it no longer has a role in the process of salvation except for highlighting sin (Rom 3:20). God now reveals his righteousness "apart from the law" (3:21), and it is faith, not the works of the law, that brings us to salvation.

Believers have died to the law "through the body of Christ," referring to the fact that he "'bore our sins' in his body on the cross" (1 Pet 2:24). As a result we "belong to another." This image goes beyond that of marriage to the mystical union with Christ. Our oneness is with the one who has indeed been raised from the dead," referring to Christ's resurrection as the "firstfruits" (1 Cor 15:20, 23), implying that this new union will be eternal.

The purpose of our union with Christ is "in order that we might bear fruit for God." Some see this as a further metaphor, the bearing of fruit representing the children born of the marriage to Christ, that is, evangelism; but as I said above such metaphors are not really part of the meaning here. Rather, Paul means that Christians will live fruitful lives as a result of their union with Christ. The proper fruit is a sanctified life, including the "fruit of the Spirit" of Galatians 5:22–23.

CONTRAST BETWEEN THE FLESH AND THE NEW WAY OF THE SPIRIT (7:5–6)

Flesh/Spirit dualism is one of the major themes in Paul's writing, as we will see when we get to chapter 8. The "flesh" is the human tendency to sin, the proclivity to giving in to self and Satan in temptation. The old self has been nullified and rendered powerless. It no longer is that controlling power within that dominates the carnal nature. Now it is an external force arrayed against us and tries to regain control through the flesh. Paul will explore this spiritual war further in the rest of this chapter.

Here Paul notes that in the realm of the flesh, "the sinful passions aroused by the law were at work in us." Law, by showing that sin was a transgression of God's legal demands, first makes people conscious of sin and then makes sin more appealing, causing it to increase in intensity (see 3:15, 20–21; 4:15; 5:20). These passions completely control the lives of nonbelievers but gain power over believers as well. The emphasis here is on the former, the lives of those under the total depravity of 1:18–32.

This verse culminates Paul's teaching on the relation of the law to sin, and it is not a happy or good one. The law defines sin, then makes people conscious of it, then brings God's wrath down on its practitioners, and finally produces increasing sin and death in this world. The law is not evil in itself, and as we will see in 7:12 it is "holy, righteous and good." However, sin uses the law for an evil purpose, and thus at times it has a sinister side to it.

All this is summed up here as the "passions" inflamed by sin and the law. These passions were at work in the "members" of our bodies (NIV "in us"). As in 6:13 the phrase refers to our total person, so these passions are self-centered desires at work powerfully "in us" when we were unbelievers, producing the temptations that lead us to sin. When we succumbed, we turned away from God and went our own way. The final result was that in contradistinction to verse 4 we "bore fruit for death" rather than "for God." The question is why in light of the incredible powers at work and the horrifying results, anyone in their right mind would ever want to return to that!

Paul transitions to the present in verse 6 ("But now"). Here we discover the true meaning of life, the "new way of the Spirit" as opposed to "the realm of the flesh" (v. 5). Followers of Christ have died "to what once bound us." This would certainly include dying to sin as in 6:2. The enslaving power of sin (6:16, 20) has been nullified in the cross. This took place at conversion when they were

"united with [Christ] in ... death" (6:4-5) and the "old self was crucified with him" (6:6). Paul is specifically talking about their having
been "released from the law," with language borrowed from 7:2
on marriage to assert we have been delivered from bondage to it.

The old era of legalistic observance is past, and the "new way
of the Spirit" has arrived. There are several different interpretations of the contrast between the "old way of the written code"
(literally "oldness of the letter") and the "new way of the Spirit"
(literally "newness of the Spirit"): It could refer to (1) a Jewish
misuse and misunderstanding of the law versus the Christian view
of the Spirit; (2) the pre-Christian life versus the Christian life;
(3) the law versus the gospel; (4) the old covenant of the letter of
the law versus the new covenant of the Spirit. There is no question that there is law/Spirit dualism here, but that only narrows
the options to numbers one, three, and four. Of these the fourth
captures the thrust best, given the salvation-historical tone of so
much that has come before. Paul is talking about the switch from
the old covenant, centering on the Mosaic law, and the new covenant age as typified by the Spirit.

Paul is not saying that the law is evil; that will be made clear
in 7:7, 12, 14, where he will emphasize the "spiritual" value of the
law. Rather, as he has said the last two chapters, the law could
only make us "conscious of our sin" (3:20). It highlighted sin and
revealed transgressions but could not bring people to salvation. In
fact, it became an agent of the very thing it was supposed to counter and caused sin to "increase" (6:19). Christ alone can solve and
destroy sin, and in doing so he completes or culminates the law
(Matt 5:17-20; Rom 10:4). The whole law is summed up in him, and
faith in him replaces trust in the works of the law for salvation.

Paul first contrasted the Spirit and the written code in 2:27-29,
where the pair defined a true Jew versus a non-Jew, characterized
by "circumcision of the heart" that takes place "by the Spirit." The
old covenant of the letter of the law has given way to the new covenant of the Spirit and of the heart, and there is now a "newness"

that typifies both the new covenant reality and the life of the people who are part of it. Once more we recognize the basic paradox of Christian salvation (see 6:16–18): we have been liberated from bondage to sin in order to give ourselves freely as bond slaves of the Triune Godhead.

THE LAW SUBJECTS THE UNBELIEVER
TO SIN AND DEATH (7:7–12)

This passage (7:7–25) completes Paul's trilogy on the problem of sin and the law (5:12–21; 6:1–23; 7:1–25). The development of thought across these passages moves from the imputation of sin from Adam to Christ, to the great battle regarding the invasion of sin and the liberation from it effected by Christ, and now to the victory over sin and the law in Christ. Yet one of the great debates in Romans centers on which victory Paul is describing: the victory of the unbeliever over sin and the law at conversion, or of the believer in the Christian life.

We must decide two preliminary issues in answering this dilemma. First is the question of whom Paul is describing in his switch to the first-person singular ("I") in this section. There are four theories:

1. *Paul himself*—Paul describes his own experience with the law and sin, either as he was growing up or perhaps relating his life as a whole.
2. *Adam* (especially vv. 7–12)—this passage describes Adam's experience and struggle with sin in the garden.
3. *Israel*—the "I" refers to Israel before and after receiving the law, especially the struggle of God's people with the law.
4. *General humanity*—Paul is referring not to any particular person or group but to all people who wrestle with God's demands on them.

The second (Adam) is unlikely because there is no type-of-Adam Christology developed here like there is in the **typology** of 5:12–21. Moreover, Paul does not hint that he intended the "I" to stand for Adam. Still, Paul probably does intend to show how the experiences of himself and of all humanity echo Adam in the garden, as I will point out in ensuing verses. The third (Israel) fits the centrality of the "law" in this passage along with the Jewish nature of 7:7-25, but it does not quite do justice to the whole passage, as we will see in the next paragraph. The fact that the "law" is at the core of this chapter does not mean that Paul intends Israel here. "Law" is also central in chapter 8 (vv. 2, 3, 4, 7), and there it is the Christian life that is the focus.

I think the best interpretation for the meaning of "I" here is a combination of the first and fourth views. Whenever Paul uses "I" in Romans he is referring to himself, yet at the same time it is also unlikely that he is speaking *only* of himself, for the language expands in this chapter to include all humanity. I conclude that Paul uses his own experience under the law to describe the basic human dilemma under sin and the law. In addition, the contrast between the old and new creations is also part of this section. In short, Paul is speaking autobiographically, and at the same time uses typology (he is a type of all humanity) to depict the plight of all of us.

The second issue flows out of the first one. Is Paul describing (1) Christians (as Augustine and other Latin fathers believed), (2) non-Christians (as Origen and other Greek fathers believed), or (3) the non-Christian in verses 7-12 and the Christian in verses 13-25 (as Calvin believed)? Scholars have been divided mostly over the first two, with a growing number seeing this mostly as the unbelieving Jewish people wrestling with the law.

While the first two are viable, I believe the third makes best sense of the text, as we will see. It fits closely the switch from past-tense verbs in verses 7-12 to present-tense verbs in verses 13-25. Paul's Jewish background was the prolegomena to his Christian life, so the idea of the Jewish person under the law is true of verses 7-12. At the same time, Paul describes "everyman" first on the basis of his Jewish past and then on the basis of his Christian present.

THE LAW IS NOT SINFUL BUT MAKES SIN KNOWN (7:7)

Paul starts with "What shall we say, then?" just like he does in 3:5; 6:1; and 9:14, and as before he uses it to clarify himself and avoid potential misunderstandings. In 3:20 he stated that the law was meant to make people "conscious of … sin"; and in 5:20; 6:14; and 7:1–6 he centered on the inability of the law to deliver one from sin. From this it was possible to conclude that the law was inherently evil, so he asks, "Is the law sinful?" If so, it would constitute an unbridgeable barrier between Judaism and Christianity and between the old covenant and the new, a charge his opponents had most likely made against him. His usual response ("By no means!"; see 3:4, 6, 31; 6:2, 15) shows his objection to such a complaint.

At the same time, he feels he must explain the link between the law and sin, since over the past couple chapters he has asserted that the law has indeed become a vehicle for sin. He must steer a clear path between the two extremes—that the law is sin on the one hand and that it is the instrument for salvation on the other. He begins by arguing generally, "I would not have known what sin was had it not been for the law." "Known" here is experiential and not just intellectual. He learned the hard way how the law produced sinful living. He then speaks specifically via a single example of sin from the tenth commandment: coveting. When the law specified, "You shall not covet" (Exod 20:17; Deut 5:21), Paul was not only aware that it constituted a sin but also attracted to it. As earlier in the verse, "would not have known" combines the intellectual realization that it was sin with the experience of committing it. Some interpreters narrow this coveting to sexual lust, but in the commandment it is broader, covering all kinds of sinful desires.

THE PROGRESS OF THE LAW TO SIN AND DEATH (7:8–11)

Paul shares in the next verses how sin exploits the law and uses it to establish an entryway into a person's life so as to accomplish its sinister operations.

Establishes a bridgehead (7:8a)

He uses a strong metaphor, describing sin "seizing the opportunity," or "taking advantage of the occasion," a military image for establishing a bridgehead or base of operations. In this verse, coveting seized the opportunity the law gave it and made "the commandment" its base of operations and "produced in [him] every kind of coveting." Paul pictures sin as the enemy force invading his life and grabbing the chance afforded by the law against coveting to produce all kinds of temptation and to defeat Paul spiritually. Human beings are attracted to "the wild side," and once they learn that self-centered desires are dangerous, they can't wait to try them.

Springs to Life and Produces Death (7:8b-9)

In the last part of verse 8 Paul introduces a twofold antithesis between the life of sin and the life of God's people. In the first half (8b-9a) sin is dead, and I am alive. Then the scene reverses in verse 9b: when sin comes to life, I die. The means by which this reversal takes place is the law.

The law, which is meant to be a spiritual force for good (vv. 12, 14), in reality has the opposite effect. It becomes the nutrient that brings sin to life. When he says sin is dead "apart from the law," Paul hardly means that sin did not exist before the law of Moses arrived. We know from 5:12-14 that sin was not just present but "reigned from the time of Adam to the time of Moses." Most scholars interpret this to mean sin was inactive or inert, looking at it in a legal sense as transgressing God's laws (cf. Jas 2:17, 26, for this use of "dead"). Without the law, people did not understand this legal sense of sin.

In verse 9 Paul says that "once I was alive apart from the law," but he later died when "sin sprang to life." There are four possible views of what Paul means here.

1. A few think this passage flows out of 5:12-21 and depicts the fall of Adam into what can be called "the primal I": "apart

from the law" refers to Adam in the garden, and the commandment refers to the order not to eat the forbidden fruit. The problem with this interpretation is the lack of any true connection between Adam and the I, as discussed in the introduction to 7–12.

2. Many have recently posited that the "I" is Israel before the law was given on Sinai, with the law in existence but not complete. This fits the third approach to 7:7–25 above, that the passage pictures Israel's struggle with the law. From this perspective this interpretation makes a great deal of sense, since it would fit the centrality of "law" here. However, I think it runs into difficulty with the idea of "I was alive," which usually in Paul refers to the spiritual life, an approach that seems correct in terms of "I died" in verses 9–10. It does not seem likely that Paul would be saying that Israel was "alive" before the law came.

3. Quite a few agree with Calvin that this passage describes Paul's life before conversion, perhaps the equivalent of his bar mitzvah. In this sense "apart from the law" could refer to that period of his youth before he truly understood what sin was or the extent to which he was a sinner. While this is closer to the thrust of the passage, I still wonder if Paul or any Jew would actually have described their youth as "apart from the law."

4. I think it best to see Paul using himself as an example of all humanity "apart from the law." He is looking at his own experience of the interplay of the law and sin to be typical of everyone. The biggest problem with this understanding is that it seems implausible that Paul ever thought of himself as "apart from the law"; but he is thinking of himself as symptomatic of every human being struggling with their finite sinfulness.

Note the progression of the ideas here. The first stage occurs as he begins, "Once I was alive apart from the law." This is the first time the emphatic *egō* (I) appears, and as I have said earlier, it probably refers to Paul's own experience as typical of everyone. Yet I still can't help but wonder if he ever thought this of himself in a culture where the law was central from birth to the grave. He often speaks of the zealous piety that characterized him at all times (Gal 1:13-14; Phil 3:4-6). The best answer is that Paul is identifying with fallen humanity and so reflects the other side of what he called his "faultless" behavior in Philippians 3:6.

The second stage occurred "when the commandment came," when he became aware of God's demands as specified in the law. At this point the third stage came, when "sin sprang to life" and sinful actions became conscious rebellion against God and his law. With awareness of the law, sin took advantage of it and established a bridgehead in his life, attacking him via temptation, thereby leading him into ever-increasing sinful deeds.

The final stage was "and I died," literally, "the I [*egō*] died." This is the opposite of the "death to sin" in 6:2, 4-6, and describes that death that results from sin. There could be an echo of Adam in the garden in this. He too was innocent and without law, but when the serpent took over and seduced him, death entered the world and conquered all humanity.

The killing mechanism: the commandment (7:10)

As we will see in verses 12, 14, the law with its commandments is "holy, righteous and good" in its purpose. Hence it is "intended to bring life," that is, to enable God's people to live rightly and experience a holy life with God. Certainly it accomplished just that for many in the old covenant period. But Paul once more shows the other side, what happened when the evil powers used the law as an instrument for their nefarious deeds. Instead of making people right with God and enabling them to live life rightly for God, its "commandments" were "found" (by Paul) in actuality to "bring death."

As sin became more and more alive, the *egō* began to die. Sin in a sense fed on whatever life the "I" possessed and ate it alive. To the Jews the law indeed would "bring life," but when deformed by sin, it was the harbinger of death. As throughout this chapter, the death Paul has envisaged includes physical death but is primarily spiritual, ending with eternal death in the lake of fire (called "the second death" in Rev 20:14).

Deceives and kills (7:11)

This verse sums up the whole of verses 8–11 and traces the progress of sin and the law in destroying the life of all who fail to turn to Christ in faith. As in verse 8, sin lay dormant without the law to turn it into legal transgression. While the law was meant to have a positive purpose and bring life, sin, "seizing the opportunity [establishing a bridgehead] afforded by the commandment," rears its ugly head.

Satan is a brilliant military strategist and even turns God's gifts to his people around and makes them into weapons of destruction. The Mosaic regulations, which allowed God's people to remain in right relationship with him, were turned into weapons of deception. It is not the law that is at fault but sin, which uses the commandments to seduce people like the serpent did Adam. It "deceived," a word Paul also uses for the seduction of Eve in the garden (2 Cor 11:13; 1 Tim 2:14). All through Scripture this is the way Satan defeats God's people, not overpowering them but tricking them and leading them astray (Rev 12:9; 20:3, 8).

Because of sin, the law became the weapon that "put me to death." Meant for life, the law led to sin and became the dominion of death. For Adam and Eve it was physical death that entered the world and reigned over it (5:12–14). For us now it is also spiritual death. Apart from Christ there is no hope. Many, even Christians, feel this verdict is unjust and that earnest people who seek God through their own religious traditions should be included in the gift of life. The problem is that all other religions in the final analysis center on works-righteousness, that is, earning salvation by our own efforts and merits. As Paul says in 3:21–26, we can never be good enough to merit salvation by our own efforts. This is why God paid the price himself by sending his Son in our stead to die as the atoning sacrifice for our sins. There is no other way (John 14:6; Acts 4:12). God is perfectly just and merciful, for he loved us enough to die for us (John 3:16; Rom 5:8).

CONCLUSION: THE LAW IS HOLY AND GOOD (7:12)

The question that began this section (7:7) was, "Is the law sinful?" Paul has concluded no, the law was the agent used by sin to produce its evil agenda. Here he proceeds to sum up ("So then") the actual verdict on the law. Rather than being sinful, "the law is holy, and the commandment is holy, righteous and good." He wants to be certain no one thinks that the law was unholy or bad. Sin is the true culprit, the actual enemy of God's people.

When he calls the law "holy" he declares that God originated the law and gave it to humankind. Holiness is the true core of the Being of God and expresses his transcendent Otherness. For people to be "holy" means that they are taken over by God and set apart for his purposes. They partake of the very character of God. With regard to the law or other inanimate objects, holiness stresses the sacred character of what God has made available to redeem this world. In this way "the law" as the general set of principles and "the commandment" as the specific regulation in the law are both "holy," and in addition the two are "righteous and good."

At first glance, calling the law "righteous" seems to contradict 3:20 and 5:20-21 (it caused sin to increase). However, the earlier passages described the function of the law (what it does), and here Paul is telling us the character of the law (what it is). In fact, making us conscious of sin was a righteous purpose of the law. There is also a double meaning in *dikaios*—the law is "righteous" in terms of partaking of God's nature and "just" in terms of being fair to his people. The term carries both connotations and here functions both ways. When Paul states that the law is "good" he looks at it as an expression of God's goodness and produces what is best for his followers (cf. Rom 12:2, God's will as "good, pleasing and perfect"). Far from being evil, the law is a sign of God's justness and goodness.

————

Romans 7, perhaps the most difficult chapter to interpret in the letter, culminates Paul's lengthy teaching on the issue of sin in the life of believers. The first section, verses 1–6, introduces the question of sin and the law with the analogy of marriage. As marriage is a lifelong commitment that is only broken by death, so God's people are bound to the law until they have died in Christ. At conversion, when they die and are buried with Christ (as stated in 6:3–4), they are freed from the law to begin life anew in Christ. We now belong to him and through that union live fruitful lives for God (7:4).

However, we still wrestle with sin. The unsaved are under the total control of sin, which inflames sinful passions, enslaves its practitioners, and leads to death (v. 5). The Christian, while free from the law and the internal control of sin, is invaded by it from the outside and must depend on the Spirit for victory. Our freedom is provided by "the new way of the Spirit" and releases us from bondage (v. 6).

In verses 7–25, Paul describes his own struggles with sin, first as an unbelieving Jew under the law (7–12) and then as a believer wrestling with sin in the present (13–25). The first portion, as we have seen, describes Paul's past as a Jew under the law and feeling the temptation of sin through wrestling with the law. It was the law that told him coveting transgressed God's law, and that very knowledge caused Paul to sin all the more, for it provided an edge to coveting that appealed to his fleshly nature.

The progress of sin is presented in verses 8–11. It depicts Paul and humanity in a time of seeming innocence when the law had not yet made them aware of sin. The law then became the instrument sin used to invade our lives. It enhanced the attractiveness of sin, with the result that sin produced more and more spiritual failure. As sin grew, we became weaker until we died. However, while the law may function as the instrument of sin, in and of itself the law came from God, in essence partook of God's holy character, and produced righteousness and goodness in our lives.

While we have not grown up with the same issues Paul is discussing here, we have all had the same struggle with sin. When we know something is wrong and should be avoided, the forbidden becomes all the more attractive, and we, like him, have to depend all the more on God's grace and strength to overcome temptation.

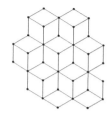

FREEDOM FROM CONDEMNATION UNDER THE LAW, PART 2:
THE BELIEVER AND THE LAW
(7:13–25)

As mentioned in the last chapter, 7:7–25 is the final of Paul's three major meditations on the problem of sin and the law (with 5:12–21 and 6:1–23). The discussion began with Christ overturning Adam's sin and making victory possible for his followers. Then Paul moved to the invasion of sin and the liberation from it we find in Christ, and in 7:7–25 he presents the struggle and eventual victory over sin and the law in Christ. There are two parts in this section; the first (7:7–12) describes Paul as a Jewish unbeliever, the model for unsaved humanity defeated by sin as it overwhelms the defenses and takes control.

The second part (7:13–25) describes Paul as a believer, wrestling with the law and sin, and now a model for Christians and their spiritual walk. He is nearly defeated, with victory coming only when he surrenders and learns to depend only on Christ. In this section it is critical to understand that even though the Christian has "died to the law" (7:4) and been "released" from it in Christ (7:3), the law is still present in our lives in a secondary fashion as fulfilled in him (Matt 5:17–20). It is culminated or completed by Christ (Rom 10:4) but still a part of our lives.

The reader should go back to the introduction to 7:7–12 in the last chapter for the arguments regarding whether Paul had in mind regenerate or unregenerate humanity in this section. Some go so far as to conclude that Paul is describing the struggle of every person, unregenerate or regenerate, with the law and sin. However, I believe it is best to see verses 7–12 describing the unbeliever and verses 13–25 describing the believer. Paul then contrasts the life of the Christian under the flesh in verses 13–25 with the Christian under the Spirit in 8:1–17. I believe the present-tense and emphatic *egō* (I), along with the movement of the three passages on sin in 5:12–7:25, favors the interpretation that Paul is depicting the Christian battle against sin and the law. This is not an antithesis between the unsaved and the saved but rather between the Christian trusting the flesh and the Christian living in the Spirit.

So this passage depicts Paul (and us) trying to defeat sin in his/our own strength and finally learning to surrender to Christ and the Spirit. I simply find it too difficult to take *egō* as an unbeliever or Israel without seeing Paul speaking of himself in some way. Moreover, both the battle with sin and the eventual victory in verses 24–25 fit the Christian too well. Very few of us have read this passage without thinking first of our own wrestling with sin and the law. In one sense, it is true that the centrality of the law in this passage seems inconsistent with the characterization of a believer, for instance "I delight in God's law" in verse 22. Yet at the same time it fits Paul's own relationship with the law after he became a Christian, as seen in Acts 18:18; 21:22–26. This would characterize a Jewish Christian quite well.

The passage progresses powerfully, tracing the battle against sin under the law. In verse 13 Paul summarizes the struggle depicted in verses 7–12 of sin using the law as a means of introducing death and defeat into the person's life. Then verses 14–17 depict the futility of trying to do good but failing due to the power of sin. Verses 18–20 describe the problem of sin living in *me*, and finally verses 21–25 picture the opponents in the spiritual war within the believer—sin versus Christ—showing how the victory is finally won in Christ rather than in the flesh.

SIN USED THE COMMANDMENT
TO PRODUCE DEATH (7:13)

In my earlier commentary on Romans I followed those who place verse 13 with verses 7–12 as a summary of the issues there.[1] However, I now believe it is a transition verse but primarily introduces verses 14–25. The question here, "Did that which is good, then, become death to me?" does indeed flow out of the twofold thrust of 7–12 (the law is good but still produces evil). However, as with other rhetorical questions in Romans, the question introduces issues that are answered in the verses that follow.

From the earlier passage it would be easy to conclude that the law, while good in intention, actually brought death to people. In verse 7 Paul asked, "Is the law sin?" Now he adds the natural next step, "Is the law death?" This question is especially relevant in light of verses 10–11, "the commandment ... actually brought death." But the answer is the same as in verse 7: "By no means!" The villain is not the law but sin. The law that was "good" became (as in v. 11) the tool sin used for its evil purposes. Paul thus introduces a twofold model of what brings death—the law as the instrumental basis, and sin as the actual producing agent.

This means the blame for bringing death into the world rests squarely on sin (as in 5:12). God has two purposes regarding sin here: First, he wishes to "reveal" (the meaning of *phaneroō*, "recognize") the true nature of sin.[2] Second, God uses the commandments of the law to prove that sin is "utterly sinful," a strong idiom meaning it is proved to be completely evil. Through the

---

1. Grant R. Osborne, *Romans*, IVP New Testament Commentary (Downers Grove, IL: InterVarsity Press, 2004), 179.

2. The NEB has a good translation: "sin exposed its true character."

law the depth of sin's perversity is realized as never before. It is both opposed to God and opposed by God. Thus the law is indeed "good," since it exposes the deep underbelly of sin. Sin is unmasked and proved to be repellent to any right-thinking person because of its demonic and supremely destructive nature.

TRYING TO DO GOOD IS FUTILE (7:14–17)

THE LAW IS SPIRITUAL, I AM UNSPIRITUAL (7:14)

In the next few verses the law continues to be central, and Paul begins on a positive note: "We know that the law is spiritual." As in 2:2 and 3:19 (also 6:16; 7:1), "we know" points to a commonly accepted truth that Paul wishes to develop further. The law is known to be "holy, righteous and good" from verse 12, and now we learn it is "spiritual" as well. Its origin is divine, not human, and it deals with the essential realities of the spiritual realm.

In contrast, however, "I am unspiritual" (literally "fleshly"). This is the first of six times in this section that Paul stresses "I" (egō). This is not inherently a negative term; it refers to his basic self and his common humanity with all of us. Yet Paul links it in this verse with his fleshly or carnal nature, that tendency in every person to choose sin. As such we belong to this world and are under the power of sin and death. Paul speaks of the "carnal Christian" in 3:3, one who is "worldly" and living for the flesh. We all wrestle with this tendency in our lives and need unceasing vigilance and strength from the Spirit to keep from capitulating to the pressure.

As "unspiritual" or "fleshly," the egō is also "sold as a slave to sin." This terrible image pictures the "I" in chains on the auction block, about to be handed over to sin, its new master. The image goes back to 6:16–23 and is at the center of the debate regarding whether Paul is describing the saved or unsaved person in this section. Many think the idea of slavery to sin is simply too harsh and negative for chapter 6, which shows the believer having "died to the power of sin" (6:2) and no longer "slaves of sin" (vv. 18. 22). However, others believe this pictures prevailing sin, the danger that Christians will be defeated by ongoing sinfulness.

There is no question that this is the most difficult part of the chapter for any theory arguing that Paul has a Christian in mind here. But I am still convinced by the argument (see the introduction to 7:7–12) that Paul has a believer in mind for verses 13–25. The answer can be found in the imagery. The Christ follower is set free from the enslaving power of sin and able under the Spirit to defeat the tendencies of the flesh, but sin keeps using the law and the flesh to counterattack and establish a bridgehead (7:8, 11).

Paul uses the slavery metaphor to hyperbolically stress the growing control of sin at times in every Christian. This is not the "normal Christian life"; that is seen in chapter 8. In this sense he develops a "straw man," a picture of believers who attempt to live the Christian life in their own strength. Romans 7:7–23 presents the Christian living by the flesh; 8:1–17, the Christian living by the Spirit. Paul wants us to realize the malevolent forces arrayed against us and the dangers of the enslaving power that can all too easily take control of us.

PROBLEM: I DO WHAT I DO NOT WANT TO DO (7:15)

The unspiritual, fleshly Christian is totally confused: "I do not understand what I do." Note the contrast with verse 14, "We know that the law is spiritual." Putting the two together, Paul is saying, "Every one of us is aware that the law is spiritual, but I can say for myself that I am unaware and confused that I fail to act on what I know. I recognize the good but then don't live it out in my life." Are there any of us who fail to identify with this? A single thread runs through these verses—conflict and self-guilt, confusion and doubt. Paul wants to do what is right but cannot get over the hump of the flesh, his carnal nature. This is the heart of the struggle between living for God and living for self: "What I want to do I do not do, but what I hate I do."

Paul uses three verbs translated "do" in the NIV. They occur repeatedly in the rest of verses 15-23. Some believe they build on each other, but it is more likely that they are synonymous and used for stylistic variation and emphasis. If we translate them literally, the verse would read, "For I do not understand what I am producing. For what I want I do not practice, but what I hate, that is what I do." Together they refer to the actions of a person who wants to do good but cannot seem to do so.

Another central term Paul introduces here is "want" (seven times in vv. 15-21). The will is at the core of Christian thinking, and Paul is distinguishing his personal spiritual desires from what is effectively carried out in his actions. He planned for the good but actually produced what he hated. This moral failure was the product of sin within along with the fleshly propensity to surrender to what he knows is wrong. It is neither sin nor the flesh acting alone but the two working in concert. Sin provides the temptation; the flesh surrenders to it. This struggle is at the heart of living the Christian life, the war we fight against evil within us and the fleshly tendency to give in to what we know is bad for us.

PROOF THAT THE LAW IS GOOD (7:16-17)

Paul fails to live up to what he knows is right, but the very fact that he desires to do what is good proves that "the law is [indeed] good" and spiritual (vv. 12. 14). The fact that he "agrees" with the law's assessment proves that he knows the difference between right and wrong stated in the law. Even when his actions go against what he wants to do, the very fact that he desires to do what is right constitutes implicit agreement to the moral goodness of the law.

The reason for all of this is given in verse 17: "As it is, it is no longer I myself who do it, but it is sin living in me." As we have already seen, Paul is saying in effect, "The law is good, but I am not." Moreover, it is not the "I" but a separate force, sin, that is at fault. His conclusion is, "it is no longer I myself who do it, but it is sin living in me." Like the law, the "I" is a dupe to the power of sin.

It does give in to the temptation and is guilty, but it is not the generating force. Paul is responsible for his poor choices, but another force interferes with his spiritual desires and reverses them.

Sin was expelled at conversion when the "old self" was nullified (Eph 4:22-24). But it has invaded, conquered, and now has made a new home in us. It has once more become an internal reality in the defeated, carnal Christian. We must remember that while Paul is painting a bleak picture, it does not have to be this way. Overall, Paul will expect the Christian not to be like this but to live a victorious life. But that will come when the Spirit takes over, as Paul describes in 8:1-17. His point here is that whenever we, though Christians, live life in the flesh, sin will be our lot.

THE SELF IS IN BONDAGE TO THE
POWER OF SIN (7:18-20)

In these verses we are at the heart of the problem. It is not just the malignant power of sin that is at fault but the fact that it has taken up residence once again in us. In chapter 6 Paul pictured sin as an invading army coming from the realm of darkness to conquer and enslave us. He carried this argument further in the first half of chapter 7, when he depicted it as establishing a bridgehead in our lives (7:8, 11). Now in 7:14-20 sin has defeated us and made its home in us. This completes the picture of the carnal Christian as enslaved in sin (v. 14), wanting to be free but unable to break out of its stranglehold (vv. 15-16), and with sin not only the taskmaster but also now indwelling the inner person (v. 17) and driving out the good (v. 18).

Nothing Good Lives in Me (7:18)

This verse repeats what Paul just said in verse 17 in a different way. Because of the indwelling presence of sin, Paul is aware ("I know") of two things.

First, he realizes that "good itself does not dwell in me" any longer. Since sin has now taken over his house, that is, his life, the good he has been seeking (vv. 15–16) cannot remain. So now sin, described as "nothing good" (NLT, NET, LEB, ESV), is now living "in my sinful nature," literally "in my flesh." The law is good (v. 12), but that is now external to him, and the internal controlling power has nothing to do with "the good" (*agathos*, at the end of the sentence for emphasis). The internal mechanism in control is no longer the Spirit but "the flesh," the proclivity to sin and attachment to the world that seeks to please the self rather than God.

Second, he recognizes that the reason for his proclivity to sin is the conflict within him: "For I have the desire to do what is good, but I cannot carry it out." This restates verse 15, "What I want to do I do not do." The *egō* has given in to the flesh and chosen to do what it detests. The true desires have been nullified, and the "I" has been virtually taken over. Now, this does not mean that the battle is over. The war between the will and the deed is ongoing.

Some think Paul reflects here the Greek repugnance toward the body, but more likely he has in mind the Jewish doctrine of the two *yetzers*, the two natures of every person: the impulse or tendency toward good (*yetzer tōb*) and the impulse toward evil (*yetzer hara'*). All moral and ethical decisions are made via the interaction between these two forces. "The flesh" is not a reference to the physical body; it is the base of operations for sin, and it is at the heart of decision-making in the self.

I Do What I Do Not Want to Do (7:19–20)

In these next two verses Paul recapitulates what he said in verses 15–17 regarding the defeat of the will by sin and the flesh. This first part repeats verse 15 and adds further clarity by specifying more precisely the opposing forces: "For I do not do the good I want to do, but the evil I do not want to do—this I keep on doing." He concretely identifies his desire as "the good," and he concretely identifies what he actually practices as "the evil."

At first glance this seems as if he has totally given up. Yet we must remember that he is emphasizing the negative side, and that he is preparing the reader for the turnaround in verse 25. There have been times in every one of our lives when we felt this way due to some prevailing sin we just couldn't seem to overcome. As a result, like Paul we "keep on doing" the wicked things that we do not want to do whenever sin is able to appeal to our flesh. But as we will soon see, when we yield to the Spirit and find strength from him, victory results.

Paul sums up the negative side in verse 20: "Now if I do what I do not want to do, it is no longer I who do it, but it is sin living in me that does it." Nearly every point in verses 16-17 is found here. The fact that deep within Paul does not wish to commit these deeds proves that it is not the "I" but indwelling sin that is the guilty party. Again, this doesn't mean he is innocent, for he has still chosen to succumb. The key is that once the culprit is identified, the rescue operation can commence.

PAUL SUMMARIZES THE WAR BETWEEN GOOD AND EVIL (7:21-25)

These final verses in the section provide the conclusion (*ara*, "so;" better, "therefore") and summary of the issues in verses 7-25, in particular the war between good and evil. It could even be labeled the culmination of Paul's teaching on the issue, period.

THE LAW OF EVIL (7:21)

Paul begins, "I find this law at work." Several think "law" here is the law of Moses, since everywhere else in verses 7-20 it refers to the Mosaic law. While this is possible, I am convinced that its more general meaning of "principle" fits better here. Note the progression of thought in verses 21-23, with an ABA pattern: Paul's delight in the Mosaic law (22) is offset by a different law or principle (vv. 21, 23). This principle, the law or ruling power of sin, has made war against him and gained control. This "other law" imitates the true law but lays down regulations that lead to evil rather than good.

So Paul echoes verses 15–16: "Although I want to do good, evil is right there with me." This evil is that self-same sin that entered the world at the fall of Adam and with its sidekick, death, reigned over sinful humankind (5:12–14). As a believer, he wanted at all times to do what was good in the sight of God. But he was unable to live up to his desire for God because evil was present in his life, leading him away from God and making him turn to sin. Sin is a counterfeit law that deceives the world into obeying false rules that produce evil rather than good. So when we try to make the morally correct decision, the flesh or tendency to sin interrupts, counters our will, and forces us to evil.

THE WAR OF THE FALSE LAW AGAINST THE MIND (7:22–23)

These two verses describe the battle between good and evil, between the true law and the counterfeit law, in all of us. The positive side depicts Paul's intense "delight in God's law," the law of Moses, at the core of his "inner being." Paul often uses this phrase to refer to the sphere of Christian awareness (2 Cor 4:16; Eph 3:16), the inner workings of the mind and heart. There is some debate as to whether this depicts the inner being of a Christian or non-Christian. If the latter, it would be the mind or spirit as opposed to the physical body. The decision is completely tied to the larger issue in chapter 7 as a whole. My earlier decision that Paul has a Christian in mind here (see the introduction to vv. 7–12) favors this being a Christian here as well.

"Delight" means to "rejoice in" a thing, describing devotion to God's revealed truths. Christians rejoice in the Old Testament law as divine revelation and as fulfilled in Christ. Jesus was clear that he had not come to "destroy" the law but to "fulfill" it, to bring it to completion and consummate its divine purposes in himself (Matt 5:17). To follow Jesus is to follow the law, and so we delight in it just as much as the Jewish people do. As we contemplate what the law meant in the lives of God's people in the old covenant age and see the parallels with his Word as taught in the New Testament as well, we too are filled with joy at what God has done and at what he continues to do. We realize anew the spiritual power and goodness of his Word in every age (vv. 12, 14, 16) and desire in the depth of our being to live up to its wondrous truths (vv. 15, 18, 19, 21).

However, the problem is that "I see another law at work in me" (v. 23). God's law brought joy to Paul, but now he turns back to "another law," a false law that masks a counterfeit reality and leads to wickedness. This other law is "at work in me, waging war against the law of my mind." The law of sin is "at war" on two fronts, against God's true law on the one hand and against my mind on the other hand, referring to both my thinking process and volition. The mind is where spiritual growth takes place. It is here where the war rages.

As Paul paints the picture here, sin is the victor in the opening battles and captures the "I" as "a prisoner of the law of sin at work within me" (literally "in my members"). So now I am a prisoner of war in a gulag of wickedness. There is some debate as to whether "members" connotes the physical body as controlled by sin or to the whole person. The latter is the thrust it had in 6:13, 19; 7:5, and it is quite likely that this continues here.

There are two opposing forces within us—the flesh and the Spirit. Here the flesh triumphs, but as we will see in 8:1-17, the Spirit will conquer the flesh every time we throw ourselves on him and fight the battle under his power and guidance. Paul is pessimistic here because he is looking at the battle from the perspective of the flesh. The carnal Christian will be defeated every time, for the priorities are skewed and the self is given sway over the Spirit.

Every child of God must understand the insidious, seductive power of sin. We should be taught about it regularly from the pulpit and in every class and small-group fellowship in our churches. Every church should have group therapies and counselors available, and everyone who attends should know they can bring up anything to the pastors and leaders, be accepted rather than rejected, and get the help they need.

The Dilemma: Who Will Rescue Me? (7:24-25)

In light of all the misery and defeat at the hands of invading sin, Paul exclaims, "What a wretched man I am! Who will rescue me from this body that is subject to death?" It is common to doubt this could be uttered by a believer since it is so filled with misery. Yet this is also in keeping with the rest of verses 7-23. Yes, there is great anguish and frustration, but that is also the natural result suffered by a Christian conquered by the flesh.

As I said at verse 19, this is a picture of the Christian who ignores the Spirit and tries to live the Christian life by their own strength. It is not hopeless when the Spirit is brought into the picture, as we will see in the next section. There will be hope, even certainty of rising above the despair. This means the question is rhetorical (like in 6:1, 15; 7:7, 13) and does not mean there will never be any answer.

"The body of this death," as in 6:13, 19; 7:5, 23, does not mean the physical body that will perish but the total person inhabited by sin and death. It is under siege and conquered by overpowering sin; physical and spiritual death are the result. In our defeated state, we long to be released from the hostile powers, but so long as we fail to trust entirely in Christ and the Spirit, that cannot happen.

However, it does not have to remain that way, and verse 25a provides the long-awaited solution. The despairing, defeated believer has ignored that "power" and "mighty strength" that God provides through Christ (Eph 1:19), and when one tries to live the victorious life in their own strength, they are doomed. Note the question and answer in all its brevity and power: "Who will rescue me?" "Jesus Christ our Lord." On this positive side Paul exclaims, "Thanks be to God, who delivers me through Jesus Christ our Lord."

But Paul then concludes by saying the war continues to rage. Followers of Christ have to continue to choose between surrendering to the lordship of Christ and deliverance (25a) or giving in to their "sinful nature" and becoming "a slave to the law of sin" (25b). This battle takes place in the "mind," which as in verses 15-16, 18-20, considers itself "a slave to God's law." However, it is opposed by the flesh or "sinful nature," which continues to guide the decisions to serve sin.

At first glance the chapter seems to end on a note of defeat. This is one of the major reasons why many conclude Paul could not be describing a Christian here. However, I do not think this is the case. Verse 25 does not end with crushing defeat but rather with continuing battle. We have died to the old realm, the old self; it has been nullified, and we have been set free (6:1-7). Yet sin is not yet destroyed, and it returns as an invading army from that realm and lays siege to us. Using the twin weapons of temptation and the flesh (our sinful nature), it can once more dominate our lives when we fail to depend on Christ and the Spirit.

That is the point of verse 25. The first half provides the solution for attaining victory over the flesh and sin. The second half reminds us that the battle is ongoing, but in the next chapter Paul will turn back to the victory and expand on the promise when we rely on the lordship of Christ—the Spirit takes over (8:1-17). There is an ABA pattern here, with the note of victory (25a [Christ] and 8:1-17 [the Spirit]) framing the battle (25b). We do not have to be defeated, for we can live the victorious life when we depend completely on Christ and the Spirit. As Hebrews 12:1 says, "Let us run with perseverance the race marked out for us," and in this race we can be "more than conquerors through him who loved us" (Rom 8:37).

This is an important passage of Scripture for the doctrine of sin. Paul uses himself as a model for all people wrestling with sin, with the unbeliever in 7-12 and the believer in 13-25. The believer wants to do what is right but does the opposite, defeated by sin, which uses the flesh to overwhelm with temptation (vv. 15–17). Still, the very desire to do good proves that the law is actually good (v. 16). However, the fact that I fail to act on that but instead capitulate to what I know is evil proves also that the bad is alive at the core of my being.

In the carnal Christian the war is nearly over. The invasion has succeeded, and the self within has surrendered, with sin taking up residence in my life and controlling my decisions (vv. 18–20). Indwelling sin is now in charge, and even though I do not want to act this way, the flesh is giving the orders, and I cannot stop the wicked practices. The impulse for evil has defeated the impulse for good within me. The war takes place in the mind, and sin wants to gain control of it, for where the mind goes, action follows (vv. 22–23). Mind control is the name of the game, and too many Christians who fail to yield to the Spirit allow the flesh to have ascendency over their thought processes. When that happens, the battle is over, and we have lost.

The overwhelmed Christian, trampled under the boots of invading and conquering sin, seems hopeless and filled with mind-numbing despair, for there seems to be no delivery in sight (v. 24). But that is wrong, and Paul jumps straight from the vanquished Christian to potential victory. He answers his question, "Who will deliver me?" immediately with thanksgiving, for in the Lord Jesus Christ there will always be triumph (v. 25). The Spirit of Christ will conquer evil on every occasion, and the way this victory will take place is the subject of the next section.

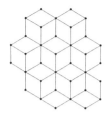

NEW LIFE IN THE SPIRIT
(8:1-17)

I n any list of the greatest chapters in the Bible, this one is always
at or near the top. The themes are wondrous—life in the Spirit,
adoption into the family of God, triumph through adversity, the
security of the believer. How can you not love it! I think of some
of my favorite movies, like *Chariots of Fire* or *Remember the Titans*,
that center on snatching victory from the jaws of defeat.

In this chapter Paul gives the answer that can guarantee the
victorious Christian life: live life under the power of the indwelling Spirit, thereby rejecting bondage under indwelling sin. The
problem of sin, the law, and the flesh in 7:7-25 provides a perfect backdrop for the power of the Spirit in 8:1-11. The term *sarx*
(the flesh) occurs twice in chapter 7 and ten times in 8:1-13, and
pneuma (spirit) doesn't occur in chapter 7 but is found twenty-
one times in chapter 8. The point is clear: to live according to the
flesh is defeat, and to live according to the Spirit is victory. When
the Spirit becomes the active force in a believer's life, the flesh is
defeated and victory ensues.

The astounding progression of themes traces the glorious presence of the Spirit and the triumph his residence in the believer provides (8:1-11), followed by one of the deepest passages in Scripture

on conversion as adoption into sonship as the new believer joins the family of God (vv. 12–17).

LIFE IN THE SPIRIT BRINGS VICTORY (8:1–11)

This passage, in contradistinction to the victory of sin and the flesh in 7:7–25, acts as a conclusion for the positive fragments in chapters 5–7. Victory is not secured until the Spirit of Christ takes residence in us. As we yield to him and live in obedience to him rather than the flesh, sin is dislodged from the center of our life, and we are liberated.

NO CONDEMNATION FOR THOSE IN CHRIST (8:1)

The introductory "therefore now" (ara nyn) makes this the victorious conclusion to all of 5:12–7:25. The war has been settled and turned around by the Spirit. In 5:16, 18, Paul said that the sin of Adam brought condemnation on humankind, and this was reversed only by the gift of justification in Christ. Paul returns to that truth here and says, "There is now no condemnation for those who are in Christ Jesus." The "now" points to the salvation-historical switch, the now-ness of the new age of salvation in Christ (3:26; 5:9, 11; 6:19, 21). The condemnation of the old era under the law has been replaced by the forgiveness of the new era in Christ. Christ has overturned the results of Adam's sin, and the condemnation has been removed for those who are in Christ (3:24; 6:11, 23; 7:4).

If we stopped at 7:25 we would be in abject despair, feeling our capitulation to the flesh and sin meant we would face nothing but condemnation for our terrible failures. Instead, Paul tells us that in reality we are "in Christ Jesus," meaning we are united with Christ and members of his body, the church. When the condemned sinner turns to Christ in faith and accepts his payment for sins, the sin penalty is covered by Christ's blood and we are forgiven. Judgment is replaced by a "life" sentence!

THE BASIS: THE SPIRIT (8:2–4)

The law of the Spirit has set me free (8:2)

The reason condemnation has ceased is "because [*gar*] through Christ Jesus the law of the Spirit who gives life has set you free from the law of sin and death." The triumph of evil proves to be short-lived when the Spirit takes over. We have a twofold liberation: the Spirit sets us free at conversion and then is present throughout life to strengthen and enable us to triumph in the ensuing battles against invading sin.

Note the antithesis between "the law of the Spirit" and "the law of sin and death." Scholars debate whether "law" here should be interpreted metaphorically as a "principle" or "rule" (as in 7:21, 23) or as the law of Moses. If we opt for the latter it will mean that without the Spirit, the Mosaic law leads to sin and death. If it refers to a principle it will connote the Spirit's power to liberate us from sin and death. Both options can make sense of the passage, but I think the metaphorical use is best. The use of "law" here is very similar to "the law of sin" in 7:21, 23, and fits better the New Testament idea of the Spirit principle/power versus the sin principle. As such it becomes a thesis statement for the Spirit-versus-flesh antithesis in 8:1–11.

The primary issue dominating 5:12–7:25 was the war of sin against the people of God, and in 6:19; 7:5, 18, Paul introduced the idea of the flesh as the means of sin's entrance into our lives. This last section (7:14–25) centered on the frustration of trying to live the Christian life under the power of the flesh rather than the Spirit. Now we see the only possible solution: turning from the flesh to the power of the indwelling Spirit. Christ through his atoning sacrifice has solved the sin problem and become the instrument ("through") of salvation, and the Spirit has become the means of liberation from sin.

There has been some difference of opinion as to whether Paul in this verse refers to conversion or the process of sanctification.

It refers to both, as the twofold liberation above makes clear. The unsaved are under the control of sin, and the defeated Christian who has given in to the flesh is dominated by sin. In both situations the liberating power of the Spirit is needed. We no longer belong to the dominion of sin and death but to the new kingdom of God and Christ, and it is the Spirit who has delivered us to that new realm.

Paul identifies five liberations in Romans: freedom from slavery to sin (6:16-22), from imprisonment (7:23), from condemnation (8:1), from the power of sin and death (8:2), and a final liberation of both God's whole creation as well as of his people at the **eschaton**, or end of this sinful world (8:21, 23). In the Spirit we are set free to resist sin (here), to pray to God as Father (8:15), to intercede in prayer (8:27), and to obey God's law (8:3-4).

The solution: the sin offering of God's Son (8:3)

This new life in the age of the Spirit cannot begin so long as we are under condemnation for sin (v. 1). Paul points out that "the law[1] was powerless ... because it was weakened by the flesh." In 4:13-15; 7:7, the Mosaic law brought wrath down upon people and could only make them conscious of sin (3:20). Thus it caused sin to increase (5:20) rather than solving the sin problem. It aroused "sinful passions" and brought forth death (7:5; 8:11), so it was powerless to remove condemnation.

Yet what it could not do "God did by sending his own Son in the likeness of sinful flesh to be a sin offering." The imagery of sending pictures the mission of a royal envoy, but here it is all the more intense, being God's "own Son." The deep relationship between Father and Son includes the idea of preexistence.

The glory of the preexistent Son is combined with the humility of the one who is "in the likeness of sinful flesh." This reminds

---

1. Note the play on words. "Law" (*nomos*) is metaphorical in v. 2 and reverts to its usual reference to the Mosaic law here.

us of the hymn in Philippians 2, where the one who was "in very nature God ... made himself nothing ... [by] being made in human likeness" (2:6–7). The "likeness" here means Jesus identified with fallen humanity by assuming the likeness of sinful humanity and dying for our sins. He did not become sinful but suffered all the ravages of finite humanity in order to pay the price for our sins.

The result of this sacrifice is that as the "sin offering," he "condemned sin in the flesh." He had to be "in the likeness of sinful flesh" to become the perfect "sin offering" and accomplish what the law could not do, namely, remove the penalty of sin, redeem fallen humanity, and procure forgiveness for sins. Jesus' sin offering both condemned sin and justified the believer. The power of sin was broken, and those who turned to Jesus in faith were declared right with God at his judgment seat.

Result: the requirements of the law met in us (8:4)

The purpose for God's sending his Son to be the sin offering was "in order that the righteous requirement of the law might be fully met in us." This could be forensic, referring to the judicial fulfillment of the law's demands on the cross, or ethical, referring to obeying God and living out the law's requirements. My own feeling is that the context refers both to the legal "sin offering" of Christ and to life in the Spirit.

The true purpose for sending Christ takes place when Christ's sacrificial death enables the law's requirements to be "fully met in us." "Fully met" is plērōthē, to be fulfilled, a divine passive that means God "fulfills" these in us. The purpose of the law comes to completion in us, meaning that we participate in its results. The idea is similar to Matthew 5:17, where Christ came "to fulfill the law," that is, sum it up in himself and lift it to a higher plane. Here the "righteous requirement" refers to the divine purpose of the law in bringing God's righteousness into this world, completed both in the sin offering that brings justification and the life of the Spirit that follows and produces sanctification.

Through the Spirit we will experience progressive sanctification and grow in righteous living for the Lord. This will take place when we "do not live according to the flesh but according to the Spirit." What Christ has done for us on the cross (v. 2) is worked out in Spirit-empowered living, and this is the true subject of chapters 7 and 8. The life made possible by the cross and lived out in the Spirit is what fulfills the law as God intends. One choice dominates the action: to live by the flesh and the world's standards or to live in obedience to God's demands and the Spirit's leading.

THE FLESH VERSUS THE SPIRIT (8:5-8)

Paul defines the conflict between the flesh and the Spirit in verses 5-6, and a diatribe against the flesh follows in verses 7-8. This passage tells why we must live according to the Spirit as stated in verse 4. Both contrasts center on the mindset of two groups, the converted and the unconverted.

The antithesis presented (8:5-6)

The NIV has "those who live according to the flesh," but the Greek literally reads, "those who *are* according to the flesh." The emphasis is on who they are rather than what they do. Those of the flesh (their fallen nature) "have their minds set on what the flesh desires" (literally "the things of the flesh"). They are attuned entirely to the self and the things of this world. This goes back to 1:21, 28, and the utter depravity that controls the thought life of fleshly people. They choose to act not from the perspective of what is right but on the basis of self-centered desires.

In contrast, those characterized by the Spirit "have their minds set on what the Spirit desires." Their thought life is directed by the Spirit and centers on the Spirit rather than the self. The old adage is quite true: the way you think is who you are, and that determines what you do.

Verse 6 states the same antithesis another way. "The mind governed by" is the same as "those who live according to," since the way we live is determined by what we think. The two phrases in the Greek are "the mind of the flesh"/"mind of the Spirit," and the two genitives ("of" phrases) could be subjective ("the mind governed by the flesh," as in the NIV) or objective ("the mind set on fleshly things"). The latter is slightly better, with the stress on whether the person's mindset is centered on the flesh or the Spirit. When the thought life is filled with carnal content, "death" in its broadest sense is the result. This is not only the final death of eternal punishment but also a state of death that reigns over the unsaved throughout their lives (5:12–15; 7:10–13).

The lives of people who are separated from God is itself a terrible type of death, for they are doomed to a lonely, self-centered existence without hope. Those who center their lives on the Spirit, however, are never alone and have the "living hope" of 1 Peter 1:3. They experience "life and peace." "Life" here is both present life in Christ and under the presence of the Spirit (7:10; 8:2) and eternal life (2:7; 5:21; 6:22–23). "Peace" with God is the result of justification (5:1) and refers to both reconciliation with God and the inner tranquility of the soul, with the right relationship with God being primary.

The problem of the flesh (8:7–8)

In these two verses Paul centers on the problem of the flesh. He wants to elaborate on the reason why (dioti, "because," omitted in the NIV) the fleshly mindset ends in death. The first reason is that "the mind governed by the flesh is hostile to God." In keeping with my translation of verse 6, I would change the NIV translation here to "the mind set on fleshly things." The carnal mindset is the enemy of all things holy, and God is set against it. Pleasing self has complete priority over pleasing God, and the resulting actions are the exact opposite of what God desires.

The basis of this hostility is the refusal of the fleshly mind to "submit to God's law." As in 7:21–23 and 8:2 there is a question whether "law" refers to the law of Moses, or God's principles in general. In 7:21, 23; 8:2, I opted for the more general "principles," but in 7:22 it referred to the Mosaic law. In light of the theme of the conflict in chapter 8 it seems better to see this in the more general sense. The carnal mind is incapable of placing itself under God's will and rules. This does not mean unbelievers are incapable of good but does state that they cannot choose the good for God's sake.

This is the point of the next verse. Because "those who are in the realm of the flesh" are incapable of submitting to God's laws, they "cannot please God." They can perform good deeds and recognize the right thing to do, but they will not live a life pleasing to God or find salvation. The flesh is the sphere of their existence, so goodness is sporadic because it does not stem from a desire to please God. In the long run, such impulses actually result from a desire to please oneself or others, and they are unable even to want to do what brings pleasure to God. This can be achieved only in Christ and the Spirit (as stated in 8:3).

THE ROMAN SAINTS: IN THE SPIRIT, NOT THE FLESH (8:9–11)

The key: the Spirit of God lives in you (8:9)

With *hymeis de*, "You, however," Paul turns from the fleshly unbelievers to the saints of Rome. Unbelievers are incapable of pleasing God because they belong to "the realm of the flesh." The saints, on the other hand, belong to "the realm of the Spirit" and are characterized by life and peace (v. 6).

The criterion for belonging to the new realm of Christ is "if indeed the Spirit of God lives in you." Indwelling sin marks the unbeliever (7:17, 20), and the indwelling Spirit marks the believer. A second clause reinforces this by stating the opposite: "if anyone does not have the Spirit of Christ, they do not belong to Christ." The "if" form in both clauses (*eiper ... ei*) does not mean Paul is uncertain. These are conditions of fact and come close to "since"— they know Christ and so have the Spirit residing in them.

Note that in the first clause he is called "the Spirit of God" and in the second clause "the Spirit of Christ." There is a hint of trinitarian doctrine here, for the Spirit is sent by and represents both the Father and the Son. When we say, "Jesus lives in your heart," it is in reality the Spirit of Jesus that is his presence in us. While certainly the Triune Godhead is omnipresent, the Bible spatially portrays Jesus in heaven with the Father (for instance, Eph 1:20–22), and the Spirit on earth and in the heart of the believer, as we see here.

Death and life in the believer (8:10)

In 8:10 Paul shifts his focus from the Spirit indwelling the saints to Christ being "in you." When Christ indwells the believer, two things intersect. First, "even though your body is subject to death because of sin" identifies the problem that must be rectified. It is possible to see this as dying to sin, but this is not death *to* sin as in 6:2, 11, but death *because of* (*dia*) sin. The body will die, but for believers that death will lead to resurrection.

The realm of sin has been nullified on the cross (6:6; 7:2, 6), and we experience victory over invading sin because of the empowering presence of Christ and the Spirit (6:17–18; 7:25). Nevertheless, we still struggle against encroaching sin and temptation (7:14–25), and as a result we face the consequences of sin, physical death. From the moment we are born, our body begins to die.

The second reality of life counters this developing death: "the Spirit gives life because of righteousness." Death reigns (6:14) over our bodies, but there dwells within us a new power, the Holy Spirit who fills us with new life, an eternal gift from God. John tells us that eternal life is not just a future reality for us but a present gift that has already begun in us (John 3:16; 6:40, 47). It is part of what we call "inaugurated eschatology"—eternal life is a present reality already in us, and yet it is not yet fully experienced. That will take place when we die and Christ returns, when we receive our glorified bodies (1 Cor 15:20–23, 51–54).

The basis of this life is "righteousness," seen in its forensic or legal sense of the justification of the believer (3:21, 24), which leads to God's declaring us innocent, forgiven, and right with him. Our bodies will die, but the Spirit is the deposit and guarantee of our new life in Christ (Eph 1:13-14), so life is our present and future inheritance and we dwell in the promise that death will lead to resurrection.

Result: life to your mortal bodies (8:11)

In this verse Paul elaborates on this promise of life through the Spirit. "The Spirit of life" from 8:2 Paul now calls "the Spirit of him who raised Christ from the dead." For the Christian, life does not end with death but continues with resurrection. Physical death is a transition to a much more glorious existence, and the Spirit is the means by which this is accomplished. Jesus was the "first-fruits" (1 Cor 15:20, 23) that guarantees future resurrection for us (Rom 6:5). Since the Spirit who raised Jesus "is living in you" (note the present tense), eternal life is already a reality in us. It is a natural conclusion for Paul to say this same Spirit "will also give life to your mortal bodies."

There is a great deal of repetition in this verse. Paul mentions the indwelling Spirit twice, and the resurrection of Jesus from the dead also twice. A syllogism (deductive reasoning to prove the validity of a truth) emerges from this:

> Major premise: The Spirit dwells in us
> Minor premise: The Spirit is life
> Conclusion: Then life dwells in us

Death will be overcome when we like Jesus are raised from the dead to life. Again, this is more than just the promise of a future event. It is a present reality experienced in the here and now by the Spirit's taking up residence in us. We have a "mortal body" that is subject to death, but awaiting us are "spiritual bodies" raised "in glory" (1 Cor 15:42-44) that will be ours forever.

THE BELIEVER IS ADOPTED
AS GOD'S HEIR (8:12–17)

The imagery of these verses is quite poignant: Converts, the moment they are justified and forgiven (Rom 3:21–24), are adopted as God's children. Like all newborn infants, they cry out to their new Father and know they are brothers and sisters of Christ, and coheirs with him. This is also the primary Pauline passage for the doctrine of assurance, telling those who doubt they are Christians that the Spirit himself will assure them they belong to God's family (v. 16).

A CALL TO PUT THE FLESH TO DEATH (8:12–13)

Scholars are divided whether these verses conclude verses 5–11 or introduce verses 14–17, a sure sign that they form a transition passage that does both. Still, I prefer to see them as introducing what follows, with the passage together describing the conversion experience. Here we see the true depravity that lies behind this sinful world in which we live. It is so evil that there can be only one proper response—a decisive and radical repudiation that can only be depicted by the image of putting it to death.

The opening *ara oun* (therefore) shows Paul is drawing an inference from verses 5–11. Since we have Christ in us and live in the realm of the Spirit, we are under obligation, but "not to the flesh, to live according to it." In 1:14 he stated he was "obligated" to preach the gospel to all peoples, and both there and here there is a debt to God to obey his calling on us and to serve him. Since this a debt to God, it must be totally separate from the flesh, the enemy of God, which can only be rejected.

Paul introduces a new image here for sin and the flesh, viewing them as a kind of loan shark demanding payment. In the first century such debts often resulted in slavery. Those who live fleshly lives are indeed "sold as a slave to sin" (7:14). Yet those who are of the Spirit eschew the life of the flesh and refuse to "live according to it." We have been set free from sin and the flesh by Christ (6:18, 22), having died to it in him (6:2–4, 11; 8:13).

Verse 13 does not complete the thought of verse 12 by describing our obligation to the Spirit. Instead, it restates verses 5–8 by warning us anew about the dangers of the flesh. Those who "live according to the flesh ... will die," with double meaning in "die." As Paul said in 6:12–14, sin has brought physical death into this world, and they reign together. However, there is a broader sense of spiritual and eternal death that is the lot of those who prefer the flesh over God. As Paul asserts in Galatians 6:8, "Whoever sows to please their flesh ... will reap destruction."

The seriousness of surrendering to the dictates of the flesh is readily apparent. One's eternal destiny is at stake! Several other passages warn about the consequences of falling away, and we must take them seriously (see John 15:1–6; Hebrews 6:4–6; 2 Peter 2:20–22). They must also be interpreted alongside other passages that show God protects his people and will deliver them in the end (like Rom 8:31–39; John 10:27–29; 1 Pet 1:5). I will discuss this further below at 8:28–30.

The answer to the flesh, of course, is the Spirit: "if by the Spirit you put to death the misdeeds of the body, you will live." This language echoes 6:2, 11, where the saints are called to "die to sin." That is the "what" of the Christian life, and in this verse we have the "how." We die to sin by putting to death the "misdeeds of the body." Here Paul uses the verb form of "death," *thanatoute*, building on the first clause to say in effect that the only way to make certain you do not die is to make sure that the sin in you dies.

Paul here says the means of your victory is "by the Spirit," the active presence of the Spirit that infuses you with the strength needed. It is neither your strength by itself nor the Spirit that takes over your life and does the work for you. It is a union of yourself with the Spirit that fortifies you so you can be "strong in the Lord and in his mighty power," with the result that you "stand your ground, and after you have done everything, to stand" (Eph 6:10, 13).

In an interesting digression Paul labels the hostile force "the misdeeds of the body," literally "the practices [or deeds] of the body," almost equating the actions of the body with the flesh. However, it is best, as in verses 10 and 11, to see "body" here as the physical body, the arena in which these sinful actions take place. When God's people unite with the Spirit and die to such fleshly deeds, they "will live," gaining new life in Christ and the Spirit now and eternal life in the future.

THE BASIS: THE NEW RELATIONSHIP IN THE SPIRIT (8:14-15)

This paragraph (vv. 14-17) is the primary scriptural passage for understanding what occurs at conversion. The basis and foundation (*gar*, "for") for this new life in the Spirit is a right relationship with God effected by the Spirit, called "reconciliation" in Romans 5:10-11. It was made possible by "the death of his Son" there and by the work of the Holy Spirit here.

New status: the children of God (8:14)

The descriptive "those" (literally "as many as" to stress the particular group) "who are led by the Spirit of God" tells how the reality Paul described in verse 13 takes place. We "put to death" the flesh and its misdeeds through the guiding presence of the Spirit in us (cf. Gal 5:16-18).

Out of this comes the phrase "Spirit-led" to portray those who are particularly effective for God. Not only does this means that the saints are guided by the Spirit as they make daily decisions, but it also has global force. These people are led by the Spirit in terms of career, choosing a life partner, and other major events in their life. This is how we define the victorious Christian life: the extent to which the Spirit is directing our actions is the extent to which we are progressing in our sanctification. The more we determine our own direction, the more we are failing the Triune Godhead.

When the Spirit is in control, we are called "the children of God" and "sons" in verses 14–15, and "children" again in verses 16–17. This does not mean that the Spirit's indwelling has force to give salvation. As in Galatians 4:5–6, the Spirit is given when we are made sons. Being led by the Spirit is not the basis of salvation but proof that salvation has taken place.

Adoption to sonship (8:15)

When we think of "sonship" or adoption as the result of the Spirit, we need to reflect on the two kinds of spirit we must choose from. Translated literally, in this verse Paul is contrasting a "spirit of slavery" with the "the Spirit of adoption," representing the two eras or realms that define life. Some conclude that "the spirit of slavery" is also the Holy Spirit at work under the old epoch of the law, enslaving people to the law. However, it is difficult to think of the Holy Spirit as being behind the enslaving power of the law, and most think rightly that "spirit" in the first instance is rhetorical, used to say that the unsaved are enslaved to sin and know only fear.

Paul depicts the Holy Spirit as the one believers have "received," referring to the conversion experience when "God sent the Spirit of his Son into our hearts" (Gal 4:6). At that moment enslavement to sin ended (6:16–22). Those who are enslaved by sin know only "fear," which includes both general worry about an uncertain future and specific terror of final condemnation. Many interpreters associate this fear especially with life under the old covenant, but I prefer a broader perspective, in which it refers to sin and the law for the Jewish Christian and the power of sin for the Gentile Christian (1:18–32).

In contrast, the believer has received "the Spirit of adoption." The Spirit is given to us at the moment God adopts us as his children. The adoption metaphor is very Pauline (Rom 8:23; 9:4; Gal 4:5; Eph 1:5), stemming from both Old Testament ideas of sonship and **Hellenistic** practices. It portrays the movement not only from slavery to freedom but also from lower class to royal

son. It provides a perfect metaphor for conversion, since under
the Roman law an adopted child had all the rights of a true son.

The Spirit produces not a sense of fear but rather that sense
of belonging and membership in a family that produces a wonder,
a security that leads us to "cry," the verb here pointing to a strong
emotion and a deep-seated joy and connected to prayer as crying
out to God (Ps 3:4; 17:6; 88:2). "Abba, Father" was one of the earliest confessional prayers, seen also in Galatians 4:6, where it is
the Spirit in us uttering this cry. Here it is our cry. When we put
the two together we have antiphonal worship: we respond to the
Spirit by echoing his cry of rejoicing that God has now become
our "Abba."

The Abba prayer is built on Jesus' prayer life. His every prayer
was uttered to his "Father," except the cry of dereliction on the
cross, "My God, my God, why have you forsaken me?" (Mark 15:34
and parallels). "Abba" was a term of deep intimacy for the father-
child relationship, and its use here depicts that intimacy between
us and our heavenly Father. Our God is our Father who lovingly
holds us in his arms and watches over us.

THE ASSURANCE OF THE BELIEVER (8:16–17)

The Spirit, when God places him in us at our conversion, empow-
ers us to cry out to God and to defeat the flesh, and then to live for
God. He also assures us of the reality of our salvation.

The Spirit's witness (8:16)

Paul now switches tenses from the moment of conversion
("received," "brought about") to the continuing life in the Spirit
("testifies"). The Spirit gives continual witness to us that we are
indeed adopted as the children of God. This and 1 John 5:10–11 are
the two primary passages on the issue of the assurance of salvation. The Spirit provides testimony to our spirit that we are God's.

Note the two uses of *pneuma* (spirit) here. The word for "testify" (*symmartyrei*) means "to testify together with." Here it means

there is not a single but a double witness: the Holy Spirit joins
our own spirit in witnessing to us that we are members of God's
family. Also, the second "spirit" is not a separate part of our being
(body, soul, and spirit) but refers to our inner being, the mental
and volitional part of our life. There is no reason to be unsure of
the reality of our salvation. We just need to listen to that twofold
witness, God's Spirit and our inner spirit, telling us we are really
and truly his.

Result: heirs of God and Christ (8:17)

Now Paul gives us another great result of our salvation: we are not
only the children of God but also the heirs of God and of Christ.
We rejoiced in our present blessings of sonship in verses 14–15, and
now we rejoice in our future blessings, the inheritance awaiting
us. Paul will cover this in more depth in verses 18–30, but the basic
truth is encapsulated here.

The inheritance theme is a major biblical teaching. It began
with the promised land as Israel's inheritance (Gen 15:7; Num
34:2; Deut 1:7–8, 38; Ps 78:55). Later Israel itself becomes God's
inheritance or possession (Isa 19:25; Jer 10:16; 51:19), and the biblical authors picture Yahweh himself as Israel's inheritance (Ezek
44:28). In later Judaism and the early church, the kingdom blessings were associated with Israel's inheritance (Psalms of Solomon
49:10; 1 Enoch 40:9), in particular the kingdom and eternal life
(Matt 25:34; Mark 10:17; Gal 5:21; 1 Cor 15:50). All this means the
earthly promised land has now expanded to the eternal promised
land, the "new heaven and new earth" of Revelation 21:1.

Paul closely connects sonship and inheritance (see Gal 3:29;
4:7). The phrase "heirs of God" looks upon God as the source of the
promise, and as his adopted children we receive this inheritance.
In fact, we are not only heirs of God but also "co-heirs with Christ."
In the Roman world the adopted child's inheritance depended to
some extent on the willingness of the natural heir to include the
adopted child. Christ as well as the Father gives us our inheritance.

All who will share Christ's glory must also share his sufferings, so Paul adds, "if indeed we share in his sufferings in order that we may also share in his glory." If we are united with Christ as sons and heirs, we are also one with him in his path to glory, which his suffering, as the Philippians hymn (Phil 2:6-11) makes clear. Elsewhere Paul calls this "the fellowship [NIV 'participation'] of his sufferings" (Phil 3:10).

The theme is simple and yet profound: suffering is the path to glory. The conditional *eiper* as in verse 9 stresses the factuality of the statement—we "indeed" must suffer with him if we hope to share his glory. Paul likely has in mind more than just persecution, for this is the harbinger of the lengthier list in verses 35 and 38, as well as in the well-known list of his sufferings in 2 Corinthians 11:23-29. Still, Christians in the first century had to expect persecution, as we see from Jesus' extended discussion in John 15:18-16:4. The "glory" we experience is comprehensive, embracing the glory we share now in being God's children (2 Cor 3:18, "ever-increasing glory") as well as the final glory we shall share with Christ (Col 3:4).

This wondrous chapter alleviates the pressure the flesh exerts on God's people according to chapter 7. The defeatism of that material disappears when the Spirit gains control and takes up residence in our lives. According to 8:1-4, sin and the old self are nullified and removed from us at conversion. Sin then must invade from outside. Christ won the first victory at the cross, but now a second set of victories is needed, and that is accomplished when the Spirit takes up residence in us and gives us the strength to be victorious.

In verses 5-8 the scene is the flesh versus the Spirit, and the battleground is the mind, for the thought life determines actions and the direction our life takes. The fleshly mindset produces both present and final death, the absence of life and peace. In verses 9-11 we see what happens when the Spirit is not part of our lives: death takes over. However, with the Spirit the opposite is the case.

Death itself becomes a transition to a new and eternally joyous life, and our present existence suddenly has new meaning.

Then in verses 12–17 Paul gives us a marvelous portrait of the conversion experience. He begins in verses 12–13 with the necessity of putting the flesh to death, meaning we not only fight against it but also overcome it and cast it out of our lives. At conversion, we both die to sin and put it to death. Then we are adopted into God's family as his new children, and the Spirit is given to us by God as the internal empowering agent. We react with absolute joy and worship as we cry "Abba, Father," celebrating our new intimacy with God (vv. 14–15). This intimacy with God leads to the assurance of our salvation as the Spirit testifies to our Spirit that we now belong to God (v. 16). Finally, we become heirs of God and share in Jesus' glory as we become coheirs with him (v. 17). Truly our salvation in Christ and the new life we have in the Spirit are beyond anything we could ever imagine!

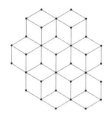

NEW HOPE OF GLORY
IN THE SPIRIT
(8:18-30)

Paul's wonderful essay on the meaning and process of conversion in 8:1-17 ended with a note that experiencing the glory of Christ involves a willingness to share his suffering as well (8:17). Paul now expands that comment into a major section that covers the groaning of creation as well as of God's people. God's creation as well as humankind was marred at the fall of Adam, and both long for that future "liberation from bondage" that will end their suffering. The question is, how can God be both sovereign and merciful when afflictions and suffering are the lot of saved and unsaved alike, as well as God's creation? Paul's answer is twofold: Christ's followers must walk in the path of their Lord, which is suffering (v. 17), and present suffering will inexorably lead to final glory (vv. 18-30).

There are two ways we could outline the passage. (1) The grammatical flow would have three sections: the hope of future restoration (18-25); the intercessory prayer of the Spirit (26-27); and God sovereignly working for our good (28-30). (2) Topically, it can be organized around the three groanings of creation (18-22), the believer (23-25), and the Spirit (26-28), concluding with God bringing us to glory (29-30). While most opt for the former on the basis of grammar, I prefer the latter since it catches the thought flow better. That is what I will follow below.

PAUL PRESENTS THE THEME: SUFFERING LEADS TO GLORY (8:18)

After telling his readers how important it is to share in the sufferings of Christ (v. 17), Paul more fully explains the critical connection between suffering and our future glory, returning to the theme of 5:2–5. Paul's opening "I consider" does not lead into his mere opinion or a suggestion for them to think about. Rather, this is his settled conviction on the matter that he believes comes from God.

Afflictions and troubles are temporary rather than permanent. Elsewhere in the New Testament, Peter states that "now for a little while you may have had to suffer grief" (1 Pet 1:6), and in Paul himself says, "our light and momentary troubles are achieving for us an eternal glory that far outweighs them all" (2 Cor 4:17). Here he calls the difficulties of the saints "the sufferings of the present time" (literal translation), a phrase found also in Romans 3:26; 11:5; 13:11 to emphasize the sacrifices that believers must make in this present age of salvation as anticipating the final glory.

These present troubles "are not worth comparing with the glory that will be revealed in us." This is another instance of the already/not yet tension between the present and the future. The troubles of life are the already, and the glories of our eternal destiny are the not yet. We are already glorified as part of God's family but have not yet been accorded our final glory. "Will be revealed" is literally "about to be revealed," stressing the imminence and divine guarantee of the final events. "Revealed in us" is better "revealed for us," and means God is preparing this glorious future for us.

THE CREATION GROANS (8:19–22)

Paul demonstrates the thesis of verse 18 (suffering leads to glory) first through creation. The glory God is preparing does not only apply to his people. God's entire creation will be transformed. To understand the point he is making, we must remember that all of creation was affected by the fall of Adam. Not only was the image of God in humankind marred; but death and destruction also affected the animal world, and entered inanimate creation as well. God's creation shares in our frustration at the incompleteness and short span of life and with the suffering and devastation that so often accompanies life.

The Eager Expectation of Creation (8:19)

Paul begins, "For the creation waits in eager expectation." The personification of creation as a living organism is common in Old Testament passages: creation can be filled with awe (Ps 65:8), rejoicing (Ps 66:1), or mourning (Jer 4:28). The Greek behind "eager expectation" (*apokaradokia*) pictures someone straining their neck to see what's coming. This does not depict a sense of anxiety but rather a confident longing to see the final transformation of this world take place.

Interestingly, Paul does not depict creation as longing for its own release but rather for the "children of God to be revealed." It recognizes that its own future is caught up with God's people. Creation will participate in their liberation, which Paul will describe in verse 21. What they eagerly await is a true apocalyptic event (*apokalypsin*, "revealed"), the final unveiling of the glory of Christ's followers. It is a spiritual reality now, but then it will be a visible event that will last for eternity, and when it arrives, creation will rejoice and be liberated along with us.

The Frustration and Longing of Creation for Liberation (8:20–21)

These two verses form a single sentence; in them Paul relates why creation longs to see the transformation of God's children at the end of history. Adam's sin deeply affected it, and as a result it has never been able to realize its original God-intended potential.

Instead, it has been "subjected to frustration." The curse of Genesis 3:17–18 ("Cursed is the ground because of you") meant that creation could not fulfill the purpose for which God designed it.

"Was subjected" is a divine passive pointing to God as the actor, as indicated in the following, "not by its own choice, but by the will of the one who subjected it." While we might think Adam was the actor, that cannot be, for Adam too was cursed. He lost his authority over God's creation at the fall. Certainly Adam's transgression was the cause of the curse that fell upon both animate and inanimate creation. However, it was God the Judge of all who pronounced the curse and carried out the punishment.

So creation joins humankind in "frustration," likely referring both to the mortality of all created things as they are subject to death and to creation's inability to fulfill its God-given purpose and destiny. Unlike sinful humanity, which rationalizes its guilt and explains away its failures, creation faces up to the results and longs for its release. Paul powerfully expresses this longing, "in hope that the creation itself will be liberated from its bondage to decay."

There is debate as to whether "in hope" (1) modifies the preceding ("by the will of the one who subjected it in hope, *because*," so KJV, NKJV, RSV) or (2) modifies what follows ("in hope *that* creation itself," so NIV, JB, NLT, ESV, NASB, LEB). However, the conjunction is clearly "that" rather than "because," so the majority of translations and commentators take it correctly with what follows.

Hope is one of the primary themes of this section (the word occurs five times in vv. 20–25), and it continues the thought of the "eager expectation" of creation from verse 19. Unlike fallen humanity, which places all its hope in itself and is doomed to failure as a result, creation is God-centered and realizes his promises are its only hope.

Since creation realizes that its future is linked to the future of "the children of God" (v. 19), it hopes that it "will be liberated from its bondage," language similar to the liberation of God's people from bondage to sin in 6:18, 22; 8:2. Creation is in "bondage to decay" (*phthora*), which could refer to the "destruction" of the earth (2 Pet 3:10) but more likely refers to the progressive "corruption" or "deterioration" of the natural world. In spite of all its beauty, natural decay enslaves God's creation, and its release is called a "liberation."

This liberation will occur as the old creation is destroyed (2 Pet 3:10, 13) and then "brought into the freedom and glory of the children of God." The disintegration of the old creation is not an end in itself but a means to its transformation into "the new heavens and new earth" of Revelation 21:1. Once more Paul ties the future release of frustrated creation to the liberation of the saints. Instead of "the freedom *and* glory of the children of God" (NIV), I prefer to translate this as "the freedom *of the* glory of the children of God." Paul's emphasis here is not on how glorious it is but on the future glory that awaits believers (8:18), that final vindication when we share in the glory of Christ. John describes this incredible state perfectly in Revelation 22:1–5, picturing the new order as a final garden of Eden with "the river of the water of life ... flowing from the throne of God and of the Lamb down the middle of the great street of the city. On each side of the river stood the tree of life, bearing twelve crops of fruit. ... And the leaves of the tree are for the healing of the nations." This is what the original garden would have been like if Adam had not sinned, and it explains the confident longing and hope of creation.

THE GROANING OF CREATION (8:22)

Paul summarizes verses 19–21 by saying, "We know that the whole creation has been groaning as in the pains of childbirth right up to the present time." When he uses "we know" (2:2; 3:19; 6:6; 7:14), he is stressing catechetical teaching—Christian truths that would have been known in any church. Paul pictures every element of creation "groaning together" (*systenazei*, a *syn*-compound verb meaning "together" in complete accord).

The key term in this section is "groaning," found in verses 22, 23, and 26, denoting a cry of agony that accompanies the frustration and pain of decay from verse 21. In 2 Corinthians 5:2, 4, our "groaning" in this finite body longs for the perfect heavenly body, paralleling the cry here. Note that this takes place "right up to the present time," emphasizing the continuous nature of this agonizing cry (for Paul and for us).

This is not a negative cry of anger but a positive cry of "eager expectation" (v. 19), for Paul links the frustration here with "the pains of childbirth." These are probably the same "birth pains" of Mark 13:8 that look forward to the second coming of Christ and the end of the world of evil. These pains lead to birth, not death, signifying the promise of the new life to come. The "grief will turn to joy," as in John 16:20-22. Creation participates in the living hope of God's faithful, who realize that their present travail is a portent of final glory and eternal peace and happiness.

THE CHRISTIAN GROANS (8:23-25)

In verses 19 and 22, Paul linked the groaning and yearning for liberation of creation to the future of believers. Here he turns to believers themselves, thereby including both inanimate and animate creation as awaiting freedom from the effects of Adam's trespass. If creation groans, how much more the believer, who is the recipient of the redemptive work of Christ.

Awaiting the Redemption of Our Bodies (8:23)

Paul says that believers "groan inwardly" (Greek: "within ourselves"), a nonverbal cry from the heart. This agonizing cry is even more a reality because we have been given "the firstfruits of the Spirit." This is the same metaphor Paul uses of Christ's resurrection as firstfruits in 1 Corinthians 15:20, 23, which in turn stems from the old covenant offering of the first part of the harvest to God (Exod 23:16, 19; Lev 2:12, 14; Deut 26:10). It means that God has given us the Holy Spirit as a foretaste in anticipation of the glory that awaits us, a "deposit guaranteeing our inheritance until the redemption of those who are God's possession" (Eph 1:14).

In light of this, we "wait eagerly for our adoption to sonship, the redemption of our bodies." We already have the Spirit within ourselves as the first installment of our future "redemption" (see on 3:24 for this term), but we do not have the promise in its fullness and long for that final manifestation. Christ has redeemed us by paying the penalty of our sin and enabling us to find forgiveness. Through his redemptive work, we have been "adopted to sonship." We had no rights before God, but he adopted us as his children out of his grace and mercy. The complete release of our suffering and the fullness of the glory that will be ours is a future certainty, but we do not want to wait. We yearn for the eternal transformation of our finite earthly bodies (Phil 3:21).

Hope and Patient Waiting (8:24–25)

We share with creation its groaning and frustration, but we even more intensely share its eager expectation and hope, especially since "in this hope we were saved." Here we learn that hope is part of the conversion process. Our past conversion initiated a life of hope in our final deliverance. Hope is not mere wish-fulfillment with an uncertain prognosis. By its very nature, hope makes us confident that what God has promised will indeed come to pass. At conversion the idea of an uncertain future has ended once for all, and we absolutely know what our final end will be.

Hope deals with what is unfulfilled and not yet here, so Paul adds, "hope that is seen is no hope at all." Its very definition demands that the object of our hope be in the future. As he says next, "Who hopes for what they already have?" That would hardly be logical. Our present life in the Spirit must be centered on this future hope. Hope is not a present-oriented reality, so

Paul is preparing his readers for a (perhaps lengthy) time of waiting before it is realized. This is where the frustration lies, not in the fact of its happening but in the process it entails. Still, as we groan in the midst of our present troubles, we do so in expectation and hope.

Verse 25 completes this thought. Our task in light of all our present trials is to "hope for what we do not yet have," basically summing up the message of verses 23–24. Paul couches it as an "if" clause to emphasize the importance of doing so. Living in this type of hope will enable us to "wait for it patiently," the primary point of this section. In the midst of our difficulties, once we know the true meaning of the hope that lies beyond them, we can find the patience to endure them.

This is the third time Paul has used *apekdechomai*, which means to "wait eagerly" (vv. 19, 23) and stresses the connection between hope and "eager expectation" (v. 19). Now he adds the theme of patient endurance, literally "eagerly wait with endurance," a major theological emphasis linked with the idea of suffering. In the midst of our earthly trials, the terrible load of sorrow we face must be greeted with perseverance. In Hebrews 12:1 we are called to "run with perseverance the race marked out for us," and in the book of Revelation all the suffering and persecution God's people must go through "calls for patient endurance and faithfulness" (Rev 13:10; 14:12). In Romans 5:3–4 "suffering produces perseverance; perseverance, character."

We know the final result and what awaits us, but the pain of the present is still hard to bear. It is one thing to realize how worthwhile the waiting will be, but quite another to actually go through the tragedy of losing a loved one or be bedridden with a debilitating illness. Yet in those times the Lord is nearer to us than ever, as we will see in verse 26. At the deeper level we "share in his sufferings," and his glory awaits (v. 17).

THE SPIRIT GROANS (8:26–28)

THE INTERCESSORY PRAYERS OF THE SPIRIT (8:26)

Paul transitions to a new subject with "in the same way," which is difficult to interpret. There are several possibilities regarding its antecedent: perhaps Paul is referring to the Spirit (v. 23), or the groaning of the believer (v. 23), or the hope that sustains us (vv. 24–25). All three make sense, but in light of the emphasis on the Spirit's work in verses 26–27, it is probable that he is referring to the Spirit. As the Spirit gives us hope, he "helps us in our weakness." The verb "helps" means to "come to the aid of" the saints. In the **Septuagint** (Greek Old Testament) of Exodus 18:22 and Numbers 11:17, this verb (*synantilambanomai*) tells how the elders appointed as judges over Israel were to "come to the aid of" or "share the burden" of leading the people with Moses.

This means it is more than the Spirit helping us. The Spirit shares the burden "along with" (the meaning of the prefix *syn-*) us. The Spirit holds us up and sustains us (Ps 89:21) in our finiteness and weakness. Some see this especially as weakness in our prayer life, but it is better to understand it more broadly of all our human frailty. This is the message of Romans 7:14–8:17: when we fail due to the weakness of the flesh, the Spirit pours his strength into us and enables us to find the victory.

Paul follows with one primary example of this weakness: "We do not know what we ought to pray for." The NIV omits *katho dei*, "as we should," but it is an important clarification that could be paraphrased, "as God deems it necessary for us to pray." It parallels the phrase "in accordance with the will of God" in verse 27. In his Gethsemane prayer Jesus cried, "*Abba*, Father, … everything is possible for you. Take this cup from me. Yet not what I will, but what you will" (Mark 14:36). Our prayer weakness is our inability to know the will of God. When we pray, we don't know for certain what will be best for us or what God wills in the situation.

Paul makes this explicit in the next phrase: "We do not know what we ought to pray for." We do not know what God wills as we come to him with our troubles. When we pray for healing, financial aid, social relationships, and so on, we cannot know whether it is in keeping with his purposes, so we must always pray the Gethsemane prayer: not what I want but what you want. We must want what God wills for us, but we cannot know whether that means a "yes" to our request or a "no," and that is our weakness.

God (not us) is sovereign over our lives and therefore over our prayer requests. Verse 28 tells us that when God rejects our prayer requests, it is for our own good. From the perspective of true faith, God's no is actually a yes, for it is an affirmation that he loves us enough to give us what we need rather than what we want. What parent would ever give their child anything they wished? That would destroy the child and prove the parent did not actually love them but just took the easy road.

This is the message of Hebrews 12:5–11, which tells us that our trials are the act of a loving Father who disciplines us "for our good, in order that we may share in his holiness" (v. 10). Let me relate a personal example. I have had chronic asthma virtually from the day I was born. I spent two childhood summers shut up in my house because my doctor (erroneously) told me I could not play outside due to the pollens. (I was locked up with a chain-smoking mother!) I have prayed all my life for healing, and several prayer warriors have anointed me with oil for healing. God has never granted me healing for my breathing problems, and now I have steroidal myopathy (muscle weakness from the prednisone I have all too often had to take). What I do know is that physical weakness made me what I am today. All I had was books, but they turned me into a scholar and a teacher and shaped my life *for the best*. God knows what he is doing even when we don't!

The most blessed thing about our prayer life, as finite as it may be, is that we are never alone. While we may be lamenting our infirmities, "the Spirit himself intercedes for us through wordless groans." Far from being unaware of our difficult circumstances, the Spirit is in that very situation petitioning God more deeply than we ever could. The phrase "wordless groans" translates a Greek term found only here in the New Testament, *alalētois*, meaning "unspoken," and often translated as "unspeakable" or "which words cannot express."

Its meaning is debated. Does it mean "too deep for human utterance," or perhaps groans that are spoken but unable to be deciphered? Several believe it to be a reference to speaking in tongues, akin to "praying in tongues" under the influence of the Holy Spirit (1 Cor 14:14–15). This is not too likely because this is the Spirit groaning rather than us (ours is in v. 23), and the gift of tongues is given to a few chosen individuals (1 Cor 12:30), while this groaning concerns all believers.

Instead, these "wordless groans" most likely refer to the Spirit's interceding too deeply for human language. This intercession takes place within the Triune Godhead, and Paul's point is that as we groan in the midst of our difficulties, the Godhead is not ignoring us but deeply involved in our situation. This intercession is expressed at the very throne of God as Father, Son, and Spirit are undergirding our travails with their deep involvement in our needs. These are the Spirit's (and the Godhead's) own intercessory intervention into our desperate situation.

We do not know the mind and will of God, but the Spirit does, so we can rest assured that in spite of our ignorance, God will be guiding us through our trials and working out what is best for us (v. 28). As we pray in an uncertain world, we have the God who is sovereign over that world guiding our affairs and the Spirit who is with us both praying for and empowering us through them.

Intercession in Accord with the Mind of God (8:27)

Now Paul gives us "the rest of the story." Not only does the Holy Spirit groan in the midst of our troubles more deeply than we do and intercede for us with God, but he also "intercedes for God's people in accordance with the will of God." God does not expect us to work out all the details of our needs and to tell him what he should do. Our prayers are intended to align us with him and help us to depend more deeply on his wisdom and sovereign action on our behalf. We share our needs and desires with him, but in doing so we yield entirely to his will. Prayer is a sacred privilege and the time of deepest communication with our God, but in this we need the Spirit's undergirding presence in our prayer life. It is so unbelievably comforting to know we are never alone when we pray!

Paul describes God as "he who searches our hearts," referring to him not only as the judge of our innermost thoughts (as in 1 Kgs 8:39; Ps 26:2; 44:21; Jer 17:10) but primarily as the one hears our heartfelt groanings and acts on them. The God who knows our hearts also "knows the mind of the Spirit." This is another reminder that the Triune Godhead is involved in every situation and need that we face (Christ's intercession is noted in v. 34 below).

The conjunction (Greek: *hoti*) could provide the contents of what God knows from the Spirit, "that" (so JB, ESV footnote), or the reason for that intercession, "because" (NIV, ESV, NASB, NLT, LEB). The latter is definitely better. God knows the Spirit's intercession "because" it is entirely in keeping with his will. This is the basis for our own security in the Lord.

THE RESULT: ALL THINGS WORK FOR OUR GOOD (8:28)

This is one of the most famous memory verses of Scripture. However, it is too often taken out of context and generalized beyond its intended meaning. We must put verses 26–28 together as a whole statement to get its true meaning. Paul wants us to realize that we are not alone, nor are our groanings isolated and for naught. Behind and much deeper than our own cries to God for help is the Holy Spirit, who is not only groaning more deeply than us on our behalf but also is doing so knowing the will of God. It is on this basis, the Spirit's deep intercession, that we can be absolutely certain that "in all things God works for the good of those who love him."

This verse continues the thought of 26–27, stating the truth that "we know" is the result of the encouraging news about the Spirit's intercession for us. Verse 28 shows the results of the Spirit's prayer for believers who are passing through the dark tunnel of despair over their overwhelming troubles. We do not know how to pray, and if we relied only on our own prayers we would never have peace. God hears our prayers as they are deepened by the accompanying intercessory work of the Spirit, and so he acts. And as a result of that divine action, the situation turns out for the best.

We must take "all things" seriously. While encompassing our present struggles, it includes even our sins and mistakes. God intervenes and turns them around as well. Certainly if we sin we will have to suffer in ways we would not have had to if we had taken the right path, but God turns even this situation around and corrects our errors. The verb "works" could mean the events themselves work together to produce the good, but that ignores God's sovereignty in this verse. It is God who turns everything around, and not fate or chance.

We should understand the "good" in terms of the already/not yet tension we have often seen in this chapter (vv. 10, 18, 19, 23). It refers to the present "good" that results from the Spirit's work in us and God's actions on our behalf, and it is also the final joy and peace that will be ours in eternity. It is also critical to realize that the "good" does not mean we will get whatever we want but rather what is best for us in accordance with God's will.

This incredible promise is given to "those who love him, who have been called according to his purpose." In the Greek the promise itself comes between these two phrases, with "those who love him" at the beginning of the verse for emphasis. One question is whether this is restrictive (it is only for those who love God), or for encouragement (it works out because they love him). The latter is more likely, since the entire passage centers on comfort rather than warning.

Paul qualifies this even further by concluding with a note on the divine calling. As the Spirit prays in accord with the Father's will, the child of God lives according to his will. The phrase "called according to his purpose" emphasizes those who follow his will and live it out in their lives. The two become an interesting pair, looking at our relationship with God first from the human perspective (our love for God) and then from the divine perspective (his will for us). God's will results from his love for us linked to his plan for us. The divine plan guarantees that all will work out for our good.

A GOLDEN CHAIN RUNS FROM FOREKNOWLEDGE TO GLORY (8:29–30)

The five stages of the salvation process named in verses 29–30 are introduced with *hoti*, "because" or "for," stating the reason why all things work together for good. God purposes to lead us through the suffering and trials we face to the glory that is ours. This list describes how God brings his people to himself and to the glorious future that he has for them. Paul repeats each term as it leads to the next, forming a golden chain of linked concepts that provide a foundation for his doctrine of salvation.

The list contains five key aspects of God's sovereign control of salvation. Each item tells how God controls the process that moves his children from their sinful state to redemption and then to glory. This movement from foreknowledge to predestination to calling to justification to glory shows how his purpose and plan are always efficacious in the life of the believer.

THOSE GOD FOREKNEW HE ALSO PREDESTINED (8:29A)

The first link in the chain, "to foreknow" (*proginōskō*), means to know something beforehand or to foresee an event, in this case the faith response and salvation of God's followers. There is debate

over the relation of this foreknowledge to the next term, predestination, and this verse is at the heart of the Calvinist-Arminian
controversy. The followers of John Calvin assert that the two terms
are virtually synonymous for several reasons. They claim that (1)
"foreknowledge" means more than mere knowledge of human
choices and includes God's decision to enter a covenant relationship with those he chooses (Rom 11:2; 1 Pet 1:2, 20). (2) Foreknowledge thus includes election to a foreordained plan (v. 28). (3) "To
foreknow" is subordinate to and a ground for the key idea, predestination. (4) It contains God's intimate knowledge and determination about his chosen people and is synonymous with his choice of
them "from before the creation of the world" (Eph 1:4; 1 Pet 1:20).
They conclude that the faith choice of every convert is determined
by God's predestined choice of them for salvation.

The followers of Jacobus Arminius believe that the more natural understanding of the two verbs would see them as stepping
stones rather than one synonymous act. In other words, God first
foreknows/foresees people's faith-decision and then predestines
them based on his knowledge of that decision. They argue that (1)
none of the other five stages in verses 29-30 are synonymous, but
each one leads to the next. This means that for Paul foreknowledge
leads to predestination. (2) The verb actually says God "knows"
about his people ahead of time, and they are the topic of 8:31-39.
This does not mean God determines their salvation but that God
knows of them. (3) Other passages on foreknowledge (Rom 11:2,
and especially 1 Pet 1:2) fail to make the two synonymous and
have the choosing based on the foreknowing. (4) The passages on
choosing "before the creation of the world" (see above) more naturally point to God foreseeing who would make a decision to follow
him than to his actual choice to bring them to himself. They conclude that God was aware before he created this world who would
respond to his salvation offer in faith, and as a result both chose
them to be his own and called them to himself.

Like most Christians I have meditated on and studied this issue most of my Christian life. After going back and forth many times, I find the Arminian approach more faithful to all the biblical data. The Holy Spirit convicts every person born on this earth and makes a choice possible. It is the Triune Godhead who allows sinners to overcome their depravity and make a choice, and for those who come in faith, God works out his salvation in their life. The point here is that before God created this world he knew how every individual sinner would react to his salvation offer. On that basis he chose them ahead of time (predestined them) to be adopted as his children.

Predestined to be Conformed to the Image of His Son (8:29b)

This verse relates the purpose of predestination and shows that it deals more with sanctification than with justification. God calls people to himself through the convicting work of the Spirit (John 16:8-11), but this calling is not effectual. Rather, it gives the sinner an opportunity to accept or reject that call. The goal is to lead to their salvation and then to holiness. "Conformed to the image of his Son" refers to the Christlikeness of Ephesians 4:13, "the whole measure of the fullness of Christ."

There is some controversy as to whether this verse refers to present spiritual growth or to the final conformity to Christ's glory at the end of this age. In light of the already/not yet tension of this whole section (see vv. 18, 23, 28) it is likely Paul intended both aspects, with the emphasis on present growth in the Spirit. Humanity was created in the image of God (Gen 1:26-27), but that image was marred due to the trespass of Adam. Christ through his atoning sacrifice has restored that image, so that we can once more be conformed to it through union with him.

A second result then takes place, as Christ becomes "the firstborn among many brothers and sisters." Christ as the firstborn is also found in Colossians 1:15, 18, where (as here) Paul's focus is on status (first in importance) rather than time (first to be born). It signifies, as in Exodus 4:22 (Israel as first among the nations) and Psalm 89:27 (David as first among rulers), Jesus' exalted status as supreme over all creation. The point again parallels "firstfruits" in 1 Corinthians 15:20, 23, where Christ's resurrection guarantees we will be raised with him. As we grow in Christ we become more and more like him and share in ever greater ways in his glory.

THOSE HE PREDESTINED HE ALSO CALLED (8:30A)

The calling of God also relates to the debate on predestination. Some believe this is an effectual call to salvation, meaning God predestines and then calls the elect to himself. If so, this refers to the doctrine known as "irresistible grace," the view that the predestined will not reject the call to salvation. Others believe the call is to a faith-decision, referring to the convicting work of the Spirit, and that while God makes a faith-decision possible, the call can be resisted or rejected.

It is doubtful that Paul had such an issue in mind. He was thinking simply of the call to become a follower of Christ, with the decision lying between this stage and the next (justification). The message would be that through the Spirit God calls and convicts sinners, then they respond to that call, and those who accept it by faith are justified by God on the basis of Christ's blood sacrifice.

THOSE HE CALLED, HE ALSO JUSTIFIED (8:30B)

From the time of Martin Luther, many have called justification the central theme of Romans and of Paul as a whole. This overstates the case, but in light of 3:21–5:11 justification by faith is one of the key motifs in Romans and indeed of all Paul's letters.

Paul's emphasis on calling in this verse presupposes the response to that call in the faith-decision of the individual. In this golden chain of 8:29–30, Paul is centering on the divine side of the equation, but the place of faith on the human side is also a critical aspect in Romans ("faith" occurs seventeen times in 3:21–4:25). However, we must realize that human depravity makes a faith response a virtual impossibility without the Spirit's involvement. It is he who overcomes our depravity through his convicting power and makes response possible.

When sinners do respond with faith and put their trust in the atoning work of Christ, it is also God and the Spirit who forgive their sins and justify or declare them righteous. God saves us; we do not save ourselves. This was the heresy of Pelagius, who said we are the basis of our own salvation. Nothing could be further from the truth.

Those He Justified, He Also Glorified (8:30c)

Glorification is another major theme of Romans, with *doxa* (glory) appearing fifteen times and *doxazō* (glorify) five times. hose who are the people of God and have become the children of the King (2:7, 10; 6:4) experience a present glory, and those who have suffered for Christ (5:2–5) and waited for God's future glory (8:18, 21) will experience an eternal glory. The final glory we will enjoy in eternity has already begun. We may be mocked and rejected for belonging to Christ, but we have already been glorified as Christ followers and will see this glory revealed when we inherit his kingdom.

Some take this verse as referring entirely to final glory, but it is unlikely Paul would leap from the benefits of our present salvation and justification straight to final glory. The verb "justified" here is the same tense as the others in this series. It describes a process that has already begun and will culminate in Christ's return. This process is firmly linked to the Spirit's work here in chapter 8 as the "seal" and "deposit" guaranteeing our future inheritance (Eph 1:13–14).

———

This wonderful section gives us a whole new perspective on suffering. When we feel alone and forgotten in the midst of troubles,

Paul wants us to know that will never be the case. Not only is the Spirit with us, but also our suffering is an integral part of the travails of all of God's creation as it groans alongside us and awaits its deliverance.

Both the inanimate creation and we who are God's people must know that redemption is coming. Creation is on its way to "the new heavens and new earth" (Rev 21:1), and we are on our way to sharing the glory of Christ for eternity (Col 3:4). In recent years our society has realized how important ecological concerns are for our future. Here we see the ultimate ecological recovery, as all of creation joins us in awaiting our deliverance from all the evils human sin has visited upon our environment.

Our groaning and the Spirit's groaning are closely linked. Every one of us has experienced the deterioration of our bodies and groaned deeply as we longed for healing. This is all the more true because the presence of the Spirit has made us acutely aware of the wonderful promise of our final liberation from suffering. As my body seems to disintegrate step by painful step, I long for the promised release. However, the antidote for frustration is hope, for the hope of the believer is not uncertain but recognizes that what God has promised will absolutely come to pass. Because of hope I eagerly wait for my liberation, but I need not despair, for I know pain is temporary and will end in eternal joy.

When we pray we may feel all alone, but that is a tragic error. In our weakness, the Spirit is nearer than we have ever experienced, for he undergirds our groans with deeper groans on our my behalf. The Holy Spirit is praying for us more deeply than we are praying for ourselves! Moreover, we don't know what God's will is or what will be best for us, but the Spirit does, and his intercession is completely in accord with God's will. If we pray wrongly, the Spirit corrects our error and ensures the incredible promise of verse 28—that what God will do in answering these prayers (mine and the Spirit's) will be for the best!

Finally, Paul wants us to understand that everything he has said about our suffering and prayer life is grounded in the sovereignty of the God who rules over all of creation on our behalf and who has given us the ultimate blessing of eternal salvation. In verses 29–30 Paul makes us aware of the extent to which God has overseen every part of our salvation. Our present salvation and our eternal glory are anchored in his loving control. Our security in our status as children of God is certain in Father, Son, and Holy Spirit, who are all at work ensuring our adoption into the eternal family of God.

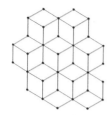

THE SECURITY AND VICTORY
OF THE BELIEVER
(8:31-39)

This is the third of the famous and beautifully written passages in this magnificent chapter. It summarizes the blessings of 5:1-8:30, and like 5:1-11 centers on God's provision for his people in the midst of their suffering. Paul's message is also similar to 1 Peter 1:3-12, telling believers that they need to place their suffering into proper perspective by meditating on the blessings of salvation. Paul says here that our security is grounded in God's love for us. The elegant style of the section may indicate that Paul got it from the liturgy of the early church, but it is more probable that Paul wrote this in his own beautiful hand. There are two sections, the first (31-34) on judicial victory in Christ, and the second (35-39) on the inseparable love of the Godhead for us. Both center on the security of God's people in him.

OUR JUDICIAL VICTORY IS DUE TO
THE GIFT OF THE SON (8:31-34)

No Opposition Due the Gift of the Son (8:31-32)

Throughout Romans, Paul often uses the rhetorical question that introduces this material, "What, then, shall we say?" to provide a critical set of qualifications for his argument (3:5, 9; 4:1; 9:30). The added phrase "in response to this" points back not just to the material of 8:18–30 but also to the teachings on salvation from 3:21–8:30. Paul has moved from sin and guilt, to Christ's atoning sacrifice, to forgiveness and justification, to the gift of the Spirit and the liberation from sin that defines the Christian life. In other words, "this" encompasses the whole of our salvation, both our justification and our sanctification.

The key affirmation comes next: "If" (a condition of fact meaning "since") "God is for us, who can be against us?" "For" translates the Greek *hyper*, "on our behalf," and describes the heart of the gospel: Christ died as an atoning sacrifice for us. He was our substitute in paying the price for our sins, with the result that the covenant God is at work *on our behalf*, and the Spirit intercedes with the Father *on our behalf*.

In light of the involvement of the Triune Godhead in our lives and for our good, the question is, "who can be against us?" Since God is absolutely faithful to his covenant people and ensures our future, those who stand against us will come to nothing. Paul's point is not that nothing can ever go wrong. He is saying that nothing that matters in the long run can stand against us. Many forces want to do us harm, and in an earthly sense they will succeed. Paul will give a list of them in verses 35 and 38. But with God on our side, all their efforts will come to nothing.

We have nothing to worry about. As Jesus said in Matthew 10:28, "Do not be afraid of those who kill the body but cannot kill the soul. Rather, be afraid of the One who can destroy both soul and body in hell." The truth is, we cannot lose! Every time Satan conquers the saints by killing them, they conquer him by being killed (Rev 12:11). Their seeming defeat is their great victory. Throughout the book of Acts, the efforts of the Jews and the Romans to eradicate Christianity actually enables it to triumph and grow. The same has taken place in China since the Cultural Revolution of the 1960s and '70s. The government program of persecution against the church has not only failed to stamp out believers but actually caused the church to grow in staggering ways. Persecution became a church-growth stimulus!

The "for us" of verse 31 carries over to the next verse, which tells why we can know that the promise "God is for us" is absolutely true. The proof of this is seen in the fact that God "did not spare his own Son, but gave him up for us all." This is a sovereign act of God; it is not something we could do for ourselves or that could be accomplished by the law. Only God could do such a thing or provide so great a salvation. This level of love is beyond human comprehension (see 5:8). God did not "allow" the cross to happen. He instigated it and deliberately "delivered" his Son to the cross for our sake.

Paul's message is that the kind of God who would surrender his Son to die for us would of course "along with him, graciously give us all things." "Along with him" (*syn autō*) means that the primary gift that guarantees the other gifts is Christ himself. In him the greatest gift of all has come, salvation and eternal life. God could make us the wealthiest person in the world, and it would be insignificant compared with the gift of Christ.

The verb *charisetai* (graciously give) points to the grace-gifts God provides (1 Cor 2:12; Gal 3:18), referring especially to the kingdom blessings given to God's covenant people. Yet it encompasses even more than this. Accompanying the gift of Christ is the promise of "all things." There are several possibilities for what Paul might be referring to: the present blessings of salvation or the final blessings to be ours at the end of this age, but most likely it connotes both present (the already) and future (the not yet; see on vv. 13, 18) blessings poured out upon God's people—both spiritual and earthly gifts to meet all our needs. This is closely related to verse 28; God works *all things* for our good by giving us *all things* that we need.

No CHARGES DUE TO JUSTIFICATION (8:33)

Paul returns to verse 31 in showing the implications of God's extensive grace-gifts to us. There he asked, "If God is for us, who can be against us?" Now he asks, "Who will bring any charge against those whom God has chosen?" There have been differences of opinion as to which of the clauses in verses 33-34 are questions—some have even made every clause a question (seven in all). However, most versions are the same as the NIV, which translates it in a question-answer format. I will follow this interpretation, with verse 33 a single question and answer, then verse 34 another question and answer.

Paul is hardly saying that no one will ever be able to bring charges against us. He means charges that will matter. Others will make countless accusations, but none of them will count in the long run. The phrase "charge against" adds a courtroom atmosphere to the scene. Satan often accuses God's people (as in Job 1-2 and Rev 12:10), and throughout history believers have often been hauled before magistrates and courts—like Jesus before the Sanhedrin and Paul before Nero. The future tense "will bring a charge" makes some think this is a charge at the last judgment, perhaps by Satan or the enemies of the saints, and others surmise that it depicts the continual opposition against God's people throughout history. It likely connotes both, but in this context Paul is stressing present earthly opposition more.

Our earthly enemies and our powerful cosmic enemy, Satan, will do us great harm but will ultimately be frustrated in their attempts to thwart the plan of God with his people. We can be mistreated and even killed now, but ultimately the triumph is ours, and we find victory even in the fact that we "did not love [our] lives so much as to shrink from death" (Rev 12:11). Our suffering and even our death is our ultimate victory over our accusers. For the elect, there is nothing that can in the end bring harm to us, for the sovereign God stands behind us and uses even these charges for our benefit (see v. 28). This will be the theme in verses 35-39 as well.

The answer to this first query is profound: "It is God who justifies." Paul continues the law court atmosphere—people (and Satan) accuse us, but God the righteous judge disproves their charges and declares us innocent. Paul is echoing Isaiah 50:8–9, "Who then will bring charges against me? ... It is the sovereign LORD who helps me. Who will condemn me?" The questions in Isaiah are future tense, but the answer, as here, is in present tense, indicating God's continuous presence with his people. The meaning of "justifies" here probably moves from the judicial act of declaring God's people righteous to his sustaining work of making them righteous (see commentary on 3:24).

NO CONDEMNATION DUE TO HIS INTERCESSION (8:34)

This verse moves from the accusations to the judicial verdict, the condemnation of the saints by evil humankind. Note the contrast between God's justification and people's condemnation. The death and resurrection of Jesus provided the basis of our justification (4:25), and the lies and charges of sinful humanity provided the basis of our condemnation. Yet all attempts to condemn believers are ultimately doomed to failure, for the death of Christ has covered their sins (3:25).

In this verse Paul lists four actions that Christ has accomplished on our behalf, and they sum up the teaching of Romans thus far. The first pair relates to his earthly work: "Christ Jesus who died—more than that, who was raised to life." His death and resurrection provided the basis for our salvation, as in 4:25, "He was delivered over to death for our sins and was raised to life for our justification." These form a single event in salvation history. Christ's resurrection guarantees our own, so we have nothing to fear from our enemies. His death and ours end with resurrection and new life.

The second pair relates to Christ's heavenly exaltation: he "is at the right hand of God and is also interceding for us." The first stems from Psalm 110:1, the most quoted Old Testament passage in the New, thirteen times (five in Hebrews alone). It provides the primary biblical underpinning for the exaltation of Jesus "at the right hand of God," the place of majesty, power, and authority. The fourth item in the list is Jesus' intercessory work. In verse 26 the Holy Spirit was our intercessor before God, and here Jesus joins the Spirit on behalf of the saints. In Hebrews 7:25 this intercessory ministry is Jesus' high priestly work, and here it is the cross that overcomes all charges, true as well as false (for instance, our sins charged to our account).

NOTHING CAN SEPARATE US FROM THE LOVE OF GOD AND CHRIST (8:35–39)

Paul's focus now changes from the forensic to the relational, from the judicial to the personal. The topic turns back to 5:6–8 and the issue of God sending his Son to die for us as a demonstration of his deep love for us. In 5:5 that love was "poured out into our hearts through the Holy Spirit, who has been given to us." Love unites the Triune Godhead on our behalf, and it is important to note that these two passages (5:5–8; 8:35–39) are the only two places in Romans thus far where Paul has mentioned love. The divine love shown on the cross and in the gift of the Spirit is now shown to be unbreakable. In both places the depth of God's love is proved in the gift of the Son on the cross.

Verses 35–36, on the inseparable love of Christ, and verses 38–39, on the inseparable love of God, surround the affirmation in verse 37 that we are "more than conquerors" as a result of the wondrous love of the Godhead for us. An ABA pattern shows that this is the key point of this paragraph:

A The inseparable love of God (8:35–36)
　　B The result of adversity: more than conquerors (8:37)
A' The inseparable love of Christ (8:38–39)

THE LOVE OF CHRIST (8:35–36)

Paul asks, "Who shall separate us from the love of Christ?" The idea of separation stems from the charges and condemnation of our enemies in verses 33–34, and the list of troubles following in verse 36 elaborates these problems. The question is whether the

charges and the troubles of life have the potential to cause an irrevocable rift in our relationship with God. Paul says they will not.

The list of difficulties—"trouble or hardship or persecution
or famine or nakedness or danger or sword"—are all found in 2
Corinthians 11:26-27; 12:10, where Paul notes the dangers he has
experienced in his ministry. This is a personal list; he is reiterating what he has gone through for Christ. The last of these,
the "sword," or death by execution, he would not experience for
about eight years (he died at the hands of Nero after his second
imprisonment in Rome about AD 64-65). Still, arrest at the hands
of the Romans was a constant threat, and he had previously been
imprisoned at Philippi in Acts 16:22-36 and probably at Ephesus
in Acts 19:35-41.

In addition to reflecting Paul's experience, the list is similar
to Old Testament lists of disasters like 2 Chronicles 6:28; 20:9.
It reminds us that God's people rarely have an easy life, and we
should all expect suffering. Natural disasters happen all the time,
and things like illnesses or economic challenges are a way of life.
Moreover, as it says in John 3:19-20, people love darkness rather
than light, and evil people hate the light. But there is no need for
despair, for while the world turns against us, God and Christ never
do so, and "nothing can separate us" from their love.

Paul anchors this truth in verse 36 with a quotation from
Psalm 44:22, "For your sake we face death all day long; we are considered as sheep to be slaughtered." He wants to show his readers that suffering for following the Lord is not a new thing. In this
lament psalm, the psalmist begins by reciting the victories Yahweh
has won for the nation (44:1-9) and then decries his delivery of
his people to their enemies (44:10-22), concluding with a plea for
God to "rise up and help us" (44:23-26).

The statement Paul quotes draws the lament section to a close
by affirming his people's sacrifices for God. For Paul the phrase
"face death all day long" probably parallels the list of difficulties
in 8:35, and "sheep to be slaughtered" equals the "sword." All that

the Roman Christians are suffering is in line with the people of the psalmist's time.

MORE THAN CONQUERORS (8:37)

In verse 35 Paul asks whether anything such as trouble or hardship can separate the saints from the love of God. His answer to his question comes in verse 37, where he implies a negative answer, made explicit by the "no" in the NIV (the Greek only has *alla*, "but"). In doing so he goes beyond a simple "no, it can't"; the adversity we experience actually makes us "more than conquerors."

"In all these things" means that in every single area where we face opposition and troubles we not only cannot be defeated; we actually thrive and triumph. Paul is thinking not only of the list in verse 35 but also of all the pressures Christians encounter. When we pass through hard times we often feel like God has forgotten about us. As we saw in 8:23–25, the truth is just the opposite. God and his Spirit are nearer than they have ever been, and we must surrender to and rely on them.

What we are can be literally translated "hyper-conquerors" (*hypernikōmen*), in a sense saying we triumph more deeply and greatly than Alexander the Great and Julius Caesar put together. Absolute victory over all our difficulties and everyone who works to do us harm (for instance, our persecutors) is guaranteed when Christ and the Spirit take over. The means of this certain triumph is "through him who loved us." When Christ pours out his love for us, including all four areas from verse 34, we are filled with "his incomparably great power" (Eph 1:19), enabling us to "be strong in the Lord and his mighty power" (Eph 6:10). With all that, how can we lose?

As throughout Scripture, Paul reminds us of our own inadequacies and the adequacy of Christ and his Spirit. Whenever we rely on our own strength (7:14–25), we are utterly defeated in the battles of life and in spiritual warfare. When we totally depend on Christ and his Spirit, we are hyper-conquerors (8:1–17, 37).

ROMANS 8:31-39

Certainly, our struggles are never "pleasant … but painful," but in the end they always yield "a harvest of righteousness and peace" (Heb 12:11). As Paul was writing this verse, he was obviously thinking of verse 28 and the fact that God always works what is best for his beloved followers.

THE LOVE OF GOD (8:38-39)

Paul now completes his meditation on divine love in the life of the Christian, turning from the love of Christ (35-36) to the love of God the Father here. It too is inseparable and always efficacious in the life of the believer. Paul begins "I am convinced" because he is giving his own witness to all God has accomplished in his life. "Convinced" means he is absolutely certain that nothing can come between himself and the God who loves him. To make his point, he provides another list of difficulties he has passed through, organized for the most part in a series of pairs, except for "powers" and the closing "anything else in all creation."

1. *Neither death nor life.* This is the key pair that leads into all the others and defines the two powers that dominate this world. In 5:12-14 Paul described death's entrance through sin and its reign over God's creation, leading creation into frustration and bondage (see 8:18-22). We can only enter life via faith in Christ. Throughout chapters 5-8 death with sin is personified as a hostile power, and death and life represent two eons at war in the believer.

2. *Neither angels nor demons.* The second term is *archai*, "rulers." Paul often uses this term in a titular sense, "principalities and powers," to label the fallen angels or cosmic powers that are the enemies of God and his people (Eph 1:21; 6:12; Col 1:16; 2:15). Christ has conquered these cosmic rulers on behalf of his church (Eph 3:10; 6:10-12; Col 2:15). They cannot overpower Christians, only deceive them (Rev 12:9; 20:3). Christ's followers have been given authority over them (Mark 3:14-15; 6:7).

3. *Neither the present nor the future.* Paul now turns to the realm
    of the already and the not yet (see vv. 18, 23, 32). Nothing
    now or in the foreseeable future can come between us and
    God's love. He could certainly attest to this, for Paul's life
    was an unending series of crises (2 Cor 11:23–29). He did not
    know it, but after writing this letter he would be arrested
    soon after reaching Jerusalem (Acts 21) and spend the
    next several years in prison in Caesarea and Rome. Upon
    his release, he would have at best a few years before his
    final arrest and execution. In all that time, God never once
    deserted him.

4. *Nor any powers.* Some have thought "powers" refers to mira-
    cles, but almost certainly it is the cosmic powers or demonic
    realm. It is difficult to know why he would refer to the evil
    powers just above and then list it here by itself. Perhaps
    spiritual warfare was especially on his mind, or perhaps
    he wished to emphasize it for the readers since he had not
    mentioned the demonic forces in verses 31–37. The primary
    point is that the realm of darkness is real, and we dare not
    ignore the "powers" arrayed against us. They cannot defeat
    us unless we allow them entry into our lives, and a good
    way to do so is to live as though they are not there.

5. *Neither height nor depth.* There are two options for under-
    standing this phrase. Some think the **Hellenistic** use of
    these for the heavens above and the subearthly realms
    below with the beings that inhabit them point to celestial
    powers. But I don't think Paul would list three straight ref-
    erences to demonic powers, and these terms are not found
    anywhere else in the New Testament used this way. It is far
    more probable that these are terms referring to the realm
    above the earth and under it, either the whole universe
    above and below our world, or to heaven and hell. Either
    way, it means nothing in all of this world or outside it can
    separate us from the love of God.

6. *Nor anything else in all creation.* Paul wants his readers to know he has left nothing out—absolutely nothing in God's created world can threaten the relationship between God and his children.

This inseparable love of God is poured out on us "in Christ Jesus our Lord," repeating a major theme that combines our union in Christ with our membership in his body, the church (see on 3:24; 6:11, 23; 8:1). However, the basic formula adds an emphasis on his Lordship, and this formula begins or ends several sections (5:1, 21; 6:23; 7:25; 8:39) with the motif of the cosmic lordship of Christ. The sovereign control of Jesus over our lives guarantees the love of God; and the security of the believer, so endemic to the last half of chapter 8, is grounded in his power over salvation history and our lives.

This is one of the primary passages in Scripture on eternal security, and the debate on this issue in Romans 8 centers on the promise that nothing "will be able to separate us from the love of God" (v. 39). The lists of verses 35, 38–39, are all external forces, and the question is whether this list implicitly includes the internal choices of the believer as well. Arminians would state that nothing can come between us and God except our free will, and we can decide to turn away from him. Calvinists say that God is also sovereign over our decisions and will not allow his people to walk away from Christ and salvation.

In context, Paul simply wants to comfort believers that the love of God and Christ will keep us secure from all dangerous forces and events arrayed against us. Still, we all must compare those verses that stress security (John 6:35–51; 10:27–30; Rom 8:28–39; Eph 1:13–14; 2:8–9; 4:30; Phil 1:6; 2:13; 1 Pet 1:5) with those that stress warning (John 15:11–6; Rom 11:18–21; 1 Cor 9:24–27; Heb 6:4–6; 10:26–31; Jas 5:19–20; 2 Pet 2:20–22) and try to develop a theology that accounts for both sides. There is no final answer, and our decision must harmonize our security in Christ with our responsibility to remain faithful to him. I will discuss this further at the end of Romans 10.

We must savor in all its richness this wonderful passage on the inseparable divine love of the Triune Godhead for us. The first half (31-34) deals with the judicial triumph that is ours in Christ. There are countless opponents and charges made to derail us, but none of them really matter. We are opposed and can be killed, but every vicious act perpetrated against us is overturned by God, and our final victory is secure. The world will condemn us as they did Christ, but we unite with both his death and resurrection, and our triumph will be eternal.

The second half of this passage (35-39) moves from the judicial to the relational. The charges our opponents make against us are intended to break our relationship with God and his Son, but Christ's love is inseparable from us (vv. 35-36), as is God the Father's love (vv. 38-39), and the result is that we are "more than conquerors" as we triumph in him (v. 37). No matter how severe the difficulties we are going through, Paul can attest from experience how God used these very areas of hardship to enable us to triumph in Christ.

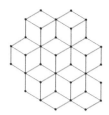

PAUL'S SORROW:
ISRAEL'S CURSE AND DIVINE ELECTION
(9:1–13)

When people think of Romans 9–11 they normally think of predestination, but that is not the reason Paul added this passage at this point in his argument. Divine election is not a focus of the section but is a part of Paul's primary argument for the justice of God. In chapters 1–5 he developed the point that Jews and Gentiles were equal as sinners in need of grace and as the objects of God's redemptive love. Then in chapter 8 he showed that God was faithful to those he loved and worked on their behalf, Jew and Gentile alike, who have been united "in Christ" to form new and true Israel. Out of the inclusion of the Gentiles with the Jews in salvation history and God's faithful love for his new people, Paul addresses his sorrow over unbelieving Israel.

God's covenant love throughout the Old Testament was poured out upon Israel, but now they have rejected their Messiah and God has seemingly abandoned them and turned his mercy upon the Gentiles. Imagine you are a Jewish Christian in Rome reading Romans 1–8. You had grown up steeped in the glorious stories of God's loving care for his people, Israel, how God had chosen them out of the nations to be his special possession and would "never leave ... nor forsake" them (Deut 31:8; Josh 1:5). Paul's words would be shocking. You would ask if Paul had established a contradiction between the God of covenant love and faithfulness you had grown up with and the new (?) God who had seemingly turned his back on his covenant promises. Is there still a "righteousness of God" (1:17)?

Some have thought Romans 9–11 an afterthought disconnected from chapters 1–8, but it is integral to the development of Paul's message. In these chapters he is responding to the Jew-Gentile controversy and the place of the law in the church. Since the law had been fulfilled and culminated in Christ (10:4), the rituals of the law were no longer needed. This meant that by rejecting both Christ and the Christian gospel, the majority of Jews were no longer a part of God's people. The result was a feeling among many Jewish Christians that God had become unjust and now favored the Gentiles over the Jews. Moreover, Paul had seemed to turn against his people and become pro-Gentile. Paul now counters these charges and shows that (1) he, Paul, still loves his people and (2) God is still faithful to his promises.

There are three major sections with a brief opening and a brief closing, so five in all. In the opening of 9:1–5 he laments the sad state of his people, under the divine curse, having thrown away all the blessings God has showered upon them. Then he closes in 11:33–36 with the opposite sentiment, a doxology of praise over the riches of God and his "unsearchable judgments."

There are three main sections in the middle portion. The first (9:6–29) addresses the issue from God's perspective, arguing that God's promises have not failed because he has sovereignly chosen to elect the Gentiles along with believing Jews as his new people. The second (9:30–10:21) addresses it from Israel's perspective, showing that the rejection of Israel is due to its own refusal to accept God's Messiah and the salvation he has brought. Jewish unbelief and rejection of God's righteousness as coming only through faith in Jesus the Christ led to divine condemnation. The third (11:1–32) points out that this sad state of affairs is temporary.

There is a righteous remnant (11:1-10), and while some branches (unbelieving Jews) of the olive tree have been broken off, with believing Gentiles grafted in (11:11-24), there is a future salvation for national Israel (11:25-32).

Tying this whole section together is a brilliant collection of Old Testament quotations and allusions. Fully one-third of all Paul's quotations from all his writings are found in these three chapters, and he uses them to show that the points he is making stem from every part of God's word. He wants the Roman church to realize that the two covenant eras cohere, and that the inclusion of the Gentiles was God's will from the beginning. These are not two covenants in conflict but in continuity with one another.

PAUL IS FILLED WITH SORROW OVER ISRAEL'S FAILURE (9:1-5)

Paul wants the Roman believers, especially the Jewish Christians among them, to understand how deeply he loves his nation and how sorrowful he is over their plight. In verses 4-5 he provides a wonderful recapitulation of the blessings Israel has enjoyed as a result of being God's covenant people. His sorrow is made worse by the fact that their rejection of their Messiah means they have thrown these privileges away. This is particularly agonizing because they are his people; he would take their curse upon himself if he could (v. 3).

HIS DEEP ANGUISH OVER ISRAEL (9:1-2)

Most likely Paul was accused of anti-Semitism for becoming God's missionary to the Gentiles, so he goes to great lengths here to stress his heartfelt concern for his Jewish kindred. He uses three doublets in these opening two verses to portray how deeply he feels—"speak the truth"/"am not lying," "in Christ"/"through the Holy Spirit," "great sorrow"/"unceasing anguish." The first doublet stresses his trustworthiness, paralleling 2 Corinthians 11:31 and Galatians 1:20. This is a virtual oath to the truthfulness of what he is claiming.

He speaks the truth "in Christ." It is the product of his union with Christ, and Christ himself is the first witness to the veracity of his deep concern for his people. The other two witnesses are his conscience and the Holy Spirit. "Conscience" refers to his inner awareness of right and wrong and of God's will for his life (see on 2:15), and its validity is grounded in "the Holy Spirit." The Spirit is the means by which his conscience becomes a valid barometer for the truth content of his feelings. His affirmation is framed by members of the Godhead—in Christ/through the Holy Spirit—so that the divine imprimatur flows through his testimony here. He is not speaking on his own but is led by the Father, Son, and Spirit in all he attests.

The focus of this personal testimony is Paul's lament over his people, Israel (v. 2). The third doublet demonstrates the depth of his concern: "I have great sorrow and unceasing anguish in my heart." Paul here echoes Jeremiah, who is called "the weeping prophet" for his tears over the apostate nation of Judah (Jer 4:19; 6:24; 9:10). Sorrow and anguish are combined in Isaiah 35:10; 51:11 as well, but there "sorrow and sighing will flee away" as God restores his people to himself. In Romans 11:25–32, Paul prophesies that this will happen: the remnant will return and all sorrow will be removed from the nation. For Paul this can only happen in Christ.

But at this point Paul's focus is on the sad state of the nation. He feels deep pain over his fellow Jews and their rejection of Christ. By adding "in my heart" he wants to communicate that he feels sorrow to the very depth of his being. It consumes every part of him.

HIS WILLINGNESS TO BE ACCURSED FOR THEM (9:3)

Paul wishes he could take the divine curse upon Israel for them if it would bring them to Christ. The phrase "I could wish" (*euchomai*) was often used in Jewish prayers during Paul's day, so some think this an actual prayer to God. However, I think this is a hypothetical statement. He is saying, "If it were possible I would be willing."

The word for "curse" is *anathema*, and it normally is translated "eternally condemned" (Gal 1:8, 9; 1 Cor 12:3; 16:22). In the
Septuagint (the Greek Old Testament) it often refers to something intended for destruction (Lev 27:28; Deut 7:26; Zech 14:11).
Since to be cursed is to be consigned to everlasting destruction,
Paul is expressing his willingness to be eternally separated from
his Messiah in order to bring his Jewish compatriots to salvation.

This may be an allusion to Exodus 32:32, in which after the
golden calf incident Moses implored God, "please forgive their
sin—but if not, then blot me out of the book you have written."
Paul identifies with Moses' concern for the fallen nation. His language is emphatic—"cut off from Christ for the sake of my people,
those of my own race." Paul used the preposition *hyper* (for the
sake of) in 8:31–32 with a substitutionary thrust (God for us). Paul
is willing to take the curse in the place of unbelieving Israel.

"My people" in the Greek is "my own brothers" (*mou tōn
adelphōn*), the first of a series of phrases in verses 3–5 stressing
the kinship of the Jewish people to Paul and especially to God. Normally he uses this term for his relationship to other Christians, but
here he uses it of his brothers and sisters in ethnic Israel. They are
also "of my own race," literally "my kindred according to the flesh,"
with "flesh" having a double meaning, both physical descent and
(with negative overtones) pointing to them as unbelieving Jews in
terms of their fleshly existence as seen in 7:5, 18, 25; 11:14.

The Privileges of Israel (9:4–5)

Paul presents the covenant blessings of the Jewish people in their
relationship with God in a series of six statements composed of
two sets of three each, with each related to its corresponding
member in the other list. The first set relates to their status before
God and the second to the gifts they have received from God as
a result.

THEIR STATUS	THEIR GIFTS
the adoption as sons	the receiving of the law
the glory	the temple worship
the covenants	the promises

This list leads into the basic problem behind Romans 9–11: If these covenant blessings were true, how can so few have been saved? Have these promises failed (v. 6), and is God unjust (v. 14)? The list begins with the covenant name for the nation, "the people of Israel." If they really are his chosen people, Israel (Gen 32:28; 35:9–12; Ps 25:22; 130:7–8), with the title always used to designate their elect status as God's special people, how could such a tragic state of affairs have come to pass? Has Israel's rejection of the gospel of Christ obviated all the blessings of God? Have these promises come to nothing because of Israel's hardness?

In Romans 9–11 Paul is not only showing that God has not abandoned his people but also that the divine promises from the old covenant have not failed. The new and true Israel of the new covenant is in direct continuity with the Israel of old, and the Abrahamic, Mosaic, and Davidic covenants are intact and continued in the new covenant of Christ.

Their status: adoption, glory, covenants (9:4a)

Paul begins his list of the blessings Israel has received with their adoption to the status of sonship. This echoes the emphasis of 8:15–17, 23, but it is not the same relationship as the adoption of Christians in 8:15–17. Instead, it describes the corporate status of the nation as God's children (Exod 4:22–23; Isa 1:2; Hos 11:1; 12:9). For Paul it is an ongoing relationship, though endangered by the people's rejection of the gospel. The status is very real, but there is no guarantee for the salvation of individual Israelites, which is dependent on faith. What is guaranteed is God's special favor toward the nation as God's covenant people. In this way there is continuity between the two groups, Israel of the old covenant and the new Israel in Christ, composed of believing Jews and Gentiles.

The second blessing is "the divine glory," a reference to the **Shekinah** presence of God among his people. The Shekinah appeared in the exodus with the pillar of fire by night and the cloud by day (Exod 13:21–22), the cloud covering Sinai at the giving of the law (Exod 24:15–17), and the cloud filling the temple at its dedication (1 Kgs 8:10–11). The glory of God "dwelling" (from the Hebrew *shakan*, "to dwell") among his people stemmed from his gracious love and was a sign of their status as the chosen people. Paul stresses the glory of God shared with his people throughout Romans (5:2; 8:17, 18, 21, 30), and is another point of continuity between the two eras of salvation history.

The third blessing is "the covenants." Some interpreters think this should be restricted to the Abrahamic or the Mosaic covenant, but the plural indicates Paul has all of them in mind— Noah (Gen 9:9), Abraham (Gen 12:1–3; 15:1–21), Isaac and Jacob (Gen 26:3–55; 28:10–15), Moses (Exod 19:5–6; 24:7–8), David (2 Sam 23:5), and perhaps the "new covenant" of Jeremiah 31:31–34. Each covenant emphasized the place of Israel in God's plan.

Their gifts: law, temple, promises (9:4b)

First in the second tier of blessings is "the receiving of the law" (Greek: *nomothesia*). While all agree that this is a reference to Sinai, scholars debate whether it refers to the giving (KJV, ESV, CSB, LEB, NASB, NET, NLT, NRSV) or the receiving of the law (NIV). Both are possible. Psalm 9:21 and Hebrews 7:11; 8:6 emphasize the giving of the law, and the context in those passages slightly favors the centrality of the blessings God has given Israel, so I prefer "giving of the law" here. Moreover, the receiving would have a negative air, as Israel rarely had kept the law, and the stress here is on the gifts of God. The law was the sign of God's favor to his chosen people and signified the wisdom and knowledge of God given to enable his people to walk with him rightly.

The second gift, paralleling the "glory" of the first set, is "the temple worship" (Greek: *latreia*). Probably this broadly refers to the entire worship system, including the sacrificial system as well as the temple services. Since the Israelites' experience of the Shekinah glory was especially evident in the temple services, that was primary. The true purpose of the temple was to enable the nation to experience the presence of God in worship, and the sacrificial system was meant to enable the people to approach God ritually clean so they could worship God in his temple.

The "promises" complete the list, paralleling the covenants in the first set. The two go together, since Scripture often speaks of the "covenant promises," especially the Abrahamic promises here in Romans (4:13, 14, 16, 20; 9:8, 9; 15:8). Paul is referring here to all the covenant promises God had given to his people. While Israel often failed to fulfill its promises to God, he never failed his people, and that is Paul's primary point in this section.

Their ancestry: the patriarchs and the Messiah (9:5)
This verse consummates the blessings listed in verse 4, as most of them relate in some fashion or another to the patriarchs (the past) and culminate in the Messiah (the present), the first and the last of God's great gifts to his people. The patriarchs (Abraham, Isaac, and Jacob) received the three versions of the Abrahamic covenant noted above, and they were in a sense the founding fathers of Israel. The promises given to the patriarchs were behind the sense of Israel as the special possession of God, so the heritage of the nation came from them. In 11:28 Paul will say that the election of the Jewish people as the beloved of God came "on account of the patriarchs." Everything they are and everything they were destined to become stems from these fathers of the nation.

Another core blessing is the messianic line, "the human ancestry of the Messiah." The Messiah is the culmination of the blessings poured out on Israel. The Greek literally means "theirs" are the patriarchs and "from whom" is the Messiah, and the antecedent is the same for both: Israel. It is the nation rather than the patriarchs "from whom" the Messiah has come. This makes the tragedy all the greater, for God sent the Messiah, originated from the Jewish people, yet they greeted this divine gift with unbelief.

Paul concludes with a note of worship that celebrates this wondrous gift of the Messiah. The question is whether this doxology affirms the deity of Christ. The key to finding an answer is the punctuation. If we place a period after Christ, the ascription centers on God rather than Christ, as in the RSV (also REB, TEV), "of their race, according to the flesh, is the Christ. God who is over all be blessed forever. Amen." If we place a comma there, it affirms the deity of Christ, as in the NIV (also KJV, NASV, ESV, NLT, LEB, NET), "the human ancestry of the Messiah, who is God over all, forever praised! Amen." Doxologies tend to be connected to their preceding context, and if God the Father was the object of worship here, one would expect that to be indicated in the context. It is Christ who is foremost in 9:1–5, so he is the object of worship in this doxology. Most of those who opt for the first reading also say that Paul does not call Jesus God in his writings, yet he does so clearly in Titus 2:13; Philippians 2:6; and Colossians 1:15. Here, too, he is praising Jesus as God.

The greatest gift of all is that God himself should become incarnate in Jesus and become the suffering servant who gives his life for the salvation of sinners (Phil 2:6–8). He is supreme "over all," meaning cosmic lordship over all creation (Col 1:15–18). As God, he is sovereign Lord over the universe, the history of this world, and all beings, good and evil, that inhabit his creation. This is the one Paul's kindred, the Jews, are rejecting. He is not only Messiah but also God himself, and so the Jewish people refuse to believe in their God, their Creator. The "Amen" is a formal closing affirmation to the validity of such worship (as in 1:25; 11:36; 15:33; 16:27).

PAUL DISCUSSES THE DIFFERENCE BETWEEN
NATIONAL ISRAEL AND TRUE ISRAEL (9:6-13)

The key to the issue Paul is addressing in chapters 9–11 is found
in 9:6, 14. From verse 6 it seems many of the Jewish Christians
in Rome and elsewhere were asking if "God's word had failed."
God's covenant promises had centered on Israel, and the Gentiles
as far as most Jews were concerned were excluded from those
promises. Now that promise had been turned on its head, and the
Gentiles seemed to have taken the central place, especially since
Paul had become "missionary to the Gentiles." The question from
verse 14 grew out of this: if God had indeed turned from the Jews
to embrace the Gentiles, was he unjust? He had promised an eternal covenant to Israel as his special people, and it seemed he had
totally reversed his position vis-à-vis the Jews and the Gentiles.

The message of 9:6–29 is that in God's economy national identity was never meant to guarantee that a person belonged to God's
family. This was a misunderstanding that grew out of the view
that only the Jews were God's elect people. But God, not Israel, is
sovereign over salvation. He alone decides and has predetermined
who will receive his mercy and love. He clearly intended the Gentiles to be part of this, as in the Abrahamic covenant (Gen 12:3;
18:18; 22:18; 26:4).

There are three parts to Paul's emphasis on God's sovereignty
in election: national Israel versus true Israel (vv. 6–13); the righteousness of God and his freedom to have mercy on whom he
wishes (vv. 14–23); and God's call of the Gentiles as well as the
Jews (vv. 24–29). We will look at the first part here, and the second
two in the next chapter.

THESIS: GOD'S WORD HAS NOT FAILED (9:6)

Paul responds to the question of whether God's word must have
failed by saying that the problem was not with God. Instead, it was
with the Jewish misunderstanding of their identity as God's chosen
people. By equating their national identity with their spiritual

standing before God, they had assumed a false reality. It is not ancestry but spiritual commitment and obedience that matters. It is God who sovereignly chooses; he has not promised salvation by birthright.

Before concluding that God's word had failed, some of Paul's audience must have assumed that Israel's extravagant privileges should result in God's wholesale acceptance of the Jewish people. In fact, they may have thought that a "conversion" should not even be needed, and that membership in the church should automatically be extended as another of the blessings accorded to the people of the old covenant.[1]

Paul responds that "not all who are descended from Israel are Israel," rejecting the erroneous belief that being the people of God was a Jewish birthright. There is national Israel, and there is spiritual or true Israel; the two are not synonymous. As he proved in 3:21–4:25, one can only join the true (spiritual) covenant people by faith. True Israel consists only of those Jews (and Gentiles) who put their faith in Christ.

EXAMPLE 1: CHOICE OF ISAAC OVER ISHMAEL (9:7–9)

In Romans 9:7–13 Paul restates the point of verse 6 (not all national Israel is spiritual Israel) via two examples: the choice between two with the same father but different mothers (Isaac and Ishmael), and between two with the same father and mother (Jacob and Esau). The second intensifies the first and proves even more strongly that it is God's sovereign choice rather than his covenant obligation that determines who his true people are.

God chose Isaac, the child of promise (9:7–8)

Just because Jews are Abraham's "descendants" does not mean they are actually "Abraham's children." Birth is inadequate for actual

---

1. Some preachers today still make this claim, and it is a heresy. Only faith in Christ, not national identity, can make a person a child of God.

sonship; only faith is sufficient. To anchor the point Paul quotes Genesis 21:12, "It is through Isaac that your offspring will be reckoned." God spoke these words when Abraham was distressed at sending Ishmael and his mother Hagar away. God reminded him that his posterity was promised through Isaac, not Ishmael, and he was to dismiss Ishmael in order to protect the messianic line.

Paul is emphasizing two things with this quotation. First, "reckoned" is literally "called," and it has a double meaning, stressing that the true successor can be recognized in Isaac and that God has chosen or elected the true lineage (Isaac) rather than the false one (Ishmael). Second, the calling takes place "in" (Greek: *en*) Isaac, referring not just to physical descent but to the spiritual offspring, the promised people who would constitute the children of the covenant (Gen 17:21, 21:2).

In verse 8 Paul interprets the Genesis quotation, beginning with "in other words" to make sure his readers understand. Isaac and Ishmael signify the contrast between "the natural children" (Ishmael; "children by physical descent" NIV) and "the children of promise" (Isaac). It is through God's "promises" and not through "the flesh" (literally "according to the flesh" in vv. 3, 5) that true Israel will be found. Ishmael came through a purely fleshly union, while Isaac was the child of promise.

The children of promise are "regarded as Abraham's offspring." This echoes Genesis 15:6, the core to the faith section of Romans 3:21–4:25, "Abraham believed God, and it was credited [= "regarded as" here] to him as righteousness." Moreover, "the promise" is reminiscent of the grace of God shown in 4:13–20, so this passage refers to the grace of God poured out on God's covenant people in bringing them to salvation. This is the principle of "grace rather than race." It provides the key to the issue of Jew and Gentile in God's plan. When Gentiles believe they become the children of the covenant and join believing Jews to form the new Israel.

God Fulfills His Promise (9:9)

This verse culminates this paragraph by clarifying the meaning of "promise" with respect to the Genesis 21:12 quotation (v. 8), showing that it refers to the promises of God fulfilled in the Jewish mission. Paul considers that quotation one of the covenant promises since Isaac's birth was a direct act of God foreseen by a divine promise (Gen 17:15–16; 21:12). This is anchored further in two further promises, Genesis 18:10, 14, which Paul has brought together and paraphrased, "At the appointed time I will return, and Sarah will have a son." The point is that the divine promise came through his choice of Isaac over Ishmael, foreshadowing God's sovereign choice in the new covenant era of some Jews (and Gentiles) over other Jews.

EXAMPLE 2: CHOICE OF JACOB OVER ESAU (9:10–13)

Had the same father (9:10)

Paul's second example of God's election is even more intense. The opening "Not only that" shows that Paul is building on the first example and taking it further. While Isaac and Ishmael had different mothers, Jacob and Esau had the same mother (Rebekah) as well as father. Both were of the promised line. They were also twins ("conceived at the same time"), and Esau was the firstborn, so God's choice reversed the regular rule of inheritance. Esau had the right of patriarchal blessing, but God chose the second son. In every legal sense, Esau had the right to become head of the family. Yet God chose to go against normal procedure and anoint Jacob as the chosen one. It was not birthright (race) but divine will (grace) that led to God's choice of Jacob over Esau.

Jacob chose not on the basis of works (9:11–12)

Paul explains the conundrum more carefully in these verses. God's choice of Jacob over Esau took place "before the twins were born or had done anything good or bad." This idea is at the core of predestination theology: God makes his choice entirely on the basis of his predetermined will, which occurs "before the creation of the world" (Eph 1:4; 1 Pet 1:20), or in this case before the individuals were ever born. God's election of Jacob was not based on who he was or what he had done but because God for his own reasons willed it so.

The purpose of God's sovereign choice was "in order that God's purpose in election might stand." Paul does not explain what constituted God's "purpose in election." From the context it is likely that it refers to the promised line that ran through the patriarchal period and led to the Messiah (see v. 5). The choice of Jacob over Esau, Paul wants his readers to understand, had nothing to do with which child had greater potential or had done better things. Neither one had much to commend them. Esau was a sensual hedonist, and Jacob lived up to his name, which meant "deceiver" or "trickster." God made the choice on the basis of his divine plan; "purpose" (*prothesis*) here is the same term as in 8:28, "called according to his purpose." God had a goal for his chosen people, and his plan unfolded by electing Jacob to the patriarchal office. His design for his people Israel demanded Isaac rather than Ishmael and Jacob rather than Esau. Note that the divine purpose/plan in the end would "stand," that is, remain certain. When we pray, "God's will be done," we have this in mind. The sovereign will of God stands sure.

Paul goes on to explain in verse 12 that election "not by works." The children had not been born yet and thus had done neither good works nor bad when God made the decision. In Genesis 25, before the twins were born, God foretold the significance of the birth, that two nations would emerge through them and that surprisingly "the older will serve the younger." For Paul this was a prophecy fulfilled in salvation history, with Jacob the father of God's chosen people who would inherit the promised land—the inheritance promised the faithful. Election is based entirely on the one "who calls" rather than external or earthly reasons.

Result: Loved Jacob, hated Esau (9:13)

This is a summary of the issues and the climax of verses 7–12. Paul quotes Malachi, a postexilic prophet, as saying "Jacob I loved, but Esau I hated" (Mal 1:2–3). Malachi is explaining why God is blessing the nation of Israel (Jacob is given the name "Israel" in Gen 32:28) and punishing the nation of Edom (Esau is called "Edom" in Gen 25:30; 36:1). In Malachi the quotation is corporate, referring to the two nations, but here Paul uses it to explain the process of predestination. God on the basis of his elect will is choosing one group descending from the patriarchs and rejecting another group, so there is both a corporate and an individual aspect here.

Still, this quotation seems overly harsh. If Paul meant the language literally, it would be. However, this language is almost certainly a Near Eastern figure of speech of acceptance ("I love") and rejection ("I hate"). God has chosen Israel over Edom in Old Testament history, from the patriarchs (Genesis) to the postexilic period (Malachi). Paul intends his readers to see in this a **typological** significance: God has chosen believing Jews (Isaac) over the unbelievers in Israel (Esau). God has the right to make his sovereign choice, and as we will see in verses 19–21, we have no right to question his decision.

Some interpreters bring up the issue of double predestination here. This is the view that God has made two choices: some for eternal life and others for everlasting punishment. Yet while this idea may be present, it is only part of the picture, and Paul stresses human responsibility in 9:30–10:21.

In fact, while a case can be made that Paul is talking about predestination (either single or double), it is too early to make a decision. Paul is not developing a systematic theology but addressing one issue. Two passages thus far in Romans have touched on election (8:28–30; 9:7–13), but we need all of the material on 8:28–11:36 before drawing a conclusion. We must consider human responsibility and the issue of faith and works before we can put together a dogmatic hypothesis. I will develop such a summary statement at the end of Romans 10.

———

This is an important passage on the issue of theodicy, the defense of God's goodness. Israel had never in its history been more faithful to the law than from 400 BC to AD 100. But when Jesus came, he was rejected by his fellow Jews, and God turned from them to embrace the Gentiles. As a result some Jewish Christians began to doubt the justice of God and thought his covenant promises to the nation had failed. Paul addresses this line of thought in chapters 9–11.

In 9:1–5 he demonstrates that God's blessings have not ceased but continue in the new Israel, those believing Jews and Gentiles who turned to Christ. God has not failed; rather, the majority of the Jewish people have failed.

The second paragraph begins Paul's presentation of why God's word and promises indeed have not failed: he has the sovereign right to choose whomever he wills. The two examples center on the patriarchal line and build in intensity. A great title for a sermon on this paragraph would be "grace rather than race," and it would apply quite well to racial issues today. God has decided that all peoples of the earth (Jews and Gentiles) are equal in his family and that racial and ethnic divides will cease. This proves not only that God refuses to play favorites but also that his family refuses to be divided by such differences. To be the children of God means to accept each other as thoroughly as God accepts us.

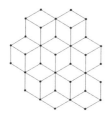

GOD CHOOSES AND ESTABLISHES
A NEW COMMUNITY
(9:14-29)

Paul has shown that God's word and promises have not failed, and that God never leaves his people. As Lord of all, he has the right to choose whomever he will. However, his will to reject many who belong to his covenant community has led to the accusation that he is unjust to his people (v. 14). So Paul turns once more to his diatribe method (as in Romans 2-3), in which he asks rhetorical questions that anticipate potential complaints and then answers them. This section reiterates the point of verses 7-13, that God is free to choose whomever he wishes. In one sense this leaves us unsatisfied, because a full defense of God's elective will should discuss the issue of human choice and the part it plays in the process. However, Paul is saving that question for later (9:30-10:21).

GOD IS FREE TO CHOOSE (9:14-23)

Verses 14-23 come in three parts: In verse 14 Paul presents the basic question regarding the justice of God, then in verses 15-18 he explains that God's justice is actually divine mercy at work. Finally, in verses 19-23 he uses a series of questions to go deeper into the issue of God's sovereign right to bring glory to himself in any way he wishes.

THE DILEMMA: IS GOD UNJUST? (9:14)

Paul has used the formula, "What then shall we say?" several times (3:5; 4:1, 6:1; 7:7; 8:31) to introduce potential misunderstandings of his teaching. This is one of the most serious errors, questioning divine justice regarding the exclusion of unbelieving Jews and the inclusion of Gentiles in God's new community. His response is immediate: "Not at all!" (see 3:4, 6, 31; 6:2, 15; 7:7, 13).

What follows is a theodicy, or defense of the righteousness of God.[1] It is natural that some would think God unjust when he accepts some (mostly Gentiles) and rejects the great majority of his covenant people, Israel. A sovereign who would ignore the merits of his own people and choose merely on the basis of his own will (9:12) would not be thought righteous, especially since righteousness would demand he be fair to his own citizens. Moreover, this would demand he be fair not only to his own people but also to his own standards and character. God had seemingly broken faith at both levels, and Paul answers both.

GOD'S JUSTICE IS ACTUALLY HIS MERCY AT WORK (9:15–18)

The word *gar* (for) introducing this passage shows Paul is providing the reason why we must reject the accusation that God is unjust. The two quotations in these verses are parallel presentations of a third illustration (after Isaac and Jacob) of God's sovereign "rightness," namely, Moses (v. 15) and Pharaoh (v. 17). God's character demands that his mercy be extended on the basis of what he decides is right. The two sections both have a citation (vv. 15, 17) followed by a conclusion (vv. 16, 18) that demonstrate the positive (Moses) and negative (Pharaoh) sides of the formula. This twofold divine will parallels "Jacob I loved, but Esau I hated" from verse 13.

---

1. The term "unjust" (*adikia*) also means "unrighteous" and suggests that what God is doing is not right.

God Chooses the Objects for His Mercy (9:15–16)

The first citation is from Exodus 33:18, where Moses asks Yahweh at Sinai, "Show me your glory," to prove to the people that his presence is with them. God responds that he will "pass in front" of Moses and "proclaim my name, Yahweh," to ratify his covenant, adding, "I will have mercy on whom I have mercy, and I will have compassion on whom I have compassion." In Exodus this meant God will have mercy and compassion on Israel even though they don't deserve it after worshipping a golden calf.

In verse 16 Paul applies this passage to the fact that God's elect will is not based on "human desire or effort" (The Greek is literally "willing or running") but entirely on "God's mercy." The "willing" happens when people decide on a course of action, and the "running" is the action that results from those decisions. This is all we humans can do, and the results are more often wrong than right. As 8:28 states, God's will arises from his perfect knowledge of what is best in any situation, and the results are never wrong and always acts of mercy.

The Example of Pharaoh (9:17–18)

In verse 17 Paul presents the negative side of the equation through the story of Pharaoh at the exodus. He cites Exodus 9:16, God's message telling Moses how to confront Pharaoh after the plague of boils has just taken place and the plague of hail is about to commence. God warns Pharaoh that he could have wiped Egypt from the earth but didn't because he had a *purpose* for Pharaoh.

Pharaoh's very existence was due to this sovereign purpose, comprising two divine intentions. First, "I raised you up for this very purpose, that I might display my power in you." Some think this is God's saving power, and others his judging power, but most likely both aspects are part of it. God's saving power was experienced by Israel (for Paul, by believing Israel), and his judging power by the Egyptians (for Paul, by unbelieving Israel).

Second, God intended that his "name might be proclaimed in all the earth." In Exodus this took place through the plagues and the exodus of Israel from Egypt to the promised land, with the known world watching (see Josh 2:9–10; 9:9). For Paul the rejection of the Jewish people led to the mission of the gospel to the Gentiles. In other words, even when human evil forces God to act negatively, incredible good results. Nothing greater could be imagined than God's power made evident and his good news proclaimed worldwide!

Paul's conclusion in verse 18 can cover verses 7–13, 15–16, as well as verse 17: "God has mercy on whom he wants to have mercy, and he hardens whom he wants to harden." Mercy and justice are interdependent aspects of God's holy character, and placing mercy and hardening side by side sums up the message of the entire section (9:6–29). Exodus states often that God "hardened Pharaoh's heart,"[2] meaning that God made him stubborn and unyielding. At the same moment in history God chose to mercifully liberate his Jewish people from slavery in Egypt, he did so by hardening Pharaoh. The hardening was used to show mercy.

The point in Exodus and Romans is that God did so to accomplish his own purposes. There has been too much debate on whether God hardened him or Pharaoh hardened his own heart.[3] In Exodus both are true, and the final answer is another one we will know only when we get to heaven. It is not an issue here. Paul's emphasis is on God's sovereign decision (and right) to harden Pharaoh.

<hr />

2. Exod 4:21; 7:3, 13, 14, 22; 8:15, 19, 32; 9:7, 12, 34, 35; 10:1, 20, 27; 11:10; 14:4, 8, 17.

3. As said in Exod 7:14, 22; 8:11, 15, 28; 9:33; 13:15.

GOD'S RIGHT TO BRING GLORY TO HIMSELF (9:19–23)

The Charge: God Cannot Blame Us (9:19)

This paragraph starts with an imaginary objector ("One of you will say to me") complaining that if God indeed does harden people, he has no right to blame anyone for doing wrong, since they are hardly "able to resist his will" and refuse to perform those evil acts God has willed them to do. As in verse 14, God is charged with injustice for acting against his covenant promises. To resist him Israel would have to refuse to act in accordance with his will. Therefore God cannot blame Israel, who has no ability to resist hardening. If all resistance is predetermined, no guilt can be assigned.

The Response: The Potter and the Clay (9:20–21)

Paul counters that the charge is illegitimate. It is not that there is no answer; rather, we do not even have any right to ask such a thing. The Greek, "But who are you, O man" (NIV "a human being") is not just a mild "my dear sir," but contrasts "man" with "God" to charge that the objector is stating things from a merely human perspective. The vast gulf that separates "man" from God renders such demurrals inadequate. Humankind has neither the right nor the wisdom to talk back to God in this way. Mere created creatures dare not tell their Creator what to do, nor should they question their Creator's decision as to how he runs *his* world.

Paul anchors this assertion in a citation from Isaiah 29:16 ("Shall what is formed say to the one who formed it"), to which he adds an echo of Isaiah 45:9 ("Why did you make me like this?"). Both passages stem from the metaphor of the potter and the clay, saying that mere mortals are nothing more than clay pots with respect to God and cannot complain to their maker for molding them in the fashion he desires. Isaiah, like Paul, was addressing God's judgment on the nation, so the parallel is exact. The point is that the creature has no place talking back to its creator.

So in verse 21 he asks, "Does not the potter have the right to make out of the same lump of clay some pottery for special purposes and some for common use?" Literally, the Greek is translated "some for honor, some for dishonor." This parallels 2 Timothy 2:20, in which Paul speaks of vessels in a house: "some are for special purposes and some for common use."[4] In one sense the lump of clay is Israel, with the honorable use being a member of God's family and the dishonorable use those destined for damnation in the sense of Pharaoh.

As in verses 6–13, there is debate as to whether this should be interpreted corporately or individually. Most likely both Israel and the church as well as individual believers and unbelievers are in Paul's mind. In light of chapter 9 as a whole, certainly Paul means this to address why so many in Israel have not found salvation. What is the national future of Israel, and how does it relate to the church? Paul's discussion also links with the question of predestination to salvation (vessels for honor) and damnation (vessels for dishonor).

God created humanity with full knowledge of the fall and so provided a Savior who would die for the sins of all humankind. Many sinners would repent in faith, but the majority would refuse and prefer to live in sin. God foreknew both and destined some to salvation and others to damnation. What we have yet to decide is the relationship between these three factors—God's foreknowledge, the decisions of individuals, and God's predetermined decision. We will continue to work at this. Did God create some sinners in order to punish them (like Pharaoh)? We will see, and draw conclusions at the end of chapter 10.

---

4. See also Job 10:9; 38:4; Ps 2:9; Isa 41:25; 45:9; 64:7; Jer 18:5–10; Sirach 27:5; 33:13; Wisdom of Solomon 15:7.

God's Great Patience: To Make His Power and Glory Known (9:22-23)

In these verses Paul unveils God the Potter's choice to honor some and dishonor others in order to make both his power (v. 22) and glory (v. 23) known. The grammar of these verses is difficult. There is an "if" clause but no "then" clause, reading literally, "If God, wanting to demonstrate his wrath ... bore with great patience." To clarify this, some have translated the verse, "What if God, although he wanted" (NIV, NLT, NASB, JB) while others translate, "because [or untranslated] he wanted" (KJV, ESV, LEB, NET, NRSV). Both make sense, but the second (causal) is better in a context emphasizing God's sovereign choice.

The verb "bore" (Greek: *pherō*) means to "bear patiently, endure, put up with"; Paul lays great emphasis on the longsuffering of God, both in this verb and then stressing it in the phrase "great patience." In Exodus the object of God's patience is Pharaoh and the Egyptians; in Romans 9 it is the unbelieving Jews. Paul is thus pointing to a salvation-historical movement, progressing from the redemption of Israel to the inauguration of the new Israel, but it is also individual, as God puts up with us in our failures.

Wrath and mercy are interdependent, for the outpouring of wrath is often the vehicle of divine mercy in bringing his people to their knees so that they return to him. This is not double predestination, for the vessels are "prepared for destruction" on the basis of unbelief, and in that very condemnation they are also "objects of his mercy" (see further below). As in 10:1-15 and 11:25-32, the present "objects of his wrath" are also the objects of God's patient call to salvation. He is truly "not wanting anyone to perish, but everyone to come to repentance" (2 Pet 3:9). The final "destruction" here is the result of unbelief and not just God's predetermined will.

Three purposes are made clear in these verses:

(1) God intends to "show his wrath," his righteous anger toward sinful, unbelieving humanity. Yet it is important to study carefully the relationship between their unbelief, God's preparing them for

destruction, and the gospel being proclaimed to them. I will continue to discuss this throughout Romans 9–11, but my tentative conclusion is that their unbelief brought about the wrath, and that there is still an opportunity for them to repent. This is not the unpardonable sin, on which see Mark 3:28–29; Hebrews 6:4–6; 1 John 5:16.

(2) God also wants to "make his power known." Originally, God displayed these acts of power in the Egyptian plagues and the destruction of their armies. The divine omnipotence was also demonstrated in the miracles of the Gospels and Acts, and those displays became part of the mission of the church. In verse 17 Paul quoted Exodus to demonstrate that God displayed his power so that his "name might be proclaimed in all the earth," a motivation that was also true in Paul's day, and still is in ours (see 10:8–10 for the word of power to the lost). God's "power" constitutes both his saving power and his judging power.

(3) The first two purposes point to this third one, which culminates the list and constitutes the primary goal, "to make the riches of his glory known to the objects of his mercy." This purpose also contrasts with the first two, which center on the negative goal of judging sinners, while this third one centers on mercy for the repentant. We turn from wrath to mercy, with the "vessels [skeuos] of wrath" (v. 22 ESV) being unbelieving Jews and the "vessels of mercy" (v. 23 ESV) being believing Jews. The "riches of his glory" connote the blessings of salvation, seen also in the "riches" of Romans 2:4; 11:12; Ephesians 1:7, 18; 2:7. In his salvation God's glory is manifested.

In the very way he "prepared" the vessels of wrath for "destruction," he has "prepared" the vessels of mercy, repentant sinners, "in advance for glory." Both sides of this are part of his predetermined will, but as I have been saying, this does not necessarily imply double predestination. Salvation is produced in the elect, but there is a dynamic relationship at both levels (wrath and

mercy) between faith-decision or rejection and God's granting
of salvation. The "glory" is both the present experience of glory
via becoming part of God's family and the final glory of eternal
life in heaven. The present glory anticipates the final glory that
will be ours.

THE NEW COMMUNITY IS MADE OF THE
REMNANT AND THE GENTILES (9:24-29)

Paul culminates this section (9:6-29) with a collage of Old Testament quotations that tells how God foretold his rejection of the
apostate nation and his turn to the righteous Israelite remnant
and the Gentiles. These citations prove his claim in verse 24 that
God from the start intended to call both Jews and Gentiles to himself. The whole of chapter 9 has progressed to this moment. People
become members of God's family not on the basis of their birthright or rights as the covenant people (vv. 3-4, 7-8) but on the basis
of the divine call (God's response to the faith of 3:21-4:25). Membership in the covenant community descended from Abraham was
no longer required for inclusion among God's people, and that was
shocking to most Jewish Christians.

CALLED PEOPLE FROM THE JEWS AND THE GENTILES (9:24)

In one sense this verse continues verses 22-23. However, it actually introduces a new issue and begins the final paragraph of this
section on God's electing a new people to himself. This chapter has
centered on the two charges of verses 6 (have God's covenant promises failed?) and 14 (is God unjust?). There the issue was the exclusion of the majority of Jews for unbelief. Now Paul adds the second
issue, God's calling people "not only from the Jews but also from
the Gentiles." This was a huge issue in the first-century church.

CHOICE OF THE GENTILES (9:25-26)

Here Paul quotes two key passages from Hosea and reverses
them for topical purposes. The book of Hosea addresses the

northern tribes (Israel during the era of the divided monarchy) and describes the wrath of God upon them for their sin. God leads the prophet Hosea to name his children *Lo-ruhamah* ("not loved," 1:6) and *Lo-ammi* ("not my people," 1:9) as illustrations of his indictment against the nation. The two citations here are part of God's promise in Hosea to the faithful remnant that he would indeed remove his judgment on his people and reinstate them as his people and the objects of his love.

In the first quotation, from Hosea 2:23, the names of the two children are applied and overturned. Those who were formerly "not my people" and "not my loved one" would be returned and forgiven. Paul uses a loose citation, changing Hosea's "I will say" to "I will call" and reversing the clauses so the citation can begin with "I will call." In this way he builds upon the call of the Gentiles in verse 24 and culminates the themes of 9:6–23 regarding the call of God to join his people. "Call" frames the two Hosea quotations of verses 25–26, beginning the first and ending the second.

Paul is using **typology** here, in which an Old Testament principle is applied and reenacted in a New Testament situation. He sees the promise to the northern kingdom of Israel as fulfilled in the new Israel that includes the Gentiles. The two major kinds of typological exegesis we see in the New Testament are applying passages to Christ and the church. Paul is applying the Hosea passage to both here, but especially the church. Salvation for the Gentiles is the proper next stage of salvation history and also a fulfillment of prophecy. Those who for generations were the enemies of God's people will now be "my people" and "my loved one."

The second citation, from Hosea 1:10 (v. 26), is drawn from the **Septuagint** (Greek Old Testament) and tells the results of the first one. Those who were formerly "not my people'" are now called the children of the living God (see Rom 8:15–16). Not only is the rejection of the Gentiles over; but it has also resulted in a radical new birthright and status as a member of God's family along with believing Jews to constitute a new and true Israel. This will happen in "the very place" where they were called "not my people." In Hosea this was probably Babylon, the place of exile, but for Paul this is fulfilled in the Gentile mission. God's call in the new Israel is inclusive of all peoples worldwide. As in Ephesians 2:14-18 "the barrier, the dividing wall of hostility," has been removed, and Christ has created "one new humanity" in its stead.

The implications are enormous. For the church, racial divides have evaporated and ethnic tensions dissolved. We should celebrate our differences and rejoice in the privilege of learning from each other. We should move out of our comfort zone: suburban churches should have a ministry presence in the inner city, and urban churches should minister to the suburbs. Tribalism can be healed in the new reality of Christ and his one people. God is calling the church to find solutions for old animosities and to relieve hatred with the love and forgiveness Christ alone can truly bring to all peoples.

A REMNANT WILL BE SAVED (9:27-28)

In these verses Paul shifts his attention from the Gentiles back to the Jewish people, specifically those "called ... from the Jews" (v. 24). A good part of the nation has been excluded, but a portion remains, and Isaiah "cries out" to that remnant. Paul takes this citation from Isaiah 10:22-23, interspersed with "the number of the Israelites" from Hosea 1:10 (Isaiah has "your people, O Israel"). Paul draws the two passages together to emphasize the church as made up of Gentiles (Hosea in vv. 25-26) and a remnant from the Jews (Isaiah).

In Isaiah these verses are part of an oracle (Isaiah 7-12) asking Israel whether they wish to put their trust in Assyria or God. If they trust in Assyria they will be destroyed, but not all of them. A remnant will be spared—but only a remnant. Paul sees in the Israel of Isaiah's day a parallel with Israel in his own day. The nation is indicted for unbelief. The vast majority of Jews will fall under God's judgment and are reserved by him for judgment.

"Only the remnant will be saved." For Paul this remnant is the believing Jews. God has called only a few to himself, and these constitute true Israel (Rom 9:6–7a). In the first century an innumerable number of Israelites ("like the sand by the sea") have been rejected for failure to keep the covenant, this time the final covenant instituted by Israel's Messiah. But for Isaiah and Paul, God is still faithful to his promises. The apostate nation has forfeited its covenant rights, and is no longer numbered among God's people. The people of Paul's day have reenacted the failure of those in Isaiah's day by rejecting their Messiah and are suffering the same fate.

However, this is not primarily a prophecy of judgment, for the real stress is on the remnant who will be spared. In this there is mercy and hope for Israel. God is keeping his covenant promises, and as in the exile God is using judgment to bring his fallen nation back to him. God is ensuring a future for national Israel, and in chapter 11 Paul will carry this theme of the remnant and national revival forward.

Still, the second half of the quotation gives serious warning to readers (v. 28), "the Lord will carry out his sentence on earth with speed and finality." The legal "sentence" (the Greek literally means "word" or "decree") is divine judgment on those who are unrepentant and guilty of unbelief. It is less clear what "speed and finality" means. The second is a rare term (here only in the New Testament and seven times in the Septuagint) meaning to "cut short" a thing. In different contexts it can refer to time (indicating here a swift or speedy judgment), number (that only a few are saved), or to a decisive or final verdict. Since these words modify the sentence that is carried out, the third makes best sense.

So I would translate, "The Lord will carry out his sentence of judgment completely and decisively [or "with completeness and finality"]." In Isaiah it is primarily the judgment on recalcitrant Israel, while here it is probably both the divine act of mercy toward the remnant and judgment on the unbelieving nation. In both instances God is faithful to his promises, for they flow out of the blessings and curses that characterize the covenant (Lev 26).

God's Mercy (9:29)

The concluding citation comes from Isaiah 1:9 and once more centers on God's mercy upon his undeserving people. Isaiah at the start of his work rebukes Israel for its rebellion (1:2, 5) and corruption (1:4), foretelling God's judgment upon it (1:7–8). In 1:9, he writes that "unless the Lord Almighty had left us" survivors/descendants, they would have been completely wiped out like Sodom and Gomorrah (Gen 19). The central term is "descendants" (or "seed"), which links this verse with Romans 9:7–9, the choice of Isaac over Ishmael and the choice to restrict Abraham's "seed" to the descendants of Isaac.

Israel in both Isaiah's and Paul's days deserved to be destroyed for its rebellion and unbelief, and only divine mercy had kept it from the same oblivion as Sodom and Gomorrah. The "seed" or descendants God had allowed to remain is the remnant of verse 27. In spite of the tragic situation, the future is hopeful: God is faithful to keep his promises (answering the charge of v. 6), and his justice is at work both in his mercy and his judgment (answering the charge of v. 14).

––––

Both parts of 9:14–29 answer the question of divine justice by emphasizing God's sovereign right and freedom to choose, a doctrine we call predestination. In the first half (vv. 14–23) Paul tells us that God's justice is his mercy at work. When God hardened Pharaoh's heart, his justice against Egypt proved merciful for Israel in forcing the Egyptians to let his people go. He knows best, not us. This is the same issue as in the prayer theology of 8:26–27. We don't know what is best for us and in our prayers must submit to the will of the One who alone does. God never fails us, and his judgments are always just and right.

God's actions with believers and unbelievers alike bring glory to his name. His patience with us demonstrates his mercy. Even the vessels of wrath (sinners and unbelievers) proclaim to all "the riches of his glory," both his love and justice. By including the Gentiles as well as the covenant people of Israel God has shown the depth of his love, and in pouring out his judgment upon those who turn against him he demonstrates his justice. The two, his love and his justice, are interdependent aspects of his holiness.

The final section of this portion of Romans, 9:24–29, centers on the new community composed of Jews and Gentiles who have come to Christ in faith. The old hatred and racial prejudices that characterize fallen humanity since Adam evaporate in a new oneness established in Christ. Differences of color and ethnic divides disappear when God's mercy and love weld together all disparate peoples and establish peace and reconciliation.

Paul's answer regarding the rejection and justice poured out upon the majority of Israel, the unbelieving Jews, is found in the concept of the remnant from Isaiah. The nation of Isaiah's day is being reenacted in the Israel of Paul's day. The majority of the Jewish people have turned from God, and he has thus rejected them, but there is still hope, for God has once more saved for himself a remnant through whom his covenant promises are still in effect. The message for us is that God is always faithful to his promises. Even when our actions have brought divine judgment down on our heads, God is acting redemptively to bring us back to him. God's acts of mercy and judgment are carried out with finality (v. 28), and in both he acts with righteousness and justice. As we experience God's hand at work in our lives, it will not always be pleasant, but it will always be fair and best for us.

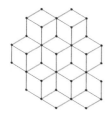

ISRAEL RESPONSIBLE FOR
REJECTING GOD'S OFFER, PART 1:
RIGHTEOUSNESS AND SALVATION BY FAITH
(9:30–10:13)

A s noted previously, Romans 9–11 is Paul's attempt to explain two seemingly contradictory realities. On the one hand, God had promised to be faithful and just to the Jews. On the other hand, few of them had been converted, and Gentiles had been inserted into the covenant people in their place. Paul answers this charge first by pointing to the sovereign right of God to choose whom he wishes (9:6–29), and second by emphasizing the responsibility of Israel to accept God's gift of salvation by faith (9:30–10:21). These two facets demonstrate God's fairness and justice to his people. Unbelieving Jews cannot blame God for their situation, for God has been faithful to his promises while they have been unfaithful in fulfilling their responsibility to accept God's Messiah by faith.

The primary emphases in this section are the call to "righteousness" (six times), and the necessity of "faith" or belief (twelve times). Righteousness is a gift from God attained only by faith, and Paul frames this section with passages placing in contrast the exclusion of Israel and the inclusion of the Gentiles (9:30–32; 10:19–21). The Jews have "stumbled" (9:33) because they sought their own righteousness (10:3), responded in unbelief (10:14), and disobeyed God's call (10:21). As a result, God turned to the Gentiles and included them in his covenant people (9:30; 10:19–20).

Some scholars who wish to place human responsibility at the forefront of God's plan of salvation make this the critical section in chapters 9–11. Others who see God's sovereignty in election as the central point make this section virtually an excursus. Both are wrong. Paul places them side by side as concomitant aspects of God's plan of salvation. This is true of the Bible as a whole. Faith is not an afterthought but an essential component of the process of justification. Faith is a gift of God made possible only by his grace and mercy, but it is still exercised by each believer. God chooses them as they choose him, and the whole is made possible by the convicting presence of the Spirit.

There are three parts to this section: righteousness by faith not works (9:30–10:4); salvation by faith rather than the law (10:5–13); and Israel's guilt for rejecting the gospel (10:14–21). This chapter deals with the first two, and the third is the subject of the next chapter.

RIGHTEOUSNESS COMES BY FAITH, NOT WORKS (9:30–10:4)

Once more Paul begins with the rhetorical question, "What then shall we say?" (see the commentary on 8:31). Here Paul is not so much answering the mistaken notion of an opponent as he is drawing a conclusion from the previous section (9:16–29) on the issue of the inclusion of the Gentiles into God's family. Here he reintroduces one of the central concepts in Romans, righteousness/justification. As in 1:16–17 and 3:21–26, he sees it in its forensic sense as the judicial act of God in declaring people to be right with him on the basis of Christ's atoning sacrifice on the cross. Paul uses this doctrine here to explain why the Gentiles more than the Jews have entered God's family and why so many Jews are no longer part of the covenant people. In her ignorance Israel has become "zealous" for the wrong thing (10:2)—a works-righteousness centered

on keeping the law rather than a God-centered righteousness
obtained by faith (10:3). They failed to realize that Christ has ended
the law as a valid approach to God (10:4).

WHY THE GENTILES? (9:30–33)

The Gentiles obtained it by faith; the Jews did not (9:30–31)

Paul establishes in the opening two verses two contrasts between
the Jews and the Gentiles.

First, the Gentiles "did not pursue righteousness" while the
Jews "pursued the law as the way of righteousness." As in 1:18–32,
the Gentiles never sought a right standing with God at all. The Jews,
on the other hand, sought (translated literally) "a law of righteousness." This phrase has been variously understood as the "principle of righteousness," or "a righteousness attained by the law," or
"the righteous law"; almost certainly it refers to the use of the law's
regulations as the path to a right relationship with God. The imagery of pursuing evokes the picture of a racecourse and running
to win a prize (as in Phil 3:12–14). As Paul argued in Romans 2–3,
the Gentiles did not seek right standing with God and found it,
while the Jews energetically pursued it by the wrong means (the
law) and failed.

Second, the Gentiles "obtained" this right standing while the
Jewish people did not "attain their goal." They believed the law
promised a right standing with God, but when the Messiah arrived,
the law ended (10:4) as a path to righteousness. Turning to Christ
by faith became the only way to a right relationship with God.
This gets back to the faith-versus-law antithesis that dominated
chapters 4–7. The only path to attaining this right relationship
with God is to realize it "is by faith"—not by keeping the law or
by ethical living but only by turning to Christ in faith and being
justified by his blood sacrifice. Since a right relationship comes
entirely by faith, it no longer matters who pursues it but only on

what basis that pursuit takes place. The Jews no longer have an advantage over the Gentiles.

Reason: the stumbling stone (9:32–33)

Having discussed the implications of God's turning to the Gentiles, Paul once again invokes an imaginary opponent and asks, "Why not?" Why has Israel failed to attain right standing with God? Paul's answer summarizes much of the material from chapters 4–8: "they pursued it not by faith but as if it were by works" (see also 3:20, 27–28; 4:2, 6; 9:11–12). Their error is not their pursuit of righteousness but their attempt to attain it by works. It is not even that they pursued the law but that they made it the locus of salvation. They rejected God's Messiah and the salvation that could come only by faith, not works.[1] Paul may have added "as if it were" to strengthen the contrast between faith and works and possibly also to stress the illusion of their failed perspective on the law.

Paul now uses imagery from Isaiah to highlight their failure. Since they pursued righteousness by works, they "stumbled," which does not mean just that they fell into sin (as in Rom 14:21) but, as in 1 Peter 2:8, that they took offense at Christ, leading to divine judgment. Some interpreters think the stumbling stone is the Torah, but certainly it is Christ, as in all the passages in the New Testament that make use of this kind of stone imagery (Mark 12:10–11 and parallels; Acts 4:11; 1 Pet 2:6–8).

Jesus' claim to be "the cornerstone" was messianic; first-century Jewish people understood Old Testament stone passages as messianic. Yet the Isaiah citation of the next verse isn't just messianic; it adds the imagery of judgment and destruction. Those who rejected the stone stumbled over it, and then it fell on them and

---

1. For the debate on this with the "new perspective" on Paul, see the discussion at 3:20.

crushed them. The early church used this analogy to depict the
Jewish rejection of Jesus ("the stone you builders rejected," Acts
4:11; cf. 1 Pet 2:7) and the fact that God made him the chief cornerstone of his church (Mark 12:10–11).

The citation of verse 33 conflates the two stone passages in
Isaiah 8:14 and 28:16. In Isaiah they describe the Assyrian threat.
The first two lines here stem from 8:14 and warn that God will
judge Israel ("a stone that causes people to stumble"). The last two
lines stem from 28:16 and promise that God will deliver his people
("a precious cornerstone for a sure foundation"). The conflated
product becomes an excellent summary of the message about
Israel in this section—those who "believe in him" will be saved,
and those who "stumble" will be destroyed.

For those Jews who have rejected their Messiah and refused
to believe, he has become "a stone that causes people to stumble
and a rock that makes them fall." Those Jews (and Gentiles) who
believe will "never be put to shame" at the last judgment. Throughout Scripture "shame" means much more than sorrow and embarrassment but refers to terrible judgment. Those who put their trust
in Christ will be vindicated when they stand before God and give
account for their lives.

WHY NOT ISRAEL? (10:1–4)

Paul's desire for their salvation (10:1)

Beginning with "Brothers and sisters," Paul shifts to another aspect
of his message by reiterating his concern for his kindred people,
the Jews. He takes no joy in proclaiming judgment, for his deep-
seated desire is for their salvation. "Desire" uses a term (*eudokia*)
that means more than merely what he wants, for its primary
thrust points to the "goodwill" or "favor" that leads to the desire.
Paul's mention of his "heart" means that his desire for their salvation comes from the deepest level of his being. He is hurt by their

animosity toward the Lord and wants them to join him in worshipping their Messiah.

This concern is reflected in his prayer "that they may be saved." Paul has said in 9:33 that those who believe will "never be put to shame," and he weeps at the thought of his Jewish countrymen standing before God in everlasting shame and judgment. He prays in the depth of his being that his people will put their faith in Christ and fulfill the hope that he will express in 11:25-26, that although "Israel has experienced a hardening ... all Israel will be saved." Paul prays that the people of his day will be part of that miraculous revival.

Zeal without knowledge (10:2)

The reason (*gar*, "for") for Paul's prayer for their salvation is his personal testimony regarding how "zealous" they are "for God." Paul is not just a witness; he was the major example of that zeal before he came to know Christ. He was one of the most ardent Jews of his day (Acts 26:4-5) and even led the persecution against the Christians in Jerusalem (Acts 8:10-11). When Christ appeared to him in a vision on the road to Damascus he was taking letters from the Jerusalem authorities giving him authority to lead the persecution outside Jerusalem (Acts 9:1-3).

"Zeal" refers to a passionate desire to serve and worship God and to uphold the traditional ways. Paul spoke of his own zeal for the law and God in Galatians 1:13-14 and Philippians 3:4-6. Though we could say that the time from about 400 BC to AD 100 was the most extended period of zealous regard to follow the law in the history of the Jewish people, the problem, especially in Paul's day, was that "their zeal is not based on knowledge." Paul's persecution of Christians was part of a zealous desire to protect the law from heretical beliefs like Christianity. Jews had developed an oral tradition that extended the law's regulations into the first century. Their entire

concern was to live the law in every area of their life, to "build a
fence around the law" and ensure that everyone could follow it.

However, when the Messiah sent from God appeared, he did
not fit their notions of what a Messiah should be, and the Jewish
leaders and most of the people rejected him. They failed to gain
"knowledge" (*epignōsis*; see 1:28) of the truth of the new salvation
God had sent them in Jesus. Their zeal was wonderful for the old
covenant period but erroneous and misdirected for the new covenant period initiated by Christ.

Rejected God's righteousness (10:3)

The switch to the new era of salvation history in Jesus required
a new kind of righteousness. Previously, following the law kept
the Jewish people in right relationship with God, but when Jesus
arrived, a new covenant era came into being, and righteousness
derived not from the law but from a faith response to Jesus. As we
will see in the next verse, the old ways were ended and a new path
to righteousness was instigated. "They did not know the righteousness of God" any longer. Since Jesus the Christ had come, the law-
based religion they had inherited had become "their own" old and
outmoded path to righteousness—no longer God's way.

In biblical times, ignorance was not understood as an absence
of knowledge so much as a studied and deliberate rejection of
God's truths (see 1:28). The Jewish people understood that God
was righteous and they need to be right with him. However, they
followed their traditional beliefs that righteousness came from
keeping the law and rejected the new truths that this came only
through faith in Christ and his atoning death. As a result, they
could never be justified and truly right with God. Instead of finding salvation in Christ, they tried to follow "their own" path to salvation through the law. They refused to "submit to God's righteousness," which now depended on Christ rather than the law, so they
failed to attain the right standing with God they sought.

Those who follow the "new perspective" on Paul (see comments on 3:20) believe this is not a diatribe against "the works of the law" (the individual view) but rather against the Jewish refusal to allow the Gentiles to share their righteousness by erecting "boundary markers" that maintain the covenant as an exclusively Jewish privilege (the corporate view). They see it as a corporate issue, dealing with the acceptance of the Gentiles into the church. But this misses the whole point of this verse. Paul is not describing Israel's opposition to including the Gentiles but rather their attempt to anchor their walk with God in their own religious approach rather than God's. The issue is Israel's own righteousness replacing that of God and Christ.

Christ the end of the law (10:4)

A righteousness based on keeping the law is insufficient because "Christ is the culmination [telos] of the law"—perhaps better translated the "end" of the law. He has put an end to the law in the sense that God gave the law to prepare for Christ and point to him, so it has been culminated or finalized in him. This does not mean the law has ceased to have any value. In 7:12, 14, Paul says the law is "holy, righteous and good," and "spiritual." According to 2 Timothy 3:16, as Scripture it is "God-breathed and is useful for teaching, rebuking, correcting and training in righteousness."

There is continuity between the law and Christ. Jesus said in Matthew 5:17-20 that he did not come to "abolish" the law but to "fulfill" it, that is, bring it to completion and lift it to a higher plane. That is the point here as well. In Christ the law has not disappeared but has become part of his being. Christ embodies the law in himself, and to follow Christ is to keep the law in its entirety. Paul is saying that Christ has put an end to any attempt to achieve righteousness by means of the law. There is only one way to be right with God: by faith in Christ alone. The law is at an end as an instrument of salvation.

This is all part of the salvation-historical switch from the covenant of the law to the covenant of grace. The result is a "righteousness for everyone who believes." Salvation is now available to everyone, but not by works—only by faith. This means that Gentiles as well as Jews can be made right with God the same way—by believing in Christ. The problem of faith and works is the same today as it was in Paul's day. Every church and Christian ministry has people who are trying to earn their way to salvation through church attendance or good works. It is every bit as crucial today as it was then to help people understand that we can never be good enough to purchase our salvation. We all must examine our hearts before we rationalize our approach to life. Our eternal destiny is at stake!

SALVATION IS BY FAITH, NOT BY THE LAW (10:5-13)

Anyone who thinks they can get to heaven by keeping the law or performing good works is doomed, for no human being born in sin can keep the law perfectly enough to earn salvation. This law-gospel antithesis has been a topic of discussion since the Reformation. Salvation cannot be attained through the law but only by the gospel (the "good news") about Christ and the cross. This paragraph unpacks the meaning of righteousness by faith, not works. Of course, Paul has stated this often in Romans, but now he wants to show that the Old Testament does so as well. He wants his readers to realize it has always been God's intention to prepare for the coming of Israel's Messiah and to include the Gentiles in his gift of salvation.

Verse 5 centers on the inadequacy of the works of the law, and verses 6-8 on the necessity of faith to be justified. Human effort can neither bring about the incarnation nor produce the resurrection (v. 7). Only the "message concerning faith" can accomplish anything of eternal value (v. 8). Then in verses 9-13 Paul explains how the process works: only confession and belief result in justification (vv. 9-10), and only faith can stave off the last judgment

(v. 11). This means that "everyone," Jew and Gentile alike, "who calls on the name of the Lord will be saved" (vv. 12–13).

FAITH VERSUS WORKS (10:5–8)

As in verses 2–3 above, this verse begins with a *gar*, "for" (not translated in NIV), meaning that Paul is drawing an inference from what has come before. The reason the majority of the Jewish people have failed to attain salvation (1–4) is that they have not turned to their Messiah in faith. Instead, they are trying to gain right standing with God on the basis of their own efforts, by seeking a "righteousness that is by the law." This builds on "the law of righteousness" from 9:31, which I defined as the use of the law's regulations as the path to a right relationship with God. This is a parallel expression meaning the use of obedience to the law as the path to remaining in covenant relationship with God.

Must Keep the Law Perfectly (10:5)

Paul asserts that "Moses writes ... about" the impossibility of obeying the law well enough to earn righteousness and cites Leviticus 18:5, where Yahweh commands Israel not to be like the Canaanites but to obey his decrees and live by them. In one sense this Leviticus passage does not seem appropriate here, since in context it urges the Israelites to keep the law in order to enjoy God's covenant blessings. Yet Paul builds on one part of the citation ("The person who does these things will live by them") and makes two interpretive changes. "Live by them" he sees as eternal life, and "the one who does these things" must do so perfectly to inherit eternal life.

There are three possible interpretations of this passage: (1) Some see a reference to Christ, who perfectly "does these things" and thereby renders it possible for his followers to "live by" faith, but there is no hint in this paragraph that the focus has shifted to Christ here. (2) Others see no contrast between the "righteousness by the law" in verse 5 and the "righteousness by faith" in verses 6–8. Since Christ culminates the law (v. 4), this verse shows how believers can keep the law in Christ through faith and remain in covenant relationship with God. However, the antithesis between doing and believing is too strong throughout Romans, and the contrast between verse 5 and verses 6–8 is too apparent here. So (3) the best view is to see an absolute contrast between keeping the law (v. 5) and believing in Christ (vv. 6–8).

Paul's point is that the one who seeks to earn salvation by works (in Paul's day and in ours) must do so perfectly. This is an impossible task in light of human depravity. Eternal life cannot be attained by mere human obedience or good works. The history of Israel proves this, for they never could keep the law well enough to remain in covenant relationship with God. Every generation for two millennia fell into sin and had to experience God's judgment. When the people returned to God, it rarely worked longer than a generation at a time.

Human effort can produce neither the incarnation nor the resurrection (10:6–7)

An initial "but" (Greek: *de*) here establishes a contrast between the Leviticus command to keep the law in verse 5 and the quotations from Deuteronomy about a faith-based righteousness in these two verses. As Israel was about to cross the Jordan River into the promised land and face seemingly overpowering opposition, God promised to go before them and vanquish all foes (Deut 9:1–3). Paul draws from this passage the opening, "Do not say in your heart" (Deut 9:4), saying that their inheritance is not due to their own righteousness but to the gracious gift of God alone.

Paul then turns to Deuteronomy 30:12, "Who will ascend into heaven?" Again the context to the Deuteronomy passage is the renewal of the covenant before crossing into the promised land. Moses is reminding the Israelites that they have God's law and know it, so they must obey it. They do not have to ascend to heaven or cross the sea to discover it, for it is theirs now and must be obeyed. Paul applies this passage to Christ's incarnation (bringing him down from heaven) and resurrection (bringing him up from the dead). Moses wanted to make certain that Israel kept its covenant responsibilities by obeying the law, while Paul takes his words and applies them to the necessity of faith in Christ.

How can Paul validly do this? Neither Christ nor faith was in Moses' mind. On the surface it looks like the arbitrary application of an old covenant passage to a new covenant reality. Some say that this is not a direct quotation but a general allusion, and that Paul is simply using the idea from Deuteronomy in light of Christ. But the use of "writes" and "say" in verses 5 and 8 indicate that these are citations (cf. 9:15, 17, 25), and the context here strongly favors Paul interpreting an Old Testament text.

A little more background will help us see what he is doing. The larger narrative structure of Deuteronomy centers on the blessings and curses for obeying or disobeying the covenant (27:1–30:1). In 30:2–10 Moses gives a prophecy of the exile and the renewal of the nation after the exile. Paul sees this return from exile fulfilled in Jesus and the new covenant age of faith he inaugurated. In other words, Paul interprets the Deuteronomy material as typologically fulfilled in Christ the Messiah and the age of salvation. Christ and the New Testament writers often take this approach (see especially Matthew, Romans, and Hebrews).

"Who will ascend into heaven?" in Deuteronomy 30:12 originally meant that God's demands were not so impossible to understand that one would need a trip to heaven to grasp their meaning. Paul with his Christ-centered interpretation sees this as going to heaven in order to "bring Christ down," or bring about the incarnation. God is giving us the gift of salvation; we do not have to go to heaven and do it for ourselves.

In verse 7 he does the same with Deuteronomy 30:13, "Who will descend into the deep?" Literally this refers to "the abyss," the unfathomable depths of the sea. The Deuteronomy text has "Who will cross the sea to get it," another metaphor added to the one in verse 12, now saying that the law's demands were not so far away that one would have to cross the sea to find out what they meant.

Paul, using the same **typology** as in his earlier citation, applies it to "bringing Christ up from the dead," understanding "the abyss" or "deep" as the place of the dead. Paul here adds the idea of the resurrection to that of the incarnation. Human effort cannot produce the resurrection any more than the incarnation. Both result from the grace of God, not the will of humankind, and so they can only be accepted by faith. The Messiah has already appeared as God's gift for our salvation. He has died on the cross for our sins and has been raised from the dead for our justification (4:25). We are asked to accept this gift by faith and in so doing forego the law and its works-righteousness.

Answer: the word of faith (10:8)

On the one hand, we cannot bring about the great events of salvation history by personal effort (vv. 6–7). On the other hand, as we see in this verse, we can hear and understand the word of faith. God has given these truths, and they can be received as a divine gift.

The final citation from Deuteronomy reads, "The word is near you; it is in your mouth and in your heart" (Deut 30:14). In its original context this verse referred to the law's accessibility to the Israelites; here it is the gospel of Christ that is now open to God's people. In the gospel God has drawn near and spoken to our hearts. We can now experience and understand God in the very depths of our being. He can be both shared (mouth) and worshipped (heart). Since Christ is the culmination of the law, the law is deepened and made more real in the gospel. In Christ, "the Word became flesh" and made its home among us (John 1:14). In verse 9 Paul will elaborate and show that this word of faith involves both confession ("in your mouth") of the deep truths of the lordship of Christ and the salvation he produced as well as the deep-seated conviction ("in your hearts") that believes in Christ.

How Faith Works (10:9–13)

The second half of this section (vv. 9–13) is closely tied to verses 6–8. Paul's purpose is to explain how the "righteousness that is by faith" actually works in the process of coming to salvation. Verse 9 begins with *hoti*, and it is debated whether it means "that," thus providing the meaning of the "word of faith" from verse 8 (NASB, LEB, untranslated in NIV, NLT); or "because," thereby telling why "the word is near you" (so NRSV, NET, ESV). I prefer "that" because the issue of faith is central to the whole context.

The necessity of confession and belief (10:9–10)

Verses 9–10 describe the proper response to the gospel, telling how people come to faith. Salvation is experienced in the twin responses of confessing ("declare with your mouth") and believing ("believe in your heart"). The order of this reflects the mouth/heart sequence of verse 8. The content of the confession is not specified here but certainly includes "Jesus is Lord," which was at the very heart of early Christian worship, such as in the Aramaic *marana tha* (O Lord, come) of 1 Corinthians 16:22. This was a central part of celebrating the exaltation of Christ and acknowledging him as the Risen One (see also Acts 2:36; 10:36; 1 Cor 8:6; 12:3; 2 Cor 4:5; Phil 2:11; Col 2:6). Calling Jesus "Lord" recognizes that Jesus was far more than a mere rabbi, more even than the expected Messiah. From the start Christians worshipped him as fully God and Lord of all (Heb 1:3; 1 Pet 3:22; Titus 2:13).

This homage to the exalted Lord is especially evident in the most-often-quoted passage of them all, Psalm 110:1, "The LORD says to my Lord: Sit at my right hand until I make your enemies a footstool for your feet" (Mark 12:36–37 and parallels; Acts 2:34–35; Heb 1:3, 13; 5:6, 10; 6:20; 7:3, 7, 17, 21 and others). This citation is so prominent because it provides the main textual support for the exaltation of Christ as Lord. Some have said it is possible to know Jesus as Savior apart from knowing him as Lord. That is actually not true on the basis of this passage. To know Jesus as Savior begins the process of coming to know him as Lord. Without lordship there is no saviorhood.

Believing is intimately connected to confessing Jesus as Lord, as indicated here, "and believe in your heart that God raised him from the dead." The resurrection of Jesus is at the core of Romans (4:24; 6:4, 9; 7:4; 8:11, 34; 10:9; 13:11). His exaltation to the right hand of God took place at his resurrection into heaven (Eph 1:19-20) and was at the center of early Christian preaching and belief (Acts 3:15; 4:10; 13:30). The cross without the empty tomb was little more than the tragic death of an innocent Jewish rabbi.

In verse 10 Paul draws together the ideas of righteousness and salvation from verses 6 and 9 and amplifies the confession and belief from verse 9: "It is with your heart that you believe and are justified, and it is with your mouth that you profess your faith and are saved." Along with the previous two verses, this forms an ABBA **chiasm**, with mouth/heart in 8-9 mirrored by heart/mouth in 10. The inner belief of the heart must lead to an outward expression.

Paul uses verse 10 to sum up his argument in verses 5-9. Faith is the only possible path for attaining a right relationship with God, and it includes the mouth and the heart—confession and belief. There can be no other way to get right with God. He has in his grace and mercy made it possible to come to him through faith in Christ, and it is the height of foolishness to think there can be any other means to find salvation (John 14:6; Acts 4:12).

This passage is often quoted when we wish to tell how anyone is saved. Salvation in verse 9 is in the future tense ("will be saved"), which could make it a reference to final salvation rather than present conversion, but it more likely describes what takes place beginning at conversion. So, there are three stages of salvation—the confession of sin and turning of our life over to Christ, then the faith-decision or believing in Christ, and following this the ongoing experience of salvation. As often in chapters 6-10, there is an inaugurated (already/not yet) thrust—salvation is present now and will be consummated at the return of Christ. This latter aspect is the subject of verse 11.

Those who trust will not have shame (10:11)

In the next three verses (11–13), Paul applies the truth of justification by faith to the question of who can be saved. The answer here is drawn from Isaiah 28:16 (used earlier in 9:33): "Anyone who believes in him." Paul adds "anyone" to the Isaiah citation to stress the universal implications of the gospel (compare "everyone who believes" in v. 4). Whether Jew or Gentile, any person who puts their faith in Christ has attained salvation. As in 9:33, Paul in this verse teaches that there will be vindication at the last judgment for those who find faith in Christ.

Conclusion: no difference between Jew and Gentile (10:12–13)

These verses constitute a brief essay on the implications of the universal salvation implicit in "anyone" from verse 11. It is organized around three consecutive *gar* (for) clauses, each one elaborating the meaning of the Isaiah quote.

(1) "For there is no difference between Jew and Gentile." In 3:22–23 Paul used this phrase negatively to explain they are alike in sin. Here it is positive, teaching that both can be justified on the basis of faith in Christ. The Jewish people had neglected the Abrahamic covenant, which clarified that they had been chosen so that "all peoples on earth will be blessed through you" (Gen 12:3; 18:18; 22:18; 26:4; 28:14). Moreover, since they had rejected God's promised Messiah they had lost that covenant relationship and could regain it only by joining the Gentiles in finding faith in him. God was gracious and accorded them the opportunity to turn from their rejection and find Christ. Jesus died for everyone, so anyone — Jew or Gentile — can be saved through faith in him (see 3:22, 29–30; 4:11–12, 16–17; 5:6–11, 18–19).

(2) "For [not translated in NIV] the same Lord is Lord of all and richly blesses all who call on him." Some have thought "the

same Lord" is God the Father, since in 3:29–30 God is God of both
Jews and Gentiles, and in the Joel quotation in the next verse the
"Lord" on whose name they call is Yahweh. However, the lordship
of Christ is uppermost here, and this is connected to the passages
noted in verse 9. Christ is also the focus of faith in verse 11, and
that continues here. Jesus is Lord of Jew and Gentile alike, and
both are the recipients of his blessings, as seen in the outpouring
of his riches on them.

Elsewhere in Paul's writings God's rich blessings are "lavished"
on his people,[2] but here it is Christ's riches (as also in 2 Cor 8:9;
Eph 3:8). These riches are the outpouring of his grace and kindness in providing salvation for "all who call on him," as in the
believing and confessing of verses 9–10. To "call on him" in secular Greek contains the idea of "invoking" the gods in prayer, meaning here the invocations to the exalted Christ in prayer, worship,
and constant dependence on him. This new life begins with calling on him in faith for salvation and continues in lifelong surrender and reliance on him.

(3) "For 'Everyone who calls on the name of the Lord will be
saved.'" This quotation in verse 13 is from Joel 2:32. The paragraph
concludes with further material (with Isa 28:16 in v. 11) in which
Paul asserts that the universal offer of salvation was God's intention in the old covenant as well as the new. The link between this
and verse 12 is "calls on," expressing the way faith is behind turning to Christ to experience the riches of his grace in redeeming
and justifying the penitent sinner.

Paul's major emphasis here is on "everyone" (also in vv. 4, 11, 12),
stressing the universal applicability of the gospel. Every person
ever born is the object of God's salvific love, and he is "not wanting anyone to perish" (2 Pet 3:9). In Joel this is part of a prophecy
regarding the pouring out of the Spirit on all at the day of Yahweh

---

2. Eph 1:7–8; see also Rom 2:4; 9:23; 11:33; Eph 1:18; 2:7; 3:16; Phil 4:19; Col 1:27;
1 Tim 6:17.

(Joel 2:28-32). In Joel "all" refers to all in Israel, while here it refers to all people, Jew and Gentile alike—everyone who "calls on the name of the Lord." The last days prophesied by Joel have dawned, so all peoples on the earth enjoy the blessings of salvation God has promised those who call on him in faith. As in Joel, this blessing includes the Spirit (Rom 8:1-17).

―――――

This is a critical section in Paul's argument that God is faithful to his covenant promises. God in his sovereignty has called people to salvation (9:6-29), and humans are responsible to respond to that call (9:30-10:21). God has fulfilled his part, but Israel has failed in her part and so can only blame herself for God's turning to the Gentiles. The problem was that the Jews sought righteousness by keeping the law and failed to realize that since their Messiah had come, the law had been replaced by faith in Christ. The Gentiles were able to attain right standing with God, while the majority of Jews had not done so.

God has established Christ as his chief cornerstone, and his covenant people have stumbled over that cornerstone (9:32-33). Judgment resulted when the stone fell on them and crushed them. The reason they rejected Jesus as Messiah was that he did not fit their preconceived ideas. The centrality of the law in the life of God's people had come to an end (v. 4), and they refused to accept that. This is exactly the case in our world today. Many people are unwilling to change their ideas of what Christ should be (namely, the kind of God who would approve the lifestyle they want to lead), and so they refuse to turn their lives over to him. They reject Christ, and as a result God rejects them.

But the wondrous truth is that "the word of faith" is near and speaks with a clear voice to those willing to listen. The path to salvation is open to us, and we walk it by opening our hearts to the gospel. To receive it we simply confess and believe in the salvation that is ours in Christ (vv. 9-10). This is a wonderful summary of

gospel truth. This salvation is available for "anyone" who is willing
to believe (vv. 11–13). It is critical in our day to realize this means
every human being ever born. No sinner is exempt, and salvation
is open to thieves, prostitutes, murderers—any and every sinner
who is willing to repent, turn to Christ in faith, and find forgiveness. But it must be received by faith in Christ; no human effort
can ever earn salvation. It is a divine gift and cannot be bought, no
matter how much fancy paper and ribbon we wrap it in!

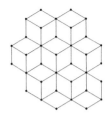

ISRAEL RESPONSIBLE FOR REJECTING GOD'S OFFER, PART 2:
ISRAEL'S GUILT FOR REJECTING THE GOSPEL
(10:14-21)

G od has promised and offered salvation equally to Jew and Gentile. However, Jewish guilt is more severe, as Paul pointed out in 2:1-3:10, because they had been given the covenant privileges. Thus when they rejected Christ, they did so deliberately and defiantly ("with an high hand," Exod 14:8 KJV). The theme of the last section was the promise that "everyone who calls on the name of the Lord will be saved" (Joel 2:32 in v. 13). But the vast majority of the Jews have not responded with faith.

Paul now traces the process of conversion in reverse order (vv. 14-15), unpacking what it means to "call on" Jesus in faith by moving from effect back to cause. The order follows the sending of a witness who preaches the gospel, leading to hearing the summons to faith in Christ, then to believing the truth, which results in calling on the Lord. Paul's point is that Israel has followed this process, but they have not responded in faith and so are guilty and accountable to God (vv. 16-17). They have greeted the gospel with obstinacy, and so God has turned to the Gentiles (vv. 18-21).

PAUL DESCRIBES THE PROCESS OF
CONVERSION (10:14–15)

This description of the process expands the promise of verse 13 in the quotation from Joel that those who "call on" the Lord "will be saved." It proceeds backward from the final step of calling out to the Lord for salvation.

The steps to conversion in these verses take the form of a series of rhetorical questions (as in 3:1; 4:1; 6:1; 7:1; 8:31; 9:14). The questions seem to be saying "one cannot do this unless," and each item becomes a precondition for experiencing the thing that precedes it. For instance, the first three say in effect, "You cannot call on the Lord unless you believe, and you cannot believe unless you hear." While this primarily refers to the Jewish people, it is true of everyone who becomes a Christian. It is the process every convert must follow.

CALL-BELIEF-HEARING-PREACHING-SENT (10:14)

Paul's first point is the impossibility of calling without faith. The necessary basis calling is belief in God and Christ, as stressed seventeen times in 3:21–4:25 alone, and in the immediate context in 10:4, 6, 8, 9, 10, 11. Paul demands here a full-fledged faith that includes belief not only in his sacrificial death for our sins but also in the resurrection and the lordship of Christ (10:9).

The precondition for belief in Jesus the Christ is hearing the gospel. Some have said it is Christ we hear, but it is much more likely that it is the proclamation of the gospel, as in "the word about Christ" in verse 17 and "the feet of those who bring good news" in verse 15. It is important to realize that hearing throughout Scripture also means responding. Both the Hebrew and Greek terms for "hearing" also refer to "obeying." We have not truly heard until we respond and begin living the truth of the message. This is especially the case with the gospel.

Of course, hearing is impossible "without someone preaching to them." Paul frequently emphasizes the proclamation of the gospel and the privilege of ministering God's good news to a lost world. Preaching Christ is at the very heart and soul of his commission from God (Gal 2:2; 1 Thess 2:9) and provides the core of his apostolic ministry (1 Cor 1:23, 15:11–12; 2 Cor 1:19, 4:5; Col 1:23). He maintained firm control and discipline both in his preaching and in living out his message in his own life (1 Cor 9:27) and considered the proclamation of the word the most important task in his life (1 Tim 3:16–17; 2 Tim 4:2).

Preaching is impossible "unless they are sent" (v. 15). The calling and commission of God are essential for a ministry to have power and validity. A person can preach a sermon without a calling from God, but the message will not be infused with power by the Spirit. The words will carry truth only by chance, for the Lord will not be behind the message. This does not mean that only an ordained minister can preach; it means God must be behind the message.

A preacher is a herald, and in the ancient world a herald had no authority apart from the sending agent. The term "apostle" (*apostolos*) is actually "a sent one," emphasized especially in John, where Jesus over twenty times calls himself the Sent One.[1] Jesus gives his apostles authority in mission in John 20:21, "as the Father has sent me, I am sending you" (see also 17:18). Jesus passes the baton to the preacher, who then passes it on to "reliable" people who are "qualified to teach others" (2 Tim 2:2). There are four stages here, from Jesus to the preacher to those the preacher trains and finally to the "others" in the church. One could add a fifth as the church members use these gospel truths to evangelize the lost.

---

1. This is a semi-technical phrase for the idea, found especially in John, that Jesus is the One sent by his Father. See, for example, John 5:23, 24, 36; 6:29; 8:16, 18, 29, 42.

PROOF FROM SCRIPTURE (10:15B)

The basis of all this is the authority of those heralds sent out to proclaim the gospel, the word of God. Paul anchors this critical process in a paraphrase from Isaiah 52:7, "How beautiful are the feet of those who bring good news!" Paul omits "who proclaim peace" from the citation and sticks to the proclamation itself here. He wants this to demonstrate that both the sending and the proclamation fulfill the prophetic mandate. Paul's purpose in using the phrase "how beautiful are the feet" is to show that the itinerant ministry of God's good news by both prophet and preacher is the highest of callings. The goal of all ministry is to "bring good news" first to the church and then to the world. Those called to preach are messianic heralds (this citation is found in the messianic Servant Songs of Isaiah), and the mission of preaching is a continuation of Jesus' own itinerant ministry.

Some think that "beautiful" should be translated "timely" or "at the appropriate time," thus giving a sense of the "fullness of time" (as in Gal 4:4) for the good news to reach all the world. However, both in Isaiah and here it is more likely that it refers to the "beautiful" event of the proclamation of the gospel, as also in the other places New Testament writers cite Isaiah (Matt 23:7; Acts 3:2, 10).

In too many churches the proclaimed word is de-emphasized, and the pastor is considered more a CEO or an entertainer than a shepherd of the flock and a messianic herald of truth. This is exactly the opposite of Jesus and the disciples, for throughout Acts and the Epistles of the New Testament they gave the message they proclaimed the highest priority. In Acts 2:42 the number-one pillar of the church is "the apostles' teaching." Pastors are first to feed their flocks (John 21:15-17) and will be judged by God on the basis of the quality of their handling of "the word of truth" (2 Tim 2:15). Moreover, all believers are called to be repositories and dispensers of these divine truths.

ISRAEL HAS NOT RESPONDED WITH FAITH (10:16–17)

God sent commissioned preachers to Israel, first the prophets in the Old Testament (as in the passages cited above) and then the preachers of the New Testament. All the conditions of verses 14–15a were met except one: faith. "Not all the Israelites accepted the good news." "Not all" means "only a few"; the vast majority of the Jewish people rejected the gospel message. The few who did respond constitute the remnant of 9:27 and 11:1–10. There is a play on words here. The nation has "heard" (*akouō*) in verse 14 but has refused to "obey" or "accept" (*hypakouō*) the gospel message. There is no true belief without active obedience.

To anchor this, Paul cites Isaiah 53:1 from the **Septuagint** (Greek Old Testament), "Lord, who has believed our message?" This is also quoted in John 12:38, which also describes Jewish unbelief. While Isaiah 52:7 in verse 15 tells how God sent his messianic herald with the good news, Isaiah 53:1 here tells how the majority of the nation has rejected that message. God sent his proclamation of redemption to Israel, but they refused to accept it. Israel has done this throughout its history and is still following that pattern, refusing to heed the good news.

In verse 17 "therefore" (*ara*) summarizes the fourfold process of redemption from verses 14–15. God has done his part in the redemptive process, sending both the messenger and the message. Israel has failed to live up to its responsibility and so stands before the Lord guilty on all counts.

First, "faith comes from hearing the message." Jesus said this powerfully: "Whoever has ears, let them hear," meaning, "If you are willing to listen and respond, you had better do so right now" (Matt 11:15; Luke 14:35). In the seven letters of Revelation this is expanded to, "Whoever has ears, let them hear what the Spirit says to the churches" (Rev 2:7, 11, 17, 29; 3:6, 13, 22). By refusing the gospel, Jewish hearers showed they did not truly "have ears."

Notice Revelation has "the Spirit says" and Paul here adds "the word about Christ." The gospel is a trinitarian message, with all three members involved. The Father sends it, the Spirit speaks it, and Christ is the content of the message.

Second, the message is "the word *about* Christ" rather than "from Christ." Paul is emphasizing the proclaimed gospel regarding what Christ has done: providing salvation through his blood sacrifice on the cross. As Acts shows well, the proclamation of the gospel to the Jewish people was thoroughly done. Nearly everywhere Paul went, he fulfilled Romans 1:16, "first to the Jew, then to the Gentile" (Acts 13:14-15; 14:1-2, 16:12-13; 17:1-4, 10; 18:2-6; 19:8-10). However, it was not received, and it did not lead to belief. Failure to receive the gospel also happens in our day, but I believe a greater problem is the large number of shallow topical messages that fail to open up the word to the people. Not too many Christians are unteachable, but many are untaught. In 1 Peter 2:2-3, teaching is a gourmet meal that feeds the flock. Too many churches are fed a fast-food diet in the word.

PAUL DESCRIBES THE OBSTINACY OF ISRAEL (10:18-21)

THEY DEFINITELY HEARD (10:18)

Paul introduces Old Testament citations in verses 18-19 with "I ask," a style he uses again in 11:1, 11. The purpose is to make his rhetorical questions more personal. He then turns to the basic issue, asking, "Did they not hear?" Two negatives introduce the question, so it could be translated, "It is not true that they have not heard, right?" This means they have heard, so immediately he answers, "Of course they did!" Paul points to their deliberate rejection of the gospel and thus intends to justify God's condemnation of them.

Paradoxically, they did not hear (16-17), and yet they did (18). These two can be harmonized by noting the three aspects of "hear" language in this context: to hear the gospel proclaimed, to understand the meaning of it, and to obey or accept it. This verse emphasizes the first two: they heard and understood the gospel.

Verses 16–17 stresses the third: they did not accept what they understood. Paul's purpose is to clarify the statement in verses 16–17 that Israel refused to truly hear the gospel.

Paul's point is that in one sense the Jews not only heard but also understood the gospel. To anchor this, he cites the well-known psalm that begins, "The heavens declare the glory of God; the skies proclaim the works of his hands" (Psalm 19:1). Yet there is disagreement as to what Paul actually means when he quotes Psalm 19:4, "Their voice has gone out into all the earth." This psalm extols natural revelation (creation), while Paul is discussing special revelation (the gospel and the word of God). However, the Old Testament is often cited in the New in terms of similar ideas (what we might call "analogous meaning"). In other words, God's revealing himself in nature is analogous to God's revealing himself in his word, and so Psalm 19 can viably be used of God speaking through the gospel as well. The same way God speaks through nature he can even more clearly speak through his revealed word. Also, the second half of Psalm 19 moves into special revelation (the law), so the psalm itself supports both emphases.

There is some debate also as to the meaning of "into all the earth." Some restrict it to the Gentile mission, but in Acts as well as in Paul the Jewish people are included in the universal mission. The mission would hardly be universal if it were restricted to Gentiles. In the same way, it is not restricted to Israel in Psalm 19. In both places Paul intended all humanity. But here too there are questions. Did Paul believe in AD 57 as he is penning the Letter to the Romans that the gospel had reached to the very "ends of the world"? This is hardly likely, as he was planning to visit Spain (15:24, 28). He certainly realized that the mission of the church to all the world was in process of completion. I would call this the "inaugurated mission" to the ends of the earth. It had already begun but was not yet complete. If the worldwide mission was being successfully accomplished, the mission to the Jews was as well. As in the Great Commission of Matthew 28:18–20, the mission to "all nations" is to Jew and Gentile alike. In the end the people of Israel have no excuse; they have heard and understood but would not believe.

THEY UNDERSTOOD AND WERE JEALOUS (10:19)

In this final paragraph of the section on the Jews' responsibility and guilt for their own failures (vv. 18–21) Paul demonstrates that they cannot use the excuse that they lacked opportunity to believe. In verse 18 Paul showed they heard the message of salvation. Now he shows they also understood that message. He uses the covenant name "Israel" to depict them, showing they were the chosen people that produced the kings and prophets who served Yahweh. As the covenant people steeped in the traditions of the Old Testament, they not only heard but also "knew" (ginōskō, translated "understand" in the NIV) the meaning and implications of the gospel preaching.

Verses 19–21 are a series of citations from those Scriptures to prove the continuity between the old and the new paths to salvation God has initiated. Paul begins these citations with "Moses says," connoting that he was the first in a long line of witnesses testifying to the extent of Israel's knowledge. The quotation stems from Deuteronomy 32:21, part of the farewell song of Moses at the end of his life. This follows the Septuagint text closely, the only change being "you" rather than "them" in the first line in order to contrast with the Gentiles, "who are not a nation."

The farewell song itself celebrates the covenant faithfulness of Yahweh in spite of the idolatry and corruption of Israel. Since the Jews made God "jealous" by turning from him to "worthless idols" (Deut 32:21), God would "make you envious by those who are not a nation. I will make you angry by a nation that has no understanding." In the Hebrew they are made envious by a "no people," probably linked in Paul's mind to similar language of Hosea 1:10, which Paul cited in Romans 9:25 ("I will call them 'my people' who are not my people").

Paul saw in both the Hosea and Deuteronomy passages a prophecy of the Gentile mission. As we will see in 11:11, 14, below, a major reason God turned to the Gentiles was to make Israel jealous. The purpose of "making them jealous" was to get them to turn back to God so they could recapture their national identity. If Israel was "angered" during the wilderness wanderings (the scene behind Deut 32), how much more now, for this is the messianic age.

God Turned to the Gentiles (10:20)

Paul imagines Isaiah prophesying "boldly," thereby stressing the incredible nature of this truth. Paul reverses the two verbs from Isaiah, perhaps to emphasize Gentile conversion ("found") as leading to a new relationship with God ("revealed"). The new relationship produces a new understanding. In Isaiah this does not refer to the Gentiles but is God's response to the rebellious nation that had complained that God had forgotten his people (63:7–64:11). God answers that in their apostasy they had not even called on his name (65:1–2). Paul applies this to the Gentiles on the basis of the principle of analogy we have seen throughout this chapter (see on v. 18). This verse is particularly apropos for the Gentiles, as they were indeed "not a nation" in the eyes of God and had "no understanding."

Because of their apostasy in rejecting the Messiah, unbelieving Jews must join the Gentiles and come to God as repentant sinners. The point here returns to the opening part of this section (9:30–31), where it is the Gentiles who failed to "pursue righteousness" but have "obtained it." Israel has now joined the Gentiles as "those who did not seek me" or "ask for me." Now they must doubly join the Gentiles and "call upon" Christ in faith (10:12–13). They have sinned deliberately, and thus have lost their privileges as the chosen people. They must repent, fall on their knees, and ask for forgiveness and salvation.

A DISOBEDIENT AND OBSTINATE PEOPLE (10:21)

In verses 20 and 21 Paul cites Isaiah 65:1-2 in succession and applies them first to the Gentiles and second to the Jews. The Gentiles "found" the Christ in faith while the Jews at all times ("all day long") remained hardened to the gospel. In Isaiah 65:2 two elements are stressed—God's continuous concern for his people ("all day long I have held out my hands") and Israel's obstinate response ("to a disobedient and obstinate people").

Paul has moved "all day long" from the end of the first line to the front of the quotation, so there is strong stress on the constant love of God for Israel. The stretching out of his hands shows God imploring his people to come to him in repentance, but in the context the primary thrust is the stubborn and stiff-necked refusal of Israel to repent. Their disobedience and guilt are set in contrast to the graciousness of God. God in his *chesed*, his gracious love, has sought to return his people to himself, but they have obstinately refused to come back and so stand before him in all their guilt.

This is a fitting conclusion to Romans 9-10, explaining why unbelieving Jews stand before God as apostates. First, God has in his predetermined will chosen to punish them and bring the Gentiles into his true Israel (9:6-29). Second, they have heard and understood yet stubbornly refused to submit to Christ and so are completely responsible for the sad state they have entered. However, Paul will show in the next section (11:1-10) that God has not forsaken his covenant people but has chosen a "remnant" for himself.

EXCURSUS: DIVINE SOVEREIGNTY AND HUMAN RESPONSIBILITY

We now have enough material from Paul to draw some conclusions regarding his view of divine election, which stresses divine sovereignty from 9:6 to 9:29 and human responsibility from 9:30 to 10:21. The debate over predestination must find a balance between these two perspectives. The key is that while God's sovereignty has priority, the two are interdependent, and I believe that God has "decreed" human choice from the beginning. God could have created an Adam and Eve who would never sin, which would mean an end to world wars, murder, prostitution, and human greed—no malnourished children, no atrocities like the Holocaust or the Cambodian slaughter, no debilitating illnesses.

But without choice there would also not be love, for love demands choice. God did not create evil, but he did demand choice, and with choice the possibility of evil is always there. God thought the possibility of evil was worth the price of enjoying love and choosing to do good deeds.

Divine sovereignty demands that God create us with free will. Yet how does this work at the level of eternal salvation, specifically in terms of the relationship between predestination and faith? Many state that due to the absolute sovereignty of God, his grace must be grounded entirely in his own free will and not depend on human choice. That is correct, but salvation is not based on "the human choice to believe" but on the Holy Spirit's universal convicting presence. We do not choose to save ourselves, but God sovereignly allows us to respond to the Spirit drawing us to Christ (John 16:8–11). There is still free choice, but it is made possible by the Spirit overcoming our total depravity and convicting us, thereby enabling that choice.

Faith is not a work (Eph 2:8–9) but an opening of ourselves to the work of the Spirit within. In my comments on Romans 8:29–30 I explained that foreknowledge preceded predestination, that God knew who would respond positively to the Spirit's convicting work and thus elected them to become his children (John 1:12). God's predetermined will is indeed operative here, and his sovereignty has priority over human choice. It is his sovereign will, in fact, that makes choice possible. We would never be able to overcome the total control of depravity over ourselves without the Spirit's enabling presence.

This is the theme of 9:1–10:21, that God has made his sovereign choice to judge Israel but that this choice is based on his foreknowledge of Israel's choice to reject the gospel. This, in fact, is also the theme of 11:1–32, as Paul says in verse 2: "God did not reject his people, whom he foreknew." God sovereignly chose a remnant whom he foreknew would remain faithful. Both God's part and their part led them to be the elect. Note that it is only the remnant, not the entirety of Israel, who were chosen.

To sum up the matter: God is sovereign, but every individual is accountable to respond positively to the universal offer of salvation. This response is made possible only by the Spirit's presence. Israel was the chosen people of God, but only those within her who responded in faith were saved. The majority lost their place among God's people because of their unbelief. Then God sovereignly turned to the Gentiles and chose from them those who responded with belief in Christ. God is sovereign, and he has sovereignly chosen that the free choice of every human being be made on the basis of the Spirit's universal convicting and enabling work.

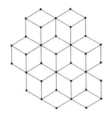

A NATIONAL FUTURE FOR ISRAEL, PART 1:
THE ELECTION OF A REMNANT FROM ISRAEL
(11:1-10)

All children go through periods when they are "naughty, not nice," and have to experience discipline from Mom and Dad. During that time they may be heard to wail, "Why don't you love me? Why can't you be nice to me?" A good parent's reply is remarkably similar to Paul's in Romans 9-11: (1) Your father has a right to do what he knows is best (9:6-29); (2) you are responsible for what you have done and have received what you deserve (9:30-10:21); (3) there is a wonderful future ahead for you, and temporary discipline is part of that promise (11:1-36).

Paul has never said all of Israel has been rejected by God. In 9:6-7 he carefully states, "*not all* who are descended from Israel are Israel"; and in 9:21 he adds, "*some* pottery for special purposes and *some* for common use." In 10:16 he says, "*not all* the Israelites accepted the good news"; and in 11:17, "*some* of the branches have been broken off." Only a portion of the nation experienced hardening, and a portion of the people were reserved for God and have become part of the new covenant community. This theme is found in verse 2: "God did not reject his people, whom he foreknew."

The first section of this critical chapter is verses 1–10, where Paul tells his readers that at the present time there is a remnant of Jews who are chosen by grace and have found Christ. The language of this section is taken from 8:29–10:21, especially its terms for the process of election—"foreknew" (2), "elect" (7), and "hardened" (7). In 9:6–29 Paul argued that God chose for eternal punishment, but here he has chosen a remnant for himself. He has not rejected all his people, only those guilty of unbelief (10:3, 14, 16–21). At the same time, he has graciously chosen out of his people a group who has not rejected his Son.

There are two sections in verses 1–10, a positive one, on the chosen remnant from Israel (vv. 1–6), and a negative one, on the hardened ones (vv. 7–10). The theological core is predestination of two groups: the chosen "who have not bowed the knee to Baal" (v. 4) and those hardened and condemned by God. The point is that God has not turned his back on the covenant promises to his people, for he has preserved a remnant for himself (see 9:6, 14).

GOD HAS CHOSEN A REMNANT (11:1–6)

God Has Not Rejected Israel (11:1)

The opening "I ask then" (*oun*) signals a major point, as in 10:18–19 and 11:11. Paul is drawing a conclusion from chapter 10. In all three passages, the "I say/ask" is followed by a rhetorical question expecting a negative answer: "Did God reject his people? By no means!" (see also 3:3–5; 9:14). In 10:16–21 Paul emphasized that Israel had refused to believe even though the people had clearly heard and understood the gospel message.

Their disobedience and guilt could easily lead to the question, "Did God reject his people?" In 9:25–26 and 10:19, Paul cited Hosea 1:10; 2:23; and Deuteronomy 32:21 to assert that the apostate nation was no longer "my people" and to contrast the fallen people of Israel with the believing Gentiles who were now the people of God.

Now the imaginary opponent is asking whether God has made Israel a "not-my-people." Paul denies this charge.

He then reminds his readers in Rome, as in 9:1–4, of his Jewish roots as a "descendant of Abraham, from the tribe of Benjamin." In 2 Corinthians 11:22 and Philippians 3:4–6, he uses an even more developed list to anchor his right to correct erroneous opponents. Here he wants to use himself as a primary example of a Jew who has become one of the elect, a member of the new Israel. If he, a primary persecutor of the Christian movement and a leader among the Jewish people, could find Christ, then God has not rejected his people.

Moreover, if God had called him, one of the leaders of the Jews, to become apostle to the Gentiles, he would hardly be abandoning his covenant people in favor of the Gentiles. Rather, God wanted Israel to become the channel by which the Gentiles were brought into his covenant community. Paul is the archetype of the people God has not abandoned but instead has called to serve the Gentiles, and through this the Abrahamic covenant will be fulfilled as the Jews bring God's blessing to the Gentiles (Gen 12:3).

The three designations Paul uses to describe himself here are interesting. "An Israelite" is the supreme covenant name for the chosen people (as also in 9:4); a "descendant of Abraham" looks back on Paul's discussion of Abraham as a major example of justification by faith (Rom 4:1–25; 9:7–8). It is more difficult to see why he labels himself "from the tribe of Benjamin." He could have noted this because the tribe had a great history. It was "beloved of the Lord" (Deut 33:12), and Saul had come from that tribe. According to the Mishnah,[1] rabbis believed it was the first tribe to cross the Red Sea and would be the means of unifying the twelve tribes. We do not know how much of this was in Paul's mind. At any rate, his

---

1. The Mishnah is the legal document in the Jewish Talmud that collected in written form many of the laws in the Oral Torah.

major purpose is to show that many Jewish people were becoming believers.

ELIJAH'S COMPLAINT THAT GOD FORSOOK HIM (11:2–3)

Verse 2 carries the premise of this section: "God did not reject his people, whom he foreknew." This phrase closely resembles Psalm 94:14 and 1 Samuel 12:22, which have the same wording in the **Septuagint** (the Greek Old Testament). There the verb is in the future tense (will not do so), while here it is in the past tense, to stress the unchanging nature of the promise.

Paul adds "whom he foreknew" to bring the election theology of chapters 9–11 into the message. This theme dominates the section (vv. 2, 5, 7). Scholars debate whether this refers to the special election of a select portion out of the nation or the general election of the nation as a whole. The Old Testament passages in the background here and several others along the same lines (Deut 7:6; Amos 3:2) favor general election in this verse, with special election in verse 5. Many in Israel have turned their backs on God and Christ (see especially the context of 1 Sam 12), but God has not turned his back on them. As we saw in Romans 8:35–39, nothing can separate his people from the love of God and Christ. God called them on the basis of his predetermined will to be his own.

The rest of this section (vv. 2b–6) brings in the idea of a remnant from within the apostate nation as the focus of God's covenant love. It begins with a question Paul often uses: "Don't you know?" (cf. 6:3, 16; 7:1). He is assuming that the readers are familiar with the career of the prophet Elijah. He was one of the most famous prophets, performing great miracles as well as prophesying and personifying the power of God at work on behalf of his people. His main purpose was to bring the nation back to God and rescue them from idolatry. In verses 2b–3 Paul cites Elijah's complaint and "appeal to God against Israel" regarding the apostasy that was disseminated throughout the land. The verb translated "appeal" is the basic term for intercession but here refers to prayers *against* apostasy.

The 1 Kings passages Paul quotes in verse 3 (19:10, 14) and verse 4 (19:18) stem from a section (1 Kings 19:1–18) celebrating events after the great victory of Elijah over the prophets of Baal in 1 Kings 18. Immediately afterward, Queen Jezebel threatened the life of Elijah, and in one of life's great ironies, the prophet who had defeated 450 prophets of Baal ran for his life into the wilderness. There he was cared for by God (19:4–8) and then traveled forty days and nights to Mount Horeb (where Moses saw the burning bush, Exod 3:1) and poured out his complaint to God: "Lord, they have killed your prophets and torn down your altars; I am the only one left, and they are trying to kill me." He had already forgotten how God empowered him on Mount Carmel!

This complaint that Elijah was "the only one left" does not reflect reality, for a hundred prophets had been hidden from Jezebel (1 Kings 18:13). It shows the deep fear and despair of Elijah; he had failed to put his trust in Yahweh. The emphasis in 1 Kings and here is less on Elijah's terror and even more on Israel's apostasy. For Paul the Israel of his day was echoing the failure of Elijah's day. The nation continues to turn against God and his chosen leaders.

God's Answer: Seven Thousand Spared (11:4)

After the lament of Elijah, God responds, "I have reserved for myself seven thousand who have not bowed the knee to Baal" (1 Kings 19:18). Elijah is not all alone. Although the majority of the nation has turned against God, God remains faithful to his covenant promises. He has "reserved" (a cognate verb of the Hebrew term for "remnant") for himself a faithful remnant. This is an example of the balance between God's sovereignty ("reserved for myself") and human responsibility ("not bowed the knee"). God "foreknew" (v. 2) that they would be faithful and so "reserved" or chose them "for himself."

Paul's emphasis is on the sovereign election of this remnant for God. Some see significance in the number seven thousand: seven is the number of completeness multiplied by ten three times (also signifying perfection). But there is little evidence Paul sees numerological meaning in this, and the emphasis is more likely the opposite: the paucity of the number out of the whole nation. Very few out of Israel remained for God in Elijah's time, and the same is true in Paul's time. Still, the victory is God's, and the future is bright. Jesus in the parable of the mustard seed predicted the greatness of the church that would arise out of his small band of disciples (Mark 4:30–34). When God is in charge, a small number like the seven thousand in Elijah's time or the Twelve in Jesus' time is in reality a vast, invincible army.

CONCLUSION: THE REMNANT SAVED BY GRACE, NOT WORKS (11:5–6)

Paul's "So too, at the present time" shows that he is contextualizing the Elijah story for his own day, drawing a **typological** link between the ancient event and the present situation. Paul sees the Israel of the first century as the antitype of Elijah's situation. He is an Elijah figure, standing firm for God and exposing the apostasy of the nation, yet finding hope in God's preservation of a remnant.

The idea of a remnant developed in the time of Elijah, the eighth century BC. It began with Amos, who foretold the doom of the apostate people, with only a remnant spared (Amos 5:3, 15). This remnant would inherit the Davidic kingdom (Amos 9:11–12). Isaiah took the idea further, also through a context of divine judgment against an unrepentant people and salvation only for the faithful remnant due to the mercy of Yahweh (Isa 37:32; 46:3), who will purge the faithful so they will be holy (4:2–3) and redeemed (11:11). God will open a highway (11:16) for those who are faithful (7:3, 9; 10:20–23) and will be their crown (28:5).

As in Isaiah's time, the faithful remnant in Paul's time and ours has been "chosen by grace," both parts of which are critical throughout Romans. Election is central in Romans 8:33; 9:11; 11:5, 7, 28; and 16:33, with synonyms like "predestined" in 8:29-30; and "called" in 1:1, 6-7; 8:28; 9:24-26. Paul emphasizes grace in 3:24; 4:16; 5:2, 15, 17, 20-21; 6:14; and 11:5-6. There is no salvation apart from grace; If humanity received what it deserved, there would be nothing except eternal damnation. Yet God's lovingkindness and mercy have led him to choose a remnant and spare us from our just deserts. God is "not wanting anyone to perish, but everyone to come to repentance" (2 Pet 3:9).

Paul clarifies the grace-not-works concept in verse 6: "If by grace, then it is no longer by works" (NIV "then it cannot be based on works"). This does not mean that in the old covenant salvation came by works. "No longer" should be seen as logical rather than temporal. What Paul is saying is that human achievement is incapable of making a person right with God because the law of sin and death is in control. No one is able to be good enough. We all fit into the category described in 7:18: "I have the desire to do what is good, but I cannot carry it out." Since we are born in sin (5:12), our very DNA makes it impossible for us to live out goodness day by day.

Paul takes this one step further: "if it were, grace would no longer be grace." If election and grace were based on human merit, salvation would cease to be by grace at all. We would have earned it rather than receiving it as God's gift. As a sovereign act of God, salvation must of necessity be his choice and not merely the payment of a contract. Human effort can have no place in it (Eph 2:8-9).

GOD HAS HARDENED THE OTHERS (11:7-10)

Paul now spells out the implications ("What then?") of verses 2-6, a remnant chosen by grace. He separates the two groups into which humanity falls, contrasting God's work among "the elect" with his work among those whom he has "hardened." Paul discussed the positive side, the remnant God has chosen to save, in verses 2-6. Now he turns to the negative side, those whom he has chosen to harden (vv. 7–10). This is based on 9:6–29, the sovereign right of God to choose an elect and to harden the others.

THESIS: ONLY THE ELECT OBTAINED SALVATION (11:7)

Paul mentions three groups here, but they are not separate groups. There is one large group, Israel, and it consists of two subgroups, the elect and the hardened. The Gentiles are not part of this, for Paul is discussing only the Israelites. In 2:17–18 Paul told how the Jews relied on the law, knew God's will, approved what was superior, and yet failed to teach themselves how to live that law and by God's will. In 9:31 Israel "pursued the law as the way of righteousness" but "have not attained their goal." In 10:2, Paul says she was "zealous for God" but without knowledge. Now he pictures Israel as seeking salvation but not obtaining it. This was the reason for his sorrow in 9:2–3. But it was a source of joy to Paul that the elect among Israel did attain right standing with God, for this meant there was hope for the nation (as we will see in 11:25–32). He uses the same term for "elect" here (*eklogē*) as he did in 9:11 and 11:5, stressing the sovereignty of God and his elect choice.

Those who are not among the elect in this verse are "the others" who "were hardened," a divine passive meaning God hardened them. This is the same issue in 9:16–18, God's hardening Pharaoh, with the conclusion in 9:18: "God has mercy on whom he wants to have mercy, and he hardens whom he wants to harden." The word for "harden" indicates a spiritual callousness toward the gospel. It is a medical term, containing the image of bladder stones or the hardening that causes bones to knit together.

GOD SENT THE HARDENING (11:8)

In verses 8–10 Paul draws on three Old Testament texts (v. 8 conflates two) from three divisions of the canon—the Law (Deut 29:4), the Writings (Ps 69:22, 23), and the Prophets (Isa 29:10)—to emphasize that all of Scripture supports this harsh reality. The first, from Deuteronomy, comes from the concluding charge of Moses to Israel before they entered the promised land. Israel had not understood the events of the wilderness wanderings because "God gave them a spirit of stupor, eyes that could not see and ears that could not hear, to this very day." As in Romans 1:24, 26, 28, this refers to the hardening process when God surrenders sinful people to the extremes of the evil they deliberately prefer. In addition to Deuteronomy, Paul may also have in mind Isaiah 6:9–10, a passage on the hardening of Israel: "They may be ever seeing but never perceiving, and ever hearing but never understanding; otherwise they might turn and be forgiven" (cited in Mark 4:12 and parallels; John 12:40; Acts 28:26–27). The result is a blend of Romans 9 and 10, combining God's sovereign choice and Israel's failure to keep its covenant responsibilities.

Together with the passage from Deuteronomy, Paul includes a phrase from Isaiah 29:10, "a spirit of stupor," from a passage of judgment upon Jerusalem for its deep sin. The term translated "stupor" is rare, found only here and Isaiah 29:10; 60:3 in the two testaments. It means stupefaction or a paralysis of thought, called in Isaiah "a spirit of deep sleep," meaning a complete inability to contemplate spiritual realities. The mind, the eyes, and the ears are no longer open to understand truth, and God is judging people by making them completely blind to his ways.

The Judgment: Eyes Are Darkened (11:9–10)

Paul takes the third text from Psalm 69:22–23, a lament psalm used often in the early church in connection with the life and passion of Jesus (Mark 3:21; 15:23, 36; John 2:17; 15:25; Acts 1:20; Rom 15:3; Phil 4:3; Heb 11:26; Rev 3:5; 16:1). It was natural for New Testament writers to use David's thoughts to describe the thoughts of the Davidic Messiah and thus to see the reflections on David's enemies in the psalm to describe the enemies of the Christ.

In both Deuteronomy and the psalm the eyes are darkened and cannot see. The image of darkness is also used in 1:21 of the total depravity of the Gentiles and in 2:19 of the Jewish pretense that they were "a light for those who are in the dark" when in fact they were equally guilty. Paul expands this imagery to include "a snare and a trap, a stumbling block and a retribution for them." Paul first draws on "stumbling block" imagery in Romans 9:33 and will return to it later in 14:13; 16:17. This imagery pictures a level of depravity that turns on itself and self-destructs. Paul is asking God to confirm their hardness, to condemn them for their unbelief.

The final part of this quotation asks that "their backs be bent forever," depicting extreme punishment in chains and under a yoke. Several translate the adverb "continually" rather than "forever," indicating that this situation will last only so long as the hardened ones remain closed to the gospel. It is more likely that this word denotes ongoing punishment, yet it is doubtful that Paul thinks the opposition of unbelieving Jews is an unpardonable sin and is asking for eternal perdition for them. (After all, he himself was converted!) Rather, he means that they will face God's displeasure and punishment so long as they refuse to believe and continue to persecute God's true people, the new Israel.

———

In Romans 9–10, Paul answered the charge that God had broken his covenant promises with Israel, showing that God, not Israel, was sovereign and had the right to both choose who were his and harden the others (9:6–29). Then he proved that in reality Israel, not God, had failed in their covenant responsibilities and stood guilty of unbelief (9:30–10:21). In this chapter, Paul sets out to prove God's justice and mercy: God has not rejected his people but has chosen a remnant from the nation as his own.

In 11:2 we find the premise for the chapter: "God did not reject his people." We would expect this, and it's a helpful summary of the whole unit, but Paul adds "whom he foreknew," summarizing also the other major emphasis, God's predetermined choice of Israel. God knew when he chose Abraham and his progeny that these catastrophes would occur and did so anyway. But God's basic promise remained true. He fulfilled his covenant promises by centering on a remnant who would join believing Gentiles in a new, true Israel.

He did not "cut off" his covenant people but turned instead to that small group within the larger Israel who would come to God's Messiah in faith. There is no need to complain with Elijah that the numbers opposed to God's true people are too powerful, for God has always accomplished incredible things with very few faithful people. The remnant of Elijah's time, of Paul's time, and of our time are more than enough to change the world.

Paul in verses 7–10 stresses also the negative side: only the elect remnant obtain salvation, and God has hardened the others. Yet this is in reality a positive point for Paul, because the presence of an elect remnant shows that God has not rejected his covenant people but has chosen the few to form the nucleus of a new Israel. In verses 9–10, Paul calls God's condemnation down on unbelieving Israel for their rejection of Christ. In both the positive and negative aspects of God's sovereign choice (choosing a remnant and hardening the others), God is proved faithful to his covenant promises. In fact, Paul is calling the blessings and curses of the covenant in Leviticus 26 down upon the nation.

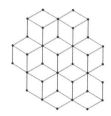

A NATIONAL FUTURE
FOR ISRAEL, PART 2:
GOD'S FUTURE PLACE FOR
JEWS AND GENTILES
(11:11-24)

As "apostle to the Gentiles" (v. 13), Paul in this section wants to place all he has said so far in chapters 9–11 in terms of Jew-Gentile relationships. Israel's failure has led to God's turning to the Gentiles for their salvation. Then, the salvation of the Gentiles was intended to make the Jews jealous (vv. 11, 14) and thereby lead to the salvation of the Jewish people (v. 26). In Paul's day, Israel was divided into a repentant minority and a hardened majority, but that is not God's plan for the future. He still has a salvific intent, and his covenant blessings will once again fall upon Israel. Even the hardening of Israel is meant to bring salvation to the Gentiles, and their salvation will eventually lead to a saved Israel and their full inclusion in the new Israel. In the future, "all Israel will be saved" and God's plan will be complete.

There are two parts to this section. (1) In verses 11–16 God's rejection of Israel has made way for the coming of salvation to the Gentiles, that is, to "the reconciliation of the world" (v. 15). The further purpose is to make Israel envious of the blessings on the Gentiles and to bring them to salvation as well. (2) In verses 17–24 Paul presents this anew through a metaphor: God has removed many Jewish branches from an olive tree and grafted Gentile branches into that tree. This should produce humility among the Gentiles, not pride, for the Gentiles are just as responsible as the Jews and can be removed in turn.

THE REJECTION OF ISRAEL BRINGS SALVATION TO THE GENTILES (11:11–16)

Paul is afraid his readers will surmise from what he has said in 11:1–10 that the choice of the remnant and the hardening of the "others" is permanent, so there is no longer any hope for Israel. His response in verses 11–16 takes four stages:

- Israel has been rejected, but this state is not permanent (v. 11a).
- The immediate purpose of this rejection is to bring salvation to the Gentiles (vv. 11b–12).
- The more distant purpose is to make Israel jealous through the Gentiles (vv. 11c, 14).
- This eventually will bring Israel back to God (vv. 14–16).

PURPOSE: MAKE ISRAEL ENVIOUS AND BRING GREATER RICHES (11:11)

As in 11:1, Paul begins this section with "I ask," followed by a rhetorical question expecting a negative answer: "Again I ask: Did they stumble so as to fall beyond recovery? Not at all!" Once more Paul's purpose is to counter a potential misunderstanding. In the psalm quotation of verse 9, Paul asked God to send a "stumbling block" to make them fall. This was stated so strongly that readers could think the fall was irredeemable and that it meant eternal damnation for all of Israel. Now Paul asks, "Did they stumble so as to fall beyond recovery?" He is countering the mistaken supposition that the rejection of Israel was final.

Paul goes a step further in correcting the error, considering the fall of Israel to be not just retrievable but an important salvation-historical stage in bringing salvation to the world: "because of their transgression, salvation has come to the Gentiles." The "transgression" is the "trespass" of Adam (used six times in 5:12-21), leading to the sinfulness of humankind inherited from Adam. The sin of falling and rejecting the gospel on the part of the Jews had a positive result—God turned to the Gentiles and included them in his new messianic community. This is now part of God's plan of salvation, as seen in the missionary journeys of Paul. The Jews out of "jealousy" placed him under the ban and cast him out of their synagogues, resulting in his turning to the Gentiles (Acts 13:45-46; 18:6-7; 19:8-10). This means the Great Commission was fulfilled partly as a result of Jewish opposition.

Yet this does not quite complete the picture. When the Gentile mission was successful, God used it "to make Israel envious." In the Acts passages noted above, the Jews wanted many Gentile conversions to prove the superiority of Jewish ways, and they were jealous that Christianity was outshining Judaism in this area. Their jealousy here is over Christians enjoying the covenant privileges that belonged to Israel. The second type of envy would lead the Jews eventually to surrender to God and Christ in faith so they could recover their place among God's covenant people.

This Jewish envy worked in two directions. It caused the Jewish people to persecute believers intensely (Acts 13:45; 17:5), but Paul's stress here is on their desire to retrieve what they had lost, their right relationship with God. This goes back to the Deuteronomy 32:21 citation in 10:19, "I will make you envious by those who are not a nation." God is using the success of the Gentile mission to remind the Jews of what they had lost because of unbelief, and thereby to stimulate their return to him.

God even uses human sin and rejection to accomplish his goals—a perfect example of all things working together for good (8:28). As we will see in the next verse, Jewish spiritual poverty will result in God's riches being given to Gentiles, but that will in turn produce Jewish jealousy and their surrender to God, so that eventually God's riches will be universally experienced by all humankind!

Result: Greater Riches for Jews and Gentiles (11:12)

Paul has frequently used "how much more/greater" to expand on the results of sin and the gospel in this world (5:9, 10, 15, 17; 11:24), and here he uses the phrase to enumerate the greater blessings that flow even from the rejection of Israel. By the salvation-historical steps emanating from their rejection of their Messiah, God would eventually bring about their full evangelization.

The rest of this subsection (vv. 12–16) addresses Gentile readers. Paul says this explicitly in verse 13, and shows it also by referring to the Jews in the third person ("they," "their"). He wants the Gentiles to understand what God is doing through them for his Jewish people. The Gentile mission, dear as it is to God's heart, is intended as a step to the critical thing, the *full* evangelization of his covenant people, Israel. In these verses, Paul explains why this is so important.

He uses two "if" clauses in verse 12 to highlight the results of Jewish rejection. Both center on the salvation coming to the Gentiles described in verse 11 and show that the basis was Israel's "transgression" (repeating the term from v. 11) and her "loss." In the Greek the latter means "weakness" or "defeat" and depicts their rejection of Christ as their "defeat" by sin. The defeat, however, produced "riches for the world" and for "the Gentiles" (synonymous ideas). These riches are the kingdom blessings promised to God's faithful, the wealth inherent to being the children of God and coheirs with Christ (8:15–17). This is not only salvation but also sanctification, "the riches of his kindness, forbearance and patience" (2:4) as well as "the riches of his glory" (9:23) and "of God's grace that he lavished on us" (Eph 1:7–8).

The last part is somewhat difficult to understand: "how much greater riches will their full inclusion bring" (literally "will their fullness bring"). It is best to see this looking forward to the conversion of the "full number" of "all Israel" in 11:25-32. Though the "defeat" of Israel because of unbelief is sad in the present, there is a glorious future harvest when all of God's covenant people return to him. This means the current opposition of the Jews is wonderful in the sense that it is bringing God's salvific riches to bear on the Gentiles. And if this is true, "how much greater" will be the joy when this in turn brings Israel back to God. Thus God's greater purpose in all this is the final salvation of the Jewish people, so that they join believing Gentiles in the new and true Israel. At present the true Israel contains very few Jews, but the future is glorious and can only be characterized by "fullness," a rich term (*plērōma*) that probably contains multiple meanings: the full number of Jews (the primary thrust), the fullness of times in God's plans (see Gal 4:4), and the fullness of riches God has in mind for his people.

Purpose of Reaching the Gentiles: Save the Jews (11:13-14)

Many think Paul takes a parenthetical turn in these verses, but I don't think so. There may be a slight tangent, but he has just addressed God's plan for using the infusion of Gentiles into the church as a means of bringing the Jews back from their spiritual "defeat" to experience once more the full blessings of being his people. Now Paul wants to tell his Gentile readers what part his own ministry will be playing in this. He also wants to remind them again of his deep-seated concern for his Jewish kin (as in 9:1-5; 10:1; 11:1-2), to the extent that his calling to be "apostle to the Gentiles" has a deeper purpose—to use the Gentile mission to bring Israel to salvation by arousing their envy.

Thus he makes explicit that he is "talking to you Gentiles" about this ultimate goal. He wants them to comprehend the motivation behind his ministry to Jews and Gentiles. An important part of his reason for ministering to Gentiles is to use it for the salvation of Israel. He was commissioned on the Damascus Road as "apostle to the Gentiles" (Acts 26:17-18), and this was confirmed by Ananias

(Acts 9:15) and then a temple vision (Acts 22:21). He considered his ministry to the Gentiles one of the great apocalyptic "mysteries" (Eph 3:3-6; 6:19-20; Col 1:26-27). It was at the core of his life, but at the same time he realized that an equally important part of God's strategy for him was to use this ministry to the Gentiles to awaken a longing for their own salvation among his fellow Jews.

In light of this he adds, "I take pride in my ministry" (literally, "I glorify my ministry"), asking them to understand how much his Gentile ministry means to him. However, he "glories" in it not only to see Gentiles come to Christ but also "in the hope that I may somehow arouse my own people to envy and save some of them" (v. 14). Paul has mentioned this "jealousy" earlier (10:19; 11:11). His desire for his own ministry is to provoke his fellow Jews to jealousy to drive them to reconsider Christ.

Note the emphasis on "*some* of them." Paul is not a universalist, thinking that every single person among Israel will turn to Christ. The theme in this section is that only some will respond positively (9:6-7, 21; 10:16; 11:17). However, 11:25-32 predicts that "all Israel" will in the end come to their Christ. Paul's hope is that each day more of his fellow Jews will turn to Christ.

THE SALVATION OF THE JEWS: LIFE FROM THE DEAD (11:15)

This verse restates the point of verse 12, creating an ABA pattern:
A riches for the world = full inclusion of the Jews (v. 12)
    B Paul's ministry to the Gentiles = salvation to the Jews (vv. 13-14)
A' reconciliation for the world = life from the dead for the Jews (v. 15)

Putting the four verses together, there are four steps as God's plan comes full circle: (1) God's rejection of Israel (2) produces Paul's ministry to the Gentiles. (3) This successful ministry in turn arouses envy among the Jewish people, (4) leading to reconciliation and salvation for Israel. The term for "rejection" only occurs one other place, Acts 27:22, where it means "loss" ("not one of you will be lost"). The point is that God "rejects" the nation (loss of salvation) for a time in order to "accept" them later. This is similar to the exile, as God had the nation taken captive by the Babylonians in order to bring them back later.

God is the active agent here. In rejecting the nation, he has "brought reconciliation to the world," meaning he has brought humankind back into right relationship with him (see 5:11). As in 5:9–10, the word "reconciliation" implies that this is accomplished by the death of Christ and the acceptance of him by the world—both Jews and Gentiles. This in turn leads to God accepting them into his kingdom.

It is critical to separate the groups carefully here: *God* has rejected *the Jewish people* in order to bring reconciliation to the world, *the Gentiles*, so that this may lead *God* to accept *the Jewish people* and bring *the Jewish people* back from the dead. At one level this resurrection is figurative (as in 6:13), referring to the conversion of Israel as bringing eternal life to those who were spiritually dead. Paul may be thinking of the valley in Ezekiel 37:2–14, where dry bones who are brought back from the dead, considering this a fulfillment of the restoration of Israel—a second return from exile, this time to full salvation in Christ. Yet at another level Paul means a literal resurrection, pointing to the return of Christ and the final resurrection of the saints from the dead. Paul will expand on this in 11:25–32, when the "full inclusion" (v. 12) takes place and "all Israel" is saved at the return of Christ.

RESULT: THE WHOLE BATCH IS HOLY (11:16)

There is considerable debate as to whether verse 16 concludes 11–15 or introduces 17–24. I think it is better to see it as a conclusion because of the theme of the small remnant reaching the whole nation (11–15). Paul uses two similar metaphors here, the firstfruits and the root. The first stems from Numbers 15:17–21, when after they entered the promised land, God told the Israelites to take the "firstfruits" of the dough used for baking their bread and offer it to him. This became the grain offering once they were in the land. Paul's probable point here, that from these firstfruits "the whole batch is holy," is not made in Numbers, but rabbinic logic would say that when firstfruits consecrated a harvest, it was consecrated to God. Therefore, when a part of the dough was set apart for the Lord, the entire batch of dough was made holy by it. This thought is similar to 1 Corinthians 5:6, "a little yeast leavens the whole batch of dough."

The second metaphor is simpler and more clear but makes the same point: "if the root is holy, so are the branches." A plant's root determines what kind of plant it is, so a holy root always produces a holy tree.

There are three primary interpretations for what these two metaphors are talking about: (1) the patriarchs who begin the story of Israel with holiness, as in verse 28 below, which says the people of Israel "are loved on account of the patriarchs"; (2) The remnant, or Jewish Christians, who are the means by which the nation will be saved (v. 14); (3) Jesus Christ as the basis of salvation. Both the patriarchs and the remnant can make sense in this context, but in light of verse 28 the patriarchs are slightly more likely. As in 9:5, the patriarchs were the source of God's special favor to his chosen people. In the first metaphor they are a sanctifying presence as "firstfruits," and the "whole batch" is the nation set apart for God because of them. As the "roots" of the Jewish people, their sanctity is conveyed to God's people. Because of their formative influence, Israel belongs to God and is loved by him (v. 28).

THE JEWS WERE REMOVED FROM THE OLIVE TREE AS A WARNING TO THE GENTILES (11:17-24)

The second half of this section builds on the idea of the root and branches from verse 16 and develops it into a corporate metaphor of the relationship between the Jewish and Gentile peoples in God's economy. Old Testament authors often depicted Israel as an olive tree (Jer 11:16; Hos 14:6). Olives are a major crop in the

Mediterranean world, so the principles of its cultivation would have been well known. Here the olive tree refers not just to Israel but to the whole church composed of Gentiles as well as Jews. A major purpose for this image is to show the importance of sustenance to a healthy olive tree; both Jew and Gentile have no hope unless they draw spiritual nourishment from God and Christ and truly become part of God's tree, the new Israel.

THE JEWS BROKEN OFF, THE GENTILES INSERTED (11:17)

This passage begins with a lengthy clause that assumes (*ei*, "if") the reality of the condition (Jews broken off, Gentiles grafted in). This concludes with a "then" clause that is a warning to the Gentiles (v. 18) against boasting in their new status and privileges. The tragedy is that "some of the branches have been broken off," referring to those Jews who have rejected the gospel. This is the point of chapters 9–11 thus far (see the introduction to this chapter). The majority have turned away from Christ, but a few, a remnant, have found Christ in faith. They remain part of the olive tree and join believing Gentiles as the new messianic community. The image of the olive tree is a corporate image, with the branches the individuals who respond either in rejection or with faith.

These believing Jews are "the natural branches." The unnatural ones (called "wild"), the Gentiles, are grafted in "among" (not "in place of," see below) these "other" branches. Each has been grafted in as "a wild olive shoot," pictured individually to emphasize each convert. They are not branches from a cultivated tree but from the wild forest. While olive trees were the most highly cultivated fruit in the Mediterranean, wild olive trees did not produce a great deal of fruit. Because of this, farmers would normally take branches for grafting onto cultivated trees. Paul is deliberately turning the image around to make his point that this is God's grace, and the Gentiles have nothing to boast about. They are wild olive shoots and have done nothing to warrant God's mercy to them. "Have been grafted in" is a divine passive and stresses God's gracious action on their behalf. Only when he takes control can the engrafted Gentiles "now share in the nourishing sap from the olive root." The olive tree was well known for the huge amount of sap it produced, so this is an apt picture of the bounty that the Christian has in Christ.

Above I pointed out that the olive tree was a symbol of Israel in the Old Testament, and here it would also seem to be a symbol of the church. In this sentence the image seems to typify Christ as the source of nourishment for his church. Yet we need to understand there are three parts to the olive tree image—the tree, the roots, and the branches. The tree is Israel and the church as an entity under God, the roots supplying nourishment are God and Christ (though the roots are the patriarchs in the next verse), and the branches are the individual members of Israel or the church. Within the olive tree, the branches receive nourishing sap from the roots.

GENTILES: DO NOT BOAST, YOU ANSWER TO GOD (11:18-21)

No superiority: the root supports you (11:18)

Since the gift of being grafted into the olive tree and receiving nourishment from Christ is entirely a gift from God and has no basis in merit, Paul warns the Gentiles, "Do not consider yourself to be superior to those other branches" (literally "Do not boast over those branches"). The word "boast" (*katakauchō*) pictures the pride of the Gentiles as they brag about their greater privileges and lord it over the Jews. Like Israel, they could become proud of their new status and begin to think they were better.

Paul earlier condemned the people of Israel for such boasting (2:17, 23), and now it is the Gentiles' turn. All glory must go to God, for it is he and he alone who saves us. Pride is one of the basic sins, and people generally want to feel superior to others in order to bolster their own egos. It is common to feel this along racial and ethnic lines. We use anything and everything to look down on another. This type of paternalism was a problem in missions in the nineteenth and twentieth centuries, when missionaries proclaimed Western civilization to the "primitives" as much as they did the gospel.

Paul reminds the Gentile Christians, "You do not support the root, but the root supports you." In verse 16 the root was Abraham and the patriarchs. He reminds the Gentile readers in this light that they are not the source of blessing to the Jews. Rather, they are the recipients of blessings only because of the Abrahamic covenant, which proclaimed blessings for the Gentiles. The movement of the blessings is from Abraham to the Jews and then to the Gentiles. In fact, the Gentiles in the church are Abraham's offspring (4:11-13, 16-18; 9:7-8) and are dependent entirely on what they have received from him.

They were broken off because of unbelief—so be afraid (11:19-20)

Paul now provides a particular instance of pride-filled claims on the part of Gentiles. Continuing the diatribe style of 2:1-3:8 and several other places, Paul chooses an imaginary opponent who echoes this sense of superiority: "Branches were broken off so that I could be grafted in." Note the centrality of "I" (Greek: *ego*). This Gentile is saying God removed the Jewish people specifically so he could make room for the Gentiles, dislodging the inferior to include the superior.

In verse 20 Paul responds with a qualified yes ("Granted"), then adds the important "But ...." God has indeed removed Israel and grafted in the Gentiles, *but* that does not mean he wanted to get rid of Israel so he could replace them with Gentiles. He actually turned to the Gentiles to use them to make Israel envious and bring them back to God. Further, "they were broken off because of unbelief," not because God wanted the Gentiles to take their place. Paul adds that in contrast, "you [Gentiles] stand by faith," not on the basis of works or merit (3:27; 4:2). The Jews fell because of unbelief; the Gentiles enter because of belief. There can be no pride when we become members of God's people. A very important lesson—and a hard one for overachieving people to learn—is that we are nothing and God is everything!

There is a way of thinking that in some circles is called "replacement theology," which would say that the Jews are no longer the chosen people but have been replaced by Gentiles. Paul has preempted such a view, because it would mean God failed to keep his covenant promises and was unjust in the way he treated his covenant people (9:6, 14). There is not a dichotomy between the two covenant peoples but a salvation-historical continuity. The truth is that only "some" of Israel was broken off the olive tree (v. 17), and they have not been replaced. Rather, the believing Jews are the natural branches still on the olive tree, and the wild branches, the Gentiles, have been grafted in to *join* them on the tree. Now the tree is made up of the natural (the Jews) and the wild (the Gentiles) branches that together make up the church, the new Israel. The church simply continues the ministry of Israel in this new economy, and the Jewish people join the new Israel when they put their trust in Christ.

Paul concludes, "Do not be arrogant, but tremble" (literally, "be afraid"). To be arrogant is to think more highly of yourself than you should (as in Rom 12:3, 16; 1 Tim 6:17). There is no Christian basis for having an overinflated view of your own worth, as in the title of the book *Famous People Who Have Met Me*. Arrogance is one of the seven deadly sins, and it is a problem we all have. It was at the heart of the first sin in the garden, and most sins flow out of a self-centered perspective on life. The antidote to arrogance is to replace the centrality of self with the centrality of God. Fear of God is the basis of "trembling" here. We know we will stand before God and give account for our lives (2 Cor 5:10; Heb 13:7), and we should be afraid of what God finds at that moment. We may have to stand before him in shame for the way we have lived (2 Tim 2:15).

It is common in our day to think of "fear of God" as reverence, but this is one of the passages where the meaning is terror. There is real danger here of rejection by God. The unbelieving Jews were removed from the olive tree, and the obvious ramification of that removal is eternal condemnation. There are three possible overtones in any biblical *fear* passage—terror, awe, and reverence. There can be overlapping between the three, but context must decide, and we must be careful not to read more into words than context indicates.

Danger: God will not spare you either (11:21)

Paul moves on to a major reason for fear: "For if God did not spare the natural branches, he will not spare you either." In ancient care of olive trees, the wild olive shoot was not as valuable as a cultivated one because it did not produce much fruit. Why would anyone think it would be given more care? If God would cast away and burn a natural branch (cf. John 15:6), how much more readily would he discard the wild olive shoots, especially since the cultivated natural branches were stronger than the grafted wild ones? The weaker branches have to be more aware of the dangers, especially because in this analogy the danger is final judgment.

The proper response to Paul's words here is the same as in Philippians 2:12, "work out your salvation with fear and trembling," realizing the dangers of inattention. Still, we are not speaking of pure terror but a reasoned sense of responsibility to God that leads us to work very hard at our walk with him in total dependence on Jesus and the Spirit, who empower us to live victoriously for him. We do so in light of the great promise of the next verse in Philippians 2:13, "For it is God who works in you to will and to act in order to fulfill his good purpose."

WARNING: THE KINDNESS AND STERNNESS OF GOD (11:22-24)

You can be cut off and the Jews grafted back in (11:22-23)

Paul now sums up verses 17–21 by telling his Gentile readers to consider both the benefits and the responsibility of their new status in Christ, that is, "the kindness and sternness of God." The removal of the majority of the nation from the olive tree is God's "sternness," and the grafting in of believing Gentiles is his "kindness." The term for kindness (*chrēstotēs*) refers to God's goodness and mercy (see 2:4), shown in his act of bringing the Gentiles to himself. The term for sternness (*apotomia*) refers to his judgment, which is completely just and at the same time final. These are the two sides of God's holy nature: his love and his justice.

His sternness is to "those who fell," showing their own responsibility for their dire predicament (see 1 Cor 10:12; Heb 4:11; Rev 2:5). Paul draws a stark contrast between the Jews who fell and the Gentiles who "stand by faith" (v. 20). The former rely on their own strength, the latter exercise total dependence on God. His kindness is reserved for those who "continue in his kindness," who persevere in their walk with God and, as in Colossians 1:23, "continue in your faith." Paul mentions God's kindness three times here; it is not just a gift but also the means of rising above our difficulties and temptations. God pours out his riches into our lives (Eph 1:7–8), and his primary gift is the faith to put our trust in Christ and maintain our relationship with him. Out of this comes the spiritual victory commanded in this verse.

Without surrender to him, the warning is severe: "Otherwise, you also will be cut off" (just as the Jews were). This is the flip side of the security promised in 8:28, 35–39. God faithfully keeps his covenant promises (9:6, 14) and shows his kindness in both adopting us as members of his family (8:15–17) and providing his secure protection through his power (Eph 1:18–20; 1 Pet 1:5). Now our responsibility is to "continue in his kindness" lest we lose it all! Ongoing faith and surrender to him gives us the power to surmount our challenges and find victory. The alternative is too frightening to contemplate. We will be "cut off" from God for all eternity.

There is a great deal of discussion regarding whether this verse warns about loss of salvation. Many think Paul is not speaking of true believers but of members of the (visible) church who by failing to continue in faith show they never truly believed. This, in my opinion, is the best Calvinist response to passages like this (see also Heb 6:4-6; 10:26-31; 2 Pet 2:20-22; Rev 21:7-8, and others). But is this enough? Those Jews who were cut off were not all of true Israel but those who never found faith in Christ. Similarly, the Gentiles who received God's kindness did not constitute all Gentiles but only those who believed. It hardly suffices to relegate this warning only to those Gentiles who were members of the church but never believed. Paul gives no hint of this here. It is better to see this as a valid warning that any believing Gentile who falls away will be cut off. As in James 1:19-20, these people may turn back to Christ and be forgiven (like the Jews in the next paragraph), but so long as they are cut off they are headed for eternal destruction.

While the Gentiles face the danger of losing all God has given them if they fail to persevere in their salvation, the Jews can return from their apostasy and be reinstated by God (v. 23). Verse 23 is the opposite of verse 22. In this case God's kindness and severity can be reversed: the Gentiles can be cut off for failure to remain faithful to God, and the Jews, "if they do not persist in unbelief, they will be grafted in." God treats both groups the same; there are no favorites. The Gentiles must *continue* in their faith, and the Jews must *stop continuing* in their unbelief.

When the Jewish people come to faith in Christ, they will join the Gentiles and be grafted into Christ's olive tree. They have lost their place in the true people of God, but God "is able to graft them in again." Jesus provided this principle when discussing the salvation of the wealthy: "With man this is impossible, but not with God; all things are possible with God" (Mark 10:27). The emphasis is on God's power—"is able" can be translated "has the power [*dynatos*] to do so," as in 4:21, "God had the power to do what he had promised," and 9:22, "choosing to ... make his power known" (also 1:4, 20; 9:17). All is made possible by divine grace exhibited in divine power. The Gentiles dare never assume they are in and Israel is out. God has brought the Gentiles into his family as part of the process of bringing Israel back to him (11:11, 14), so there is no place for pride.

The natural branch can easily be grafted in again (11:24)

Paul concludes his olive tree metaphor by referring to ancient cultivation techniques one further time. He begins, "if you were cut out of an olive tree that is wild by nature, and contrary to nature were grafted into a cultivated olive tree." It was seldom done that way because it was a tricky process. However, God is the master gardener who is able to do so. If God can successfully graft in the wild Gentiles, "how much more readily will these, the natural branches, be grafted into their own olive tree." This continues Paul's contrast in verse 21 between the wild and the natural branches. The wild is less productive than the natural, and it is against nature to graft it into a natural olive tree. If God has the power to bring the "wild" Gentiles to himself, he certainly can bring the "natural" Jews back to himself.

At the same time, this does not mean God cares more for the Jewish people than the Gentiles, nor that the Jews have an advantage over the Gentiles. Just the opposite—Paul is responding to some Gentiles who thought the advantage was theirs and had begun to boast. This was likely a real problem in the Roman church, with some Gentiles thinking they were superior to their Jewish Christian brothers and sisters (as we will see in 14:1–15:13). This comes from a racist mindset and is always a huge mistake. We all equally need the grace of God and to care for each other.

In this magnificent section, Paul continues to answer Jewish queries about God's intentions for his old covenant people. He sees in the remnant of Israel, the believing Jews, God's predetermined mercy for the fallen nation. He goes a step further here, showing there can be joy even in the majority who have greeted Christ with unbelief. In this we see the full extent of God's mercy and grace, for his plan of salvation has made way for a four-stage evangelistic miracle arising from Jewish rejection. (1) Jewish unbelief has led God to reject them, turn to the Gentiles, and bring them into the kingdom. (2) God in turn does this to make these now-unbelieving Jews jealous of the covenant privileges that were lost and now belong to the Gentiles. (3) As a result of this jealousy, the former covenant people will come back to Christ and experience national revival (11:25-26). (4) In this way, the universal church will come to completion and achieve all a merciful God has intended. In this process, we can see that our own mission to the world is part of this goal. God's plan is for a holistic church to spread throughout the world. Our goal in mission is the salvation of individual souls but also the uniting of a fallen, divided humanity into one new humanity under Christ (Eph 2:15).

In the second section (vv. 17-24) Paul develops the analogy of the olive tree to picture the relationship of Jews and Gentiles in the church. In the new covenant period, most Jewish people fell into unbelief and were no longer Israel. God broke them off and removed them from his olive tree. Out of their rejection God created the new and true Israel, depicted here as God's olive tree in which two entities were combined, the natural branches (believing Jews) and wild olive shoots (believing Gentiles). The Gentiles did not replace the Jews but joined the remnant among them to become one people, the messianic community. This pictures the plan of God presented in verses 11-16 to show the two becoming one people in Christ. Paul warns the wild shoots that they have earned these privileges not on their own merits but by the grace of God. They dare not brag of their importance, lest they too lose their place in the olive tree.

In light of this, we are to remember the consequences of our actions (vv. 2-4). God pours out his kindness out on those who come to him in faith, relying entirely on the Spirit's empowering presence. His sternness is experienced by those who are immersed in themselves and ignore him in their lives. The judgment they face is harsh—the loss of everything. Yet God's power is indeed greater than anything we will ever face, and we can remain faithful and continue to walk with him in victory. God's strength is more than enough to enable us to persevere in the midst of everything a lost world can throw at us.

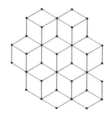

A NATIONAL FUTURE
FOR ISRAEL, PART 3:
FUTURE SALVATION FOR ISRAEL
(11:25-36)

T hese verses form a natural conclusion for chapters 9-11. The issue all along has been the justice of God and whether his covenant promises have failed in light of his rejection of Israel. The second question is whether Israel's failure is final. Paul's answer is that the rejection of Israel is not irrevocable, and God continues to be faithful to them. God has not cut off all Israel, only the unbelieving Jews. There is a glorious future awaiting his people. These verses provide the final astounding revelation of a chapter with mind-numbing surprises, a section that has to be one of the most exciting in Scripture.

There is now a remnant that God has secured out of the apostate nation (11:1-10). Even the "stumbling" of Israel has worked out for good in the sense that it has unleashed the power of God, leading to the four-stage progress of salvation history: the rejection of Israel leads to the conversion of the Gentiles; the success of the Gentile mission leads to Jewish jealousy as they want to recapture the blessings that had been theirs; this will lead to national revival and conversion; and finally this revival will complete God's plan for a worldwide church composed of people from every nation.

In this section, Paul will ground this future salvation of all Israel in the Old Testament promises (vv. 26-27), the irrevocable nature of God's call (vv. 28-29), and God's mercy to the disobedient (vv. 30-32). It is true that the time of rejection not only is in the days of Christ and Paul but also has lasted up to the present, but the time of national revival is still in the future, in keeping with the return of Christ. This revival will constitute the final fulfillment of God's promises to his old covenant people.

GOD HAS A PLAN FOR THE FUTURE SALVATION OF ISRAEL (11:25-27)

ISRAEL HARDENED UNTIL THE FULL NUMBER OF GENTILES ARE SAVED (11:25)

The opening "for" (*gar*, omitted in the NIV) shows that the regrafting of the natural branches into the olive tree in the previous verse is now anchored in the truth of "this mystery" God has revealed to Paul. A mystery is an essential truth that God has kept secret but is now revealing to his people in these last days. "Apocalyptic," a word derived from the Greek word for "revelation" (*apokalypsis*), describes the process and the kind of literature it is. "Mystery" (*mysterion*) describes the contents of the revealed truths.[1]

The primary mystery is Jesus Christ himself and his work of salvation (Rom 16:25; Eph 1:9, 6:19; Col 2:2, 4:3; 1 Tim 3:16) and then the Gentile mission (Eph 3:3-6; Col 1:26-27). There is disagreement as to whether Paul knows this through special prophetic revelation or his study of the Old Testament, but there is no reason to choose between them; both divine inspiration and general reflection on Scripture were likely involved. Here the mystery likely focuses on future rather than present salvation and concerns the Jews rather than the Gentiles.

Paul's purpose is once more (see vv. 18, 20) to counter the problem of Gentile arrogance. "So that you may not be conceited"

---

1. See the discussion in the commentaries in this series at Eph 1:9; Col 1:26-27.

is literally, "lest you be wise in your own eyes," stemming from the view of many Gentiles that they displaced the Jews in God's family and so were superior. In other words, they were spiritual racists and proud of themselves, an attitude seen too often in our churches as well, as we Westerners tend easily to lord it over Christians from Africa or Asia or Latin America.

Paul counters this Gentile arrogance by revealing to them God's "mystery" that "Israel has experienced a hardening in part until the full number of the Gentiles has come in, and in this way all Israel will be saved." There are three parts to the revelation, which form a continuum of salvation: (1) Israel is hardened, leading to the Gentile mission. (2) It forms the salvation-historical core of the current mission, when that mission is complete and the "full number" of converts are brought in. (3) Then national revival will take place, and all Israel will be saved.

First, Israel's hardening is partial and temporary. Paul first explores the idea of the hardening in 11:7–10, linking it to the hardening of Pharaoh from 9:14–18 and making the point that God hardens whomever he wishes (9:18). The "in part" could modify "Israel," meaning that only some of the Jewish people have been hardened, or it could modify "hardened," meaning it is only a partial hardening, or it could modify "experienced," meaning it has only partially fallen on Israel. This last is most likely, because the phrase modifies the verb: "Israel has experienced in part a hardening." Still, more than one aspect is implied. Only unbelieving Israel has been hardened, and that is not eternal but a present judgment making way for the Gentile mission.

Second, as a temporary hardening, it will continue until the "fullness of the Gentiles" has arrived (the literal translation of the Greek). It is difficult to be certain what "fullness" means (see also in v. 12). The idea could be the completion of the Gentile mission, the "full number" of Gentiles destined for salvation (NIV), or the full blessing God intends. Most opt for the full number of Gentiles in light of the parallel with 11:12, and that fits well. This idea was well known in the first century, as evidenced in Revelation 6:11, which stresses the full number of martyrs destined to die before God's final vindication of the saints (so also the contemporary Jewish writings 4 Ezra 4:35–37 and 2 Baruch 23:4). This means the great national revival and restoration of Israel will take place at the end of history after the times of the Gentiles. In Luke 21:23–24 Jesus prophesied that Jerusalem would be trampled "until the times of the Gentiles are fulfilled," also referring to the Gentile mission.

Third, at that time, "all Israel will be saved." "And in this way" means that by bringing the Gentiles to himself, God would "in this manner" reach the Jewish people for himself. This is the salvation process outlined in verses 11–14. The great conversion of the Gentiles in the church's mission would arouse Israel to envy and cause them to return to their Messiah. It is important to realize that "all Israel" does not refer to the Jewish people down through the ages but to the nation at the end of history.[2] I used to believe these verses predicted the gradual evangelization of the Jewish people throughout church history, but that is not the case here. It will take place at the God-determined end of this world, when the Gentile mission has been completed; at that time "all Israel will be saved." The text does not say how this will come about but simply prophesies the event, and Paul's citation of Isaiah in verses 26–27 tells us this event is connected with the second coming of Christ in some way.

Paul has developed the promise of a future salvation for Israel throughout this section (11:1–24). During the church age there is a remnant who have come to Christ (called "messianic Jews" today), but the majority, unbelieving Jews, have been hardened by God. Yet the purpose of this hardening has unleashed a powerful divine movement that has brought the Gentiles to God and grafted them

---

2. This also does not necessarily mean every single Jewish person at that time. Note that it says "all Israel" not "every person from Israel." It will be a national event but not necessarily everyone involved.

into the olive tree. This has been divinely intended to make the Jews envious to the extent that they have repented of their sins and turned to Christ in faith. The result is that at the completion of the Gentile mission, in keeping with the return of Christ, Israel will experience a national revival and be converted to their Messiah.

All Israel Saved at the Second Coming (11:26–27)

As throughout Romans, Paul wants his readers to understand that the Old Testament supports what he is saying. Now he cites material, respectively, from Isaiah 59:20–21 and 27:9. The first passage centers on the sinfulness and injustice of the nation as confessed to Yahweh, resulting in his putting on his armor (59:17) and repaying his enemies among Israel (59:18) while forgiving those who repent. Israel in this section is called to feel sorrow for sin and repent, warning of judgment for those who refuse and promising restoration for those who do.

As he often does, Paul creatively cites the first Isaiah passage ("The deliverer will come from Zion; he will turn godlessness from Jacob") to make his point. The "deliverer" ("redeemer" in Isa 59) in Isaiah is Yahweh, while here it is Christ. In Isaiah Yahweh "will come *to* Zion" as the Divine Warrior to redeem the penitent, and here Christ "will come *from* Zion" to deliver newly converted Israel. Some think Paul is adding material from another passage, perhaps Psalm 14:7 on redemption coming from Zion, but it is more likely that he is making the change himself, adding the motif of the "heavenly Zion" from which Christ will return (Heb 12:22; see also Gal 4:26; Rev 3:12, 21:2). It is clearly the **parousia** (return of Christ) that Paul has in mind with this alteration.

When Christ comes, "he will turn godlessness away from Jacob." In Romans 11 this would be the unbelief of verse 23 and the hardness of verse 25. It is another way to describe the conversion of "all Israel" in the first part of this verse. When "turn away" is used of us, it connotes repentance as turning away from sin. Describing the action of Christ, it means removing the power of evil from the new convert.

Christ will also establish "my covenant with them," also from Isaiah 59:21 but probably including the new covenant prophecy of Jeremiah 31:31-34 (quoted in Heb 8:8-12), when God will "put my law in their minds" and "forgive their wickedness." The old covenant was fulfilled in the new covenant of grace established by Christ. Here that new covenant is brought to completion with respect to Israel. The new covenant reality has already come in the first advent of Christ, but it has not yet been consummated in this world, and that will happen in keeping with the **apocalyptic** event described here.

Paul now adds a final clause to the citation from Isaiah 59:20-21, taken from Isaiah 27:9, "when I take away their sins." This Isaiah passage, like the previous one, also describes the deliverance and forgiveness of Israel as God's judgment of the nation brings about her repentance. In both passages the divine condemnation and hardening has redemptive purposes, leading to penitence and forgiveness and then to deliverance.

These verses make clear that the Jewish people will realize Jesus is the Christ, repent of sins and unbelief, then be forgiven and restored to their covenant relationship with God. However, we are not told how this will take place. In verses 11-24 we are told only in a general sense—the four steps from the rejection of the Jews to the Gentile mission to Jewish jealousy and desire to recapture their former glory to final repentance and national revival. We must leave the details and method with God, who has not deigned to reveal them to us. Other passages on the parousia detail the resurrection of the saints (1 Cor 15:51-57; 1 Thess 4:13-20) and the destruction of God's enemies (1 Thess 5:1-10; 2 Thess 2:8-12; Rev 19:17-21) but not how the conversion of Israel will take place. We know it will happen, but will have to wait to see how God brings it to pass.

GOD'S CALL IS IRREVOCABLE (11:28–29)

Verses 28–32 are a single unit in which Paul defines the theological meaning, though not the method, of the conversion of Israel. In them we see more clearly God's purpose in showing grace and mercy to the Jewish people in spite of their hardening. Because of the deep love of God for his covenant people, those who were once enemies and disobedient will receive mercy and be called to Christ.

These verses also summarize chapters 9–11, reiterating how God has brought not only the Gentiles but also the Jews back to himself. Verse 28 consists of two clauses made up of three word pairs: gospel/election, enemies/those loved, and on your account/on account of the patriarchs. The first clause says, "As far as the gospel is concerned, they are enemies for your sake." The "gospel" refers to the gospel of Christ being proclaimed throughout the world. The Jewish people by opposing the preaching of the gospel have become "enemies" of Christ and the church, and therefore the objects of God's wrath. The idea of "enemy" here stresses both the active (they hate God) and passive (they have become God's enemies) sides of their opposition.

Note the themes of chapters 9–11 here: Israel rejected the gospel (9:3–10:21) and thus was rejected by God (9:6–29). This took place "for the sake of" the Gentiles, as the rejection of the Jews meant salvation and reconciliation for them (11:11–15). When the natural branches were broken off, the wild shoots were grafted in (v. 17). God's plan of salvation was at work—the rejection of the Jews leading to the inclusion of the Gentiles, which in turn produces jealousy on the part of the Jews, leading to their conversion as well.

This latter part of the theological emphasis is the subject of the second clause: "as far as election is concerned, they are loved on account of the patriarchs." God's gracious election of Israel is a hallmark of biblical truth (11:5–6), and throughout the Old Testament Israel is the chosen people because of God's unswerving love of them (2 Chr 9:8; Ps 102:13; Isa 14:1). Even though the majority have forsaken Christ and become his enemies, God still loves his covenant people.

It is important that this love continues "on account of the patriarchs." It is not that the patriarchs did anything to merit God's love. Abraham tried to give Sarah to Pharaoh to save his own skin. The name "Jacob" means "deceiver" or trickster, and he lived up to his name. God's love for the patriarchs was grounded in his grace, not their works (11:6). They are mentioned here because the covenant promises were given to the nation through them (Gen 12:1–3; 13:14–17; 15:1–21; 17:4–19; 22:16–18 [Abraham]; 26:3–5 [Isaac]; 28:10–15 [Jacob]). They were the source of God's covenant blessings to the nation, and it is those promises that are the basis of his elect will.

Paul in verse 29 goes on to tell his readers that Israel in spite of its rejection of Christ is still loved by God, because "God's gifts and his call are irrevocable." The gifts and the call could be separate items, a single entity, or the call could be seen as a special kind of gift. In light of the emphasis on the call to salvation in this section, the latter is slightly more likely. The "gifts" are the covenant privileges and blessings Israel has experienced as God's covenant people, enumerated in 9:3–5. The greatest of the gifts was God's call to be his covenant community.

That call was "irrevocable," a strong term meaning God will never regret calling them to himself. God will never change his mind regarding his promises to Israel. His unchanging faithfulness is a constant in Scripture (Num 23:19; 1 Sam 15:29; Job 12:13; Ps 33:11; Jer 4:28). This does not mean God will never reject those who have turned against him. In verse 28 Paul refers to individuals who have become his enemies. His call is corporate; he will remain faithful to the nation. His judgment and rejection are reserved for individuals. He is faithful to the nation even though he has to condemn many within it.

GOD SHOWS MERCY TO THE DISOBEDIENT (11:30-32)

MERCY FOR THE GENTILES LEADS TO MERCY FOR THE JEWS (11:30-31)

Addressing especially the Gentile Christians in Rome ("you"), Paul tells how God's great love has manifested itself in spite of (and because of) the disobedience of so many in Israel ("they"). These two verses comprise a carefully constructed "just as ... so ... too" sentence reiterating the point made in verses 11-15: God has used the disobedience of Israel to save the Gentiles and now is using the mercy shown the Gentiles to save the Jews. He begins, "Just as you who were at one time disobedient to God," referring to 1:18-32 and the description of the total depravity of the Gentiles. They were indicted because of their refusal to follow God and their constant yielding of their minds and bodies to fleshly pursuits.

Even though they deserve condemnation and judgment, they have "now received mercy," with "now" referring to the new covenant period in which God has turned to the Gentiles. Paul considered this new messianic era a "mystery" (v. 25) through which God revealed a new salvation-historical era, centered in Christ and the Gentile mission (Eph 3:3-6; Col 1:26-27). When this was first revealed to Paul, it took three revelatory events to enable him to accept it—the Damascus road vision (Acts 26:17-18), confirmation by Ananias (Acts 9:15-19), and a vision in the temple (Acts 22:21). Yet even this was made possible "as a result of [Israel's] disobedience," a major stress in this chapter (vv. 11-12, 15). Jewish unbelief led God to turn to the Gentiles and graft them into the olive tree (v. 17).

Paul then turns from the situation of the Gentiles to that of Israel. I will reorganize the NIV of verse 31 to demonstrate the three-part message more clearly: "So now they also have disobeyed for the sake of God's mercy to you, so that they also may now receive mercy." The first two parts sum up verses 1-24 of chapter 11, saying that Jewish disobedience has resulted in God's mercy via the Gentile mission. The final part is the theme of verses 25–32—the conversion of Israel.

Yet this is not the case at present, when Israel had "become disobedient." However, Paul uses two "nows" here, the first detailing their present disobedience but the second complicating the point: "that they too may *now* receive mercy as a result of God's mercy to you." This second "now" refers to the future, the **eschatological** "Now" that will constitute the end of history and bring the conversion of "all Israel" at the return of Christ as in verses 25–26.

It is difficult to know whether Paul is referring to just the final event or also the gradual progress of the Jewish mission. What makes this possible is that the gospel is "first for the Jew," which Paul stated in 1:16. I think this includes both the progress of the mission through history and its culmination in the conversion of all Israel at the end of history. I see it as part of inaugurated eschatology: the ongoing mission to the Jews in the present is an anticipation of the final harvest at the end of the age.

Purpose: Mercy for All (11:32)

This verse draws to a close Paul's argument thus far. Paul describes a twofold purpose of God's judgment in these chapters. First, it continues the theme of 1:24, 26, 28, regarding the punishment upon sinful humankind for its depravity, namely, God "giving them over" to even more serious sin. Both Jews and Gentiles have chosen unbelief, so God has "bound everyone [Jew and Gentile] over to disobedience" so they could taste the bitter fruits of their folly. Second, his final purpose all along is "so that he may have mercy on them all." Divine judgment is redemptive at heart, as shown in the exile under the Assyrians and Babylonians, as God moved his people through those terrible times to restoration and the return from exile. The purpose of the condemnation is to wake them up and bring them to repentance so that some from both Gentiles and Jews may be saved.

The phrase "mercy on them all" does not entail universalism, the view that in the end every single person will be saved. All of Romans attests to the error of this view. It does mean that God's purpose in the entire process is to graft in branches to the olive tree from both Jewish and Gentile groups. The result is God's "mercy on them all" and converts from both groups in the church.

Paul's emphasis here is on the grace of God exhibited in his sovereign initiative in confining or "shutting all people up" (the meaning of "bound everyone over") in disobedience. Note the balance in God's imprisoning people in the very "disobedience" they have chosen for themselves. Once again we have God's sovereign will (9:6-29) and human responsibility for their own actions (9:30-10:21). Here we are told that God's true purpose is not final condemnation but "so that he may have mercy on them all." The word "all" is corporate (shown to Jew and Gentile alike) more than individual (all saved). Still, individuals from both groups experience God's mercy in salvation.

PAUL CLOSES WITH A DOXOLOGY ON THE DEPTHS OF GOD'S MERCY (11:33-36)

Many think this doxology was written out of Paul's confusion and even frustration at the mystery of God's predestining will, but I think the truth may be just the opposite. God's incredible mercy and the conversion of people from every segment of humanity are more than Paul can handle, and so in the depths of religious ecstasy he composes a hymn to the grace and mercy of God. Far from frustration, he exhibits wonder and asks his readers to join him in rejoicing at the mystery of the inscrutable mind of God. The main theme of the doxology is praise to the great God who has shown unworthy Jews and Gentiles his wondrous mercy. His reflections on human sinfulness have led to ever-deeper realizations regarding the depths of God's mercy in spite of their terrible depravity and disbelief, and so he breaks out in song at the "depth of the riches" of his grace and the "unsearchable" nature of his judgments.

The nine-line hymn is constructed as a series of threes. Three exclamations (v. 33, the first naming three divine attributes); three questions on our inability to comprehend the mind of God (vv. 34–35); and a threefold prepositional formula on God as the source and goal of all things (v. 36).

God's Great Plan (11:33)

The hymn begins with an awestruck exclamation at "the depth of the riches of the wisdom and knowledge of God." There are three, not two, attributes here—riches, wisdom, knowledge. "Depth" refers to the inexhaustible immensity of God's attributes. All the universe is summed up in them, and none can comprehend the vastness of who he is. His "riches" looks back to 2:4; 9:23; 10:12; and 11:12, detailing his mercy and grace, the spiritual blessings of the heavenly realm that according to Ephesians 1:3, 7–8, are "the riches of God's grace ... lavished on us." Through these riches God brought salvation to us.

Many separate God's "wisdom" and "knowledge" into separate ideas, and this is somewhat correct, but the two are closely intertwined throughout Scripture. Here all three attributes relate to God's great gift of salvation. The stress is on God's "wisdom" exhibited in his great plan of salvation as unpacked in 3:21–8:39, the working of his wise will in the atoning sacrifice of Christ on the cross and the offer of salvation to sinful humankind, Jew and Gentile alike. The meaning of the "knowledge of God" is not our knowing him but his knowing us and electing us to be his children and members of his church. In one sense "knowledge" refers to his omniscient knowledge of all truth, specifically his foreknowledge (8:29; 11:2) of us. His wisdom is his gracious plan, and his knowledge results from that plan in his choice of us to be his people.

The next two lines develop further the theme of God's wisdom and knowledge. The two parallel each other in a **chiastic** fashion, that is, A (unsearchable), B (his judgments), B (his paths), A (beyond tracing out). God's judgments are not his acting as judge (as in 2:2, 5:16) but his decisions in general, especially his decision to bring salvation to humankind, both the sternness and the kindness of 11:22. These actions of his will are "unsearchable" or "inscrutable," impossible for the human mind to fathom (see Job 42:3; Ps 147:5; Isa 40:28). God knows us, but we do not understand God. All we can do is trust his greater wisdom as we encounter the mysteries of life. We will never solve them, but he will lead us over the rough roads.

The phrase "paths of God" (NIV "his paths") describes the action side of his "judgments." As his decisions act themselves out in our lives, they are "beyond tracing out," meaning they are beyond our ability to understand or control. We, believers and nonbelievers alike, will never fully comprehend God's sovereign work, especially his salvation-historical actions. The mysteries Paul has explored in Romans will only be fully clear when we get to heaven. For now we must leave it all with God, be thankful for all he has done, and accept his greater wisdom.

I have spent some time in this commentary working on the divisive issue of divine sovereignty and human responsibility (see the comments at 8:28-30 and at the end of ch. 10), and this verse is an important reminder about such debates. Human pride makes us not only certain about our own theological preferences but also judgmental toward others. We do not know the mind of the Lord on many issues, and we must recognize that all truth does not begin with us. One scholar has even said that all Arminians are going to hell because by definition they have to deny the sovereignty of God. This is not true theologically, and such hubris and pride is a sin in itself.

We must all work out our views on critical doctrines like eternal security or predestination, but we also must remain humble and realize God has not given us final answers on many issues. The cardinal doctrines like the Trinity, the deity of Christ, and substitutionary atonement are taught unambiguously in Scripture, but many others are not because God wants us to wrestle and find the balance between issues like sovereignty and responsibility. There are important passages that speak of both, and we must respect each other and become "iron sharpening iron" as we debate the sides. It is time to quit going to war and realize we "know in part and we prophesy in part" (1 Cor 13:9) on many issues. This does not mean we cannot take a strong stance (I do on this issue in this commentary), but we must be humble and show respect to the other side. Some of my closest friends are Calvinists, while I am more Arminian. I tell them I am predestined to be right on this!

THE INABILITY OF HUMANITY TO COMPREHEND HIS THOUGHTS (11:34–35)

Three rhetorical questions in these verses go further on this theme of the ultimate unknowability of God and his ways. The first two questions allude to Isaiah 40:13, part of the well-known turning point of Isaiah that begins, "Comfort, comfort my people" (40:1). Rescue in Isaiah's day seemed impossible, for the Babylonians seemed invincible. God was reminding his people not to question his actions and to trust in him. Paul may well have that entire section in mind, and he draws a parallel with his own day in which deliverance also seems impossible.

Yet now that Christ has come, God is going to save Israel in a far more significant way. Once more no one "has known the mind of the Lord," and no one "has been his counselor." God is indeed incomprehensible, and we human beings can only watch in awe as he does his work and performs his will.

In ourselves we cannot cope with the complex world around us. But God in Christ gives us the Spirit, so the ability to cope with this world rests on a trinitarian act. God's knowledge of salvation history, that is, how God's salvation guides us through world history, is absolute while ours is finite and inadequate. No one of us can be "his counselor." Instead, we depend on his knowledge and his will, so we must conduct our lives in complete Christ-dependency and follow the Spirit's guidance in every area of our lives.

The third rhetorical question (v. 35) is Paul's paraphrase of the Hebrew text of Job 41:11, "Who has ever given to God, that God should repay them?" In Job this is found near the end of Yahweh's speech (Job 38–41), telling Job that he is sovereign over everything. This could almost be called the moral of the story in Job: "Everything under heaven belongs to me." Job is confused, asking God why and how everything in this world has turned against him. As Job doubts God's wisdom, God declares that he alone has the wisdom to oversee this world and the affairs of Job as well. Job is being told to surrender his life to God's superintending wisdom.

Paul is faithful to Job here, for "given" means to "give beforehand," thereby obligating God to repay us. No one has ever been able to give anything to God in such a way as to create a debt requiring God to pay them back. God owes no one. God's wisdom and knowledge (v. 33) are completely beyond us (v. 34), yet they come to us as a free gift on his part (v. 35).

THE UNIVERSAL MAJESTY OF GOD (11:36)

All Paul has said in this doxological hymn (vv. 33–35) is grounded (*hoti*, "for") in the fact that God is the source (*ek*, "from"), instrument (*dia*, "through"), and goal (*eis*, "for") of "all things" (cf. 1 Cor 8:6 of God, Col 1:16–17 of Christ). This undergirds the sovereignty of God over all things in creation and provides a fitting climax not only to this doxology but also to all of Romans 9–11. God determines everything in his created order, so while no one can know his mind, they can rely on his greater wisdom made available to his followers. He alone reveals all truth, so none can be his counselor, but they can listen to and follow his counsel. He is the sole giver and is sovereign over salvation history.

There can be only one conclusion: "to him be the glory forever." The One who has given us salvation and made us his children, who has brought Jew and Gentile together and united fallen humanity in Christ, is the one who deserves glory above all else. As the Westminster Confession says, God created humankind to "glorify God and enjoy him forever." It is our privilege to magnify his name and to enjoy his loving presence every moment of our life here on earth. Paul closes with "amen," which affirms the validity and echoes the truth of the doxology (see 1:25; 9:5).

———

This final paragraph in Romans 9–11 is the most astounding promise yet, a truly apocalyptic revelation of the true future for Israel. It is the final piece of the puzzle, telling us not only that God will keep his covenant promises to his chosen people but also that there is a national future, a God-sent revival that will ensure an eternal reward for the faithful. The promised reality, which had to bring tears to Paul's eyes, was that even the present hardness experienced by the vast majority of Jews had a redemptive purpose. The success of the Gentile mission, far from a judgment meant to keep Israel from God, was intended to make Israel envious and lead to a renewed Jewish mission that would culminate in national salvation at the return of Christ.

We must also recognize that God's final intention is the salvation of all peoples, Jew and Gentile (v. 32). It is not that the Gentile mission only took place when the Jewish people turned against Christ. The reason God made Abraham and his progeny the chosen people was so they could be the channel of his blessings to the Gentiles (Gen 12:3). If Israel had obeyed this command, the Gentile mission would have already been taking place by the time of Paul. Still, the Gentile mission was not an end in itself but a means to a larger end: Jewish conversion and a one-world church composed of all groups brought into a new Israel in Christ.

In these chapters Paul has dealt with an exceedingly difficult issue, and with the doxology of verses 33-36 he wants his readers to know he is well aware of our finite knowledge about divine sovereignty and human responsibility. The key is to recognize that all truth is God's truth, and we must yield ourselves to God's greater wisdom on such issues. God has all truth, not us, and we have to surrender to the mind of God. As we engage in debate over issues like the security of the believer or predestination, we must keep in mind this wonderful doxology and quit destroying the harmony of the church with endless debate over theological dogma we can never know fully.

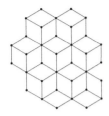

LIVING LIFE IN THE SPIRIT:
EXHORTATION TO LIVE THE CHRISTIAN LIFE
(12:1-8)

The first thing we do every morning is examine ourselves in a mirror to see what changes we need to make when we present ourselves to the world. It would be foolish to look at ourselves, shrug our shoulders, and say in effect, "What you see is what you get." As James 1:23-24 says, the word of God is the mirror of the soul, and we look into it to determine what changes we need to make to be presentable to God. When we are changed by the gospel, we must show these changes in our daily conduct.

This is what Romans 12-16 is all about: the changes in our life that our new commitment to Christ must bring about. The first eleven chapters describe what God has done for us in Christ. These final chapters command right conduct in light of the new life Christ has given us. Now Paul tells us in detail what this means—what life in the Spirit looks like.

This movement from indicative to imperative was normal for Paul, seen also in Galatians (1-4, 5-6), Ephesians (1-3, 4-6), Colossians (1-2, 3-4), and 1 Thessalonians (1-3, 4-5). The issues Paul discusses in these chapters are not general but reflect specific problems in the churches, like spiritual gifts (Rom 12:3-8), relation to opponents and persecutors (12:14-21), relation to govern-

377

ment (13:1–7), and conflict between Jewish and Gentile believers (14:1–15:12). There are two subsections: exhortations to live the Christian life (12:1–13:14) and the conflict between the strong (Gentile Christians) and weak (Jewish Christians) over meat offered to idols (14:1–15:12).

THE CHRISTIAN LIFE INVOLVES TOTAL TRANSFORMATION (12:1-2)

These two verses provide a transition from the meaning of the gospel to its implications for Christian conduct and is certainly one of the most profound and meaningful passages in all of Scripture. The introductory "therefore" (*oun*) tells us this is a conclusion or inference from all that has come before (1:18–11:36). The strong verb "I exhort" (*parakalō*) is a better translation than the NIV "I urge" in this context. This is an authoritative proclamation that demands serious attention. It is a favorite verb of Paul in teaching contexts and tells the reader both to listen and to act on what is being said.

OFFER YOUR WHOLE SELF AS A SACRIFICE TO GOD (12:1)

The phrase "in view of God's mercy" hearkens back to the emphasis on the mercy of God in 11:30–36 but actually sums up all eleven chapters on how God has brought salvation to humankind through the death of Christ. Though Paul mentions God's mercy only in chapters 9–11, it is the basis of everything in Romans. Grace is often defined as "undeserved mercy," and the gospel itself can be labeled the results of God's mercy to sinners.

Our total commitment to God is based on the totality of his mercy to us. Paul expresses this in sacrificial imagery, "offer your bodies as a … sacrifice." The verb "offer as a sacrifice" has sometimes been misunderstood as a "once-for-all" action. This has contributed to a "second work of grace" view of salvation, which encourages believers to seek a crisis-induced spiritual transformation that (like conversion) occurs only once. This is erroneous.

As an infinitive ("to offer"), this verb draws its force from the main verb, the present-tense "I exhort," and it is followed by two present-tense imperatives in verse 2. This means there is no one-time action in it. If anything, it has an iterative (repeated) force, exhorting us to frequently consecration ourselves to God.

The metaphorical force of the image pictures us at God's altar baring our necks as a sacrifice to him. This word picture is frequent in the Bible—for instance, "sacrifice thank offerings to God" (Ps 50:14, 23); "may the lifting up of my hands be like the evening sacrifice" (Ps 141:2); the "sacrifice of praise" (Heb 13:15); and "spiritual sacrifices" (1 Pet 2:5). The content of the sacrifice is "your bodies," which some think is the physical body dedicated to God, but more probably it refers to the whole person. This better fits the context of the dedication of every aspect of our beings to God. We must offer every area of our lives to God and let him infuse us with his Spirit (v. 2) in order to empower us for service to him.

There are three aspects of this sacrifice:

1. It is a "living sacrifice," looking at the dedication of ourselves not only as a dynamic process and an ongoing force but also as a spiritual state, a new "life" in the Spirit. As in 6:3-6, we die with Christ and then live in the Spirit. The sacrifice of ourselves to the Triune Godhead is part of that dynamic act.

2. It is "holy," meaning that we are wholly consecrated to him, "set apart" from the world and completely belonging to God. As a holy sacrifice, there is a sacredness to our service to God and his church.

3. It is "pleasing to God," building on the image of the sacrifice as giving off a "pleasing aroma" for God (see, for example, Exod 29:18, 25, 41; Lev 3:16; Num 28:6). The idea is divine pleasure, both in the Old Testament and the New (2 Cor 5:9, "we make it our goal to please him"; also 2 Cor 2:15; Eph 5:10; Phil 4:18).

Each of these is an important aspect of the Christian life, and we must strive always to live out the new life of the Spirit so we might be set apart for him so as to bring him pleasure.

At the close of this verse, this sacrifice of our total self to God is defined as "your true and proper worship." A great deal of discussion has attended the meaning of the Greek *logikēn* (translated as "true and proper"). It was a popular term in Greek philosophy for a concept that was logical, based on rational truth. It was borrowed in **Hellenistic** Judaism (for example, Philo) to combine the spiritual and rational sides of worship. There are three main possibilities: "spiritual" in the sense of proper and rational worship; "spiritual" in the sense of heart worship; "rational" in the sense of logical or reasonable worship. Probably the best is to combine the rational and spiritual sides and see this as a spiritual act that is the only logical way to live the Christian life.

Our whole life should be considered an ongoing act of worship. God is part of everything we think, say, and do, and we celebrate him at every moment, seen as an act of serving and enjoying his presence. *Latreia* (worship) is a cultic or ritual term describing the experience of worship not only in the community but also in everyday life. This is especially the case when we label this act a "spiritual" one, combining the ideas of rational thinking and spiritual living to describe the "reasonable" nature of serving God at all times. This is closely related to the inauguration of the new age in Christ, an era where daily conduct is depicted as one's spiritual life. The corporate celebration of Sunday worship is lived out every day of the week, and the two aspects are inseparable parts of a larger whole—serving God in every area of life.

DON'T BE CONFORMED BUT TRANSFORMED (12:2)

In verse 1 Paul describes the *what* of the Christian life (offer yourselves as a sacrifice to God), and in verse 2 he describes the *how* (by refusing to conform to this age and letting yourselves be transformed by the Spirit). The two interdependent aspects of the sacrificed life involve both the negative (not conformed) and positive (be transformed). Scholars used to define "conform" (*syschēmatizō*) as the outward side dealing with appearances and "transform" (*metamorphoō*) as the inward, powerful side, but that has been disproved. The first means to pattern oneself after another person or thing; J. B. Phillips translates this well: "stop letting the world squeeze you into its mold," as does the NLT, "Don't copy the behavior and customs of this world."

The forces of "this age" (the time in which sin reigns, 5:21; 7:17, 20, 23) are invading and gaining control, forcing believers and unbelievers alike to conform to its ideals—consumerism, the desire for status and success, the pleasure principle, sex and good looks, and so on. Peter describes this process in 1 Peter 4:4—the people of this world "are surprised that you do not join them in their reckless, wild living, and they heap abuse on you." This is a perfect definition of peer pressure. The only viable solution is to refuse and turn to the Spirit for the strength to rise above the pressure. We also need to make certain our closest friends are solid believers who will be there to add their strength in our moment of weakness (Heb 12:12-13).

The antidote for conformity to the world is to "be transformed by the renewing of your mind." There is a passive sense to this in which the transforming power is the Holy Spirit, who penetrates to the very core of our being and reshapes us into a new creation (2 Cor 5:17). The Greek term (*metamorphoō*) has given us the English *metamorphosis*, meaning to "change us step by step" into a new being in Christ as a harbinger of what we will be for all eternity. The Spirit is the change agent, enabling us to overcome temptation and live victoriously in service to God. This is a trinitarian event, part of the process by which we become Christlike (Eph 4:13) and Spirit-filled (Rom 8:5-17) children of God.

Paul describes this process as "the renewing of your mind," meaning our mindset is renewed (literally "made new again and again") by the Spirit, a lifelong process in which our thinking is rescued from the influence of the world and reprogrammed to "have in mind the concerns of God" (Mark 8:33). There is a great deal in Romans on the mind. According to Romans 1:18-32 the mind is the center of depravity, and in 7:23, 25, the mind is the sphere of battle between the desire to serve God and the fleshly proclivity to sin. In 8:5-7 this war takes place in the mind between the flesh and the Spirit. But the mind is also the place where spiritual growth takes place. There we make decisions that determine our spiritual direction and destiny.

The ongoing conduct of each one of us is based on our reaction to input from both the world (v. 1) and the Spirit (v. 2). We can label this conflict "mind-control versus the Spirit-controlled mind." This determines whether we live lives of spiritual defeat (7:14-25) or Christian victory (8:1-8, 37). In fact, this is one of the primary purposes of Christian fellowship, which counters the temptations of the world.

The purpose (*eis to*, "so that"; "then" in NIV) of the renewing of our mind is so that we can "test and approve what God's will is." The verb means to examine something so as to live according to it, involving both discernment and practice. We observe what gives us the strength to rise above these earthly pulls and to decide to follow what truly helps us. "God's will" connotes the direction and guidance that comes from God, that moral and ethical leading regarding proper Christian thoughts and conduct in his eyes.

God's will is "good, pleasing and perfect." We should seek God's will because it will always be best for us (8:28). So long as we seek what is convenient and advantageous we will fall short and be disappointed. Only when God is in charge and we are following his directives can we be sure we are doing the right thing. The meaning of "pleasing" is difficult to determine. In verse 1 "pleasing to God" meant that we seek to please him in all things. Does this word echo that thrust (as most scholars believe), or does it go the other direction—what is pleasing to us? It makes a great deal of sense to say that as we please God, he pleases us. Since the other two are directed to us—God's will is good for us and perfect for us—we can say that as God's will works in our lives to accomplish what is perfect in our lives, this brings us pleasure.

MINISTER TO ONE ANOTHER IN THE CHURCH (12:3-8)

With a transformed and renewed mind under the control of the Spirit, it is impossible to be arrogant and self-centered. Rather, our mind will be centered on pleasing others rather than manipulating them to please ourselves. In humility and a spirit of giving we will use our gifts and strengths to minister to each other.

THINK SOBERLY ON THE BASIS OF YOUR MEASURE OF FAITH (12:3)

Paul moves on to call for "sober judgment" regarding our place in the messianic community. He begins with "the grace given me," a reference to his Damascus road conversion (Acts 9), where God called him to faith in Christ and commissioned him to go to the Gentiles (Acts 26:17-18). In essence Paul is appealing to his apostolic authority. So when he says, "I say to every one of you," it is not just a gentle request but an authoritative command. "Every one" of his readers with their renewed minds must be renewed in their judgments as well.

If, he says, you are conformed to this world, you will "think of yourself more highly than you ought," that is, be conceited and self-important. If you are transformed by the Spirit, you will "think of yourself with sober judgment," that is, be humble and seek to serve rather than be served (Mark 10:45 of Christ). To think soberly is to have the divine perspective—we are slaves to God (Rom 6:16, 18, 22) and to those around us (Gal 5:13), wanting always to use our gifts to serve them. We place ourselves under others rather than over them (see Phil 2:3-4).

A proper estimate of ourselves takes place when "the measure of faith" is operating in us (NIV "in accordance with the faith God has distributed to each of you"). There are two ways of

understanding this: The "measure" could be the standard of our
shared faith in the community. We examine ourselves on the basis
of that common faith God has allotted to each of us. On the other
hand, it could be that different measure or "apportionment" given
to us as God wills and as we have accepted "by faith" (see also v. 6).

The solution must emerge from the context of verses 4–8 and
the spiritual gifts given to each believer so they might serve the
church. The measure of faith in this sense is the faith given all
Christians to receive those gifts God has for them. God has given
each the same faith, but we use it to accept the different gifts he
has for each one of us. The faith is the same, but the gifts differ.
In this sense both options are viable, for each fits one of the two
sides of the coin. In either case, we must have a proper humility
when we examine ourselves in keeping with the different gifts
God has apportioned to us. There can be no pride, for all gifts are
important to God and needed in the church. As such they are to
be received by faith, and we use them as servants.

The Body-Life Image of the Church (12:4–5)

The tendency to pride and conceit is especially evident with
respect to the more public gifts (like music or speaking or leading). They garner a lot of attention, so they easily lead to false
pride, especially in a central community like Rome. In verses 4–5
Paul presents a theology of spiritual gifts similar to that in 1 Corinthians 12:12–26. The central metaphor is one of the most important pictures of the church, the body of Christ. The human body
as well as the body of Christ is composed of "one body with many
members, and these members do not all have the same function."
The body is a single mechanism that depends on all the members
functioning together to work, yet at the same time each member
performs a different task. If any of the parts of the body tries to
function other than the way it was intended, the body is crippled.

All of us members are meant to "form one body," the church,
and to work together in unity to function as the church. As the

members come together as one body, "each member belongs to all the others," so that there is both unity and diversity in the church. God does not want us to be rugged individualists but wants us to think of ourselves as differing parts of one body. Vertically, we belong to Christ as part of his body (1 Cor 6:19-20). Horizontally, we belong to each other. This is the principle of the many and the one: many members that form one body and are interdependent.

Our "different gifts" are the way we blend into one body, with each of us playing a critical part. Since in the eyes of God no gift is more important than another, there is no place for pride or for churches that treat certain gifted individuals (by definition every believer is a gifted individual!) above others. The tendency in many churches to make their pastor a virtual demigod is a serious sin. None of us can function properly in the church without the other gifts at work blending with ours.

Studies have shown that in the average church about 15-20 percent are active in giving and serving in the church. If only 20 percent of a person's physical body was functioning, they would be virtually a vegetable. Our churches are crippled by the unwillingness of so many members to use their gifts to minister to each other (Eph 4:12, 14). The key is for all of us to recognize we are "one body ... in Christ" and to live as if that were so. Only in union with him and with each other can we gain the humility and the strength to function in unity as part of the body of Christ.

God Gives Each Differing Gifts (12:6-8)

Paul stresses the unity of the body in verses 4-5, and diversity in verses 6-8. He begins, "We have different gifts, according to the grace given to each of us." This repeats verse 3, telling us these are grace-gifts (or *charismata*) that stem from God, not from our natural abilities. Still, natural abilities become grace-gifts when they are dedicated to God and used under the empowering presence of the Spirit. To use myself as an example, I have always had the gift of gab; speaking and writing come easily to me. But they are spiritual gifts as well, for I want to use these abilities for the glory of God and the benefit of the church.

In this passage Paul is telling us four things: (1) We have gifts and abilities. (2) The gifts vary among us. (3) God and the Spirit distribute them to us (1 Cor 12:11). (4) The gifts are not intended to benefit the individuals who possess them but to benefit the body of Christ. These are ministry gifts rather than status gifts. We are all meant to be servants who use them to help and bless the other members of the church.

Only two of the seven spiritual gifts Paul mentions are mentioned in other lists (prophecy, teaching). This list is not exhaustive; it is representative of all that God graciously grants his followers. The gifts are trinitarian in the sense that all three members of the Godhead are involved in their presence among his people.

(1) *Prophesying.* Prophecy was an important office in the church (1 Cor 12:28; Eph 4:11). In many circles today it is linked with preaching or teaching, but that was not the case in the early church. Paul mentions teaching third in this list, and thus it is a separate gift. Prophets are the divinely chosen messengers in the Old Testament as well as the New through whom God gives specific orders to follow. These directions are not always canonical (that is, written in Scripture) but are often general and occasional. For instance, the two revelations given through Agabus (Acts 11:28; 21:10-11) are only in the canon because Luke included the story in Acts.

Paul says prophets should exercise their gift "in accordance with your faith," meaning in proportion to their faith. This could mean that prophecies should be made either according to the standards established by true doctrine (with "faith" referring to the content of the Christian faith) or perhaps according to the amount of faith God has given prophets so as to use their gift properly. On the basis of the discussion of "the measure of faith" in verse 3, the latter is slightly more likely. Prophets must use their gifts to serve God and the church; it is a charismatic gift under God's control, not the prophet's.

(2) *Serving.* Many think this is the type of service associated with the specific office of a deacon, but more likely it refers not just to the ministry of a particular office but also to the ministry of all believers. In Ephesians 4:12 pastors "equip [God's] people for works of service, so that the body of Christ may be built up." This would encompass a wide range of services, like discipleship, youth work, and children's ministry as well as practical helps like carpentry, plumbing, and so on. Those called to all types of ministry are being called to give themselves up to that task, recognizing it is a high calling to serve the saints any way God directs.

(3) *Teaching.* Teaching is also listed among the spiritual gifts in 1 Corinthians 12:28 and Ephesians 4:11. In Acts 2:42 it is one of the four pillars of the early church—the first one of the list. In the Pastoral Letters (1–2 Tim, Titus) this is an essential component of the life of the church, undoubtedly due to the serious problem of false teaching there.

Teachers differ from prophets in that they transmit the traditional biblical truths to the church, while prophets relay specific messages for the moment from God. Teachers maintain the truths of God's word for the next generation. According to Ephesians 4:11, the pastor is also a teacher. It is critical today for pastors to exercise their teaching gift because of the number of heretics and shallow preachers all over the world. We desperately need to ground our churches in the word and turn them into churches like those in Berea, who "examined the Scriptures every day" (Acts 17:11), caring deeply for biblical truth.

(4) *Encouraging.* "Encouraging" is better translated as "exhorting" because of its place next to "teaching." In keeping with its use in 12:1, it denotes the office of grounding people in the word. Exhortation includes the idea of comforting and consoling hurting Christians, yet it also connotes admonition. It refers to verbal care in general. The main difference with teaching is that while teaching is sharing the content of Scripture, exhortation concerns itself with the practical application of scriptural truths to daily

life. Doctrines are not only to be understood but also lived out in daily conduct.

(5) *Contributing to the needs of others.* "Giving" in the NIV, this could refer to an official who distributes the church's resources to the poor (as in Acts 6:1–7 or 1 Tim 5:16) or a believer who shares his own possessions with others. The language here, as in "serving" above, would favor the more general sense. Paul asks those who share with the needy to "give generously," or perhaps "simply," in the sense that there are no ulterior motives in the act of giving. When God's people seek to help others, the purpose is to provide for their needs and not to gain credit from others or God (see Acts 2:44–45; 4:32–34).

(6) *Leadership.* We might expect leadership to be near the top with prophets and teachers, but it is doubtful that Paul is hierarchically ordering the gifts. Nor does its placement between sharing with the needy and showing mercy mean this refers to a person who merely comes to the aid of others. Paul always uses this term (*proistēmi*) of those in leadership (1 Thess 5:12; 1 Tim 3:4–5; 5:17; Titus 3:8, 14). In this context of ministry, it likely refers to those who manage the church. In our modern context this would be any kind of Christian leadership, both pastoral and otherwise. Paul's admonition is to govern the church "diligently," with zeal and eagerness to do a good job. It involves a willingness to work hard and do our best to serve God's people with all the strength we possess.

(7) *Showing mercy.* Mercy has a general sense of caring for those in difficult circumstances, whether it be the social ostracism, economic hardship, illness or old age or any other misfortune. This is quite close to sharing with the needy above. Those able to help others are enjoined to do it "cheerfully," a term found in 2 Corinthians 9:7 for a "cheerful giver." Those who relieve the needy must never do it grudgingly. There should be the joy of the Lord in the heart, recognizing the grand privilege of being used by the Lord

to alleviate suffering. We should be thrilled to be allowed to make a difference in people's lives, to give back a small amount of what God and his people have given us.

————

Few portions of Scripture have managed to portray so deeply what it means to be a member of the body of Christ as Romans 12:1–8. This may well be the single most succinct and meaningful summary of the Christian life in all the word of God. Paul presents the process in terms of the what (offer yourself as a sacrifice to God) and the how (Spirit transformation). This is another way of stating the truth of Romans 6—dying with Christ to sin and entering into a brand new spiritual life.

Two aspects characterize this life in the Spirit. First, it is a transformed new existence in which nothing will ever be the same. The old conformity and humdrum existence in which you lived a cookie-cutter life of sin is over forever, and you begin an exciting life of adventure you had never before imagined that will continue in eternity. Second, you will finally experience true pleasure. Before, when all you had was a life of self-centered living and repeating the same old sinful clichés, you convinced yourself that such a life was filled with "fun" and that you wanted to keep doing the same old things. Suddenly you realized there was nothing meaningful about that old life. Now you will discover that God has taken over and filled you with *his* pleasure, and it will last forever.

Life in the Spirit should be highly visible in the church, for every member will be consumed with serving others. We are the many who live as one, for we take all our individual gifts and place them at the service of those around us. I want to use everything I am and everything I have to enrich the lives of my brothers and sisters in Christ. There is no place for arrogance or self-serving actions, for we are all seeking to benefit each other in everything we do. A life of giving is so much more satisfying than a life of taking, and as we begin to discover how much we have to offer those around us, we realize we find greater ways to live joyous lives in the church.

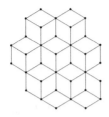

EXHORTATION TO LIVE THE CHRISTIAN LIFE IN LOVE
(12:9–21)

Romans 12, with its discussion of spiritual gifts and admonition to live in community under the law of love, is quite similar to 1 Corinthians 12–14, with its lengthy presentation on the *charismata* (chs. 12, 14) and the centrality of love (ch. 13). Since Romans and 1 Corinthians were written at nearly the same time (AD 55 to 57), several believe that they address similar situations involving a group of overenthusiastic charismatics who elevate their movement more highly than they should (with Rom 12:3 especially addressed to them). Others believe that the section on love here in Romans is focused on the problem of the weak and the strong in 14:1–15:13 and the desire to alleviate the tension by anchoring internal relationships in the church on love.

However, the section is better seen as a general one. Paul discusses love from several vantage points, not just spiritual gifts or the weak versus the strong. Paul emphasizes internal love in the community (9–13), but also loving enemies (14–21). This is general ethical admonition, but especially with the Romans in mind. Paul wants them to work at anchoring their relationships (both inside and outside the community) in love.

This passage is characterized by a clipped style common to ethical material, with few conjunctions and several short exclamations on similar topics. There is a loose structure revolving around the twin issues of the internal (vv. 19-13) and external (vv. 14-21) need for love. Within this overarching framework, Paul stacks loosely related sayings upon one another (vv. 11-12, 15-16). Thus he has combined general ethical teaching with the topics of relations with those inside and outside the church.

CHURCHES HAVE AN INTERNAL NEED FOR LOVE IN THE COMMUNITY (12:9-13)

Love Clings to the Good and Honors Others (12:9-10)

This opening verse is strange, for Paul begins by saying "sincere love" without a verb or other modifiers as if it is a heading for the section. The normal translation is correct, "Love must be sincere," with the ensuing material telling what that means. "Sincere" love is literally "unhypocritical" and so is related to being genuine. In the first century, hypocrisy pictured the actor's mask by which one would play another role, something that was not them. Paul wants to make certain no one puts on a "mask" of love and pretends to care for others when they don't. Jesus calls the proper level of love "a new command" (John 13:34) not because it was a new teaching (Lev 19:18, "Love your neighbor as yourself") but because it was now anchored in the new covenant reality of Christ, bound up with his love for us. This new messianic love existed first between the Father and the Son and then between the Godhead and us. Through it we are recipients of a level of love not heretofore seen on planet Earth, a love that transforms our whole being.

The rest of the verse consists of two participles that function as commands—we "hate what is evil" and "cling to what is good." This is the expected conduct when love is truly operative in the community. This contrast is frequently stated in Scripture, as in Psalm 97:10 ("Let those who love the LORD hate evil") or Amos 5:15 ("Hate evil, love good") or its opposite, Psalm 52:3 ("You love evil rather than good"). The true Christ follower grounded in love will abhor all wickedness, as in Romans 13:2, "put aside the deeds of darkness" (see also 1 Cor 13:6; Col 3:8; 1 Thess 5:21–22; 1 Pet 2:1). At the same time as we cast out a spiteful spirit, we must cling to goodness with every ounce of strength we possess.

Genuine love also centers on the brothers and sisters of the messianic community, leading us to "be devoted to one another in love." "Devoted" occurs only here in the New Testament but was fairly common in the Greco-Roman world for the tender affections of family life. The Greek term (*philostorgoi*) comes from *stergō*, describing the deep affection between members of a family, and both it and the second term, "brotherly love," share the *philo*-prefix, indicating family and brotherly love. Paul is bringing to the forefront the family relationships that serve to deepen love at the core of the community. The family dimension of love in the community is the basis of everything else.

There are two viable translations of the phrase Paul uses at the end of verse 10: (1) with the NIV, "honor one another above yourselves," showing preference for our fellow believers; or (2) with the RSV, "Outdo one another in showing honor." This would mean we should strive with all our strength to show respect to each other. The difficulty is that this verb occurs nowhere else in the New Testament. Its basic meaning is to "go before something and show the way." The idea of preferring others is not well attested, so the second is the better understanding.

We should be known for the pedestal onto which we lift our fellow saints. In other words, we should not be tooting our own horns or using others to lift ourselves up. It is not our own status in the community that matters, but we should go out of our way to esteem others and make them feel important. As Paul says elsewhere, "in humility value others above yourselves, not looking to your own interests but each of you to the interests of the others" (Phil 2:3–4). This is desperately needed in an age of personal achievement when most of us feel unappreciated. To go out of our way to lift others up is one of the most powerful ministries we can have.

ZEALOUSLY SERVING THE LORD (12:11)

The fervency that love nearly always exhibits leads Paul to move naturally from the definition of love to the metaphor of a fervent spirit. He tells the Romans that they should "never be lacking in zeal" (literally, "in zeal be not lazy or timid"). "Zeal" was translated "diligently" in terms of leadership in verse 8. It means not only to be excited about a thing but also to work hard at accomplishing it. There is a human tendency to be excited early in a new venture but to lose focus and energy as we move into it. At the beginning of our Christian adventure we move ahead rapidly, but all too soon we are just going through the motions. If we had any inkling of the reality awaiting us, we would have no problem with motivation. It is greater than anything we could ever imagine, and that realization alone should provide all the zeal we should ever need.

The way to maintain zeal is to "keep your spiritual fervor, serving the Lord." This stresses the great energy needed to put spiritual gifts to work. This was the problem with the Christians in Hebrews, who were slow to learn or lazy in their spiritual lives (Heb 5:11; 6:12). It was also a failure on Timothy's part in the Pastoral Letters as he failed to use "the gift of God" he had been given at his commissioning service because he was "timid" (2 Tim 1:6–7). Living for the Lord is hard work and takes discipline.

"Spiritual fervor" could also be translated "the Spirit's fire."[1] The Spirit taking over our lives is common in Scripture, as in 1 Corinthians 12:13 ("we were all given the one Spirit to drink"), Ephesians 5:18 ("filled with the Spirit"), or 1 Thessalonians 1:6 ("joy given by the Holy Spirit"). With the idea of fire, we could add

---

1. Several scholars consider these an either-or and debate which is the better translation. However, I think it more likely there is a deliberate double meaning, and Paul intends both understandings here.

Matthew 3:11 ("he will baptize you with the Holy Spirit and fire") and 1 Thessalonians 5:19 ("do not quench the Spirit"). The Spirit demands complete control of each of us.

Imagery of Pentecost is likely behind this, where the Spirit came with "tongues of fire" (Acts 2:3). When the Spirit takes us over, we are set aflame and begin "serving the Lord." There is a circularity to this: when we are on fire for the Spirit, we will always serve the Lord; and when we serve Christ, we must be filled with the Spirit. The result will always be a transforming ministry that will bring glory to God.

Patient and Faithful in Prayer (12:12)

The three exhortations in verse 12 are interrelated, all dealing with life's difficulties and trials. Paul often combines the ideas of hope, endurance, and prayer, as in 5:3-5 (the chain of suffering-perseverance-character-hope) and in 8:23-27 (prayer and hope in the midst of infirmities). At the outset he calls his readers to "be joyful in hope." This could also read "because of hope" or "by means of hope," which would make hope either the basis of our joy or the means by which we feel joy in troubled times. It is probably best to see hope as the sphere within which our difficulties are turned to joy. Due to the Spirit's strengthening presence, we see life's struggles as opportunities for us to learn anew the truth of Romans 8:28, that all things, no matter how dire, will end up working for our best.

In God our hope is actualized in the midst of affliction, and we learn to endure (niv "patient"). God controls our future, so we can say with Peter that we "greatly rejoice" in the midst of grief and trials because we know that he is in charge (1 Pet 1:6-7; see also Jas 1:2-4). In the midst of life's problems, we can endure. God's keeping us secure in Christ doesn't mean he makes our difficulties go away. Jesus said in Mark 10:29-30 that those who sacrifice family or home will inherit a hundred homes and family members (= the church), but "along with" them will come "persecutions." Trials are a necessary part of the Christian life; they stimulate faith and force us to depend on God. I would go so far as to say that trials are one of the necessary ingredients in spiritual growth. They force us out of ourselves and into complete reliance on the Lord.

Trials make it necessary to be "faithful in prayer." The verb *proskartereō* ("to be faithful") means to "persist" or "continue" in prayer. Faithful, diligent prayer is the antidote to the worries of life (Phil 4:6–7) and the only way to surmount life's hard knocks (Acts 1:14; 2:42; 6:4; Eph 6:18; Col 4:2). Prayer is faith in action, and without it we would be steamrolled by the seemingly random problems that seem to surround us at all times. With prayer the complications of life are robbed of their force before they can defeat us.

BASIS: ONE BODY (12:13)

In verse 13 Paul returns to the question of community relations with which this section began. If the Romans are truly devoted to one another (vv. 9–10), they will "share with the Lord's people who are in need" and "practice hospitality." This verse also rehashes giving and showing mercy from verse 8. The word behind "share" is the verb cognate of "fellowship" (*koinōneō*); Paul is calling his readers to have fellowship by sharing their blessings with others. To the church this was a natural outgrowth of true Christian community, and this is desperately needed today in our entitled and narcissistic generation. When the church shows concern and Christian charity, it is an incredible showcase of the difference Christ makes.

Paul likely had in mind also the collection for the poor he was soon to take to Jerusalem (Rom 15:25–28; 1 Cor 16:1–4; 2 Cor 8–9), but his injunction here goes beyond that to enjoin a general concern all believers should have for one another. Three spheres of the ministry of helps are obligatory for us, in degrees of intensity: to one's own nuclear family, to one's church family (here, Gal 6:10), and to the non-Christian community (also Gal 6:10). At every level— the patriarchs, the people of Israel, the church—God required his people to be channels of blessing to those around them. The need to "practice hospitality" is closely connected to sharing with the needy. Hospitality arises naturally from love (Heb 13:2; 1 Pet 4:9) and is a requirement for leaders in the church (1 Tim 3:2; 5:10; Titus 1:8). In the first century, inns were both expensive and dangerous as well as filthy—in one Greek play the characters compare inns on the basis of which one has fewer cockroaches. Jesus' mission for the church demands that his followers practice hospitality as part of evangelism. As with the first part of this verse, this too is needed in our day because of how many people are lonely and truly need someone who cares. In our individualistic society we need more Christians who are willing to share their homes.

CHURCHES HAVE AN EXTERNAL NEED FOR LOVE OF ENEMIES (12:14–21)

From relations and ministry in the community, Paul turns to relations with outsiders, in particular with persecutors and enemies of the church. While it seems he turns to the opposite action, from fellow believers to persecutors, this is actually a continuation of the thesis from verse 9, showing the transformed mindset of the believer, as the sincere love of the believer is first extended to "one another" (v. 10) and then to oppressors (v. 14).

EXTERNAL: BLESS PERSECUTORS (12:14)

Paul's command to "bless those who persecute you" is a remarkable demonstration of the Christlike mind. To "bless" a person is to call down divine blessings upon them. Rather than seeking vengeance (that will be the subject of vv. 17–20), the first things saints do is ask God to bless enemies.

This is likely taken from Jesus' teaching in the Sermon on the Mount (Matt 5:44; Luke 6:27–28), "Love your enemies and pray for those who persecute you." This is demonstrated in Jesus' cry from the cross, "Father, forgive them, for they do not know what they are doing" (Luke 23:34). Stephen prayed likewise (Acts 7:60),

"Lord, do not hold this sin against them." Blessing them probably includes both spiritual blessings (vv. 17–21) and divine favor, as seen in Paul's addition to "bless and do not curse." This means to ask God to pour out his blessings rather than call down his curses. These would be the covenant curses (Deut 27–28). The blessing probably centers on a prayer for conversion but could include something akin to 1 Timothy 2:2, asking for prayer for government officials "that we may live peaceful and quiet lives in all godliness and holiness."

Primarily, this asks God's blessings to pour down on the unsaved as proof that God loves all his children, not just those who are his people. This is a radical command and counter to our natural inclinations. When we love our enemies, it becomes one of the most powerful tools for reaching the lost. As Peter says, "Live such good lives among the pagans that, though they accuse you of doing wrong, they may see your good deeds and glorify God on the day he visits us" (1 Pet 2:12).

INTERNAL: HARMONY WITH THOSE WHO REJOICE OR MOURN (12:15–16)

These two verses return to the issue of internal relations in the church, beginning with "rejoice with those who rejoice; mourn with those who mourn." Though most agree this likely includes unbelievers, it is primarily the saints who have this empathy for one another. While it seems out of place in a context of outsiders, there is a real chance that Paul has the results of persecution especially in mind. Opposition had sprung up in Rome (this was seven to eight years before the terrible times under Nero), and so the love and sharing of verses 9–13 were especially needed. The result is that all the saints have shared in the sorrows caused by persecution as well as the joys of the beleaguered saints.

When our brothers have something wonderful go their way, we often get jealous and say, "Why them and not me?" Yet when we truly care, we are thrilled for them and share in their joy. In negative times, it is even more critical to share in their sorrow so they know they are not alone. This was true then, and it is true now.

In verse 16 this becomes even more clear: "Live in harmony [literally "think the same thing"] with one another." This begins with the thinking processes, as in Philippians 2:2, "make my joy complete by being like-minded, having the same love, being one in spirit and of the same mind." However, Paul is not speaking just of unity of mindset, for a careful look at the text tells us it is not "harmony *among* [that would be *en*] one another" but a "united mindset *toward* or *with* [the preposition here is *eis*, "to"] one another." This unity of mindset calls for a unity of heart and mind in concern for those around us. Our attitude toward others should be integrated in concern for their needs and in accepting those of a lower socioeconomic status (as we will see next). When our minds have been renewed by the Spirit (12:2), and we have gained sober judgment (12:3), that transformed mindset will produce true harmony in the church.

This harmony will be impossible to achieve so long as pride rears its ugly head. This returns to 12:3 and the danger of thinking "of yourself more highly than you ought" (also 11:20; 1 Tim 6:17). There is no place for elevating ourselves. We already saw in 12:4–8 that any ability we possess is a gift from God and is meant to allow us to serve Christ and the church. That which gives us status and lots of attention should in reality lead us to humility and to the joy of helping others.

The central admonition here is the importance of associating with the lowly. "Lowly" could be neuter, "lowly things," as well as masculine, "lowly people" (NIV "people of lowly position"). The latter is best in this context, but Paul could well be referencing both. The early church had an especially large number of former slaves in it (seen in the names of Romans 16, most of which are known to have been slave names). It was critical for the church to care for the poor in its midst. This has not changed; economic prejudice is part of fallen human nature. The solution is to "associate with the lowly," meaning both lowly people and lowly things. Too many people today have homes that are too big and cars that are too fancy. They can never have enough, and they wish to identify only with those who have as much as or more than they do.

Jesus taught that true leaders are known for their servant attitude (Mark 9:35; 10:43–44), and preferred the lowly over the haughty (Matt 11:19). We must also reject a lifestyle centered on the things of the world. We must seek and think "things above" rather than earthly things (Col 3:1–2) and "treasures in heaven" rather than on earth (Matt 6:19–21). To do so we must "have in mind the concerns of God" rather than a merely human perspective (Mark 8:33).

It is not a sin to have material possessions. Abraham and Job were wealthy and yet loved by God. Paul famously said, "For the love of money is a root of all kinds of evil" (1 Tim 6:10), but he did not say that money constituted evil in itself. The key is to recognize that God calls certain people to distribute his largesse to others. They have been given a spiritual gift of "helping" (1 Cor 12:28) in the financial sense. God blesses them financially in order to use their resources to help others. In the same way as God has called me to use my teaching and writing gifts for the church, he is calling them to use their monetary gifts to aid the church and help the needy.

Not Vengeance but Doing What Is Right (12:17–19)

Now Paul returns to relations with non-Christians. He addresses how God's people should respond to mistreatment and persecution, commanding, "Do not repay anyone evil for evil." This is the flip side of verse 9, "Hate what is evil." When the unsaved do what is evil to us, we are not to seek to get even with them. In verse 14 Paul told his readers to "bless and not curse," and here they are to refuse to retaliate in any way. If believers do this, we become no better than the perpetrator of the evil deed. Christ rejected this eye-for-an-eye attitude (Matt 5:38–39; Paul may well allude to that here), as did the early church (1 Thess 5:15; 1 Pet 3:9). Christ himself provided the perfect model in his refusal to "retaliate" but instead "made no threats" and "entrusted himself to him who judges justly" (1 Pet 2:23).

Paul then presents the positive side: "Be careful to do what is right in the eyes of everyone." The verb translated "be careful" means to "think beforehand" and calls for careful thought and attention to what is the right thing to do when faced with mistreatment or being cheated by someone. We are to do not only what we know to be right but also what "everyone," including the oppressors themselves, knows to be right. Paul may be alluding to Proverbs 3:4, "Then you will win favor and a good name in the sight of God and man." Our response should always be to take the high road. As in 1 Peter 2:12, our slanderers will "see [our] good deeds and glorify God" as a result. Our good response will convict them, then convince them, and finally convert them.

Some have doubted the NIV translation here, since it seemingly has unbelievers providing the standard for Christian reactions. They prefer to translate "do what is right to everyone" rather than "in the eyes of everyone." However, it is best to leave it as it is. This does not mean the unsaved set the agenda but rather that what we do is recognized by everyone, including the unbelievers themselves, as perfect behavior.

In verse 18 Paul continues to enjoin actions that will commend believers to the nonbelievers around them. If they "do what is right in the eyes of everyone," they will naturally "live at peace with everyone." Once more, as in verses 14 (bless persecutors) and verse 17 (vengeance), here too we have a saying of Jesus reflected, namely, Mark 9:50 ("be at peace with each other") and Matthew 5:9 ("blessed are the peacemakers"). The theme of peaceful relations with others is frequent in Scripture.[2]

---

2. Ps 34:14; Rom 14:19; 2 Cor 13:11; 1 Thess 5:13; Heb 12:14.

Paul realizes it is not always possible in a fallen world to maintain harmonious relations, so he qualifies: "if it is possible, as far
as it depends on you." All we can do is try to live in peace with
others; we cannot force peace on those who are bent on conflict.
We cannot "live at peace" unless our neighbors want it as much
as we do. The very topic of this section assumes it will often not
be possible for peace to reign for long. If our neighbors decide
they hate us and take actions against us, there is nothing we can
do about it except make certain none of the fault for their hatred
falls on our shoulders.

In verses 17-19 the positive challenge (to peace) occurs in the
middle, and it is surrounded on either side by the exhortation
not to seek vengeance. Paul returns to that topic in verse 19, "Do
not take revenge." This is a difficult mandate, for human beings
by their nature turn against each other, and all of us often want
to get even.

Israel, like many nations in the ancient world, established
"cities of refuge."[3] These were places of asylum where those who
had accidentally killed someone could be kept from harm while
the situation was being sorted out. The Torah stipulated that in
some cases a murderer could be executed by an "avenger of blood"
(Num 35:19-21; Deut 19:12), a family member of the victim chosen
to execute the guilty party. In the case of accidental death, the
perpetrator was protected from this avenger by the city of refuge.

Things changed with the advent of Christ. In the place of personal revenge, God's people must now "leave room for God's wrath,"
the subject in Romans 1:18; 2:5, 8; 3:5; 5:9; and 9:22. The actual wording in verse 19 is "give place to wrath," so it is possible Paul is
speaking of our own wrath or even of our enemy's, but that is
doubtful. Most places in Romans, "wrath" has dealt with final judgment, but here it is the ongoing wrath of God that brings justice
to his mistreated and oppressed people. The justice of God against

3. Exod 21:12-14; Num 35:6-34; Deut 4:41-43; Josh 20:1-9.

present sin anticipates the final moment of human history, when such depraved behavior will be eradicated once for all. God will determine when such wrongs are righted, whether now or later or at the return of Christ. Our task is to place all injustices in his hand and allow him to decide when to vindicate us.

To anchor this critical injunction, Paul quotes Deuteronomy 32:35, "It is mine to avenge; I will repay." This appears near the end of the Song of Moses, where Yahweh promises that he will vindicate his people and avenge their blood. Paul's point here is that only God has the right to avenge wrong and the moral rectitude to do it correctly. This is difficult to do, for it screams against our human desire for revenge. The person deserves to suffer, but to "repay ... evil for evil" (v. 17) will render us no better than the one who hurt us in the first place. The only answer is to leave the vengeance to God.

The means by which we can do this is through a petition that leaves the vengeance with God and asks him to bring justice for us. This is exemplified in the "imprecatory psalms" (Pss 12, 35, 52, 57–59, 69, 70, 83, 109, 137, 140), and also in Revelation 6:10, "How long, Sovereign Lord, holy and true, until you ... avenge our blood?" These kinds of prayers are not a product of an ancient ethics that was sub-Christian. In actuality, they leave the vengeance with God rather than taking it into the pray-er's own hands, and they ask God to do what he has promised here: "repay" the hurt. It is not so much retaliation as vindication the injured child of God is seeking. This cry for justice is not an end in itself but a means to an end. When we leave the hurt and vengeance with God, knowing that justice will indeed be done, we find the strength to forgive those who do not deserve it and to free ourselves from a life of bitterness.

FEED YOUR ENEMY: COALS OF FIRE (12:20)

With the desire for vengeance behind us, Paul says we can fulfill the next aspect of his requirement for us: doing good and showing love to our enemies (vv. 9, 14, 17). He turns to Proverbs

25:21-22 to anchor this: "If your enemy is hungry, feed him; if he is thirsty, give him something to drink." Food and drink are frequent scriptural symbols for good works, and Jesus in his Sermon on the Plain (Luke's counterpart to the Sermon on the Mount) had a whole list of concrete things to do so as to show love to enemies (Luke 6:27-36). If we have yielded all thoughts of retaliation over to God, we are free to do the unexpected—return good for the evil shown us. We are asked to show love to our enemies via acts of kindness, but Jesus did far more than this: "While we were still sinners, Christ died for us" (Rom 5:8). This gives us a model for the rest of our lives.

Scholars are divided on the meaning of Paul's next phrase: "in doing this, you will heap burning coals on his head." It could connote shame caused by the good deeds as they are returned for evil actions, or it could refer to the judgment of God poured on our enemies' heads for the evil they have done. I don't believe this is an either-or but a both-and. Both interpretations fit the biblical imagery as well as the context. Fire is a frequent symbol of judgment, and good deeds often convict people of their sins and bring about conversion.

The two interpretations—shame and judgment—describe the two outcomes depending on how perpetrators respond to the good deeds done to them. If they respond with shame and conversion, God forgives and saves them. If they reject the kindness, God pours his judgment on them. This passage may well supply a missing aspect from 1 Peter 2:12, in which sinners see the good deeds of believers and "glorify God on the day he visits us," assuming their conversion. This makes clear that the good deeds bring conviction and shame for their evil acts, leading to their conversion. Those who refuse to repent come under divine judgment.

CONCLUSION: OVERCOME EVIL WITH GOOD (12:21)

This section culminates with a mandate not to be "overcome by evil, but [to] overcome evil with good." This theme has reverberated through Romans 12: "hate ... evil" and "cling to ... good" (v. 9), "bless" rather than "curse" persecutors (v. 14), seek peace (v. 18), and leave the vengeance to God (v. 19). Especially when we give food and drink to our enemies (v. 20), we overcome their evil deeds with good. If we seek vengeance and add our evil deeds to theirs, then the evil that was perpetrated against us will conquer us and turn us into replicas of our enemy. We may have the satisfaction of "winning," but in reality we will have lost everything.

There may be a double meaning here as well. Being "overcome by evil" could refer both to the evil act perpetrated against us and to the evil bitterness in our own heart. John 16:33 speaks of overcoming the world, and in Revelation 2–3 each of the letters to the seven churches ends with a promise to the "overcomer" (NIV "the one who is victorious," 2:7, 11, 17, 26; 3:5, 12, 21). By paying back the evil person with goodness, the Christ follower becomes a victor in the race of life.

————

This passage is nearly equivalent to 1 Corinthians 13 in the depth of its description of love at the core of the church family. In relations with fellow believers and unbelievers, love is a deep commitment and concern for those around us. We give ourselves entirely to building others up and making them feel wanted and appreciated, and at the same time serving God with all our strength by allowing love to reign in us. The one flows into the other, as our service to Christ is reflected and made real in our service to his people.

These verses are a guide to true Christian living. Nearly everything is here—caring for others out of a deep walk with Christ, set on fire with the Spirit. Our walk with Christ and the Spirit precede our actions. When we are fervent to serve the Lord, it becomes natural to serve our brothers and sisters in Christ as well as those who have not yet turned to Christ, including those who mistreat us. This will enable us to live rightly even when the trials of life overwhelm us, for our joy in Christ and our ability to persevere through hard times will allow us to live triumphantly through thick and thin.

Our service to the Lord is not just exemplified in our ministry to the church. It is also reflected in the way we treat unbelievers, even our persecutors. Our concern is not to get even but to be the channels of God's blessing to them, undoubtedly meaning primarily prayers for their conversion. Here we live in harmony and do good to all around us, but especially with our brothers and sisters in Christ.

Every one of us has been deeply hurt in our life, and in some cases we have neither forgotten nor forgiven the despicable act committed against us. This passage makes it essential to do so both for our sakes and for the kingdom's sake. We must be ready to take Christ's model and apply his forgiveness of us to our forgiveness of others. It is a kingdom requirement, for the church's witness in the world is at stake. Our own peace of mind and walk with Christ is forfeit if we allow our baser nature to reign. The imprecatory prayer through which we leave our desire for revenge with God is a wonderful answer, for it enables his forgiving heart to guide our reactions.

The blessing of verse 14 is spelled out in verse 20. Acts of kindness bring conviction to the hearts and minds of the unsaved, and they take one of two paths. Either they reject the convicting presence of the Spirit (John 16:8–11) and face the fiery coals of divine judgment, or they turn to God in response to fiery conviction, feel remorse, and be converted to life in the Lord. Even our suffering has a redemptive purpose—to bring about the salvation of our persecutors. This is what it means to overcome evil. The key to this is a life of love, beginning with the love of God, proceeding to the triumph of love in the church, and finally to our relations with nonbelievers.

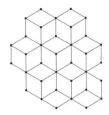

RESPONSIBILITY TO
GOVERNMENT AND NEIGHBOR
(13:1-14)

This topic comes at the reader out of the blue, and so some have thought it was added to Romans some time later. However, this hypothesis is unnecessary. It would be logical for Paul to follow up a discussion on persecution with a section on the major source of persecutors for Christians, the Roman government. The challenge in 12:9, 14, 17, to respond to evil oppression with good deeds would naturally lead to this section, so it makes perfect sense just where it is.

There had not been any official persecution as yet, but a great deal of anti-Christian sentiment had taken place. This was just at the end of the three missionary journeys (Acts 13-19), and Paul is writing Romans during his stay in Macedonia on his way to take the collection for the poor to Jerusalem (Acts 20:1-3). It was AD 57, and the young church had experienced quite a bit of opposition in each of the missionary journeys. So it would make a great deal of sense for Paul at this juncture to explore the church's relationship to the secular government, which had the power of life and death over them. At this time Nero was on the throne, but he had not yet turned into the evil despot he became a few years later. Still, there were signs of unrest and an anti-Christian sentiment to come. Claudius had expelled Jews and Christians from Rome due to Jewish rioting against the church in AD 49, and Acts describes local problems in nearly all the cities Paul had evangelized.

Several also see a connection with 12:2, "Do not conform to the pattern of this world." Some of Paul's readers may have understood that injunction to reject any connection with the world at all, including the secular authorities. Paul wants them to realize that God wishes us to remain apart from the world, but to still be a part of it. The old adage is still correct—we do not want to be so heavenly minded that we are of no earthly good. Jesus clearly lays out the principles of the relationship of Christians to the state in his teaching, and Paul is clearly quite familiar with it. In Matthew 17:24–27 Jesus stated that while at one level the children of God are exempt from earthly duties like taxes, they will pay them anyway as part of their witness to the world, to show everyone that they support the secular structures God has set up in his world. Then in Matthew 22:15–22 Christ taught that his followers are responsible to "give to Caesar what is Caesar's." Both Paul and Peter in 1 Peter 2:13–17 are part of the Christian catechetical tradition that developed from Jesus' formative principles. The Christian duty is not disengagement but transformation of society. They must reform the evils in society and be involved in removing evil from it rather than neglecting it.

There are two parts to Paul's teaching on government in verses 1–7, first an essay on submitting to the secular powers as part of one's submission to God (1–4) and second a clarification on the importance of submitting for conscience's sake and a set of examples regarding paying taxes (5–7). Two sections on living the Christian life close out the ethical emphasis in this chapter, first the responsibility of the church to be knit together in love (vv. 8–10) and second the importance of living in light of the Lord's soon return (vv. 11–14).

BELIEVERS SHOULD SUBMIT TO
THE AUTHORITIES (13:1–4)

The major debate in this section is over the relation of the three "for" clauses in verses 1, 3–4. Most likely they form three stepping stones, each adding information in turn. In the first two verses Paul says the person who refuses to submit will be judged by God. Then in verse 3 he clarifies that miscreants will also be judged by the state and should be afraid of the God-appointed rulers, and in verse 4 he adds that the officials are God's "agents of wrath" against those who flaunt their rebellion against the established laws.

God Has Established the Authorities (13:1)

Paul's basic command is to "submit" or "be subject" to the governing authorities. This verb (*hypotassō*) is behind husband-wife as well as citizen-government passages, and means to voluntarily place oneself under those whom God has given authority. Paul is asking the Romans to accept the secular authorities over them and to be willing to take their proper place in the social strata of their day.

There are three critical caveats to Paul's argument: (1) Submission does not indicate inferiority but a willing subordination; in Ephesians 5:21 believers are told to "submit to *one another*." (2) In Acts 5:29 Peter tells the Sanhedrin, "We must obey God rather than human beings" (cf. 4:19). The power of government over the saints is not absolute. Whenever society's rules contradict God's will, believers are obligated to pursue civil disobedience. (3) Submission does not depend on how "good" government is, and the Christian does not get a pass on submitting if government is evil. Paul here is commanding submission to a supremely evil government at a time when one of the most evil emperors in history, Nero, was coming into power. God removes an evil government, not us, but we can oppose its bad decisions and warn it of divine judgment to come.

The two terms for government here are "authorities" (vv. 1–2) and "rulers" (v. 3). Some think this is equivalent to Paul's "principalities and powers" in 1 Corinthians 15:24; Ephesians 3:10; 6:12; Colossians 1:16; 2:10, 15, where he describes the demonic powers. This was Martin Luther's view. If so, Paul would be depicting both government and the cosmic powers that underlie the secular world. However, few take that approach any longer for several reasons: (1) whenever "authorities" refers to celestial forces it is always combined with "rulers." (2) Taxes are never paid to demonic forces. (3) No one would ever require submission to demonic powers. In short, these are Roman government officials and not cosmic forces. There is no hint of demonic possession of human authorities here.

The reason believers should submit is that "there is no authority except that which God has established." God's authority is not restricted to the religious sphere. This is his created world, and he is in final charge over it. Officials do not possess authority inherently or due to political connections but entirely because God has given it.

Moreover, the "authorities that exist" have to include evil governors as well as good. This is the combined teaching of the Old Testament (Prov 8:15–15; Isa 45:1; Dan 2:21, 37; 4:17; 5:21); Judaism (Wisdom of Solomon 6:3; Sirach 10:4; 17:17; 1 Enoch 46:5); and the New Testament (1 Pet 2:13–14). Even the "beast," or antichrist, in Revelation 13:5, 7, "was given" his authority from God. Unworthy rulers will indeed be judged—but in God's time, not ours. The saints surrender to their God-given authority and let God take care of the rest.

Since rulers have been "established by God," they bear his authority. Paul states this twice for emphasis. They are "appointed" by him and rule in his place, and they answer to him. This does not mean God's people stand idly by and say nothing in the face of evil governments. The point is that evil in government calls for prophetic warning rather than active revolt. Our task is to call authorities to accountability and warn them of judgment if they refuse to follow God and govern righteously. This is what the prophets did with the evil rulers of Israel and Judah. Their reaction was not armed insurrection but condemnation before God and to seek for reform.

THOSE WHO REBEL ARE JUDGED BY GOD (13:2)

God has established the rulers of this world, so the one who "rebels against the authority," and the laws that God has instituted, rebels against God and brings judgment down upon their head. The Living Bible translates verse 2 well: "those who refuse to obey the laws of the land are refusing to obey God." There is a play on words between "established" (*tassō*) and "instituted" (*diatassō*), so that we can paraphrase, "God has *ordained* them, so when we rebel against them we are actually rebelling against the *ordinances* of God."

This rebellion is not just a single act but a settled attitude, an ongoing life of opposition to the things of God. People's continuous refusal to obey God's laws will "bring judgment on themselves," probably both divine judgment and the legal penalties of the law courts. In reality, since human officials are "God's servants, agents of wrath" (v. 4) who do his bidding, the earthly judgments are God's judgments. With the already/not yet perspective stressed so often in Romans, the emphasis is on immediate punishment (the human side) leading to final judgment (the divine side).

THE RULERS ALSO JUDGE THE WRONGDOER (13:3)

The first reason for submitting to the secular authorities is that God has established their power himself (v. 1). Now Paul explains a second reason: they are a source of fear for lawbreakers, because God has made government his instrument to punish all who do wrong. Yet they are not a terror for "those who do right." God has also made them his instrument of commendation for good citizens. This is similar to 1 Peter 2:14: "Governors ... are sent by him to punish those who do wrong and to commend those who do right." Government is a friend to the righteous, but it is the enemy of evildoers, who face nothing but punishment for their crimes.

Some may say this passage is naive, but Paul has not had only good experiences with government at this time of writing. He has seen the ugly side in Acts 16:22–23, 37 (Philippi); and 2 Corinthians 11:25–26 (his deprivations in ministry). He is deliberately positive here because he is centering on God's will and the responsibilities of the state to God. God will take care of the terrible decisions rulers can make and asks us to trust him to do so. Paul demands that his readers ask themselves whether they "want to be free from fear of the one in authority." The only way is to "do what is right and you will be commended."

There are two options: terror for the one who does wrong and commendation for the one who does right. "Commend" means "praise," and here too it comes both from the secular authority and from God. Some interpreters think Paul is calling not only for good deeds but also for what was called "benefaction," that is, performing civic deeds and giving gifts to the city that would ensure the welfare of the citizens. This was commended in the Roman world and would endear Christians to the public. It would certainly have been included in the good works Paul is encouraging.

The Ruler Is God's Servant, an Agent of Wrath (13:4)

Paul now spells out the true relationship of government to God, and explains in a final way why believers should submit to authorities. By definition they are "God's servants," and for criminals they are God's "agents of wrath." The consequences are extremely serious for flaunting the rules that govern society. The officers that oversee the rules are God's "servant" or "minister" (*diakonos*, rendering them the secular equivalent to "ministers" of the church), and this verse is framed by their twofold work as both a servant for good and a servant for wrath.

"Agents of wrath" is actually "avengers [*ekdikos*] for wrath," a cognate of the term "revenge" in 12:19. Only God can avenge wrong, but the state is his servant in bringing his revenge upon evil people. This image pictures serious punishment carried out against those who ignore God's laws that govern society. Those who do wrong should rightly "be afraid," for these officials "do not bear the sword for no reason."

The power of the sword was reserved for Roman officials, and Roman law was labeled *ius gladii*, "the law of the sword." A person who broke the law could count on being punished. "Bear the sword" primarily connotes the death penalty, but actually the whole emphasis of Roman justice was on the fairness of the system. Lawbreakers would receive only what their crimes deserved, and it was called **lex talionis**, "the law of retribution," meaning the punishment was to exactly fit the crime. This does not mean that it ended up always being fair, but it did strive to be so.

PAUL PROVIDES A CLARIFICATION AND AN EXAMPLE OF SUBMISSION (13:5-7)

CLARIFICATION: SUBMIT ALSO BECAUSE OF CONSCIENCE (13:5)

Paul now restates his basic argument, "it is necessary to submit to the authorities, not only because of wrath [NIV "possible punishment"]" and then adds a further clarification, "but also as a matter of conscience." Paul had explained the "wrath" motivation in verses 2-4, and now he adds conscience. The unbeliever will be most influenced by the "possible punishment," the danger of facing the wrath of the government and a fine or prison time, whereas the Christian will be influenced more by conscience.

In 2:14-15, Paul defined conscience as the inner awareness of right and wrong that God had placed in the hearts of the Gentiles. Here it is an inner awareness of God's will, which for the believer is informed and transformed by the Spirit (12:1-2). It is the ability to discern what is right and the motivation to pursue what God would have us do, including obeying the laws of the land. This adds a cognitive dimension, knowing what is required of us as citizens and how we are expected to respond to those rules. It is also a spiritual response, for as Jesus said, we are also to obey the laws as part of our witness, "so that we may not cause offense" (Matt 17:27).

EXAMPLE: PAYING TAXES (13:6–7)

"This is also why" points back to both the God-given authority behind government (vv. 1–4) and the conscience (v. 5) as the reasons why Christians should pay taxes. Paul then calls public officials God's "servants" (*leitourgoi*), which contains religious connotations, quite appropriate for the idea of government doing God's work. As servants of God, these officials "give their full time to governing," literally "devote themselves to this very thing." Since officials give themselves to serving God in governing the people, God's people are obligated not just to the state but also to God himself to support them by submitting to their authority and by paying taxes.

Taxes were especially onerous for Jews in the first century because the Jewish people had to pay Roman taxes (v. 7) as well as the temple tax. According to Exodus 30:13, every Israelite was to pay a half shekel (a third of a shekel in Neh 10:32–33) to the temple, an amount equal to two drachmas in Matthew 17:24. A drachma was a day's wages for an average worker. There was growing resistance to this in both Rome and Judea, and it eventually led to a tax revolt in Rome in AD 58, shortly after this letter was written.[1] Paul is telling his Roman readers that God required them to pay these taxes as a sign of their submission to both him and the state. In doing so Paul echoes Jesus, especially his pronouncements about paying taxes as part of correct stewardship (Matt 17:24–27; 22:15–22).

This section concludes with the observation that believers must "give to everyone what you owe them." The language here reflects monetary obligations, literally "pay back a debt." "Everyone" means every government worker, so paying taxes is seen as payment rendered to officials hired to fulfill a public need. This

---

1. According to the Roman historian Tacitus, in his *Annals* (13.50).

alludes to Matthew 22:21, "give back to Caesar what is Caesar's, and to God what is God's." The context there is also paying taxes.

In the list of taxes in verse 7, there are four tax obligations in two pairs; the first two refer to the specific tax obligations from verse 6, and the second pair looks to the general attitudes of verses 1–5. The first were called the "direct taxes" (*phoros*, "taxes"), referring to the direct tribute paid to Rome by a conquered nation, including the property tax and the poll tax (a census tax on individuals) collected by such tax collectors as Levi/Matthew (Mark 2:14). Roman citizens did not have to pay such taxes. Second, there is the "revenue" or indirect taxes, in which everyone had to participate, such as sales tax, customs duty, and tolls.

The second category includes proper attitudes toward government, namely, "respect" and "honor." "Respect" is literally "fear," "awe," "reverence" (*phobos*). Since in verse 3 Paul told us government has "no terror" for those who obey the laws, some believe the respect/fear is directed to God and the honor to government, as in 1 Peter 2:17, "fear God, honor the emperor." However, in this context one should not differentiate in this way; government is seen as an instrument of God. We respect government because it is God's instrument of punishment, and we honor it as an instrument of God.

Bad interpretations of this passage have had some deleterious effects on the Western world through the centuries, as despotic rulers have used it to justify totalitarian governments and demand submission to evil policies. The doctrine it teaches, however, that the Christian is duty-bound to respect and submit to government as an instrument of God to stabilize the secular realm, is very important. Taxes are a primary mode of respect for government. Many Christians think they can hold back taxes when they disagree with the government use of that money. It is clear here that this is wrong. We *owe* that money to support the civil authorities, and it is not optional. To refuse to pay it is to sin against God's will, not just to break the laws of the land.

The major question is how a believer submits to a government that is not following God. Some have thought God's people are not to submit in such a case, and that Paul wrote when relations with Rome were at their zenith. When that changed, the argument goes, the responsibility ceased with it. However, that is not the case. The Roman government was anti-Christian throughout the first century and beyond, and Nero was evil from the start. When government is evil, the Christian places it in the hands of God, and he removes it in his own time.

Yet "we must obey God rather than human beings" (Acts 4:19; 5:29). We submit to an evil government so long as doing so does not force us to disobey God. God's word demands submission but not blind obedience. Whenever a government contradicts the Lord's will, we refuse to submit—but only in those areas where its rules contradict God. This is also where prophetic warning comes into play. In the same way the Old Testament prophets warned the evil Israelite kings of judgment, we warn our current rulers when they are circumventing the Lord's will. We always do so out of respect for their authority and love for the nation we share.

LOVE IS THE FULFILLMENT OF THE LAW (13:8-10)

THE ONLY DEBT: LOVE ONE ANOTHER (13:8)

Paul begins these next verses by rephrasing the opening to verse 7, "Let no debt remain outstanding." Christians are obligated not just to society but also to God to pay all debts in full. Now he extends that point metaphorically to include the debt that love for others places on us. This is the only debt that can never be paid in full; love's demands never cease. Yet at the same time it is the only debt that we willingly and joyfully embrace.

The primary difference here is that Paul makes love all-inclusive; "love one another." When love guides our relationships, we give of ourselves so thoroughly that we are virtually in debt to each other. As love governs our interactions, our obligation to care and sacrifice for each other continues as we virtually say, "I owe you my very life."

There has been some debate as to whether Paul has primarily believers or unbelievers in mind. Certainly the mandate covers both, with a slight emphasis on the Christian community, as in Galatians 6:10, "do good to all people, especially to those who belong to the family of believers." In 12:9–13 the love was focused within the community, but in 12:14–21 it was extended to outsiders, even to those who were enemies of God's people. So the obligation is to love everyone around us (Matt 5:44, "Love your enemies"), but to maintain a special tie to fellow saints. By emphasizing "one another," Paul shows he especially has Christian relationships in mind.

This is so critical for believers that Paul says, "Whoever loves others has fulfilled the law." He introduces the issue of the law to prepare for the subject of meat offered to idols in 12:1–15:13. The solution for that divisive issue in Rome is to allow love to guide the community. Paul wants his Roman readers to realize that the law has already been fulfilled in Christ and the new law of love he has brought into this world (cf. John 13:34). When we give ourselves to others in the love of Christ, the law is completed in us.

By "fulfill the law" Paul could mean that the believer who loves keeps or performs the law perfectly, but it more likely carries the connotation of **eschatological** fulfillment. The loving Christian enters the new age of fulfillment in Christ, and we experience the last days in a new way when we allow the love of Christ to guide our community relationships. This goal of perfect love is not finally attainable in this life, but we are to strive for more and continue to grow in it.

The Commandments Fulfilled in "Love Your Neighbor" (13:9)

To deepen the idea of love as fulfilling the law, Paul shows that love sums up the second table of the Ten Commandments. The first table (numbers one to four) centers on relations with God, and the second (five to ten) on relations with others. He cites in order here the seventh (adultery), the sixth (murder), the eighth (theft), and the tenth (coveting) commandments. When we love our neighbors in Christ, that love encapsulates the second half of the Ten Commandments in us!

Paul is echoing Jesus' teaching (Mark 12:29-31), where he said the law comes to completion in two principles, "love the Lord your God" (Deut 6:4-5, summing up the first table) and "love your neighbor as yourself" (Lev 19:18, summing up the second table). "Neighbor" both here and in Mark 12 refers to believers and unbelievers. "As yourself" assumes that people basically love themselves and mandates that the same effort be extended to caring for others.

This self-sacrificial love "sums up" the law, another way of saying that it "fulfills" the law. It does not mean this is merely a new focus for the law but that it is a new law which at the same time completes the old and replaces it. When we love in Christ we join ourselves to the new covenant and follow the new "law of Christ" (Matt 5:17-20; Gal 6:2).

CONCLUSION: LOVE FULFILLS THE LAW (13:10)

In 12:9-21 Paul argued that love is doing good to and for others; here he restates it negatively for effect: "love does no harm to a neighbor." This is the God-ordained purpose of the law vis-à-vis relationships. In this sense the love commandment sums up the true purpose of the law, to enable God's people to experience the good he has for them and the good that they are privileged to do for each other. With respect to the family of God we are "devoted to one another" (12:10), and with respect to non-Christians we "bless and do not curse" them (12:14). We show love to our every neighbor and try to guarantee that no harm comes to them. As we do so we fulfill the law.

LIVE IN THE LIGHT BECAUSE OF CHRIST'S NEAR RETURN (13:11-14)

Paul brings to a close his section on ethical exhortation in 12:9-13:14 by reminding his readers of a truth that has dominated this letter:

we are living in the interim period between the already and the not yet, between the two advents of Christ, and the time is near. The need to live rightly according to God's will is especially urgent. This theme reverberates throughout the New Testament. Christ will come at a time we do not know, and when he comes he will hold us accountable for the quality of our walk and our spiritual condition. In the parables of Matthew 25 all God's people are judged on the basis of their readiness for the Master's return, and the message is clear—God demands that his people be prepared at all times for Christ's arrival.

Therefore, the saints must be spiritually vigilant, living for God rather than for the things of this world (1 Thess 5:2-3; Heb 9:28; Jas 5:7-8; 1 Pet 4:7; Rev 16:15). In Romans 5-7, Paul argued that the age of Adam gave way to the age of Christ, the age of law was replaced by the age of grace and faith, and the age of sin was conquered by the age of righteousness. The past age gave way to the present age of Christ and salvation. Now we move to the next step, the final transfer of realms, as the present time is soon to be replaced by the age of victory in Christ. In the present we have a foretaste of what is to come, yet at the same time we "groan inwardly as we wait eagerly for our [final] adoption" (Rom 8:23). These verses consider the Christian's ethical actions from the perspective of the future reality.

Wake Up from Your Slumber (13:11)

Paul's opening "And do this" likely refers not just to the injunction to love in verses 8-10 but to all the ethical exhortations of chapters 12-13. It could be paraphrased, "live for Christ in this way." We must live rightly by "understanding the present time" (literally "knowing the time"), a phrase used in 3:26; 8:18; 11:5 for the present age of salvation that anticipates the final age of glory. The time is short and the return of Christ is imminent, as in Hebrews 10:25, "and all the more as you see the day approaching."

In light of the nearness of Christ's return, Paul states forcefully, "The hour has already come for you to wake up from your slumber." Paul's emphasis is on "already come." There is no basis for doing what we do every morning we can—lying in bed for an extra hour, putting off the busyness of the day. The clock is ticking, and every minute counts!

This is similar to the hymn of Ephesians 5:14, "Wake up, sleeper, rise from the dead, and Christ will shine on you." In Ephesians the sleepers are unbelievers, while here they are believers. There waking up is conversion, while here it is beginning to live fully for Christ. In 1 Thessalonians 5:6–8 Paul uses the image of sleeping for pagans whose lives are defined by those who "sleep at night," while Christians "belong to the day." Rising up from slumber means refusal to participate in these dark deeds and a determination to live in the light of the Lord.

Paul is accusing many Christians of resembling pagans. These people have been asleep spiritually, and when they should have been alert and at work for the Lord they have been doing nothing of any worth. This is no time for spiritual laziness, "because our salvation is nearer now than when we first believed." Paul makes the comment here not just because time has passed but also to make a theological point, emphasizing the imminence (for the issue, see v. 13) of the **eschaton**, the "end" of history, when Christ will rid the world of evil. Then the saints will be delivered and vindicated, but they will also give account for the quality of their life. In the present time, they must make certain they are spiritually awake and active for the Lord.

THE DAY IS NEAR, SO PUT ON THE ARMOR OF LIGHT (13:12)

Paul returns to the image of day and night to anchor his warning: "The night is nearly over; the day is almost here." The night is a common symbol for the darkness of sin (Ps 139:12; Isa 21:11–12; 1 Thess 5:2, 5, 7), and the day is the day of the Lord, the time when judgment will fall on the enemies of God and his people (Joel 1:15; Amos 5:18; Rom 2:5, 16) and vindication will come for believers (Joel 3:18; 1 Cor 1:8; Eph 4:30). The message of imminence continues, with the end of the age fast approaching, when good will conquer evil once and for all.

There is only one way to prepare for that day: "Stand firm. Let nothing move you. Always give yourselves fully to the work of the Lord" (1 Cor 15:58). To illustrate this, Paul turns to the image of taking off filthy old clothes and putting on clean new ones: "Let us put aside the deeds of darkness and put on the armor of light." He uses this metaphor often to picture ethical change, replacing bad habits with good ones.[2] In Ephesians 6:14 and 1 Thessalonians 5:8 he uses it for putting on God's armor. Paul is warning against putting on nightgowns when we need armor.

The "deeds of darkness" would be the sins that characterize this present evil age (2 Cor 6:14; 1 Thess 5:4–5). We are to throw off all such evil tendencies and clothe ourselves with his armor of light. The armor, as in Ephesians 6:14–17, contains both defensive weapons that protect us from Satan's deceptive sword thrusts and offensive weapons that enable us to defeat the powers of evil. So "the armor of light" protects us from the powers of darkness and gives us the weapons to produce victory in the cosmic war.

In the midst of the cosmic battle against Satan we cannot pretend to achieve neutrality. We are in battle fighting for the Lord, or we are destroyed by the dark forces. Paul is calling for a wartime attitude of sacrifice and a single-minded focus on the seriousness of the war. There is no time or place for lazy, ineffectual soldiers or for deserters in God's army.

BEHAVE DECENTLY (13:13)

To live appropriately as God's denizens of the day, we need a new type of Christian behavior. As Christ's soldiers on a wartime footing (see 2 Tim 2:3–4), our duty is to "behave decently, as in the daytime." "Decently" (*euschēmonōs*) literally means "of good

---

2. Eph 4:22, 24; Col 3:9–10 with respect to putting off the old self and putting on the new. See also Eph 4:25; Col 3:12.

appearance," but Paul is not stressing the idea of external appearance here. Rather, the stress is on appropriate or proper conduct, as in 1 Corinthians 14:40, "everything should be done in a fitting and orderly way," with the "orderly way" determined by God's ethical standards.

Paul uses another of his favorite metaphors to illustrate this, the idea of "walking" ("behave" in the NIV translates Greek *peripateō*, "to walk"). Christians should live such exemplary lives that when people examine them, their conduct is beyond reproach (see 1 Pet 2:12).

"As in the daytime" continues the already/not yet tension we have seen often in Romans (8:18, 19, 28; 11:26–27; 12:19). We as the children of God walk in the present days he has given us but do so in light of the final day, when we meet the Lord in the air and begin eternity. In the present we experience all the blessings of being the children of the new covenant (Eph 1:3), and in this new reality we are obligated to live appropriately (= "decently") in God's eyes.

Paul then turns and enumerates a vice list of the "deeds of darkness" we are to "put aside" (v. 12), stressing the opposite of proper conduct. He provides three pairs of items that could be labeled "sins of the night":

1. *Not in carousing and drunkenness.* Some combine these into one category, "drunken carousing," but it is better to keep them separate since Paul lists these all in pairs. They describe the wild parties and binge drinking so popular in Paul's day and in ours. Sadly, it has become epidemic on college campuses today, virtually expected behavior. Paul uses plural nouns to demonstrate the repeated nature of these sinful practices. The wild parties of the emperors and the murals on many Roman walls uncovered by archaeologists exemplify the excess he has in mind.

2. *Not in sexual immorality and debauchery.* The first pair described the uninhibited parties, and now Paul turns to the sexual sins that characterized them. These were wild

orgies with every kind of perversion taking place. The first term (*koitais*) describes the sexual sin itself (transliterated as the English word *coitus*), and the second term (*aselgeiais*) the lifestyle that follows. The sins of these first two pairs go together and return to the list of depraved humanity in 1:18–32.

3. *Not in dissension and jealousy.* This turns from the party life to social sins, denoting the envy that characterizes unredeemed humanity and the quarrelling that results. There was no place this fit better than in the political infighting and petty bickering of Rome itself. Whenever an entire population devotes itself to "looking out for number one," jealousy and strife will dominate. This is as big a problem today, and even many churches are torn apart by such selfish infighting. In this third category Paul is looking ahead to the division of the Roman Christians over meat offered to idols in 14:1–15:13.

Clothe Yourselves with Christ (13:14)

In verse 12 Paul urged the Roman believers to "put on" a new set of clothes, the armor of light. Now the new set of clothes is Christ himself: "clothe yourselves with the Lord Jesus Christ" (see John 8:12, "I am the light of the world"). Many think Paul has baptism in mind, as in Galatians 3:27, "all of you who were baptized into Christ have clothed yourselves with Christ." Yet this goes further and includes the entire process of conversion, as in Romans 6:3, "all of us who were baptized into Christ Jesus were baptized into his death." In Christ we have died to sin and its evil practices. The Christian life is defined as discarding the filthy clothes of sin and putting on Christ.

When we are converted and then baptized into Christ, we throw off the old and put on the new self (Eph 4:22–24). When that takes place, we join ourselves to the death, burial, and resurrection of Christ (Rom 6:3–6) and begin a lifetime process of putting this world behind us and becoming more and more like him. Our minds are transformed by the Spirit (Rom 12:2), and we become servants of Christ and his people (Rom 12:3–8).

Paul's injunction here centers on the present spiritual life that results from being clothed with Christ, involving the process of becoming like Christ. Some have considered it a once-for-all event on the basis of the Greek aorist tense, but this misreads the force of that tense, which looks at an event as a single whole rather than a once-for-all action. Here the verb is global, looking at the investiture with the person of Christ as a process of becoming. We are brought into God's family, and at conversion we put off the old self and put on (= clothe ourselves with) the new (see v. 12 above). Thus begins a lifetime of day-by-day becoming more like Christ as well as making him more and more the Lord of our life.

The negative implications of this are that we "do not think about how to gratify the desires of the flesh." The things of Christ and the things of the flesh are completely antithetical. In 8:1–17 Paul defined the flesh as the sinful tendencies we all have, the desire to live for self and the things of this world. This provides a summary of the problem of sin developed throughout verses 11–13, for the vices of darkness could be labeled "the desires of the flesh." The war between the flesh and the Spirit was the subject of 8:1–17 (eleven times there), and this issue is at the heart of the victorious Christian life. The power of sin in our lives can only be overcome in Christ through the power of the Spirit.

To win the victory over the flesh, we begin with the thinking process. We must "think" carefully of the dangers when we allow ourselves to seek to "gratify the flesh" and consider seriously how to overcome this destructive dark force through the empowering presence of the Spirit. Instead of seeking fleshly gratification, our transformed thinking process embraces the things of Christ rather than the flesh, and the victory is ours.

———

This section details the responsibility of God's people to those around them, both the government and one's neighbors. Paul develops here a comprehensive picture of Christian relationships in every facet of society, beginning with submission and respect for the rulers of the land and moving to love for every inhabitant in the land, believer and unbeliever alike.

His command to submit to government authority is revolutionary. Every human authority, even if part of a totalitarian regime like Rome's, is actually placed in office by God. We submit to their decrees, and when those pronouncements are not in keeping with the will of God, he will reverse them and remove the evil rulers in his own time.

We must both yield to the government's laws and trust God to reverse them when needed. Paul warns us that if we flout those rules that come simultaneously from God and the state, we will receive just retribution. Taxes are an important example of the respect and honor we owe our governments. We pay them not as an optional sign of our honor but as our part in obeying God with respect to running our nation. It is more than a secular duty that we may ignore; it is a requirement if we are to obey God.

On the local level, God has placed us in this world to live out his love in community relationships. When we love those around us, we bring to completion his own laws for relating to others in the second half of the Ten Commandments. This is not possible until his love guides our responses to our neighbors.

We must put the forces God has made available to us to work in our lives and go to war against the dark forces that control this world. Once we realize that we are living in the last days and that we have weapons of light available, we should "put on the full armor of God" (Eph 6:10-18) and engage in battle with the powers of this world. While we submit to government, we also go to war against the dark forces that are often guiding the decisions that run this world. This seeming paradox is what it means to be a spiritual Christian in a secular age.

If we are children of the day rather than creatures of the night, our lifestyle must be characterized by the ways of Christ. We will throw off the wild life of the party people around us and live a life of love for the glory of God. Our goal in life is to gratify and please God rather than the flesh, and our pleasure comes not from indulging the flesh but from serving God and his people.

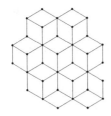

LOVE AND UNITY IN THE COMMUNITY, PART 1:
THE COMMAND TO STOP FIGHTING
(14:1–12)

The church of Rome had probably been founded by Jewish Christians who traveled there in the years after Jesus' death and resurrection.[1] In the early years it was majority Jewish with a growing number of Gentile converts. Then in AD 49 after a series of riots against Christians by the Jewish community of Rome, the emperor Claudius expelled both Jewish Christians and Jews from Rome. The church became a Gentile church. Five years later Claudius died, many of the Jewish believers like Priscilla and Aquila (Rom 16:3) returned, and tensions ensued. The Jewish Christians were still faithful to Torah, especially in observing the food laws and the holy days. The Gentile Christians felt they did not have to observe these practices since Christ had fulfilled the law.[2]

---

1. See "Recipients" in the introduction.

2. There is some debate about whether Paul is addressing a specific situation in Rome (the majority of interpreters) or a potential problem. If it is the latter, he would be drawing material from 1 Corinthians 8–10 to warn the Romans. However, the material in 14:1–15:13 is not dependent on Corinthians, and the situation seems specific enough to describe an actual problem in Rome.

The issue was one of tolerance versus intolerance. Paul wanted both sides to be tolerant of the other, but neither wanted to be. They were both accusing the other of being unfaithful to their calling. Three issues divided them—eating meat (14:2), observing sacred days (14:3), and abstaining from wine (14:21). Paul calls the Jewish Christians the "weak" group, and the Gentiles the "strong" group. This stems from the incident of the clean and defiled hands in Mark 7:19 in which "Jesus declared all foods clean," meaning that he had removed the binding nature of the food laws so that the people of God could now eat any meat. The "strong" faith of the Gentiles allowed them to accept this pronouncement, while the "weak" faith of the Jewish Christians would not let them do so.

Nevertheless, God honors their level of faith and expects them to live up to it (14:13–16). God exemplifies tolerance and accepts what we offer him in faith, however inadequate our human perspective might be. The weak are to stop being judgmental (14:10), but the strong must accept their weaker brothers and sisters and respect their convictions. God accepts them, so the strong must follow his lead. They must refrain from placing undue pressure on the weaker members and respect their right to live at the level of their faith.

There are four subsections in this larger section: (1) In 14:1–12 Paul describes the conflict between the two groups and demands that they stop fighting. (2) In 14:13–23 he admonishes the strong against offending the Jewish Christians and causing them to stumble by demanding their freedom to worship their way. (3) In 15:1–6 he commands the strong to understand and tolerate the weak. (4) In 15:7–13 he asks both groups to tolerate and accept the other on the basis of Christ's acceptance of Jew and Gentile.

PAUL DESCRIBES THE CONFLICT
OVER THE FOOD LAWS (14:1–4)

This section can be organized around the problem (vv. 1–4), specifics behind the problem (vv. 5–9), and a concluding admonition against judgmentalism (vv. 10–12). The NIV omits the opening "but" (*de*), but it shows that Paul views this judging attitude as antithetical to the command to "love one another" that dominates 12:9–13:14. He sees it also as a further result of the "flesh" in 13:11–14. The strong and the weak are not viable Christian movements but are "fleshly" groups, since they are ignoring love in their squabbles.

ACCEPT THE WEAK WITHOUT JUDGING (14:1)

The "strong" Gentiles may still be the primary power group in Rome, so Paul commands them to "accept the one whose faith is weak." By "accept," he means the strong need to consider them fellow believers and equal in the eyes of the Lord. They had been marginalized in the fellowship. This section is an exhortation for unity and harmony in the church, so the strong must receive the weak as a vital part of the church and as brothers and sisters in Christ.

Paul uses the pejorative title "the one whose faith is weak" to describe believers whose ascetic tendencies and dependence on the food laws were looked down on by the majority Gentile Christians. These were not Judaizers, whose problem was that they replaced Christ with the law and were therefore more Jewish than Christian. If that were the case, Paul would have condemned them as he did his opponents in Galatians and Philippians 3. Their use of the law was not a basis for salvation, but a part of their required worship. The regulations were not the basis of their Christian faith but the result of their faith.

By "faith," Paul means that they believed they had to follow these practices in order to walk with Christ properly. Many Jewish Christian congregations today would fit this description, since they still follow the food laws as part of their worship and lifestyle. For Paul "accepting the weak" meant that neither group passed judgment on the "disputable matters" of food (14:2), holy days (v. 5), and drinking wine (v. 21).

This doesn't mean that debates were prohibited in the early church. Luke held up the Berean Christians, who "examined the

Scriptures every day to see if what Paul said was true," as a model
(Acts 17:11). Instead, acrimonious debates were outlawed. Paul is
calling for unity in the midst of diverse beliefs, a search for truth
that reflects acceptance of one another and our differences without judging each other. We should debate doctrinal issues; we are
always searching for truth. But unless we are dealing with the
core truths of the faith, we must be "iron sharpening iron" and
accept differences without judging, realizing we could be wrong
and respecting other views.

DIFFERENT TYPES OF FAITH IN THE FOOD LAWS (14:2)

The primary disputed matter concerns the food laws. "One person's faith" (Gentile Christians, who believed the food laws had
been abrogated) "allows them to eat anything, but another, whose
faith is weak" (Jewish believers, who believed the food laws were
still required) "eats only vegetables."

Few Jews were vegetarian, for the law demanded meat from
which the blood had been drained properly, and there was no
reason to give up meat altogether. Most vegetarian movements
in the first century were Gentile, so some have wondered if this
was a Gentile movement. This makes little sense, and it is likely
the answer lies in historical contingency. From the time of the
Maccabean revolt in the second century BC, the food laws were a
major test of faithfulness to God and his law. Moreover, since they
had been expelled from Rome a few years earlier, after moving
back Jews may have found it difficult to obtain kosher meat. They
thought it better to become vegetarian than to take a chance of
eating meat that wasn't kosher. At any rate, the Gentile believers looked down on them for not having enough strength to surrender their Torah restrictions in the new era of Christ and faith.

THE STRONG: NO CONTEMPT; THE WEAK: NO CONDEMNING (14:3)

Paul started by addressing only the strong; now he admonishes both groups. The strong look down on the weak or "treat [them] with contempt," and the weak "condemn" or judge the strong. Those with no dietary convictions thought the others inferior. Christ had negated the food laws (Mark 7:19), so they felt disdain for the ignorance of the Jewish believers. Those with strong convictions thought the Gentile believers broke the laws of the Lord and so condemned them for sinning "with a high hand" (Num 15:30 ESV; "defiantly" in the NIV). Note the **inclusio**: verse 1 begins with the command to "accept the weak" while verse 3 closes by telling the weak that "God has accepted" the strong. Paul warns both groups to quit judging each other because God has accepted them both.

It is a sin to reject those whom God has accepted. I grew up in a church that often fought over legalistic issues like playing cards (I could play Rook but not games that used face cards), going to movies (even movies like *Ben-Hur* or *The Sound of Music*), social dancing, or drinking. While this is a close parallel to the legalistic issue in Romans 14, the principle also applies to quarrels over doctrines like the charismatic issue, the rapture of the church, and Calvinism versus Arminianism. We must learn to agree to disagree over noncardinal issues. It is not that they are unimportant.[3] Rather, it is that God has accepted both sides, and so we must accept each other even while disagreeing.

GOD ACCEPTS THEM: DO NOT JUDGE (14:4)

This opening section concludes with a strong challenge: "Who are you to judge someone else's servant?" Based on verse 3 Paul is especially speaking to the weak who are "judging" the strong, but

---

3. See the discussion of predestination at 8:28–30 and the end of chapter 10.

the sentiment encompasses both groups. Paul castigated the Jews for judging in 2:1, since their firm hold on the rituals of Torah led them to set themselves up as the judges of all other groups. Still, Paul is probably addressing both sides here and leading into the material of verses 5–9. In Romans 11:18, 20 Paul also warned his Gentile readers against arrogance, considering themselves "superior to those other branches," for God would not "spare you either."

The hubris of anyone thinking themselves superior enough to set themselves over others offends Paul deeply. The term "servant" (*oiketēs*) is a "household slave," and the master is certainly God. In the Roman world it was the worst sort of manners for a person to interfere with someone else's slave. How much more true is this when the master of that slave is God himself?

Paul's point is that a slave will "stand or fall" only with respect to "their own master," not an outsider. All approval (standing) or rejection (falling) comes from God, so it is wrong for anyone else to meddle in our relationship with God. This must be applied very carefully in light of other passages in Scripture that may seem to contradict this, such as Hebrews 3:13, "admonish one another daily, as long as it is called 'Today,' so that none of you may be hardened by sin's deceitfulness" (my translation). We are supposed to prayerfully get involved in each other's lives so that we encourage when encouragement is due and challenge when challenge is due. We do this out of love and for the harmonious unity of the group. The key is to refuse to judge others. When we admonish we do so out of love and avoid judgmentalism.

The weak are not being led by the Spirit but are passing judgment on those with whom they disagree. This constitutes what James labels "discrimination," so that they become "judges with evil thoughts" (Jas 2:4). Rather than being concerned for the welfare of those they challenge, the weak here are concerned only for what they assume is right. They want to win rather than get to the truth. There is no love, only contempt for the other.

Only God's judgments matter, and Paul demands that the weak realize that "the Lord is able to make them stand." God's people will be approved because the Lord is with them. As Peter says, they are "shielded by God's power until the coming of the salvation that is ready to be revealed in the last time" (1 Peter 1:5). The strong are not merely accepted but also shielded by God's power ("is able" = "has the power"). God's presence in their lives is based not on their external activities (what they eat) but on their internal trust (the one in whom they believe).

This issue illustrates the importance of tolerance in our day as well. This last century has been an unceasing example of fighting over nonessentials in the church. Going forward, the one thing we can be sure of is that Satan will continue to want us to fight over the wrong things!

PAUL DISCUSSES FURTHER THE ISSUES DIVIDING THE CHURCH (14:5-9)

THE HOLY DAYS: BE CONVINCED (14:5)

The weak person "considers one day more sacred than another" while the strong "considers every day alike." Literally, the weak "judge one day more important than another" for religious reasons, while the strong "judge each day the same." It is difficult to know for certain the background to this dispute over days. Some interpreters have thought a Gentile view of magical powers associated with certain days the gods have blessed could be behind it, but almost certainly this is a Jewish-Christian issue. Perhaps it is the Jewish festivals like the Day of Atonement or the Feast of Tabernacles, or perhaps it is a debate over the Sabbath.

If it is the Sabbath, Paul could be talking about the first-century debate over Saturday (the Old Testament *Shabbat*) versus Sunday (the New Testament worship on the Lord's Day) observance. The weak group would have followed the Jewish practice of worship on Saturday, while the strong chose Sunday. (Worship on Sunday began quite early in the history of the church, as we see from Acts 20:7; 1 Cor 16:2; Rev 1:10.) In the church at Rome the two sides were divided over such things, but Paul says it should be an open issue. Whatever position one prefers, "each of them should be fully convinced in their own mind." Both approaches are viable, and the only requirement is to be faithful to the Lord and true to your convictions.

In fact, Paul's teaching here may well be a reapplication of "renewing your mind" in 12:2. With the Spirit transforming the thought processes of every child of God, the two sides should think through the issue carefully, allowing the other side to force them to look at the issues anew, and then make up their minds accordingly. There is no single truth in matters such as this, and Paul wants each side to respect the other.

This is a healthy way to think through many doctrinal issues. I have used this perspective to examine issues like the rapture, the charismatic issue, predestination or the security of the believer, and women in the church. The word of God can be seen to support both sides, and we will never solve them completely. Paul calls for a deeper unity and respect for the other side in each instance. This doesn't mean we can't reach a conclusion; I have firm views on each of these issues. It means we cannot be absolutely certain, and the other side's view is viable.

EAT MEAT OR ABSTAIN, BUT GIVE THANKS (14:6)

It is hard to overstate the importance of this verse for understanding differences between churches. Most groups feel that they (and perhaps they alone) are correct in their doctrinal and practical demands. God puts up with the others (at times), but is not happy with them. Paul may have the "strong" especially in mind here; they know they are right and look with contempt on the weak (v. 3). He makes clear that so long as the weak truly seek to glorify the Lord in their practices, God will honor them, and he accepts both them and their views. If only we realized the truth of this, a great deal of acrimony could be avoided between our separate movements.

The key is for both groups to make certain that whatever they feel convicted about, they express it "to the Lord," meaning in high and holy worship. As long as God and the worship of him are central, they will please him. Paul provides three examples in verses 5 and 6—observing holy days, eating meat, and abstaining from meat. Both the weak and the strong groups are acceptable to God provided they are sincerely trying to honor the Lord in these practices. They may be wrong about having to follow the food laws, but God honors them and their convictions because they are using their views to worship and serve him.

One's overriding concern must not just be the desire for truth but also glorifying God in every area of life. Whether they eat meat or abstain from it, God will accept them provided they "give thanks to God," which Paul repeats to emphasize the divine reception. Whichever side of the debate they embrace, they can be assured of God's pleasure if the practice is accompanied by sincere thanksgiving. Paul uses a special example of the prayer of thanksgiving at mealtime (the Jewish people offered two prayers at mealtime). So long as they are "fully convinced" (v. 5) and deeply thankful (v. 6), they can be assured of God's blessing whichever side they choose.

Whom did God prefer—Luther or Calvin or Wesley or Menno Simons? Paul would say God loved and accepted and used each of them equally. Moreover, God uses all the groups they founded today and is pleased with each of them, provided they seek truth and to glorify him in their church life. It is true that the issues in verses 5-6 are practices rather than doctrinal beliefs, but dogma is deeply behind both practices, and the two cannot be separated. Practices always stem from beliefs.

However, we cannot take this principle to mean any movement that calls itself Christian must be tolerated and accepted. There is such a thing as heresy, and Paul said in Galatians 1:8-9 that anyone who proclaims "a gospel other than what you accepted" is "under God's curse." The movements we are talking about above agree on the cardinal issues—the Trinity, the deity of Christ, substitutionary atonement, the necessity of the cross for forgiveness of sins— but differ on noncardinal issues like sovereignty versus responsibility or the timing of the second coming. On these we can respect each other and disagree without rancor.

We Live and Die to the Lord, Not Ourselves (14:7–8)

Paul theologically anchors his admonitions of the previous verses in verses 7–9, extending the truth of "to the Lord" in verse 6. The point is that "whether we live or die" (v. 8), we do it not for ourselves but for God. Everything in life relates to God and not just to ourselves. Both the weak and the strong had forgotten this. Their purpose had become proving the superiority of their own movement rather than to glorify and worship the Lord. We shouldn't do anything in life just to benefit ourselves or our movements. Conflict between groups might have the benefit of talking people into leaving another group and joining ours, but it will never glorify God.

This echoes Romans 1:21 that those who join such religious disputes exemplify the "futile thinking" and "foolish hearts" of the world but do not honor God. This is especially true with respect to our death, for God alone controls that event, and all we can do is surrender to his will and make certain that we are so centered on him in life that our death will also glorify him. Our goal at all times is not the glorification of our group but devotion to God and honoring only him.

Paul concludes, "So, whether we live or die, we belong to the Lord." We do not belong to our denomination or even to our ministry. Rather, we minister within those parameters in devotion to God so as to magnify his name. We are not the central figure; we are not even needed. Rather, we are placed where God has us in order to proclaim his truths and honor his name. God does not need us; he has allowed us to serve, and we rejoice at our privilege.

At the end of verse 8, Paul reminds his readers that they "belong to the Lord." They are his children (8:14-17) and his slaves (6:15-22). It is natural that the servant live to please the master (14:4), and that is all that matters. Conflict takes energy away from our true goal and purpose, and replaces God with our own group as a central focus. Truth does matter, but debates are only worthwhile so long as we respect each other and refuse to allow the debate to degenerate into sectarian conflict.

This passage reminds us that God honors and uses both groups. Everything from the onset of life to its natural closure in death is the Lord's. We are not the focus of anything we do, nor is our movement. Rather, our activities and achievements, including the movements to which we have devoted ourselves, serve only the Lord and must honor only him. They dare never become an end in themselves. If they do, they have failed to meet their true purpose.

CHRIST, THE LORD OF THE DEAD AND THE LIVING (14:9)

The core of everything in verse 8 was the fact that we "belong to the Lord," and Paul follows this by reminding the Romans that this is why "Christ died and returned to life." With his blood he purchased us for God; as 1 Corinthians 6:19-20 tells us, "you are not your own; you were bought at a price." To place our own agenda ahead of God's is a sin, for it denies our true relationship with him and ignores the implications of the redemptive death of Christ.

Christ died and returned to life so that we might belong to God (v. 8), and so that "he might be the Lord of both the dead and the living." His death was a ransom payment (3:24) that bought us for God, and as a result he was raised to glory as the Lord of all, the dead as well as the living. He is Lord of the dead because he will be the Judge at the final judgment, and he will be the Lord of heaven.

A lot more is at stake here than community harmony. If Jesus is Lord of the church and of every one of its members, the kind of conflict the Roman church experienced should not be possible. If each of us is one with him, then we are one with each other. Church disputes are much more serious than just corporate tension; they endanger both the glory of God and the lordship of Christ.

As I said in my comments on verse 6, we must distinguish cardinal doctrines from noncardinal issues. The church exercised severe discipline when the key doctrines of the faith were involved, like the Judaizers in Galatians or Philippians 4 or the heretics in 1-2 Timothy or 1 John. Noncardinal debates demand dialogue and tolerance, as Paul exemplifies here over observing the law. When the Judaizers made keeping the law a means of salvation in Galatians, Paul deemed it a heresy. The Roman Jewish Christians kept the law not as a means of salvation but as a mode of worship, and it was not heretical.

PAUL GIVES CONCLUDING ADMONITIONS (14:10-12)

DON'T JUDGE—GOD IS JUDGE (14:10)

In verse 10 Paul returns to his earlier diatribe style (see 2:1-4, 17-24). He begins with a biting question and rebuke in reverse order of verse 3, calling out the Romans for judging and despising each other. He calls the opponents in each case "your brother" to stress the fact that this is a fellow member of God's family they are rejecting. They have set themselves up as judges, and they have no right to do so in the community of God.

In verses 7-9 Paul reminded them that Christ is Lord of all, and everything answers to him. He extends that image here by reminding them that "we will all stand before God's judgment seat." Only God is the judge, and those who take that role on themselves will stand before God in judgment. Their fellow Christians answer only to him and not to other Christians.

In 2 Corinthians 5:10 Paul says that "we must all appear before the judgment seat of Christ," not the judgment seat of other Christians, and there "each of us [will] receive what is due us for the things done while in the body, whether good or bad." This provides another critical warning not to judge each other when we disagree over nonessential (noncardinal) issues. Some of us may prefer a high church worship style, others a low church worship. Some prefer hymns, others loud praise songs. God blesses every group and style that honestly worships him. Yet we continue to fight over such things!

ALL WILL BOW BEFORE GOD (14:11)

The point of verse 10 is that God alone is the judge. To anchor this Paul cites Isaiah 45:23, "'As surely as I live,' says the Lord, 'every knee will bow before me; every tongue will acknowledge God.'" Paul's quotation follows Isaiah closely except for the opening "as surely as I live." This is a common introductory formula (see especially Isa 49:18 and also Jer 22:24; Ezek 5:11).

Paul probably uses it here to draw together the contexts of Isaiah 45:23 and 49:18, where God addresses the complaints of Israel that he had forsaken his people by promising that his exiled children would be returned to their mother. In Isaiah 45 he promises that he will sovereignly redeem his people and force the nations to bow before them. In both contexts he alone is in sovereign control as judge over the nations and his own people.

The judgmental Christians of Rome will either "bow before" the Lord and "confess" (the meaning of *exomologeō*, "acknowledge" in the NIV) their error to God, or face God's judgment seat in the future. While "confess" can mean giving homage to God ("praise" or "acknowledge"), in the context of judgment in verses 10 and 12 there is an implicit warning in verse 11 that makes "confess" fit quite well. To give homage to God, we must first confess our sins.

For Paul, the weak and the strong were under indictment for the sin of hubris in judging each other. They needed to confess their error and get right with him.

WE WILL ALL GIVE ACCOUNT TO GOD (14:12)

This verse makes explicit the point of verses 10–11—"each of us will give an account of ourselves to God." The emphasis is on "each of us," stressing the fact that every human being will stand before God's *bēma* (royal judgment seat) and answer for their lives. All believers as well as unbelievers will be examined and tested for the quality of the way they lived their lives.[4] This theme is called **lex talionis**, "the law of retribution," and it means that we will be paid back by God with perfect justice for what we do with our lives—the perfect punishment for sins and the perfect reward for righteous conduct.

If we judge each other, our actions are of this world and we will be judged in turn by God. If we allow God to be Judge, as Scripture demands, we ourselves will be judged righteous, and unity in the church will be restored. Then the result will be reward.

————

In 14:1–12, Paul addresses the Jewish and Gentile believers' fighting over the binding nature of the law. The Gentiles realized Christ had negated the food laws (Mark 7:19), while the Jewish followers thought them still binding. They were judging and condemning each other over the issue, and Paul is demanding tolerance and acceptance of each other. This is not merely an interesting historical situation; we have just as vociferous infighting today over

---

4. This teaching is incredibly frequent in the Old Testament (2 Chr 6:23; Job 34:11; Ps 28:4; 62:12; Prov 24:12; Jer 17:10; Ezek 18:20; Hos 12:2), in Second Temple Jewish literature (1 Enoch 41:1–2; Psalms of Solomon 2:16; 17:8; 2 Esdras [4 Ezra] 7:35, 8:33; 2 Baruch 14:12) and in the New Testament (Matt 16:27; Rom 2:6; 14:12; 1 Cor 3:12–15; 2 Cor 5:10; 11:15; 2 Tim 4:14; 1 Pet 1:17; Rev 2:23; 11:18; 14:13; 20:12; 22:12).

issues like church music, the place of women in the church, or Calvinism versus Arminianism.

These and similar issues do not have an easy solution, and believers will debate them until the Lord returns. Paul provides a brilliant solution. So long as both sides are truly trying to live for the Lord and exercise their views to honor him, God accepts them, and so should the rest of us. We must both respect and accept others and realize God is using them as much as he is using us to serve himself.

When we judge others over such issues, we are taking for ourselves the authority that belongs only to God, and our group is replacing God as the central focus of our ministry. Even if our opinion on the issue is right, but those on the other side are serving God and refusing to condemn us, then they are the ones God honors, not us. Christ is Lord and Judge, and all we do must be Christ-centered. This is what the weak and the strong in Rome were forgetting.

Every one of us will stand before God and answer not only for how we are serving the Lord but also for how we are treating each other. There must be a deeper unity in the church than has heretofore been seen. God is watching our relationships with each other. He wants to use our church factions in the same way he used the weak and the strong in Rome; he wants to blend us together into an evangelistic weapon to defeat Satan and win the lost. He demands this unity, and we will all answer to him at the final judgment for how we treated each other and whether we worked together for his glory.

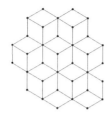

LOVE AND UNITY IN THE COMMUNITY, PART 2:
DON'T BE A STUMBLING BLOCK
(14:13-23)

The friction between the strong Gentile believers and the weak Jewish Christians continues, but now Paul addresses specifically the strong, whose freedom from having to follow the law has posed a problem. They have become so smug in their superior position that they have wielded it as a weapon, and the absence of Christian love has made the truth a negative instrument threatening to destroy the faith of many of their weaker brothers and sisters. The admonition is to build up the faith of others rather than tear it down. Sometimes being right has its drawbacks, especially when it leads to an arrogant assumption that everyone is supposed to accept your superiority and do what you tell them.

It is common to see this passage organized around a **chiastic** framework:

A Warning against being a stumbling block (v. 13)
   B Nothing is unclean (v. 14)
      C Do not destroy another by stressing your freedom (v. 15)
         D God's kingdom means peace and joy (vv. 16–18)
         D' Seek peace and mutual edification (v. 19)

C' Do not destroy the work of God (v. 20a)
B' All food is clean (v. 20b)
A' Warning against being a stumbling block (vv. 21–23)

DO NOT JUDGE OR BE A STUMBLING BLOCK (14:13–18)

Paul begins this section by rebuking the Romans for judging, which sums up verses 1–12. The problem in Rome was the animosity between the Gentile and Jewish converts over keeping the Old Testament law, and they were judging and condemning each other over it. In 14:3b, 10, the ones guilty of judgmentalism were the weak, and in 14:3a, 10, the strong are guilty of despising the weak. Here Paul chastises both groups for judging each other. In the following verses the strong are the objects of the rebuke, and Paul states the thesis of the section in verse 13—don't do anything that will hurt another believer.

THE WARNING AGAINST STUMBLING BLOCKS (14:13)

The strong were supposed to lead the way in the church by dialoguing with the weak on the issues. Instead, they exacerbated the situation by looking down on their adversaries. After he instructs both groups to stop passing judgment, Paul uses a terrific play on words to turn the attention to the strong and their responsibility in the situation. He tells them that instead of "passing judgment" (krinō) on the weak, they should "decide" (krinō; "make up your mind" in the NIV) "not to put any stumbling block or obstacle in the way" of the weak believers. The verb can mean both to "judge" and to "determine" or "decide" a thing. He exhorts them to decide not to condemn the weak (v. 13a) or hurt them (v. 13b) but to build them up. Instead of negative judgments, he wants the strong to make positive discernments.

Paul tells them not to put two things before the weak that are virtually synonymous. A "stumbling block" (proskomma) is an obstacle in a person's life that leads them to fall spiritually into sin. An "obstacle" (skandalon) pictures a trap or snare that captures a thing. Both terms refer to a series of transgressions that destroy a person's faith and lead to apostasy.

Paul does not specify how this takes place, but there is general agreement as to the likely process that would cause the faith of many of the weak Christians to fail. The obstacle is related to the food that the weak believe is unclean (v. 14). The forceful arguments of the strong could cause many of the weak to violate their consciences by eating meat without being "fully convinced in their own mind" (v. 5). When that conviction was overturned, the faith of the weak was overturned. They would abandon not just their beliefs regarding the food laws but also the Christian faith as a whole.

From this we must learn to respect the honest religious convictions of those around us, so long as they are anchored in the word and in the Triune Godhead. A good example would be the beliefs some Christians have about alcohol, movies, card playing, and dancing. Those who feel free to engage in such things while exercising their judgment should never mock or put down those who believe differently. Making them adhere to your standards could hurt them spiritually and cause their downfall. In short, the strong are not to flaunt their freedom in front of the weak and so hurt them spiritually. Rather, we should respect their consciences, realize God accepts them as they are, and not engage in drinking alcohol, going to movies, and so on when we are with them.

No Food Unclean Unless Someone Believes It Is So (14:14)

Paul next makes a clear statement about the laws of clean and unclean and shows unequivocally that he is in full agreement with the strong. The Old Testament law regarded some things as "common" and causing defilement. Such rules defined what was holy, or set apart for God. When Christ came, all such differentiations centered on him. The laws of clean and unclean were no longer necessary since Christ fulfilled or completed their purpose in the divine scheme of things. Paul realized this both through his experience of Christ and through Christ's teaching about the law (Matt 5:17–20; Mark 7:19).

While Paul agrees with the strong in their freedom from the law, he adds a very important caveat that the strong did not understand: "If anyone regards something as unclean, then for that person it is unclean." The strong must respect the conscience of a person who disagrees with them on this, for any person's religious conscience is essential for their own walk with the Lord. The strong must understand that people differ in their ability to grasp a truth and see where the arguments are leading. The exercise of freedom is not always the best way to go, for it can seriously damage another Christian with a different conscience. We must honor another person's convictions above our freedom to do what we think best for ourselves.

THE THESIS: DON'T DEMAND YOUR FREEDOM AND DESTROY ANOTHER (14:15–16)

Here Paul goes further, switching to the second-person singular "your" for greater impact. The strong should not just refrain from arguing their case too strongly around the weak; they should even refrain from exercising their freedom around them. Both sides are brothers and sisters to each other, and no sibling wants to bring unnecessary distress to their own family members.

These Jewish Christians were "scandalized" (NIV "distressed") at the so-called Christian liberty of the strong to ignore the Old Testament law and eat any meat they wished. When the strong forced the issue, they both upset the conscience of the weak and hurt them spiritually. These weak-faithed Christians are first told (and some are convinced) that they are wrong, and then they see the strong eat forbidden foods, and their conscience is further turned upside down. Paul's progression in this verse is emphatic— as the weak see the strong exercise their freedom, they are first terribly hurt ("distressed") and then "destroyed," meaning they depart from their Christian beliefs entirely.

Paul asserts that the strong "are no longer acting in love" when they "by [their] eating destroy someone for whom Christ died." There is no concern for the person's faith or spiritual life, only for winning the debate and proving the other wrong. Paul makes this even more emphatic by adding that the one being destroyed is someone "for whom Christ died." Jesus surrendered his life on the cross as an atoning sacrifice for this person's salvation, and the strong have glibly brought them to spiritual ruin for the sake of exercising their Christian liberty and winning the debate.

Christians should not exercise their freedom in any way that could hurt another person spiritually. To do so is to fail to "walk according to love" (the literal Greek in v. 15), the essential characteristic of the true Christ follower (12:9–21). In differences of theological conviction, God's people must respect the convictions of others by refraining from doing what offends them. Paul felt free to eat what he formerly viewed as unclean foods but was also free to refuse to do so when other Christians with him were convicted against doing so. Christian freedom is also seen when we refrain from an action!

Paul concludes his point in verse 16 by stating, "do not let what you know is good be spoken of as evil." Literally it says, "Therefore, do not let your good thing be blasphemed/slandered." While some think "the good thing" is meant generally of all God's covenant blessings (or perhaps the gospel), it is more likely that Paul intends specifically to sum up the knowledge of the strong that the food laws were no longer in force. The freedom to eat any and all foods is indeed a good thing, but if this freedom ever led to the faith of fellow believers being destroyed, then the name of Christ would be "blasphemed" or "spoken of as evil" both within and outside the church. The very name of Christ would be maligned as a result of the spiritual devastation wrought by these overzealous "strong" Christians.

What is good in itself can have terrible consequences if not used wisely. The spiritual damage inflicted by the debate would result in the church and the Christ it served being reviled by many. Most of all, it is mandatory that both sides of the conflict live on the basis of love by honoring and respecting the honest convictions of the other side. The strong should consider the weak not pawns to be manipulated into the "truth" but brothers and sisters whom they want to help grow and who they utterly respect in terms of their walk with the Lord. Too many unbelievers say, "Why should I be a Christian? You don't get along with each other, so why should I think being a Christian will bring me peace and happiness?" We must change this perception, which is based on too much valid data. We have to earn the right to be heard.

THE GOAL: RIGHTEOUSNESS, PEACE, AND JOY (14:17-18)

Issues of legal observance like eating and drinking are not what the kingdom is all about. Paul reminds the Romans of what really matters to God, and it is not divisive issues like the food laws. I wonder if God will be saying something very much like this to us today: "You should not have wasted the church's energy and time fighting over things like movies, which worship music God prefers, or even the rapture or predestination." They are definitely worth discussion and study papers, but they must never become ends in themselves or divide churches.

Paul makes his point clearly: "For the kingdom of God is not a matter of eating and drinking, but of righteousness, peace and joy in the Holy Spirit." The Roman church should not be stressing peripheral matters. They are not utterly worthless, but they should be on the periphery time-wise. The essential aspects of the kingdom should be in central focus. Interestingly, this is the only place in Romans Paul mentions the kingdom of God, and it is here because of the discussion about central kingdom issues. The kingdom is breaking in to this world as proof that the last days are here, and it is time to get serious about what really matters.

The church should be experiencing harmony and a unity centering on "righteousness, peace and joy in the Holy Spirit"—exactly what the dissension was endangering. Each of the three represents a critical aspect of what Romans is all about.

1. *Righteousness* is the central theme of the book and is the core of **soteriology** (the doctrine of salvation). It refers to both the justification of the believer and the righteous lifestyle that results (see 1:17; 3:21–26). There are three stages: we are declared right by God when we are justified on the basis of the atoning sacrifice of Christ on the cross, then we are made right by the Spirit as we are sanctified or made holy by his empowering presence, and then we live rightly for God as we put into practice the new life Christ has given us.

2. *Peace* results from justification (5:1) and the presence of the Spirit in our lives (8:6, 14–17). Paul wants to replace the conflict and dissension at Rome with the peace of God. This will only come when the individuals who are at odds with each other turn their lives over completely to Christ and begin caring for each other.

3. *Joy* appears here for the first time in Romans, but Paul will conclude this section with a prayer that "joy and peace" will "fill" the Roman church through the "power of the Holy Spirit" (15:13). Joy is the natural accompanying emotion to the presence of the Spirit in our lives. Even our trials are meant to produce an inexplicable joy as the Spirit takes over and turns everything around on our behalf (Jas 1:2–4; 1 Pet 1:6–7).

Divisive situations are reversed when the Holy Spirit takes over. Destructive conflicts will not be turned around by mere human effort, but with the guiding presence of the Spirit righteous behavior can finally bring the church the peace it needs and the joy that will provide proof that the kingdom of God has once more triumphed. To accomplish this the strong Gentiles must temper their arrogant demands and begin caring more about the spiritual development of the weak than they do about their precious freedom.

In verse 18 Paul tells the Romans how they can achieve this goal. They must begin to serve "Christ in this way" (literally,

"serve Christ in this"). There is some question as to exactly what
"this" refers to here. It could mean (1) "serve Christ in this matter,"
namely, in the conflict; or (2) helping the church seek "righteousness, peace and joy" rather than victory over each other in the conflict; or (3) "in the Holy Spirit"; or perhaps (4) in bringing the kingdom focus to bear on the issue. In the context, the "this" most likely
refers to the whole of verse 17—the kingdom living that produces
righteousness, peace, and joy. Until the Christians at Rome realize the centrality of the kingdom, they will never solve the problem. The same can be said of similar issues in our day. The Spirit
must replace our narrow dogmatic hobby horses with broader
kingdom values, and then we can place our sectarian debates in
their proper perspective.

When that happens, the two groups will unite in one church
and finally fulfill their divine purpose vertically (they are "pleasing to God") and horizontally (their service "receives human
approval"). When the strong subordinate their freedom to more
important kingdom truths, then God will indeed be pleased with
them. In this Paul alludes back to 12:1, where the presentation of
the whole self to God pleases him. Like that presentation of self
to God, this is a self-sacrificial act. Then approval will come from
those around them, likely the same who would have "blasphemed"
them for destroying the weak Christians in verse 16. The picture
seems to be that people are testing them to see if they are deserv-
ing of condemnation or approval. When they serve Christ and
bring peace into the community by following the leading of the
Spirit, they win the approval of others.

SEEK PEACE IN THE COMMUNITY (14:19-21)

PEACE AND MUTUAL EDIFICATION (14:19)

After discussing the implications of their infighting and the need
for another path for their energies, Paul turns back to exhortation and tells them what they need to do: "Let us therefore make
every effort to do what leads to peace and to mutual edification."

The reality of God's kingdom in their midst calls for harmony between the diverse groups that make up the church. The verb translated "make every effort" is *diōkōmen*, which in the continuous present tense has the idea of unceasing effort to produce a thing. The church is mired in dissension and bad theology, and it will take a great deal of Spirit-led work to get things moving in the right direction.

The idea of pursuing peace is frequent in the New Testament.[1] It is an essential aspect of life in the Spirit. Paul's point is that peace in the community takes tremendous energy, so they must pursue it with all they possess and do so under the strength the Spirit supplies. The strong have until now sacrificed peace for their Christian liberty.

Peace is achieved by pursuing the things that make for "mutual edification." If the strong will work to build up the weak rather than flaunt their religious freedom in front of them, peace will be the natural consequence. Paul says this well in Ephesians 4:12-13, where the leaders are to "equip [Christ's] people for works of service, so that the body of Christ may be built up until we all reach unity."

This is done individually through mentoring, but Paul likely is thinking corporately of the whole church with its focus altered to center on the united people of God growing together in Christ. The weak and the strong must stop focusing on winning the debate and center on building each other up in Christ to achieve peace and a united worship and joy in Christ.

EAT NOTHING THAT CAUSES ANOTHER TO STUMBLE (14:20-21)

Paul draws his challenge together by stating unequivocally, "Do not destroy the work of God for the sake of food." It is a sin to

---

1. 2 Tim 2:22; Heb 12:14; 1 Pet 3:11; see also 2 Cor 13:11; Eph 4:3; 1 Thess 5:13; Jas 3:18.

damage a fellow believer spiritually just so you can flaunt your freedom. The conscience of the weak gives them no choice: they cannot eat meat since it might not be kosher. The strong have the choice: they can eat it or not. It is up to them to resolve this issue, and Paul expects them to do what it best for the weaker believers and for the community as a whole.

He states it strongly because the repercussions are serious: they could "destroy the work of God." The danger is not just offending someone's overly sensitive conscience. "The work of God" includes the redemptive work of Christ and the work of salvation in these weaker believers. If they don't get their act together, two destructive forces will be unleashed—individual believers will be destroyed spiritually (vv. 15-16, 20b), and the work of God in the community as a whole will be destroyed (v. 20a).

So verse 21 provides the solution: "It is better not to eat meat or drink wine or to do anything else that will cause your brother or sister to fall." Paul reverses his mode of speaking for effect—it is bad to eat meat if it will harm another, and it is good to refrain from partaking if it will help the situation. This is the only time Paul mentions wine in this passage. In the Old Testament, only people who had taken a Nazirite vow abstained from drinking wine, and there were no Torah regulations against it (Num 6:2-4; Judg 13:7). In the Roman church, most likely the same hyperconservative Jewish Christians who avoided meat because it might not meet kosher standards avoided wine because it might have been used in drink libations to the gods. The strong should be willing to surrender eating meat and drinking wine rather than hurt the conscience of a fellow believer. Paul expands this by adding "or anything else" to show that a universal principle is involved. The mature Christian will not do anything that can harm another believer spiritually.

LIVE AT THE LEVEL OF YOUR FAITH (14:22-23)

KEEP YOUR VIEWS TO YOURSELF (14:22)

Paul's command here is a little mystifying on the surface. Literally he says, "The faith that you have, keep between yourself and God." At first glance it looks like Paul is telling the Romans not to share their Christian faith with others. But throughout chapter 14, the "faith" is not saving faith or the Christian faith in general but the "faith" of the strong and weak groups to believe what Christ said about the law no longer being binding on God's people. This faith is a conviction about the place of the law in the Christian life as it relates to the three issues in this chapter—eating meat, observing holy days, and drinking wine.

He is instructing the strong Gentile Christians to form their convictions carefully but not to force them on the weak Jewish Christians. They understand that the food laws and other restrictions no longer apply in the new covenant era under Christ. But to trumpet them in such a way that the weak Christians are damaged spiritually is a serious sin; therefore the strong Christians are to keep their beliefs between themselves and God. God honors their views and the Christian lifestyle that results from them. However, he will not honor anything that causes dissension and damage.

In the rest of verses 22-23 Paul addresses the strong and the weak in turn. He gives the strong a beatitude, "Blessed is the one who does not condemn himself by what he approves." There are three possible understandings of this: (1) Paul might be challenging the strong to make certain they won't have to blame themselves for causing the weak to stumble; (2) he could be encouraging the strong that once they have carefully examined themselves they are indeed free to partake of the food and wine without condemnation; or (3) he could mean for both the weak and the strong to act on what their conscience is telling them and not to castigate themselves for doing so. It is unlikely Paul is addressing both here, and the language does not quite fit this being a challenge. So most likely Paul intended this verse to encourage the strong to do what is right (the second position). He is telling the strong that they can be confident that God is indeed blessing them when they follow their conscience and "approve" of the meat and the wine as they partake of them. He believes their beliefs are correct, and there is no need for him or anyone else to judge these practices.

Paul then in verse 23 warns the weak to be faithful to their own consciences. What would be right for one group would be wrong for another group, for all Christians are responsible to God to live according to the level of their faith. To them the point is that "whoever has doubts is condemned if they eat, because their eating is not from faith." Their conscience has given them a faith system that cannot accept that the Mosaic law is no longer binding. Now they must live by that faith.

For the weak to eat meat would lead to divine condemnation because they would not be doing it according to their faith. They would be eating in "doubt"—without the faith that makes it right in the sight of God. Paul's conclusion is that "everything that does not come from faith is sin." God expects every one of his children to live up to the level of faith they have attained. While it is true that all meat and drink are acceptable to God, those whose faith does not allow it would fall into sin if they partook. And it would indeed be sin, for they would be acting against their God-given consciences.

———

The conflict in Rome is similar to many similar debates today, with strong believers realizing Christ has freed us from the bonds of the law but tending to lord it over the weak. The problem is that when they break down the arguments of the weak and prove their case, they do more harm than good. They destroy their weak understanding, but in doing so they also destroy their Christian faith. In addition, the good name of Christ was being slandered in the community by these terrible results. In such debates, concern for the spiritual life of our adversaries should take precedence over merely winning the argument.

Whatever enhances the spiritual life of the kingdom community must be our priority. If exercising our freedom hurts another Christian, we must forego exercising our freedom on that issue. The goal of the Christian life is not exercising our liberty at any cost but rather doing what will bring righteousness, peace, and joy to the people of God. The self-sacrificial surrender of rights for the sake of the kingdom will bring pleasure to God and win approval from those around us.

We should work with all our energy to stop fighting and start building each other up in Christ. That will bring peace to the fractured community and enable us to become one people of God rather than a divided community. In debates like the one at Rome, the strong are free to exercise their understanding and enjoy the results but should keep their understanding between themselves and God and refrain from forcing it on weak Christians (v. 22). The weak must honor their level of faith and refuse to partake of anything if they have doubts about it (v. 23). In the movie *Chariots of Fire*, for the Olympic runner Eric Liddell it would have been wrong to eat out or play sports on Sunday. God honored his convictions, and living up to them gave him a power in running few possessed. The strong must understand this and honor that conviction. The weak must allow it to guide their lives. All of us must live our convictions and follow the dictates of our consciences, seeking to build up those around us and establish peace and harmony in God's kingdom community.

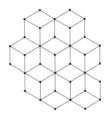

LOVE AND UNITY IN THE COMMUNITY, PART 3:
BEAR THE BURDENS OF THE WEAK
(15:1-13)

This chapter contains two units of Paul's address to the Roman believers regarding their conflict over the food laws and holy days. The first (vv. 1-6) contains his final address to the strong about their responsibilities to the weak Jewish Christians among them, and in the second (vv. 7-13) he addresses both groups, commanding them to accept each other and learn to worship God together.

The primary burden is still on the strong, as it should be. Some interpreters think Paul is speaking generally in this section about caring for others in a church conflict, but most recognize that this is still specific for the problem in Rome. Paul's point is that our concern should be for the spiritual needs of our opponents, not just for ourselves. If both groups are seeking to serve those on the other side, the conflict will take care of itself. When we seek spiritual edification rather than victory in the debate, God is pleased with us.

THE STRONG MUST BEAR THE
BURDENS OF THE WEAK (15:1-6)

The issue, as we have seen throughout chapter 14, is the Roman Christians' ability to accept the new covenant reality in which all foods are clean and there is no longer an obligation to observe the Jewish holy days (14:2, 5, 14). Many Jewish Christians were unable to grasp that truth, and this caused problems in the Roman church. However, the greatest problem was not the deficient faith of these Jewish Christians but the overzealous reaction of the strong Gentile believers, who castigated their deficiencies and forced their freedom on many of the weak Christians, destroying their walk with Christ in the process.

DON'T PLEASE YOURSELVES BUT THE WEAK (15:1)

Paul has been increasingly revealing his own agreement with the strong faction, and now he comes right out and makes the identification explicit, beginning this verse with "we who are strong" (*dynatai*, the adjective cognate of *dynamai*, "am able" or "have the strength"). Paul then commands the strong to curtail their overreactions and to "bear with the failings of the weak." The "failings" are their weak faith that forces them to obey the food laws, holy days, and other regulations. Paul is using language reminiscent of Galatians 6:2, "Carry [= "bear"] each other's burdens, and in this way you will fulfill the law of Christ."

It is difficult to know exactly what Paul is asking of the strong. He certainly does not want them to show the weak the error of their ways. That is what has been causing the difficulties, as he makes clear in chapter 14. He told the strong in 14:13-18 to accept the weak and not to hurt their faith. At the least he is exhorting them here not to dominate the weak but to shoulder their burdens. This means more than just tolerance for their views; the strong should attempt to understand where they are coming from and why, as well as adopt a loving approach to them on the whole.

Paul wants empathy toward the weak and a sympathetic aware-ness of the problem.

As they turn with compassion to the weak Jewish Christians, the strong are "not to please [themselves]." They must refuse to flaunt their freedom and trumpet their superior position with no consideration for the convictions of the weak. It is a call for restraint, compassion, and a deep awareness of how important the issue is for these Jewish Christians. They should want to build the weak up, not tear them down, and go the extra mile to do so. This is in reality a general Christian obligation (NIV "ought to") that includes us all. God requires it of us.

Please Your Neighbor (15:2–3)

In verse 2 Paul states the same thing two ways. We should "bear with the failings of the weak," which means we refuse to please ourselves but instead seek to "please our neighbors," namely, the weak, "for their good." Certainly Paul has the core command of Leviticus 19:18 in mind, "Love your neighbor as yourself," going back to his teaching in Romans 13:8–10. While he may be address-ing both groups here, the context shows his primary focus is still on the strong, who had the greater obligation (v. 1). Love is rede-fined as a desire to please the other.

The strong must come to understand the Jewish Christian mindset, and their goal must be to bring the weak spiritual plea-sure (see Rom 12:1–2 on the "pleasing" will of God). This pleasure is defined in two ways—their good and their edification (as in 14:19). This means to seek what is best for them spiritually and, as in 14:15, what will not bring them the type of spiritual harm that can destroy them. The goal is to help the weak grow in the Lord, to "build them up" in Christ, strengthening their fellow believers in the Lord. The strong must stop castigating the weak for their deficiencies with regard to the law and start helping them to max-imize the Spirit's work in their lives. This is an important lesson for us. If Calvinists and Arminians or dispensational and Reformed would attempt to understand and appreciate each other with this kind of depth, there would be fewer church splits than there are.

Paul turns to the example of Christ in verse 3: "For even Christ did not please himself." He did not live his life to meet his own desires but lived to serve others. This was the heart of the temptation narratives (Matt 4:1-11 = Luke 4:1-13), in which Satan tempted Jesus to seek his own glory and to please himself rather than his Father. This temptation is at the core of the meaning of sin, the self-centered desire to live for yourself.

Now Paul cites Scripture, and one would expect a passage pointing to Jesus' self-sacrificial lifestyle and death for us. It is therefore a little surprising that Paul cites Psalm 69:9, a passage on Christ experiencing mockery and slander for the sake of God: "The insults of those who insult you have fallen on me." In this context, "you" is God the Father and "me" is Christ.

Psalm 69 is a lament psalm of David depicting the trials of the righteous sufferer, and Paul saw it fulfilled in Jesus. It is one of the most frequently quoted Old Testament passages used of Jesus' death on the cross (Mark 15:35-36 and parallels; John 2:17; 15:25; Acts 1:20; Rom 11:9). The "insults" here refer to the mockery Jesus endured on the cross, the supreme self-sacrificial act—see Rom 5:8, where Jesus' death at the hands of his enemies "demonstrates [God's] love for us."

Paul is saying that when the Messiah willingly bore reproach on the cross, it became the model for us all of a life lived to please God rather than self. If Christ endured such insults, indeed a sacrificial death, for the Roman Christians, why couldn't those whose faith is strong endure the loss of a few freedoms for the sake of the weaker Christians among them? The judgments of the weak against them should be borne with equanimity. It is for the greater good of the church so that God's name will be honored and the church strengthened.

ALL WRITTEN IN THE PAST IS MEANT TO TEACH US (15:4)

Paul briefly diverges from his topic to explain why he cites the Old Testament so often: "For everything that was written in the past was written to teach us." It has been fulfilled or brought to completion in Jesus (Matt 5:17-20) and no longer has salvific force because salvation has come through Christ (Eph 2:15), not the law. However, it still plays a role as divine revelation for the instruction of God's people. The Old Testament canon points to Christ and is essential to God's plan. In 2 Timothy 3:16, "teaching" is the first of four purposes of the inspired Scriptures (followed by rebuking, correcting, and training). Thus the Roman Christians should listen closely to its instruction.

For Paul the basic purpose of the Old Testament is "so that through the endurance taught in the Scriptures and the encouragement they provide we might have hope." This might seem a bit out of place in a section centering on pleasing our neighbor rather than ourselves, but in actuality the context of 14:1–15:13 is the need for harmony and togetherness in the church rather than division and conflict, and hope is a primary binding force in the church. In fact, it is the major theme of this final section. The weak and the strong alike are facing persecution and hard times and need to unite under the banner of hope in Christ, as Paul has often stressed in Romans (4:18; 5:2-5; 8:20, 24; 12:12). With pressure from outside (persecution) and inside (dissension), they need the hope of the gospel more than ever. Hope in Romans provides a concrete certainty that God's presence will triumph, and it gives the church the strength to try the impossible.

The basis of Christian hope is the work of Christ and the witness of the Scriptures to him, both of which Paul emphasized in verse 3. There is a twofold means "through" (Greek: *dia*) which this hope has come to us, first "endurance" and then "encouragement." In steadfastly enduring the difficulties of life, the people of God experience the hand of God delivering and vindicating them in the crucible of a sin-sick world. The chain of 5:3–5 illustrates this, as suffering produces endurance, which in turn leads to proven character, out of which emerges hope. The path to hope is paved with suffering and endurance. Christ is the archetype of this process, and as his followers learn to follow his example, they find hope to be the antidote to despair.

The second means through which hope is gained is the encouragement provided by the Scriptures. In the many occasions of trouble and sorrow in this life, the word of God provides needed comfort and consolation as it reminds us that God is still in control and evil is doomed. We need to be reminded constantly that the Triune Godhead is at all times supremely involved with us and that as a result "neither death nor life, neither angels nor demons … nor anything else in all creation, will be able to separate us from the love of God that is in Christ Jesus our Lord" (Rom 8:38–39).

Paul wants the Roman church to realize anew that they have experienced these things together, not separately. Both endurance and comfort have been theirs only when they face their problems together. Hope is endangered when the church is fractured by conflict. The strong are obligated before God (v. 1) to go beyond their differences with the weak in order to establish harmony in the church. They share both Christ and the word, and they need to find unity in their hope in Christ.

PRAYER: MAY GOD GRANT YOU UNITY (15:5–6)

Unity is the overriding concern of this section and now becomes the subject of a prayer-wish (as in 2 Thess 3:5; 2 Tim 1:16; Heb 13:20–21) Paul utters for the Roman church. It plays two roles. It is an actual prayer Paul wants them to pray with him, and it forms a concluding exhortation that draws together major themes of the section and encourages the Roman believers to work for these goals. In verse 5 Paul repeats the two ways hope comes to the church—endurance and encouragement—for emphasis. God is the source of both. The Roman Christians will never move on from the divisions that are so endangering the church until they focus on their common need for these things and are able to rise above their differences. They must realize that they cannot endure or find comfort in their present problems without each other (yet see 16:17–20 for the one exception to this demand for unity).

Paul prays that God will "give you the same attitude of mind toward each other that Christ Jesus had." The "same attitude of mind" doesn't mean they must come to agreement about the food laws and the holy days, but they must agree to disagree. They should determine not to fight over the issue or treat each other as enemies. This is the same instruction as 2 Corinthians 13:11 ("be of one mind") and Philippians 2:2 ("of one mind"). It is to have the mind of Christ, who thought of himself as the slave of those he came to save (Phil 2:7).

As in 14:13–18 and 15:1–2, the Roman Christians must learn to live with their differences and focus on the major areas of commonality, respecting the small areas where they do not agree and refusing to let things degenerate into conflict. The key is to cultivate a particular attitude of thinking toward "each other" (*allelois*), a word Paul uses ten times in Romans to describe the united fellowship of the saints (1:12; 12:5, 10, 16; 13:8; 14:13; 15:5, 7, 14; 16:16). The basis of this unity is that both sides follow "Christ Jesus" and center on the salvation and Christian life he wrought with his atoning sacrifice. When both sides are walking the Christward road together, they will not allow a few minor differences to cause them to stumble. When a few of their beliefs differ, both sides will seek a single-minded harmony derived from the essentials of the faith and place their differences in perspective.

The core of this unity is in verse 6, to function as a united church "with one mind and one voice." The first (*homothymadon*) is a political term describing a government body making decisions "by common consent" and "with one accord." It is used often in Acts of the church meeting together in harmony (1:14; 2:46; 4:24; 5:12) and unanimously agreeing on a thing (Acts 15:25). Paul is in a sense asking these Roman believers to go back to the earlier period of unanimity in the church.

"With one voice" (literally "mouth") means that the inner disposition determines the outward discussion. The true purpose of both the inner and the outer aspects of church life is not to expose our differences but rather to "glorify the God and Father of our Lord Jesus Christ." The goal is not theological triumph but united witness. This is the heart of the entire book of Romans. The glory of God is the final goal of everything, and the Romans were endangering this as they turned theology into a wrestling match.

"The God and Father of our Lord Jesus Christ" is a liturgical title used often in the opening salutation of the New Testament Letters (2 Cor 1:3; Eph 1:3; Col 1:3; 1 Pet 1:3) but used elsewhere as well (2 Cor 11:31; Eph 1:17; Rom 15:6). The idea of the Father being "the God of Jesus" makes sense as a reference to Jesus' incarnate state of being and helps us understand the offices of the Father and Son within the Trinity. "The God of our Lord Jesus" (Eph 1:17) is the God Jesus worshipped and who raised him from the dead. Paul's calling Jesus "Lord" unites him with the God of the Old Testament.

By using the word "glorify" Paul may be alluding to 1:21, where he said that depraved humanity refused to glorify the Lord as God. In the conflict Paul is addressing here, both sides were acting like pagans. When we have the mindset of holding all things in common we place our differences and disagreements in perspective and discover respect and love for each other in the Spirit, whichever group we belong to. We find a larger unity behind our different theological persuasions since we worship the same Lord and focus on the same essential doctrines.

THE GOAL IS MUTUAL ACCEPTANCE (15:7-13)

This unit (14:1-15:13) began with Paul's command to "accept the one whose faith is weak." Now in the final paragraph (15:7-13) he takes up that command and universalizes it: "Accept one another."

Christians have a history of fighting over the most trivial of issues, and it has brought serious disrepute to the name of Christ. We have got to learn to separate major from minor issues. We must not divide the church over anything but the cardinal doctrines, and then because issues like the deity of Christ or salvation through Christ's sacrificial death on the cross are at the very heart of Christianity. On all other issues we must "accept one another" and join the united church in Christ.

This section both concludes the unit on the strong and the weak and draws the letter together as a whole, especially regarding Jew-Gentile relationships. Mutual acceptance is the thesis of this final paragraph, and it is the ultimate solution for the bickering of the weak and the strong.

COMMAND TO ACCEPT ONE ANOTHER (15:7A)

Now Paul draws his challenge to a close. The exhortation to "accept one another" frames the whole unit, beginning it (14:1) and now concluding it (15:7). In 14:3 the basis of this command is that "God has accepted them." There are two small differences from chapter 14: There Paul addressed only the strong, while here he includes both groups; and there it was God receiving them, while here it is Christ.

THE REASON FOR ACCEPTING ONE ANOTHER (15:7B)

In the second part of the verse, Paul's command moves from the horizontal dimension (the church on earth) to the vertical (the God-human relationship) and continues the theme that the internal harmony of the people of God is vital for their walk with God as a whole. It is at the heart of the New Testament doctrine of the fellowship of believers, as seen in Acts 2:44 ("All the believers were together and had everything in common") and 4:32 ("All the believers were one in heart and mind"). For this to happen, the saints have to disregard their petty differences and "accept one

another ... as Christ accepted you, in order to bring praise to God."
They are part of the family of God and members of the same body.
All this has been accomplished to the glory of God, and all this is
at stake in our harmony as a people of God. Without the oneness
of each faction as part of a whole family, the glory of God on earth
is threatened.

THE TWO GOALS OF MUTUAL ACCEPTANCE (15:8–9a)

There are two ways we can picture the organization of this passage. (1) It could contain two parallel ideas: that Christ has become
a servant of the Jews while the Gentiles are glorifying God; or (2) it
could present Christ as servant of the Jews for two purposes: to
confirm the covenant promises, and to enable the Gentiles to glorify God. In light of the context of 14:1–15:13, the latter option is
more likely.

This passage is connected to one of the primary truths of the
New Testament: Christ has introduced a new era of salvation history, in which he has become the means of salvation and of the
unity of the church. These verses unpack the meaning of his fulfilling the old covenant law with his coming. They also show how
this included the Gentiles in the church so as to fulfill the basic
covenant promises given to the patriarchs in the Abrahamic covenant (Gen 12:3). Thus the inclusion of Gentiles is a covenant reality and necessity.

The opening, "I tell you," introduces a critical doctrinal truth
supporting the new reality that Jew and Gentile are equal recipients of the work of Christ. This is supported by a basic statement
(v. 8), a twofold purpose (vv. 8b–9a), and four citations from the
Old Testament (vv. 9b–12). The first thing Paul states is that "Christ
has become a servant of the Jews on behalf of God's truth." This
stems from Jesus himself, who asserted he was "sent only to the
lost sheep of Israel" (Matt 15:24; see also Gal 4:4–5). In Matthew
this defined Jesus' early ministry in Galilee, and for Paul this is an

ongoing work but not the sole work of Jesus (he has come for the Gentiles as well, as in v. 9a). The point here is that Christ has not abandoned his Jewish heritage but came to be a "servant" (*diakonos*) to the Jews.

This reflects the "to the Jew first" priority of Romans 1:16 and means that Christ's work among his people is not finished (see 11:25–32). It is generally agreed that "God's truth" is a reference to his covenant faithfulness. God is true to his covenant promises and will not cast away his covenant people. The two purposes or goals elaborate this theme of God's faithfulness to the Jews.

The first purpose of God's plan is "so that the promises made to the patriarchs might be confirmed." This means more than proving their reliability or truthful character but contains also the idea of Christ fulfilling the promises in himself. Both the certainty of the promises and their fulfillment in Christ are intended. God's covenant faithfulness is proved by the reliability of his promises as finalized in Christ and was the primary issue in Romans 9–11 (see 9:6, 14; 11:1, 11). Paul's message is that these promises are still valid, and God has not forgotten his people.

At the same time the second purpose is also important: "that the Gentiles might glorify God for his mercy." This is the second part of 1:16, "first to the Jew, *then to the Gentile*." In 10:19–11:32 Paul revealed a complex plan of God—he has rejected the Jew and turned to the Gentile in part to make the Jews jealous and through it to bring them into the kingdom themselves. Those who had been "objects of his wrath" have now become "objects of his mercy" (9:22–23) and have been grafted into the olive tree (11:17) so that they might praise God for his mercy (here).

Both Jew and Gentile are included in God's plan of salvation and are recipients of Christ's redemptive work. The two are one in God and Christ and must become one in heart and mind in the church (15:6). It is in oneness that the church will grow and begin to reflect the unity of the Godhead. In fact, without oneness, the church will have failed in its true purpose. The church today must think about this the next time we fracture ourselves over an issue like how to interpret the days of creation.

OLD TESTAMENT CITATIONS ON WORSHIPPING GOD TOGETHER (15:9B-12)

Paul now quotes four Old Testament passages, all of which focus on the place of the Gentiles in God's plan and center on the unity of Jew and Gentile in the worship of God. Paul's goal is to help the Romans understand that the unity of the two groups was always essential to God's covenant purpose. The first three citations flow out of verse 9 in that they describe the Gentiles praising God and rejoicing. They are linked together by the repetition of "and again" before each citation, showing they are joined by the same theme of worship. They are well chosen, since they represent every part of the Old Testament—the Law (v. 10), the Writings (vv. 9b, 11), and the Prophets (v. 12)—thereby showing that the entire Old Testament supports what Paul is saying. Clearly God had always intended the Gentiles to join with the Jews, as the Abrahamic covenant had already shown (Gen 12:3; 18:18; 22:18; 26:4).

Praise God with the Gentiles (15:9b)

Paul's first citation is Psalm 18:49, which is also quoted in 2 Samuel 22:50 and celebrates David's defeat of his enemies by extolling God's mercy as "the God who avenges me … who saves me from my enemies" (Ps 18:47-48). David thanks God for the victory, promising, "Therefore I will praise you among the Gentiles; I will sing the praises of your name." Paul is saying that the Jewish Christians in Rome are to follow David's model and praise God along with the Gentiles. In the psalm it is the defeated nations that are called to join in the praise of the Divine Warrior, Yahweh, and here the converted Gentiles join the Jewish Christians in this worship.

Several scholars believe that Paul sees this as **typology**, in which the "I" is Christ who fulfills David's worship, conquering the nations (now redemptively) and bringing them together with his Jewish converts to worship God. However, this is difficult to prove, and more likely Paul intends simply to declare the inclusion of the Gentiles in God's plan from the beginning. The "I" is not Christ but David in the psalm, corporately identified with the nation and providing a pattern for Jewish Christian worship in the church at Rome. Just as the Jewish nation participated in David's victories, so the Jewish Christians now participate in worship with the Gentiles.

The Gentiles Join Israel's Praise (15:10)

Deuteronomy 32:43 is the final verse of the Song of Moses, a cry of victory that calls on the nations to rejoice with Israel that God has delivered his people. Paul sees this depiction of the nations rejoicing with the covenant people fulfilled in the New Testament reality of Jew and Gentile worshipping together in Christ. This is similar to the Psalm 18 citation above in centering on God's subduing the nations and defeating Israel's enemies, but it also moves the action forward. In the psalm citation God is praised "among the Gentiles," while here the Gentiles join together "with his people," the Jewish Christians, in worship.

Jews and Gentiles Worship Together (15:11)

Psalm 117 is a short psalm of praise celebrating God's love and faithfulness. Echoing the citation in verse 9 praising God for his mercy, this too thanks God for his steadfast faithfulness to his covenant people. The two lines contain synonymous parallelism: "Praise [*aineite*] the Lord, all you Gentiles, let all the people extol [*epainesatōsan*, "praise"][1] him." This also moves the action forward, as in the first two quotations the Gentiles participate in worship with the Jews, while here they worship God on their own. The emphasis is on "all" the peoples (in both lines), so this

---

1. The second verb contains *aineō* and so is a cognate of the first verb.

is universal worship with no one left out. This is similar to Revelation 7:9, where the "great multitude" before the throne are from "every nation, tribe, people and language." In Revelation and here this depicts an **eschatological** scene at the end of history, looking forward to the final victory of God and Christ over evil.

Christ's Rule Brings Hope to the Gentiles (15:12)

This is the only one of the quotations to include the author's name, probably because it contains a messianic prophecy. Isaiah 11 begins with the "Root of Jesse" and prophesies the coming of the Davidic Messiah. The Root of Jesse is itself a messianic title (Jer 23:5; 33:15; Sirach 47:22), depicting the One who will be filled with "the Spirit of Yahweh," giving him wisdom and understanding (11:2, quoted by Jesus in Luke 4:18–19). This messianic figure would deliver God's people (Isa 11:1–9), bringing about the return of the remnant from exile (Isa 11:11–16). This culminates the emphasis on God's plan of salvation in verses 9–12, showing it was prophetically predicted as a messianic act.

The Messiah, the Root of Jesse, would bring it to pass by "rising up" (NIV "spring up"), a possible allusion to Jesus' resurrection, though I find that doubtful in this context. This messianic figure is intended to "rule over the nations." Christ is "lord" of all (v. 6), and so now "in him the Gentiles," echoing the "hope" that is the focus of verse 4. It is this hope that will produce unity and peace between the warring factions in the Roman church, and this hope is the product of their worship and praise. Since they share the same hope, they can overcome their differences. The ability of the Gentiles to worship God in union with the Jewish believers is the direct result of the work of the Root of Jesse.

A Prayer for Abundant Hope through the Spirit (15:13)

Just as Paul concluded the first section with a prayer-wish (15:6), so he closes this section with one as well, beginning with "the God of hope." The Triune Godhead is the major force in all that we are and have, especially in the hope that binds everything together. The Root of Jesse gives the Gentiles hope (v. 12), the God of hope gives his people joy and peace (13a), and the power of the Holy Spirit enables the saints to overflow with hope. The "God of hope" does not so much mean "the God who *is* hope" as "the God who *gives* hope." As in verse 4, hope is the result of God's work in our midst.

Paul then defines God's work that will "fill you with all joy and peace as you trust [believe] in him." Each term draws together material from the rest of this chapter. Peace and joy refers to the internal harmony and joyous spirit that infuses every believer as a result of the infilling of the Spirit as in 8:14–17 and 14:17. This prayer-wish was already in process of coming to fruition due to God's work in the community, and now a so-called second work of grace was needed as the Spirit especially empowered them to bring peace and joy through solving the conflict caused by the two warring factions in the church.

This work of grace only comes "as you trust in him," meaning their total dependence on the power of God given through the Spirit. This alone makes it possible for them to overcome their failures. "Trust," or belief (the phrase in Greek is temporal, "when you believe"), stresses the ongoing faith of the community (3:21–4:25), the key aspect of the work of the Godhead in the life of the people of God. Their part is a total reliance on God in all they think and do.

"Faith" in 14:1, 2, 22–23, is that belief in God that enables us to understand his covenant promises and appropriate the lifestyle that reflects them. In this sense the weak and the strong had differing degrees of this faith, and Paul appeals to both groups to apply the larger fact of faith in Christ to bring peace and joy to the situation by molding the two groups into the one body of Christ, allowing them to rise above their differences and achieve harmony in Christ. The differences remain but are no longer divisive.

This is only possible when both sides live "by the power of the Holy Spirit" and tap his strength to forge a greater unity out of these very differences. In chapter 8 Paul identified the work of the Holy Spirit as the enabling presence in the church and the individual that allows the saints to defeat the flesh. Since it is the flesh that is behind the conflict between the weak and the strong, only the Spirit can give them the strength to overcome these fleshly tendencies.

Without the continuous presence of the Spirit and his power, peace and joy are beyond their reach. With the Spirit in their midst, they do not just have hope but "overflow with hope," meaning that their cup of hope is full and running over. In 5:15 the grace of God and the gift of salvation "overflow," and in Ephesians 3:20 God is "able to do immeasurably more than all we ask or imagine, according to his power that is at work within us." The result is that in our mutual salvation hope overflows to us all and gives us the spiritual strength to "accept one another" (15:7).

The specific details of this situation in Rome have limited relevance to us today, for the problem was not just a difference of theological opinion but the limited ability of the Jewish Christians to adjust to the reality of the new covenant. However, the first-century issues do apply more broadly to current issues on matters of adiaphora, that is, issues that are neutral, open biblically with scriptural support for both sides. These are issues on which we can agree to disagree.

There are two ways in which we may apply biblical material to our own context: at the specific level (the food laws, wine, and holy days of Rom 14:1–15:13) or at the general level, in which we apply the principles to issues that parallel the biblical situation.[2] As discussed in this chapter, there are two areas that fit the general situation—noncardinal doctrines (see on 14:3, 5, 9) and practical

2. See Grant R. Osborne, *The Hermeneutical Spiral: A Comprehensive Introduction to Biblical Interpretation*, 2nd ed. (Downers Grove, IL: InterVarsity Press, 2006), 321–22.

life situations (see on 14:13-14). In both these areas Christians must learn to accept each other and forge a larger unity that recognizes and allows such differences.

The impact of this passage on contemporary issues is startling and magnificent. The truth is that 14:1–15:13 solves a major problem in the church—the tendency of most of us to separate into theological enclaves, like Calvinists or charismatic Christians or dispensationalists or fundamentalists, and then to go to war with each other on issues God never meant for us to fight over.

Christ demands that we be a united church (John 17:21-23), and this passage tells us how to accomplish that seemingly impossible task. Like the strong addressed in 15:1-6, we must bear with the failings of the other side, come to empathize and understand why they hold the position they do, and respect them as they serve God from that perspective. Christ is our model, who came to serve and willingly bore the insults heaped upon him. Our goal is to become servants of those on the other side and to do what will build them up in Christ rather than tear them down on the basis of an overzealous desire on our part to show them the error of their ways. We must work for unity rather than division and try our best to harmonize with our opponents. As in the prayer of verses 5-6, we on both sides seek a harmonious Christian mindset that allows us to disagree on some nonessential doctrines so that we can hold "one mind" and "the same attitude" that Christ had and achieve unity.

When the church is truly praising and glorifying God, there is no place for disunity. I have close friends who strongly disagree with me on the issues of the security of the believer, the existence and nature of charismatic gifts, and the rapture of the church. We have never allowed disagreement to become dissension, and there is no reason to do so. I have read professional papers on these issues side by side with friends. I have taught for forty years in a seminary known for the breadth of its coverage (Trinity Evangelical Divinity School). We have faculty from Calvinist, Arminian, charismatic, dispensational, and several other divisions of the church. We are all good friends, and we respect each other's positions and work in harmony for the cause of Christ. One time Wayne Grudem and I deliberately wrote papers on using inclusive language in Bible translations for the same issue of *Christianity Today* so we could show that friends can disagree without becoming enemies.[3]

When we learn to emphasize unity and place our disagreements on the periphery where they belong, we can finally achieve mutual acceptance of one another (vv. 7–13). We must accept each other because God in Christ has accepted us both. This is stated clearly in verses 8–9, for Christ came to serve the Jews, but in doing so that mandated his bringing the Gentiles into the covenant people in order to make the Jews jealous and stimulate their coming back into the new Israel. There can be no new covenant without both Jew and Gentile accepting one another. This had always been God's intention, shown in the Abrahamic covenant (Gen 12:3) itself. This is as true today as it was in Paul's time. So long as the small factions in our churches are battling each other over these issues, the church can never achieve its God-intended purpose to represent Christ in this world.

This is especially demonstrated in the four Old Testament citations of verses 9–12, which show a growing intensity of worship, as the Gentiles are first included in worship with the Jews (Ps 18:49) then worship together with the Jews (Deut 32:43) and then worship God on their own (Ps 117:1). Finally, it is this united worship through which the messianic Root of Jesse brings hope to the Gentiles (Isa 11:10). We must learn to worship in harmony with believers of diverse backgrounds and opinions. Would that this were more widespread in the church!

---

3. Wayne Grudem and Grant Osborne, "Do Inclusive-Language Bibles Distort Scripture?," *Christianity Today*, October 27, 1997, 26–39.

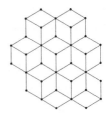

PAUL'S MINISTRY PLANS
(15:14-33)

Paul has finished his letter proper, presenting his gospel to the Roman church and addressing the problem areas that needed to be explored, including the meaning of salvation in the new covenant age and the place of the law in the Christian life. All that remains is to return to the material he first mentioned in the introductory section (1:1-17). Interestingly, he addresses them in reverse order, beginning with his travel plans (15:14-29 = 1:11-13), then requesting prayer (15:30-32 = 1:8-10), and finally including an extensive list of greetings (16:1-27 = 1:1-7). He adds a few items not found earlier but drawn from the body of the letter, like a prayer for peace (15:33 = 14;17; 15:13), along with new material such as the warning against false teachers (16:17-19).

This is the longest of Paul's letter closings, probably due to the circumstances.[1] His third missionary journey has just ended, and he is returning to Jerusalem with a significant collection for the poor (15:25-27). He is in the process of a major change of focus and a new arena for ministry. One could almost call this a midlife crisis, but one centering on kingdom values. He plans to visit Rome on his way to the next stage of his mission plan, the

---

1. See "Purpose" in the introduction.

evangelization of the western half of the Roman Empire. He hopes that the Roman church will sponsor this next missionary journey (15:24, 28), replacing Antioch in the east.

In this section he elaborates on 1:11–13 and presents his mission to the Gentiles, reflecting on his past ministry (17–21) and describing his future missionary journey from Jerusalem to Rome to Spain (22–30). It is interesting to compare his plans with what actually happened. In his farewell to the Ephesian elders in Acts 20:25 he told them "none of you ... will ever see me again." His goal was to deliver the gift collected from the Gentile churches in Asia Minor to the poverty-stricken saints in Jerusalem and then begin his fourth missionary journey through Rome to Spain. He prayed the gift from the Gentile Christians to the Jewish Christians in Palestine would forge a new unity between the two groups and initiate a new era of peace in the church.

From the remainder of Acts we know what actually transpired: riots and arrest in Jerusalem, followed by four years of imprisonment in Caesarea and Rome. He did get to Rome, but not the way he had hoped. Still, it is clear how God used those events in the long run. We will find out the why when we get to heaven, but one thing we know—God's will is superior, and he worked it out in line with Romans 8:28, "all things work together for the good" for the church and God's plan.

PAUL DESCRIBES HIS PAST MINISTRY TO THE GENTILES (15:14-21)

Paul is sending this letter and planning to visit a church that has never met him. He does not want to give them the impression that he is asserting his authority over them and ordering them to do his bidding. He plans a long relationship with them as his sponsor for years to come, so he wants to begin on the right foot and establish a good working relationship with them.

COMPLIMENTS THEM ON THEIR GOODNESS AND KNOWLEDGE (15:14)

He starts here by calling them "my brothers and sisters" and complimenting them for their spiritual wisdom and the depth of their walk with Christ. Some think this is insincere flattery, but that hardly fits the tone of this passage or of the letter as a whole. Paul instead is showing them the kind of courtesy and respect he exhorted the factions to show each other in the previous section of this letter (14:1–15:13). He is "convinced" of three things: (1) They are "full of goodness," a term (*agathōsynēs*) that stresses their kindness and generosity and perhaps also their honesty toward others. (2) They are "filled with knowledge," referring to a comprehensive knowledge of God and the gospel truths (including what is in this letter). (3) The result is that they are "competent to instruct one another," meaning their knowledge is deep enough to make them "teachers," a technical office in the early church. "Instruct" is not only general instruction in the gospel truths but also more specific admonition or exhortation in putting these truths to work in one's daily life.

They are the opposite of the group of Roman Christians in Hebrews 5:12 who have been believers so long that they "ought to be teachers" but in reality "need someone to teach you the elementary truths." The level of their knowledge and the depth of their maturity make them paradigms of the teachers of wisdom prized since the days of the prophets in Israel. Paul is stating his complete confidence in them, that they have not only accepted but also understood and acted upon all he has told them in the letter. In other words, he is certain he can trust them to be with him all the way.

THE BASIS OF HIS BOLD REMINDER (15:15–16)

The church at Rome may have been surprised that Paul had written so long and so striking a letter, so he wants to show his awareness of this. He admits, "Yet I have written you quite boldly on some points to remind you of them again." He realizes he may have offended some, but he wants them to know that he was led to do so by "the grace God gave me." His purpose was "to remind you of them again," that is, to make them aware anew of the truths of the gospel as they address the Roman situation.

It is human nature to have selective memories, and this was especially true in the conflict between the strong and the weak in 14:1–15:13. They both knew of the need for tolerance and unity in the church but forgot about them in the heat of the moment. So Paul had to "boldly" exhort them to remember these principles and follow them once more. We all need to be reminded of basic truths and their relevance in our lives on a regular basis, and in fact that is one of the purposes of the Sunday-morning sermon.

The reason Paul could have such boldness in challenging a church he had never met was "because of the grace God gave me to be a minister of Christ Jesus to the Gentiles" (vv. 15–16). In fact, this asserts the basis of the authority behind the letter as a whole. Paul was able to write authoritatively to a church he had never visited because God in his infinite grace had made Paul "apostle to the Gentiles" (Acts 22:21; 26:17-18; Rom 1:5; 1 Cor 3:10; Gal 2:9; Eph 3:2; Col 1:25).

But here it is interesting that Paul calls himself not an "apostle" but a "minister" to the Gentiles. He uses a term (*leitourgos*) that, though it can refer to a minister or servant, often connotes a priestly office (as in Isa 61:6; Neh 10:40; Sirach 7:30). Some interpreters see this in terms of Christ's high priestly office, with Paul serving as a Levite under Christ. However, this goes beyond what the context will allow. It is best to see Paul using priestly imagery for his apostolic ministry. This priestly aspect fits the context here quite well. In his priestly work Paul is "proclaiming the gospel of God" to the Gentiles and making them "an offering acceptable to God." This encapsulates the basic **soteriology** of Romans, as Paul brings them to salvation through the gospel (especially 3:21–26) and then presents them as an offering to God.

The Gentiles are now "acceptable" or "well-pleasing" to God, used also in 1 Peter 2:5 of the acceptability of "spiritual sacrifices" to God. God is pleased with the offering of the Gentiles, but it is essential that these offerings be "sanctified" or "set apart" for God. This can only be done by the Holy Spirit, who enters at conversion and makes the new convert a child and heir of God (8:14–17). In the words of 1 Peter 2:9, they become "a chosen people, a royal priesthood, a holy nation."

GLORIES IN HIS SERVICE (15:17)

Paul's bold posture in this letter is not due to his achievements or the fame he has gained but is entirely due to God's calling him to be a minister to the Gentiles, including the church at Rome. So Paul can "boast" (*kauchēsin*; NIV "glory") in Christ Jesus "in my service to God" (literally "the things concerning God"). While boasting in one's own success is wrong, boasting in Christ is not. Paul is thrilled and proud of all God has done "in Christ Jesus" in the Gentile mission. Paul's emphasis on God in Christ is reminiscent of 5:11, "in God through our Lord Jesus Christ."

Paul more than any other New Testament writer meditates on "boasting in Christ," with fifty-seven of the sixty-three New Testament references occurring in his writings, forty-eight of them in Romans and 1–2 Corinthians. He "boasts" over the Corinthian Christians (1 Cor 15:31), in the mutual relationship with the Corinthians (2 Cor 1:12–14; 7:4, 14; 8:24), in the Corinthians' willingness to give to the collection for the poor (2 Cor 9:2), in his own mission to the Corinthians (2 Cor 10:13–17; 11:10–21), and even in his own weaknesses (2 Cor 11:31). Paul is proud of all Christ has done for him and in him. The Roman letter stems from that pride in the work of Christ in him and in the Roman church.

THE EXTENT OF HIS MINISTRY (15:18-19)

Paul wants to make it clear that his pride and joy is only in Christ. He will speak of nothing except "what Christ has accomplished through me in leading the Gentiles to obey God." He begins, "I will not venture to speak"; "venture" is the cognate of "boldly" in verse 15, so it could be translated, "I will not be so bold as to speak." It would be presumptuous of him to boast of anything other than Christ regarding his successful ministry. Christ alone is the active agent in accomplishing the incredibly productive Gentile mission. Paul was the instrument but Christ the force that got the results.

These results are powerful, "leading the Gentiles to obey God by what I have said and done" (literally, "in word and deed"). The obedience of the Gentiles here refers not only to their conversion but also to a lifetime of following Christ, as in 1:5, the "obedience that comes from faith" that was the purpose of his Gentile ministry. Obedience is also stressed in 5:19; 6:16; 16:19, 26, as the proper response to Christ and the Spirit. The gospel includes not only evangelism but also discipleship as its goal. Paul seeks to ensure that the Gentiles surrender their lives to Christ in every way.

Still, Paul refuses to brag about all he has accomplished because he realizes there would be no results without the Lord's presence, intervention, and guidance. He did indeed speak and act, but behind every word and deed was the empowering presence of Christ and the Spirit. There is a trinitarian emphasis in verses 16-17 and again in verses 18-19, and all we say and do draws its eternal results from their work in the Christian worker.

Paul enumerates the deeds themselves in verse 19—"by the power of signs and wonders"—and the basis of those works is made clear—"through the power of the Spirit of God." "Signs and wonders" is a common phrase for miracles, taking place first at the exodus (Exod 7:3; 10:9-10; Deut 4:3-4, and others), then elsewhere in the Old Testament (Ps 78:43; Jer 32:20-21) as well as in the New

Testament (Acts 2:19; 4:30; 5:12; 6:8; 7:36; 2 Thess 2:9; Heb 2:4). It refers to Paul's miracles in Acts 14:3; 15:12.

"Signs" and "wonders" are fairly synonymous, though in a sense the "signs" are the Godward aspect pointing to the power behind them, and "wonder" is the human response to the power-ful, heaven-sent deed. The term "power" is found twice here, first in the powerful miracle itself and second in the basis of the mira-cle, the "power of the Spirit of God." The Spirit undergirds every-thing Paul accomplishes, including his miracles, and brings the Gentiles into the sanctifying presence of God.

The result of the Spirit's work (*hōste*, "so") is the extensive geographical area Paul has covered in his ministry of gospel proclamation, "from Jerusalem all the way around to Illyricum." Translated literally, the Greek says he "fulfilled the gospel of Christ," which could mean he had "fully proclaimed the gospel" (as in the NIV) in these areas but more likely means he had "com-pleted his gospel ministry." This does not mean he had reached every town and village, but he had finished his pioneer mission work of bringing the gospel to every region of the eastern half of the Roman Empire. His strategy was to plant churches in cen-tral cities and use them as hubs to reach the rest of the area. He had completed that task.

The geographical boundary markers of Jerusalem and Illyri-cum are somewhat puzzling. Neither was a part of his missionary journeys as recorded in Acts. They could have designated the geo-graphical extent of his mission, with Jerusalem the southernmost point and Illyricum the northernmost, as it was north and west of Macedonia (modern Yugoslavia and Albania). While no journey to Illyricum is mentioned in the New Testament, Paul perhaps went there during his trip through Macedonia to Greece in Acts 20:1-3 (that would be just before he wrote this letter). The Roman road from Ephesus to Corinth went through part of Illyricum, so he could have been briefly in that province at that time.

Although he is never said to have made Jerusalem a mission-ary focus, especially as part of his Gentile mission (the central point here), we know he ministered there in Acts 9:28 ("speaking boldly in the name of the Lord") and visited there also in Acts 11:30; 15:1–21; and 18:22. So the phrase "from Jerusalem ... to Illyricum" most likely indicates the extent of his missionary work: from the borders of Jerusalem to the borders of Illyricum.

Another issue should be discussed, the meaning of "all the way around to Illyricum." Some see this as describing the Pau-line mission as a circle from Jerusalem building on the table of the nations in Genesis 10 and fanning out from Jerusalem to the nations; others picture it as an arc as the gospel moved through-out the Gentile world. However, these read too much into a single word ("around"). This simply describes Paul moving "around" the nations bringing the gospel to the Gentiles. We scholars are often guilty of reading too much theology into individual words in our zeal for depth of interpretation.

Paul is making two statements: first, all of this incredible min-istry was only possible because of the power of the Spirit; the title of Acts should actually be "the Acts of the Holy Spirit through the Apostles." Second, he had finished his mission in the eastern half of the Roman Empire, and it was time to turn his evangelistic focus to the west. This is the purpose in 15:14–33, to enlist the church at Rome in the next phase of the Gentile mission.

MINISTRY GOAL: PIONEER MISSION WORK (15:20–21)

Here Paul explains further what he means by saying he had "com-pleted" his mission. He doesn't want anyone thinking there was nothing else to do: "It has always been my ambition to preach the gospel where Christ was not known." The translation "been my ambition" is a little strong. The term (*philotimeomai*) means to "strive after, be zealous." His primary desire was to be the first to reach the lost in a region and to form the strategy for planting Christ anew everywhere he could. He expected others (like Apollos at Corinth) to pastor the new churches, and he would then go on to another new region. As he said in 1 Corinthians 3:6, "I planted the seed, Apollos watered it."

"Where Christ was not known" doesn't mean not knowing he ever existed or even not knowing there was a religious movement called Christianity. "Knowing" Christ means worshipping or confessing his name, to be part of the Christian movement. It connotes an area that has not been evangelized. Paul wanted to go where no church had been planted because he did not want to build "on someone else's foundation." This is the same metaphor he uses in 1 Corinthians 3:10, "I laid a foundation as a wise builder, and someone else is building on it." When you begin a ministry at an established church, you have to accept the kind of church it is. Some aspects you have to tactfully change. Paul wanted the freedom to act on his strategy in his way.

In verse 21 Paul anchors his church-planting philosophy in a citation from Isaiah 52:15, part of the best-known of the Servant Songs (Isa 52:13–53:12), regarding the Suffering Servant who is disfigured (v. 14). This servant will "sprinkle many nations" (v. 15), and as a result, "Those who were not told about him will see, and those who have not heard will understand."

In Paul's situation, the nations "who have not heard" are the Gentiles, and the servant of Yahweh is the Messiah. In this same vein Isaiah 49:6 tells Israel, "I will also make you a light for the Gentiles, that my salvation may reach to the ends of the earth." Paul wants his Roman readers to see that he is fulfilling this aspect of the Servant Songs in the Gentile mission. The Gentiles who "were not told about him" and "who have not heard" will finally "see" and "understand" through Paul's pioneer mission to them. He has laid the groundwork in the eastern half of the Roman Empire, so he is turning to the western half while the Gentile mission in the east is taken to the next stage as local pastors come and water what he has planted there (1 Cor 3:6).

PAUL DESCRIBES HIS FUTURE PLANS:
JERUSALEM, ROME, SPAIN (15:22-29)

Since Paul has completed his ministry in the east, his vision has turned west, to the lands that have still "not heard." His discussion of that vision is framed with his desire to visit the Roman church (vv. 22-24, 28-29), but his actual hope is that Rome will become the sponsor of a mission to Spain (vv. 24, 28). In the meantime, he has to deliver the collection for the poor to the hurting saints in Jerusalem (vv. 24-28).

Hindered from Coming (15:22)

He first tells his readers why he has gone so long without visiting Rome—he has been "hindered from coming" (see also 1:10, 13). It is likely that the mission in the east has forestalled a visit. Perhaps "was hindered" is a divine passive meaning that it was not God's will for Paul to go earlier. His work in the east was not yet finished, and he could not leave until it was.

Romans was written at the close of Paul's third missionary journey, after his two-plus-year ministry in Ephesus. If we peruse Acts 13-19, which covers his three journeys, it is difficult to find a time when he could have pulled up stakes and sailed to Rome. He, like most people, divided the Roman Empire into east and west, with Rome the gateway to the west. Reaching Rome involved a lengthy sea voyage, and he likely felt that God would not have him interrupt the needs of his ministry in the east to do so.

His Work in the East Finished (15:23)

While his ministry in the east would not allow Paul to go, he had "for many years" now been "longing" to do so. This desired trip to see the Roman Christians has now been made possible by the fact that "there is no more place for me to work in these regions." He had planted churches in all the strategic towns in the east. Moreover, as the list of friends in 16:1-16 shows, he knew an amazing number of people who were now residing in Rome. Since Rome was the capital of the empire and the center of everything for the Roman world, the churches in the east were regularly kept abreast of events there. Paul would have been acquainted (second-hand) with the Roman church.

"No more place for me to work" hardly means he had been forced to leave or had worked himself out of a job. He had finished his pioneer mission task and was ready to move on to new territory. The absence of a place to work is due to his own mission strategy. Everything is ready for the next stage—church growth—in the east. The place for establishing churches is now in the west, and that is where he is headed.

PLAN TO VISIT ON THE WAY TO SPAIN (15:24)

We don't know why Paul wanted to go to Spain; it is only mentioned in verses 24 and 28 in all of Scripture. He may have viewed his actions as a fulfillment of Isaiah 66:19, "I will send some of those who survive to the nations—to Tarshish." Tarshish was a major ancient center of trade associated with Spain. Yet it is unclear why Paul would choose that location over the others listed in that verse: "the Lybians and Lydians ... Tubal and Greece ... distant islands that have not heard of my fame." Probably since it was the most westward part of the Roman Empire, it became a symbol of God's plan to take the gospel to the world. Expanding his mission to Spain was in keeping with Paul's calling to plant the gospel in new territories.

While it is not recorded in the New Testament, there is a possibility that Paul actually managed a visit there, as suggested in a letter written to the church in Corinth in AD 96. The letter says that Paul, "reaching the limits of the west he bore witness before rulers" (1 Clement 5:7). However, it is difficult to know when he could have gone to Spain since he returned to the churches of Macedonia and Asia Minor after his imprisonment (see Phil 2:24 as well as 1–2 Timothy and Titus). A couple years later he was arrested in the province of Asia (2 Tim 1:15), where he went after the Roman imprisonment. A short time later, according to tradition, he was executed by the Romans during the persecution under the emperor Nero. The only way there would have been time for a trip to Spain is if Paul's arrest and execution took place after Nero's reign. In short, it is an interesting possibility but cannot be proved.

When Paul comes to Rome, he only plans on "passing through" on his way to Spain. This seems different than his purpose in 1:11, where he wants to "impart to you some spiritual gift," and in 1:15, where he is "eager to preach the gospel also to you who are in Rome." Still, they do not have to be at odds, for there is room in "passing through" for a short stay there. We must remember that in both chapter 1 and this section, Paul is simply telling his intentions. They are not yet a hard and fast itinerary, so he could have gone back and forth on how long a stay in Rome he would have.

Paul's goal is to enjoy "your company," that is, have a time of fellowship with them; and to "have you assist me on my journey there." New Testament writers often used "assist" for missionary support (Acts 15:3; 20:38; 21:5; 1 Cor 6:6; 2 Cor 1:16), and so he is asking not only for prayer support and a commissioning for the upcoming mission but also for financial support. He may even be asking for assistants who would know the areas and be able to guide him on the journey. In other words, Paul wants to develop a mission team like the ones that went out from Antioch on his first two missionary journeys.

IMMEDIATE PLANS: TAKE THE COLLECTION FOR THE POOR
TO JERUSALEM (15:25-29)

Purpose: to serve the saints (15:25)

One very important duty remains before Paul can come to Rome—delivering the collection for the poor he had been gathering from the Gentile churches for months. "In the service of the saints" (NIV "the Lord's people") probably states the purpose of the trip. He wants to serve the saints with the offering. This was the second such collection. Paul and Barnabas delivered the first in AD 48 after Agabus's prophecy of an empire-wide famine (Acts 11:27-30 = Gal 2:1-10). This was Paul's second trip to Jerusalem. At that time the "pillars of the church"—James the Lord's brother, Peter, and John—affirmed Paul as apostle to the Gentiles and asked only that he "remember the poor" (Gal 2:10). This must have had quite an effect on him, and he spent a great deal of time collecting another gift from the Gentile churches for the poor in Jerusalem.

The contribution for the poor (15:26)

Poverty was an ongoing problem for Palestinian Christians. There were several factors like famines (it is estimated that there were ten famines from 100 BC to AD 100), the general poverty of Judea, and the persecution of Christians (Acts 8:1-3; Jas 2:5-8). Paul's depth of concern for the poor led him to concentrate on the collection during his third missionary journey, so that it was a major focus during his two-plus-year time in Ephesus.

He wrote 1 Corinthians toward the end of that stay (AD 56) and just before the penning of Romans. He had already told the Corinthians about the collection (perhaps in an earlier letter), and in 16:1-4 he encouraged them to take weekly offerings and set the money aside for the gift to the Jerusalem poor. In 2 Corinthians 8-9, written several months later, they still had not done so, and Paul reminded them of the sacrificial giving of the much more poverty-stricken Macedonian churches (2 Cor 8:1-5). They must have responded after that letter, for Paul says here that "Macedonia and Achaia" (the province that Corinth is part of) "were pleased to make a contribution for the poor" in Palestine.

A little while after writing 2 Corinthians he visited Corinth (2 Cor 2:3; 9:5; 12:20-13:1), where he wrote his letter to the Romans.[2] The collection had to have been going on for some time, for Acts 20:4 mentions delegates from Galatia and Asia, and they accompanied Paul with the funds (collected mostly while Paul

---

2. See "Author and Date" in the introduction.

was in Ephesus). This collection involved most of the Gentile churches from his missionary journeys; those delegates from Galatia represented the first missionary journey. He does not ask for the Roman church to participate, likely because there is insufficient time before he heads to Jerusalem and they are too far out of the way.

Why does Paul take so much time talking about a collection to which the Roman church will not be contributing? He clearly wants the Roman church to be involved, probably in praying for the collection. He believes this will become a major paradigm for unity between Jews and Gentiles as it symbolizes the coming together of the two groups. This example of unity provides an important model for the Roman Christians who had experienced Jew-Gentile tensions (see 14:1–15:13).

The obligation of the Gentiles to contribute (15:27)

Paul and the church had five goals for the collection:

First, in verse 26 he calls the "contribution" a "fellowship" (*koinōnia* has a double meaning here), which indicates a unity or oneness as a result of sharing in the gift of the Gentiles to the Jews. Paul hoped it would bind the groups together and show the love the Gentiles had for their Jewish siblings in the church. Fellowship is more than social and spiritual togetherness. It means sharing in every area of life, including finances and quality of life.

Second, the need to show their unity of sharing with the Jews produced an obligation ("they owe it to them," v. 27) on the part of the Gentiles to contribute to this financial need. The necessity of establishing a new sense of unity and family gave this task a real priority and dominated Paul for the extended time he spent putting the collection together.

Third, in verse 27 he develops a philosophy of sharing: "if the Gentiles have shared in the Jews' spiritual blessings, they owe it to the Jews to share with them their material blessings." This is stated well in 2 Corinthians 8:14, "At the present time your [material] plenty will supply what they need, so that in turn their [spiritual] plenty will supply what you need. The goal is equality." The Jews have provided the blessings of the new age in Christ and the gospel, and now the Gentiles can share with them their earthly material blessings. Such mutual sharing would go a long way in solving the tensions between the two groups. This provides a model for the church today, as each person shares areas of strength with others in the church.

Fourth, this may well have been meant as a further provocation of Israel to "envy" or jealousy (Rom 10:19; 11:11, 14) as a step to the conversion of Jews. The gift for the poor would be seen as fulfilling the prophecy that has the Gentiles bringing gifts to Zion (Isa 2:2–4; 60:6–7, 11; Mic 4:13). We cannot know whether this was in Paul's mind, but it would fit the larger context well.

Finally, this was also an act of joy, with Paul asserting that the Macedonians and Achaians, indeed everyone privileged to participate, were "pleased to do it." In a beautiful statement in 2 Corinthians 8:2, he said of the poor Macedonian churches, "In the midst of a very severe trial, their overflowing joy and their extreme poverty welled up in rich generosity." It simply cannot be stated better than this.

This has implications for us. Every church should have a care ministry, and church leadership must communicate how important it is for the church as the body of Christ to care for its hurting members. There is so much more lasting joy in helping others than there is in buying new baubles for ourselves. Today's new toy will be tossed onto tomorrow's trash heap, while the joy of knowing we have enriched a life never departs from us.

The Plan to Come to Rome (15:28)

Now Paul returns to the main point of the section—his impending visit to Rome on the way to Spain. Here again he plans a short stay in Rome, to "visit you on the way." His true objective is a fourth missionary journey to the west, ending with Spain. Before that can happen, he states a final time, he must have "completed this task and have made sure that they have received this contribution."

Paul stresses three things in this verse: (1) He has to complete "this task," which could mean he considers it a religious obligation (v. 27). More likely, though, he simply means he must finish this aspect of his ministry before he can come to Rome. The second and third are lost in the NIV translation. The Greek has "put a seal on this fruit for them," while the NIV unpacks the metaphors and translates, "made sure that they have received this contribution." I believe too much is lost in this and prefer to keep the metaphors. (2) He plans to "seal" the collection (*sphragizō*; NIV "made sure"), a term Paul uses elsewhere for the seal of the Holy Spirit (2 Cor 1:22; Eph 1:13), to authenticate or provide a mark of ownership. Here it probably means he plans to accompany the gift and personally authenticate it to the Jerusalem saints. (3) The offering is a "fruit" (*karpos*; NIV "contribution"), likely meaning it is the "harvest" from the spiritual legacy the Jewish people have given the Gentiles, perhaps also the visible demonstration of the "fruit" of Paul's mission to the Gentiles. The successful harvest of the Gentiles has now produced fruit for the Jews, as they share their material wealth in exchange for the Jewish spiritual wealth given to them.

Certainty: the full measure of Christ's blessing (15:29)

You can almost hear Paul's relief as he verbalizes his certainty that God will indeed work everything out and get him to Rome shortly. This peaceful security in God's upholding strength would have helped him on that tumultuous trip to Jerusalem when his associates told him that the Spirit had told them (!) that he should not go to Jerusalem because of the Jewish threats to kill him there (Acts 20:3, 23; 21:4), especially after Agabus gave his famous prophecy that Paul would go to Rome in chains (Acts 21:10–12). There were two interpretations of his prophecy, one by his associates that the Spirit was warning Paul not to go (the wrong understanding), the other by Paul himself, "Why are you weeping and breaking my heart? I am ready not only to be bound, but also to die in Jerusalem for the name of the Lord Jesus" (Acts 21:13)—the correct understanding.

The same assurance reflected here in Romans led him to rightly interpret the Spirit behind Agabus' prophecy. He provided the basis earlier in Acts 20:23, "I only know that in every city the Holy Spirit warns me that prison and hardships are facing me." The Spirit was not telling Paul not to go but telling him what awaited when he did go. This provides an important model when we are in similar situations. Not only do we have to listen to the Spirit; but we also have to pray that we will rightly understand the Spirit.

The one thing Paul knows is that he will arrive in Rome "in the full measure of the blessing of Christ." He does not know how he will get there, only that God will go before him and watch over him. "Full measure" refers to the overwhelming fullness of the divine blessing he was certain would accompany his coming. In fact, it is a double blessing, for the Romans would be blessed through him, and he would be blessed by them.

PAUL REQUESTS PRAYER (15:30-33)

Paul regularly in his letters requests prayer, but often it is a general list of items. Here he is quite specific, with these requests linked to the collection for the poor. Here we see how important the delivery of the collection was to Paul. The future unity of Jew and Gentile in the messianic community was linked to it, and he felt he could not turn to the next phase of his apostolic ministry until it was successfully completed.

PLEA: JOIN IN MY STRUGGLE FOR PRAYER (15:30)

Paul asks for two things—protection from his Jewish enemies and a favorable reception of the offering by the Jerusalem saints. He doesn't ask but "urges" or appeals to them for prayer. His request comes on the basis of two things: "our Lord Jesus Christ," namely, the authority of Christ and his lordship over the church; and "the love of the Spirit," which could be the Spirit's love for us but more likely means the love the church experiences as made possible by the Spirit (= "love from the Spirit").

Since the Roman believers are one in Christ, and since they have inherited that sense of brotherly love made possible by the Spirit, they should pray for Paul and his mission. When they pour out their prayers to God for him, they will "join … in [his] struggle" (literally "agonize with me"), a wrestling metaphor picturing intense effort in prayer (see Col 4:12). Prayer becomes a partnership as intercessors participate in needs by bringing them before the Lord.

The Twofold Request (15:31)

His first request is for his personal safety. There had been numerous plots against him by his Jewish enemies (Acts 9:29; 13:45; 14:2–5, 19; 17:5–9, 13; 18:12–17; 19:9), and so he asks intercession that he "be kept safe from the unbelievers in Judea." He knew his Jewish enemies were lying in wait for him. A short time later he learned of a plot against him as he was about to board a ship for Syria (Acts 20:3), so he was aware of potential problems. We know from the rest of Acts how well-founded Paul's concern was, as we read of the riot in Jerusalem and demand for his death shortly after he arrived there (Acts 21:27–36).

In fact, the prayers were efficacious. His arrest by the Romans saved him from the mob. When the next plot took place (Acts 23:12–15), Paul's nephew learned of it (miraculously, it seems), and Paul was taken to Caesarea (Acts 23:16–24). The prayer was answered, though in a way that was hardly expected.

The second request is for the Jewish believers to accept the "contribution I take to Jerusalem" from the Gentile churches. The term behind the NIV's "contribution" here is *diakonia*, "service" or "ministry." It could be meant generally for all that Paul accomplished in Jerusalem, including the sacrifices in the temple. However, it more likely refers specifically to the offering itself. This too was a valid concern, for he had been opposed by many Jewish Christians, especially the Judaizers in Galatians and Philippians 3. They would have rejected a gift from Gentile churches.

This prayer was granted as well, for in Acts 21:17, 20, Luke tells us that Paul and his team were "received ... warmly," and the Jerusalem elders "praised God" at the report of the Gentile mission. Neither does Luke mention the collection, but since everything is positive at this point, it is likely that the Jerusalem elders received the offering favorably as well.

PURPOSE: COME TO ROME WITH JOY (15:32)

Since this begins with the same *hina* ("that/so that") as verse 31, this could be a third prayer request, but in the context it is better to think of it as the purpose of all Paul is doing at present, namely, to enable him and his team to "come to you with joy, by God's will, and in your company be refreshed." The deliverance from his enemies and the reception of the gift from the Gentile churches, in Paul's mind, would fill him with joy as he finally arrived in Rome.

It is ironic that, as with his deliverance from his enemies, this did take place—but not the way Paul envisaged. All the tumult in Jerusalem, the two years of imprisonment in Caesarea, and the unbelievable ship journey to Rome (Acts 22–27) must have made him wonder many times whether God had rejected this request. Yet the key phrase is "by God's will," and that was clearly evident at every stage of this rocky road to Rome.

There is little doubt that Paul arrived "with joy." Acts 28:15 relates how a group of Christians came down to meet Paul on his way, and "at the sight of these people Paul thanked God and was encouraged." Even though he was a prisoner about to stand a capital trial before Nero as an enemy to Rome, Paul had *joy* because God was in charge. After all that had happened he knew beyond a shadow of a doubt that everything was going to take place as God wanted it. In fact, the walk from the shipping port of Puteoli up to Rome was almost another "triumphal entry," as Paul was in an earthly sense a human prisoner with few rights but in the real sense was a conquering soldier of God's army come to claim Rome for Christ.

It was in nearly every way a triumphant two years in Rome. Paul summed it up in Philippians 1:12-14 when it was all over that through his imprisonment he had evangelized the entire Praetorian guard (the elite soldiers of Rome) and Christians everywhere had become more bold in sharing their faith. They undoubtedly reasoned that if God could do all he did through one man chained to Roman guards for two years, what couldn't he do through them?

Paul also hopes here that he might be "in your company be refreshed" during his time in Rome. He desires a great time of fellowship with the Roman Christians, as he said in 1:12, "that you and I may be mutually encouraged by each other's faith." There is no direct evidence that this took place, but the pictures of Paul in Rome in Acts 28 and in 1 and 2 Timothy show a person who most probably is indeed spiritually refreshed. He certainly had many times of fellowship with Roman believers. Just the list of friends in Romans 16, as we will see, makes a very rich and fruitful time there a certainty.

CLOSING PRAYER (15:33)

Paul concludes his discussion of his future plans (15:14-33) with another prayer-wish. Here he addresses God as "the God of peace," that is, the God who gives peace to his people. The term for "peace" (*eirēnē*) is very rich and in Romans connotes both the vertical (that harmonious relationship with God that salvation produces) and the vertical (corporate togetherness in the church and a tranquility of soul) dimensions. Both are part of the meaning here. The God of peace is a major theme in the Old Testament (Lev 26:6; Judg 6:24; Ps 29:11; Isa 26:12) and in Paul (2 Cor 13:11; Phil 4:7, 9; 1 Thess 5:23). The idea is closely linked with Paul's plea for peace in the Roman church in 14:17, 19. Paul's prayer is that God with his peace might make residence "with you" in his worshipping community.

Often when we get to material like this, we think it less important than the spiritual exhortation passages earlier, but it is very
important for an understanding of the historical situation behind
the letter. Here we see how the mind of Paul operated in the pressure cooker of the critical events that took place in AD 57–58 at the
end of the third missionary journey. As we read what Paul had
hoped would take place and put it alongside what actually did
occur, we are given an incredible glimpse into the mind of one of
the greatest saints who ever lived. As you conclude this chapter,
ask yourself, "How would I react if everything went wrong in my
life like it did for Paul?" We have here one of the truly great models
for reacting to trying times!

———

Paul is hoping to enlist the Roman church as partners in his future
ministry. He wants them to be aware of his bold ministry to the
Gentiles and of his deep pride in the ministry Christ has given
him (vv. 15–19). He is still filled with wonder at the power of Christ
and the presence of the Spirit behind everything he has said and
done, including the unbelievable "signs and wonders" the Spirit
performed through him (v. 19a). He wants to stress the Holy Spirit
as the true, active agent in all this successful ministry, and to tell
the Romans that he is switching to the western half of the empire
because his ministry in the eastern half is complete.

He emphasizes the plan of God behind the timing of his coming
to Rome. God had not allowed him to come but had "hindered" his
visit (v. 22) so he could finish his work in the east. He wanted to
have a brief ministry in Rome and a time of fellowship in which
Rome would join his team and sponsor the missionary journey
establishing churches all the way to Spain (vv. 23–24). This never
transpired because of the events of Acts 22–23.

The collection for the poor is important enough to warrant several verses (vv. 25–28a), because it fits the emphasis in this letter
on the oneness of Jew and Gentile in the body of Christ. It also

fits a primary goal of the church as a whole, namely, giving sacrificially in order to care for needy members among God's people. Paul emphasizes the joy of giving.

It is interesting to have a concrete example in verses 30-33 of how God reacts to prayer and what forms his answers to prayer can take. Paul has two requests for prayer, and God grants both. Only the second, that the collection be favorably received by the Jerusalem saints, is granted directly. The first, that he be kept safe from his Jewish enemies, certainly appeared to be met with a resounding no by God. In actuality, he was kept safe. No harm came to him, and in fact, his imprisonments were a resounding success, as Rome was evangelized and Christian witness strengthened greatly by Paul's chains (Phil 1:12-14).

This has an important message for us. God hears our prayers and always responds, but his response may not be what we want or expect. We must have the faith of Paul, as we too realize he always responds in the way that is best for us. Every step of Paul's most difficult journey from Jerusalem to Rome was orchestrated by God and turned to victory by the Holy Spirit. Not many of us could handle such a series of seeming disasters, but in reality it was a triumph for the cause of Christ. What an example for us as we pray and look for how God responds!

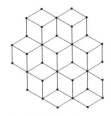

CONCLUDING GREETINGS

(16:1–27)

I t is common for Paul to close his letters with a series of greetings both to his acquaintances in the church and from members of his team to the church. However, nowhere is there a list so extensive as here, and as a result many think Paul did not write it. I argued in the introduction that this is indeed the authentic ending of this letter, and accept that conclusion here.[1] Paul has never visited the church at Rome, and he wants to establish a personal relationship with them by showing all his contacts in the church. These are all people he knows in ministry, and the list shows he is indeed quite involved with the Roman church.

He commends Phoebe (vv. 1–2), greets coworkers (vv. 3–16), then digresses into a warning against false prophets (vv. 17–19) and an **eschatological** promise (v. 20a). This is followed by a benediction (v. 20b) and a list of greetings from many leaders (vv. 21–23). Concluding it all is one of the more beautiful benedictions in the New Testament (vv. 25–27).

---

1. See "Unity and Integrity" in the introduction.

PAUL GREETS THE LEADERS AND COWORKERS IN ROME (16:1–16)

COMMENDATION OF PHOEBE (16:1–2)

This is the only place in the New Testament where Phoebe (a Gentile name) is mentioned. She was a leader in Cenchreae (the port city of Corinth, Acts 18:18) and probably the one who carried this letter to Rome. Paul had spent eighteen months in Corinth during his second missionary journey and wrote Romans from there. These two verses are similar to Philippians 2:19–30, in which he commends Timothy and Epaphroditus as bearers of that letter. Such letters or sections in a letter were often used to introduce an unknown member of the team. When Paul led the persecution of Christians outside Judea, he went with similar letters showing he came with official authority to conduct the anti-Christian campaign (Acts 9:2).

Phoebe is called his "sister," indicating she is a dedicated believer, but she is more than another church member. She is also a *diakonos*, a term that denotes a "servant" or "minister" of the church. Women did hold that office (1 Tim 3:11) at times, and Phoebe was clearly an outstanding example. While the term could have a general thrust describing her as a believer who serves God and the church, it is more likely that it describes an officer of the church, a "deacon" or "minister" as described in 1 Timothy 3:8–12. We don't know their duties, but there it is said they must (1) not be "pursuing dishonest gain" (3:8), perhaps indicating financial responsibilities; (2) "keep hold of the deep truths of the faith" (3:9), indicating they are teachers/preachers, and (3) "must manage ... his household well" (3:12), possibly indicating administrative duties in the church. Some think it indicates she was the pastor of a congregation, but there is too little evidence the word *diakonos* was used of the pastoral office. It probably indicates a ministry dealing with the practical needs of the church.

Paul asks the Romans for two things regarding Phoebe: first, they should "receive her in the Lord in a way worthy of the saints" (NIV "his people"). He wants them to show her Christian hospitality, to welcome her and give her adequate lodging. "Worthy of the saints" adds a spiritual dimension, to show her fellowship and welcome her into the life of the church. She is to be given the respect she deserves as an officer of the church and should be allowed to minister in their midst.

Second, they should "give her any help she may need from you." This could be specific, and several interpreters think it refers to assistance in a legal case in which she is involved. The term for "help" is *pragma*, which can mean "matter" or "deed," and in 1 Corinthians 6:1 it is used of a lawsuit. If that is the case, she would be coming to Rome as a litigant in a case. However, that does not really fit this context, and most agree it is intended generally here. Paul is simply asking that they help her in any need she might have.

He bases this on a further commendation, saying, "she has been the benefactor of many people, including me." The term behind "benefactor" is *prostatis*, and while it could generally refer to a person who "helps" or "gives aid to" others, it also has a semitechnical use for a wealthy patron who gives assistance to people. The term can also mean to "direct" or "lead" a group, and some translate this "leader" in a manner similar to Lydia at Philippi, the patron of the church there. Still, it is difficult to think of Phoebe as the leader of Paul, and better to recognize her as the benefactor or patron who helped many in Cenchreae in the areas of housing, finances, and general aid.

Cenchreae was a busy seaport, which would make it critical that someone in the church there be engaged in so practical a ministry, much like the women in Luke 8:1–3 who were "helping to support" the apostolic band. The needs would be immense. Visitors as well as residents would desperately need a wealthy woman of social status in just such a position. This would mean she was a leader in the church (again, like Lydia) and worthy of all the assistance the church at Rome could render her.

GREETINGS TO THE LEADERS OF THE CHURCH AT ROME (16:3–16)

Paul occasionally passes on his greetings to individuals (Col 4:15; 2 Tim 4:19), but nowhere else does he greet the number of people he does in chapter 16—twenty-six individuals, two families, and three house churches. Nine of these are women, and two hold offices: Phoebe is likely a deacon (see on v. 1), and Junia is "outstanding among the apostles" (in v. 7). The implications of Junia and Phoebe for women holding office today are definitely present but also highly debated. While settling this debate falls outside the scope of this commentary, it is certain that Jesus and Paul gave women a much higher place in the church than first-century society did generally.

Paul wants the people in Rome to know that while he has never been there, he has close contacts within the church and has remained involved in the life of their church through these friends. These people can vouch for him, so when they consider whether to become the sponsor of his mission to the west, they already know he is a friend of their church.

The names themselves are fascinating. Not only did names in the ancient world reveal ethnic origin; but they showed social status as well. Certain names were reserved for the wealthy and powerful, and others were used for slaves or freedmen (those who had formerly been slaves). Only two in this list are Jewish (Mary and Herodion). The rest are Gentiles, which says a lot about the leadership of the Roman church. Also, most of the names belong to slaves and freedmen, revealing that while all socioeconomic groups were represented in the church, most came from the lower classes. Finally, it is clear that Paul was not writing to churches as we know them but house churches. The use of homes for churches was universal until Constantine legalized Christianity in the fourth century. The church of Rome was composed of numerous gatherings of about fifty to eighty people (the maximum a home could contain), and many were quite a bit smaller depending on the size of the house.

Those identified with Paul's mission (16:3–7)

The first six names and one of the house churches are connected with Paul's mission teams. Most were probably forced to leave Rome when Claudius expelled many Jews and Christians over riots in AD 49. They returned after AD 54, when Claudius died and his edicts were no longer in force.[2] They especially were in a place to support Paul's request, as they had been a part of his ministry for a long time and could explain him to the others in Rome.

(1) *Priscilla* (Greek: *Prisca*) *and Aquila* (vv. 3–5a). Paul calls this husband-and-wife team "my co-workers in Christ Jesus," a semiofficial title for a leader who worked with Paul in ministry and who deserved pay (1 Cor 9:14) as well as respect and obedience (1 Cor 16:16, 18). They were especially close to Paul and were major figures on his teams. The fact that they are named first shows their status in Rome and the Pauline teams. Also, that Priscilla is first in four of the six times the couple is named together may indicate she either had the higher social status or perhaps the more significant ministry of the two. The order of names was significant in the ancient world.

Paul met them in Corinth on his second missionary journey, after their expulsion from Rome by Claudius (Acts 18:2). They were fellow Jews and wealthy[3] tentmakers with a business that Paul joined while there. They both worked and ministered together throughout his eighteen months there (Acts 18:3), using their home for a house church (1 Cor 16:19). When he went to Ephesus on his

---

2. See "Recipients" in the introduction.

3. In every town they had purchased a large home, which Paul was able to use as a house church.

third journey, they went with him, and they continued to minister together. There too they had a significant ministry and on one occasion took Apollos aside, correcting his mistaken views on baptism and explaining "to him the way of God more adequately" (Acts 18:26).

Now they are back in Rome, possibly for several reasons: to renew their business there, to enter once more into the life of the church in Rome (including using their home for a house church), and possibly to help spearhead Paul's visit as well as Rome's entering into partnership with him on his next mission. In commending them, Paul says, "they risked their lives for me" (v. 4), probably meaning that at some point they used their status and influence to help him, possibly saving his life at risk of their own. The most likely occasion was during the riot at Ephesus a year earlier (Acts 19:23-41).

He adds, "Not only I but all the churches of the Gentiles are grateful to them." This could mean for saving Paul, but I think it is for the significant ministry they conducted on behalf of Christ for those several years in Corinth, Ephesus, and Rome.

(2) *Their house church* (v. 5a). Paul adds, "Greet also the church that meets at their house" (v. 5a). It seems likely their house hosted a church before they had been expelled from Rome, and this could be the same house. It may have been one of the more prestigious house churches at Rome. Paul may have been intending to join this congregation when he arrived there.

(3) *My dear friend Epinetus* (v. 5b). Paul could have been especially close friends with Epinetus, though he is quite positive in all the greetings. As the first convert (the Greek is literally translated "firstfruits") in the province of Asia, he was most likely a convert under the ministry of Priscilla and Aquila. Paul had left them in Ephesus to begin the ministry there while he completed the second missionary journey, going to Jerusalem and then returning to Antioch and then Ephesus (Acts 18:19-19:1). It may be that

after a successful ministry in Ephesus, he accompanied Priscilla and Aquila to Rome.

(4) *Mary* (v. 6). Mary was probably a Jewish Christian, though at times Gentiles also took this name. We have no idea if this is any of the other Marys named in the New Testament (for instance, the mother of Jesus, Mary Magdalene, Mary the sister of Lazarus). It seems likely that Paul would have certainly said more if this was a Mary who had known Jesus. The same is true if this were Mary the mother of John Mark who wrote the second Gospel, and whose home was one of the earliest house churches in Jerusalem (Acts 12:12). She is probably a previously unknown Mary. Paul says that she "worked very hard for you," making her a longtime leader of the Roman church and a hard worker for the Lord. The term "work" doesn't indicate any particular ministry but indicates she was a tireless laborer. Still, since she is the first described this way (cf. v. 12), she obviously played an important role in the life of the church there.

(5) *Andronicus and Junia* (v. 7). These are Paul's "fellow Jews" mentioned only here but with great stature in the early church. The Greek is *syngeneis*, translated by some as his "relatives" but more likely referring to "kinsfolk" or "fellow Jews" (as in the NIV). "Andronicus" is a **Hellenistic** Jewish name, but "Junia" (Greek *Iounian*) is quite debated, for it could be either the masculine "Junias" or the feminine "Junia" depending on how the Greek term is accented. Until the twelfth century the feminine was preferred, and then from the twelfth to the middle of the twentieth century the masculine was the choice. However, in recent years the feminine form has again been strongly preferred, as Junia was much more common than Junias for this particular form. This means they were a husband-and-wife team similar to Priscilla and Aquila.

Paul describes them as "fellow Jews who have been in prison with me." The only recorded prison incident before Romans was written was in Philippi (Acts 16:24–34), but 2 Corinthians 11:23 says

Paul had been in prison "frequently," and it was written near the time of Romans. Many also believe Paul had been imprisoned in Ephesus. Though Luke doesn't ever say this in Acts 19, it is possibly indicated in 1 Corinthians 15:32 and 2 Corinthians 1:8–9. If true, that would provide a plausible occasion. The post–New Testament letter 1 Clement says there were seven imprisonments in all (5:6), but we don't know which one this refers to. Two further possibilities are worth a mention: first, this could be metaphorical, indicating they were "prisoners of the Lord," but this does not really fit the context here. Second, it could mean they were imprisoned like Paul was, rather than in prison with him. This is a viable possibility, but there is no way to know for sure. In the context, I prefer to see this as a time in prison with him, as all the greetings describe concrete, literal situations.

He next commends them as "outstanding among the apostles," and this too is debated. The preposition is *en*, which could mean they were esteemed "by" the apostles (meaning they were treasured workers) or "among" the apostles (meaning they were apostles). While "by" is technically possible, the general consensus is that "among the apostles" is the superior translation. They were likely two of the group of apostles named in 1 Corinthians 15:5, 7 (Jesus appeared to the Twelve and later "to all the apostles").

Still, it is difficult to know what level of meaning for "apostle" Paul indicates in 1 Corinthians 15:7 and here. There are the Twelve, along with Paul and Barnabas and a few others, and there is also a use of "apostle" for wandering missionaries and official church representatives. This is the thrust in 2 Corinthians 8:23 and Philippians 2:25, where the NIV translates the term "representatives" and "messenger," respectively.[4] Most believe that is the meaning here. Even if this is the case, this would still constitute an office in the early church, and Junia along with her husband is an "outstanding" example of such a leader.

---

4. This is also the sense in the second-century work Didache 11:3–6.

Finally, they were "in Christ before [Paul] was," meaning they had been converted before him. If they were among the "apostles" of 1 Corinthians 15:7, that would mean they had been followers of the Lord himself. They also could have been among the Hellenistic Jewish Christians expelled from Jerusalem in the persecution of Acts 8:1-3. That would mean they had been leaders in the church for some time.

Friends and acquaintances of Paul (16:8-15)

Here Paul lists some in the Roman church he had either known or heard about. With the exception of Urbanus in verse 9, they are not described as leaders.

(1) *Ampliatus* (v. 8). Ampliatus is a name used for slaves or freedmen. Paul calls him a "dear friend" (Greek: "my beloved," see also v. 5b) "in the Lord." He may have been the Ampliatus named on the tomb of Domitilla, the niece of the emperor Domitian. If so, he was highly esteemed in society as well as the church.

(2) *Urbanus* (v. 9a). Urbanus is another slave name, and like Ampliatus he may have been a member of the imperial household. As a "co-worker" of Paul's, he would also be a leader in the church of Rome.

(3) *Stachys* (v. 9b). We know nothing about Stachys, though he was probably also a slave in the imperial household.

(4) *Apelles* (v. 10a). Apelles is another we know nothing about, though he is described as one "whose fidelity to Christ has stood the test." The Greek simply has *dokimon en Christō*; the term *dokimon* means to be "tested and approved" by a trial of the faith. We don't know the circumstances that led Paul to call him this, but it must have been well known in the Roman church.

(5) *The household of Aristobulus* (v. 10b). Aristobulus is a fairly common name, but it is generally agreed among commentators that this is the Aristobulus who was the brother of Herod Agrippa I and a grandson of Herod the Great. He would have accompanied his brother as a hostage and lived in Rome with his brother.

Agrippa died in AD 44 and Aristobulus in AD 48–49. He was not a believer, but many in his household that remained in Rome after his death were Christians. Paul is greeting them here.

(6) *Herodion* (v. 11a). Paul is linking the two connected with the Herods; next he greets Herodion, whom he calls (as in v. 7) a "kinsman" or "fellow Jew." He was a slave or freedman in Herod's family. Slaves often took the name of their owner or patron, especially if they were foreigners.

(7) *The household of Narcissus* (v. 11b). Paul is not greeting the whole household but those in it who are "in the Lord." Most interpreters believe this is that wealthy and prominent Narcissus who was an aide to the emperor Claudius. When Nero became emperor in AD 54, his mother Agrippina conducted a purge, and Narcissus was forced to commit suicide. The household would have become part of the imperial family but allowed to retain the name.

(8) *Tryphena and Tryphosa* (v. 12a). From their names, we know these two women are also slaves or freedwomen. They were likely sisters and perhaps twins, since in the ancient world parents often gave siblings and especially twins names from the same root, as people do today. The names mean "dainty" and "delicate," respectively. Paul describes them as "women who work hard in the Lord," similar to verse 6, perhaps indicating they had the gift of helps.

(9) *Persis* (v. 12b). Another slave or freedwoman, Persis means "Persian woman," perhaps indicating her country of origin. Her greeting is unusual in that she has a double commendation, combining the "beloved" of verses 5 and 8 with the "worked hard in the Lord" of verses 6, 12a. Moreover, Paul says she worked "*very* hard," possibly meaning she was a tireless worker and an outstanding leader in the church (like Mary in v. 6).

(10) *Rufus* (v. 13a). It is likely (though it can't be proved) that this is the Rufus of Mark 15:21, which says of Simon of Cyrene, the man who bore Jesus' cross, that he was "the father of Alexander and Rufus." Mark's naming his sons means they were well

known to his readers. Since most believe that the Gospel of Mark was written in Rome, that would indicate Alexander and Rufus were prominent Christian leaders there. Paul calls him "chosen in the Lord" here, which could indicate he was greatly respected but more likely has its usual meaning describing him as one of the Lord's elect. Either way, it refers to the great respect he had in the Roman church.

(11) *Rufus's mother* (v. 13b). Paul describes her as "his mother and mine" (NIV "who has been a mother to me, too"). This could refer to special motherly affection she had shown Paul at some point. He may have stayed with their family in Jerusalem, or she may have been a frequent traveler who met Paul on her trips. We do not know, but Paul is stressing a close personal affection between them.

(12) *Asyncritus, Phlegon, Hermes, Patrobas, Hermas and the other brothers and sisters with them* (v. 14). Like most of the names above, these were names used for slaves or freedmen and possibly leaders of a house church. Paul's added "and the other brothers and sisters with them" shows that Paul's emphasis here is not on the individuals but the house church of which they are a part. We don't know Paul's connection with this church. The link could be with one of Paul's team as well as with Paul himself.

(13) *Philologus, Julia, Nereus and his sister* (v. 15a). This might well be a single family, with the father Philologus, his wife Julia, and their children Nereus and his sister (Paul probably did not know her name). On the other hand, these could be four siblings. We do not know. The first option seems better, with this being a family who are patrons of a house church.

(14) *Olympus and all the Lord's people who are with them* (v. 15b). If Philologus and Julia are patrons of a house church, these likely constitute the church that met in their home. Olympus was a leader in that church, with "the saints" (NIV "the Lord's people") being its members.

A call for general greetings (16:16)

The greetings to people and house churches in the Roman church whom Paul knew are now complete, so he concludes this section with a general request for everyone in Rome to "greet one another with a holy kiss." This was a request in many of his letters (1 Cor 16:20; 2 Cor 13:12; 1 Thess 5:26). Such a greeting was common throughout the ancient world, and in Jewish circles in particular, as kissing was a sign of great affection and friendship.

Several interpreters think the kiss here was part of a worship service in which the letter was read and followed with a "holy kiss" that came between the prayers and the Eucharist. It signified love, honor, and respect between the people, and stressed the solemnity and spiritual significance of the greeting. Tertullian called it the "kiss of peace," but it is wrong to translate it that way here (as in the NEB), for in our day it signifies a loving, Christian greeting.

When Paul adds, "All the churches of Christ send greetings," he is clearly using hyperbole, for he must mean all the churches established as part of his mission. He wants the church of Rome to be more closely connected to those churches that are part of his apostolic circle. It also tells them that there are churches everywhere that are involved with him, and his hope is that the Roman churches join that growing number.

PAUL WARNS THEM ABOUT FALSE TEACHERS (16:17-20)

This is quite similar to Paul's warning in Acts 20:29-31, where he tells the Ephesian elders, "savage wolves will come in among you and will not spare the flock." Here too the warning comes in the form of a prophecy of evil teachers before they appear. The strange thing is that he has not said a thing in the letter thus far about heretical movements or teachers. Some therefore think this was not originally part of the letter, but there is no evidence for its being a later addition, and such general warnings do occasionally appear (1 Cor 16:13-14; 2 Cor 13:11). He may have heard that some false teachers were on their way to Rome, or he is aware of their presence in other churches (2 Cor 10:13) and wants the church to be ready at all times.

It is unclear exactly what group Paul has in mind. He centers more on the type of people they are—divisive, self-centered, using flattery to gain followers, countering gospel truth. Three different groups have been suggested:

1. Proto-Gnostics. These would have associated salvation with the possession of secret knowledge (like the opponents in 1 John), but their theology had not developed into the full-blown Gnosticism of the second century.
2. Judaizers. These would have associated salvation with obeying the law (like the opponents in Galatians and Philippians 3).
3. The strong and weak parties at Rome (see 14:1–15:13).

The third is not a heresy, but the other two are possibilities. Still, Paul may not have in mind a particular group at all but wants to give a general warning to be alert and ready for whatever comes.

KEEP AWAY FROM DIVISIVE LEADERS (16:17)

Paul "urges" or "exhorts" (see 12:1) those he calls "brothers and sisters" to stress his close relationship with them. He commands them to "watch out" or "be alert," calling for spiritual vigilance so they will recognize false teachers when they arrive. They can come at any time, and they are exceedingly dangerous. This is a warning sign posted along a trail: "Warning—rattlesnakes! Be on the alert!"

Paul's description is like telling people to watch and listen for the rattler; these are the characteristics that will enable the Romans to identify them soon after they arrive: (1) they "cause divisions" or dissension in the community. Their teaching is divisive and they cause church splits wherever they go. (2) They also put "obstacles" or stumbling blocks in front of believers that cause them to fall away from the Lord. As stated in 9:33 and 11:9, these

people are part of cosmic forces that destroy people's faith and
can lead to apostasy.

Heresy is not merely error but actually destroys people's faith.
Paul emphasizes this here in his added comment that it is especially "contrary to the teaching you have learned." It contradicts
the cardinal doctrines of the Christian faith. Heresy is not a discussion of issues like eternal security or the timing of the rapture of the church but an attack on central tenets like the deity of
Christ or the cross as the basis of our salvation.

The only valid response is to "keep away from them." This is
a lot more than just avoiding them, as that would indicate a bit of
tolerance for them like that discussed in the section on the weak
and the strong in 14:1–15:13. This command demands direct and
active opposition, involving both censure and discipline. It could
infer a type of excommunication like that found in Matthew 18:17,
"treat them as you would a pagan or a tax collector," or 2 Thessalonians 3:14, "do not associate with them." Such discipline should
be done gently, with the purpose of bringing them to repentance
(2 Tim 2:24–26), but it still should be firm. The goal is not primarily to remove them from the church (though in serious cases that
is indeed a part of it), but to wake them up and help them both to
get right with the Lord and to straighten out their theology.

THEIR SELF-SERVING ATTITUDE (16:18)

The reason (*gar*, "for") the Romans must respond so strongly to
the very presence of false teachers in the church is that they "are
not serving our Lord Christ, but their own appetites" (literally
"their own bellies"). This is similar to Philippians 3:19, "Their god
is their stomach." Some interpreters think this refers literally to
people who live gluttonous and greedy lifestyles, or to people with
a Jewish background centering on the food laws (as in chapter 14).
But it is much better to see this as describing people with a greedy,
self-centered ministry that serves their own interests rather than
the Lord's. Paul's statement that they are not serving "our Lord

Christ" makes it clear that the sovereign power in charge does not come from the secular world, nor from the teachers themselves, but entirely from Christ, the Lord of all. So long as these teachers serve only their own interests, they are headed for disaster.

Another reason they must oppose these false teachers is that they are not teaching the substantive and life-changing truths of God's word but "smooth talk and flattery" by which they "deceive the minds of naive people." Satan is the great deceiver (Rev 12:9; 20:3), and Paul will make the connection with Satan in verse 20. Paul had spoken of deception in 7:11, "sin ... deceived me, and through the commandment put me to death."

These heretics manipulate truth to suck in the foolish or simple-minded. As in Ephesians 4:14, these are spiritual infants who fail to understand the deep things of God and are easily led astray by the eloquence and high-sounding promises of false teachers. They are unable to distinguish between flattery and truth. What the false teachers say appeals to their egos and sounds so plausible and convincing that they are drawn in by half-truths. This is why it is so easy for a David Koresh (Waco, Texas) or a Jim Jones (Guyana) to find adherents.

I once wrote an article on why cults seem to draw so many of their followers from evangelical churches.[5] One reason is the lack of true fellowship and caring in too many churches, and another is the lack of theological awareness and knowledge of what the Bible means. When naive people hear false teachers twisting Scripture, they cannot tell that God's truths are being compromised. Church leaders must deliberately develop Christians who search the Scriptures daily to see if these things are true (Acts 17:11). We need Bible studies in our churches to help our people treasure the truths of God and recognize when they are being twisted. We need groups that make studying the Bible exciting and interesting. We need

5. Grant Osborne, "Countering the Cultic Curse," *Christianity Today*, June 29, 1979, 22–23.

preachers who proclaim the word of God and its meaning and relevance for our lives. Then people will know when it is being misused, and will be less susceptible to "smooth talk and flattery."

THE NEED FOR WISDOM AND INNOCENCE (16:19)

In contrast to these evil teachers, the Roman Christians are widely known ("everyone has heard") for their "obedience." The heretics wreak havoc and bring dissension, but the saints in Rome are known for following the Lord, so Paul "rejoices" over them. He is confident that they will more than meet the challenge of these heretics. The point seems to be that if they are truly obedient to God and his word, they will have to shun the false teachers. They are known for their doctrinal purity, and that will spur them to be even more vigilant in protecting their reputation.

The way they will protect their church is to be "wise about what is good, and innocent about what is evil." There is a play on words, with near synonyms between "naive" in verse 18 and "innocent" in verse 19: be innocent about things, especially teaching that is evil, but do not descend to naïveté or simple-minded gullibility to those false ideas. Learn how to discern good from evil, not only with respect to ethical conduct but also with respect to theological truth.

This tells us how important the teaching ministry of the church is. Preoccupation with trivial pursuits is incredibly dangerous, for the loss of theological concern is the first step to the destruction of the vitality of the church. Sometimes churches feel that dogma is boring and that they ought to focus on all kinds of innovative programs that have no basis in biblical truth. Now, theology *can* be boring. But if that is so, it is the teacher that is boring, not the truths themselves. When the good is mingled with wisdom, it is life-changing, as in Matthew 10:16, "be as shrewd as snakes and as innocent as doves."

THE ESCHATOLOGICAL PROMISE (16:20A)

There is a debate as to whether Paul's promise that "the God of peace will soon crush Satan under your feet" is general (promising the church victory over the cosmic forces of evil in every area) or specific (relating to victory over the false teachers). As is so often the case, it is a false debate, for the defeat of the heretics will be a specific area of the universal triumph God's people will have over Satan.

This verse also relates to the issue of the strong versus the weak in 14:1–15:13. The emphasis there is on the discord caused by the infighting among the two groups, and Paul here calls God "the God of peace," a title he will use in the doxology of 15:33 and that is closely connected to his plea for peace in 14:17, 19. The promise that Satan will soon be crushed is an allusion to the *protevangelium* (first gospel) of Genesis 3:15, the cursing of the serpent, "he will crush your head, and you will strike his heel." Paul sees the false teachers as emissaries of Satan and is stating that their power and influence are both temporary and doomed. The demonic inspiration of heretics is a common motif in Paul's writings, as in 1 Timothy 4:1, "in later times some will abandon the faith and follow deceiving spirits and things taught by demons." John also links the two in 1 John 2:18, "as you have heard that the antichrist is coming, even now many antichrists have come."

At the same time, there is stress on the tension between the already and the not yet seen so often in Romans (for instance, 8:18, 23, 30). The crushing of Satan has already begun in spiritual warfare, but the battle will not be finished until the **eschaton**, or end of all things, when Satan will be first bound (Rev 20:3) and then thrown into the lake of fire (Rev 20:10). The Jewish understanding was that God and his angelic army would defeat the serpent or dragon, Satan (Testament of Simeon 6:6; Testament of Levi 18:12; see 1 Enoch 54:6), a view found in Revelation 12:7–9, in which the archangel Michael and the angels cast Satan and his fallen angels out of heaven.

Paul is saying that Satan can be defeated now when the pernicious teaching of false teachers is exposed and they are put under church discipline. The "crushing" of Satan sees this defeat of heretics as a fulfillment of the promise in Genesis 3:15. This present defeat also anticipates the final defeat of Satan and the forces of evil at the end of history. This great victory will take place soon, the same view of imminence seen in 13:12—"the day is almost here."

PAUL PROVIDES A CLOSING BENEDICTION (16:20B)

Paul provides a prayer-wish at the end of every letter, and here it reads, "The grace of our Lord Jesus be with you." Grace could be called the central tenet of the letter as a whole, for our salvation is the result of the grace of God leading him to send his Son to die on the cross so that our sins could be forgiven. This is the same grace of God and of Christ that formed the initial greeting (1:7), and Paul is now praying that this grace might continue in the lives of the Roman Christians. Only in Christ can his readers experience the peace and victory over Satan that is theirs by divine right.

PAUL SENDS GREETINGS FROM HIS COWORKERS IN CORINTH (16:21-23)

In verses 3-16 Paul sent greetings *to* the leaders in Rome. Now in verses 21-23 he sends greetings *from* leaders in Corinth. This is found in many of his letters. The names here are those of team members who are with him in Corinth in Acts 20:2-3 at the end of his third missionary journey, along with a few of the leaders of the church there.

(1) *Timothy* joined Paul's team on the second missionary journey while he was still a young man in Lystra (Acts 16:1). He later became one of Paul's most trusted lieutenants. Paul had sent him to Corinth from Ephesus (1 Cor 4:17; 16:10-11), most likely constituting the Macedonian trip of Acts 19:22. Timothy returned before

2 Corinthians was written (2 Cor 1:1) but accompanied Paul back to Corinth for the trip here in Acts 20:1–3. Later he would be sent to Philippi (Phil 2:9–14), where Paul first went when he was released from prison, and then to Ephesus (1–2 Timothy), where Paul was arrested and imprisoned for the final time.

(2) *Lucius, Jason, and Sosipater* are fellow Jewish Christians (see comments on v. 7). Lucius could be Luke, Paul's coworker and the author of Luke-Acts, or perhaps "Lucius of Cyrene," the prophet from Syrian Antioch (Acts 13:1). There is no way to be sure. Jason could be the one whose home Paul stayed in in Thessalonica (Acts 17:5–9), and Sosipater may well be the same as Sopater, the representative of the Berean church who accompanied the collection for the poor when Paul left Greece shortly after this letter was penned (Acts 20:4).

(3) *Tertius* is the secretary who "wrote down this letter" as Paul dictated it. Paul's poor eyesight meant he could not pen his letters himself and had to depend on others (Gal 6:11; 1 Cor 16:21; 2 Thess 3:17). There are three levels at which such an **amanuensis**, or secretary, functioned in the ancient world—total freedom to write the letter; guidance as to what should be said but freedom to use his own words at times; and pure dictation. The similarity of style in Galatians, Romans, and Corinthians likely means Tertius dictated these. A greeting from such a person is unusual but not unheard of. He likely knew some of the saints in Rome.

(4) *Gaius* is the Gaius of 1 Corinthians 1:14, one of the two converts baptized in Corinth, since Paul wrote Romans from there. This is more likely than the Gaius of either Acts 19:29; 20:4 or of 3 John 1. This could be the same person as the Titius Justus (full name Gaius Titius Justus) who hosted Paul in Corinth after he left the synagogue in Acts 18:7. He was probably the designated host to travelers passing through Corinth on behalf of the church, and so Paul stayed there while writing this letter.

(5) *Erastus* was an important official, the "steward" (*oikonomos*) or treasurer of the entire city. He is evidence that the church was

not entirely made up of the poor but contained many high officials (compare the Roman proconsul Sergius Paulus of Acts 13:6-12). It is possible that he is the team member sent from Ephesus to Macedonia in Acts 19:22 (see also 2 Tim 4:20), but it is hard to see a high city official having time to do such things. Many scholars link him with an inscription in Corinth of a wealthy donor who paid for a marble pavement so he could be promoted to "aedile," or commissioner of public works, for a year (thus the NIV translation "director of public works"). This is a real possibility and would fit here well.

(6) *Quartus* we know little about. Calling him "our brother" does not mean he is literally Erastus's or Tertius's brother but simply that he is a Christian brother in the Lord.

Some ancient manuscripts (labeled "western manuscripts" because they originated in western parts of the church—Codex Bezae and a few others) have included a prayer-wish that has been followed by the King James Version, making it verse 24: "May the grace of our Lord Jesus Christ be with all of you. Amen." However, this verse is missing in nearly all of the older and better manuscripts (Codex Sinaiticus, Codex Vaticanus, and many others). It was almost certainly added later, so in most versions verse 24 is omitted and the text goes straight to verse 25.

PAUL WRITES A CONCLUDING DOXOLOGY (16:25-27)

This is a longer doxology than usual; Paul uses it to summarize the implications of the gospel and recapitulate the central motifs of the letter. It is quite similar to 1:1-7, thus framing the letter with the theme of the revelation of God's salvation in Christ Jesus. The Roman Christians are to rejoice in all God has done for them and pledge themselves anew to serving him with all they have as he strengthens them in his salvation.

There is considerable difference of opinion as to whether and where this doxology should be added to Romans. Some think Paul never wrote it and it was added by a later editor, but it is too widely present in the manuscripts for that. It is found after 16:23 in the older manuscripts like Codices Sinaiticus, Vaticanus, Ephraemi, and even Bezae along with a couple older and reliable papyri, and most who doubt it do so on the basis of its so-called non-Pauline character, arguing that phrases like "hidden for long ages past" or "the eternal God" are unlike Paul. However, in reality the language does resemble the introduction in 1:1–17. It fits Romans well as placed here to frame the letter with these themes.

ATTRIBUTION TO GOD (16:25A)

This begins the same way as the doxology in Ephesians 3:20, "Now to him who is able to," noting that God alone has the power (*dynamai*, "able to" = "has the strength to") to perform mighty deeds. The first assertion, "him who is able to establish you," also means "able to strengthen" (*stērixai* = "establish, strengthen"), implying that the Christian's strength is completely grounded in his strength. This could be translated "strengthen and establish," for both are part of its meaning here. We have the spiritual strength to anchor ourselves in Christ only through his empowering presence in us. This is the strength to live the Christian life and to understand and apply the revelation of divine truth in his word (v. 26a).

The basis of this strength is "my gospel, the message I proclaim about Jesus Christ." In other words, the gospel can be defined as proclaiming Christ (as Savior and Lord). The source of strength for serving the Lord is found in the gospel, which is the core of Paul's preaching, and the gospel is grounded in the message about Christ. This was of course the teaching in 3:21–8:39, where Paul provided in-depth coverage of the gospel. The Greek "proclamation of Jesus Christ" is better "preaching *about* Jesus" than "preaching *by* Jesus," for in this context Paul is summarizing the content of the gospel rather than its origin in Christ's teaching ministry.

BASIS: REVELATION OF THE HIDDEN MYSTERY (16:25B–26A)

Paul further defines the gospel as "in keeping with the revelation of the mystery hidden for long ages past." In the gospel God has made known his hidden mystery. As seen in the comments on 11:25, a mystery is a salvation-historical event that was unknown before but is now revealed to God's people. This is apocalyptic language, with "revelation" (*apokalypsis*) the process and "mystery" (*mystērion*) the content of what is revealed.

This mystery is Jesus Christ himself, further described in three ways:

(1) He is "hidden for long ages past," meaning that full understanding of him was not given to Israel in the past. They knew their Messiah was coming but little more. They constantly speculated about the details. First Peter 1:10–11 says it well, as the prophets "searched intently and with the greatest care, trying to find out the time and circumstances to which the Spirit of Christ in them was pointing when he predicted the sufferings of the Messiah and the glories that would follow." They only knew partway what was to come and longed to have the full reality.

(2) He is "now revealed and made known through the prophetic writings" (v. 26a). Note the seeming contradiction in saying the revelation is hidden and yet revealed in the prophecies. This is in fact the case, with a part "revealed and made known" but a great amount concealed until Christ actually appeared. For instance, the Jewish people expected a conquering King rather than a suffering Servant in spite of Isaiah 52–53. In addition, the Abrahamic covenant said all the nations would be blessed, but the Jewish people never understood or accepted that the Gentiles were to have a special place among the covenant people.

(3) He has come "by the command of the eternal God." It is the divine will that underlies this new uncovering of the mystery, and it has come to pass as a result of the divine decree. He is "the eternal God," and this means the uncovering of this essential

truth for salvation was part of God's plan before this world began (Eph 1:4; Heb 4:3).

PURPOSE: ALL NATIONS BELIEVE (16:26B)

God is doing all this "so that all the Gentiles might come to the obedience that comes from faith." This is a major theme throughout this letter. *Ethnē* means both "Gentiles" and "nations," and both fit equally well here. Christ has come for all nations and peoples, and both Jew and Gentile stand before him as sinners in need of the grace and mercy of God. Christ died for all humankind, and the new covenant era he introduced has united Jew and Gentile into one body, the new Israel. Justification by faith has brought all humanity, every nation, together into one. This is Paul's purpose in 1:5, "to call all the Gentiles to the obedience that comes from faith for his name's sake."

Paul emphasizes the moral and ethical side of salvation throughout Romans. To put your faith in Christ is to live for him. There are three interdependent aspects of justification language: we are declared right by the redemptive work of Christ; we are made right by the sanctifying work of the Spirit; and then we live rightly by the strength supplied by the Triune Godhead. Justification is the first moment of sanctification, and that launches our walk with Christ. Right belief leads to right standing with God, which produces right living for God.

CLOSING WORSHIP (16:27)

The letter closes with praise: "to the only wise God be glory forever through Jesus Christ! Amen." This could be understood as referring to two of God's attributes ("the only and wise God"), but all translations take the phrase as one idea, "the only wise God," meaning that only God is wise. In 11:33 Paul meditated on "the depth of the riches of the wisdom and knowledge of God." Throughout Scripture divine wisdom is one of the most frequent topics, particularly the wisdom of his creation work and his plan of salvation.

Wisdom in Paul's writings is similar to wisdom in Proverbs, where it means living life in God's world on the basis of God's rules. In 1 Corinthians 1:17–2:16 and 3:18–20 he contrasts the wisdom of God with the so-called wisdom of the world that is actually foolishness. The point is that God alone is wise, and his people will only find wisdom in him.

The only way to end this letter is to ascribe glory only to God and to recognize it is his forever. Eternity can be summed up with the praise-cry, "Glory be to God!" He deserves eternal praise. As the Westminster Shorter Catechism says, God created us "to glorify him and enjoy him forever." It is our sacred privilege to give him the glory that is his for all eternity.

This is how Revelation 7:15 pictures our eternal destiny: we will stand "before the throne of God and serve him day and night in his temple" (also 22:3). Heaven in one sense will be an eternal worship service, with the mind-blowing difference that Father, Son, and Spirit will be completely present. Moses could not look on God and live (Exod 33:20; John 1:18), but we will look on his face for all eternity and rejoice!

This praise is only possible "through Jesus Christ." This provides a fitting end to this letter, which dwells on the fact that all salvation is possibly only through Christ and the cross. It was his act of love (5:8), his atoning sacrifice (3:25), that has brought all this about, and our faith in him (3:21–4:25) that brings us justification to eternal life (4:25; 6:23).

As the old saying goes, "You can't have too many friends." That was definitely the case for Paul, as this closing greeting shows. I think Paul must have been an extrovert, judging from the number of people he could name as friends and coworkers. It is surprising how many he could name in a city he had never visited.

The purpose of Paul's greeting is to show the people of the Roman church that even though he had never visited, he was highly involved with their church through his many friends there. Many who read the list today might get bored and wonder if there is anything of value in this type of material. There is, but it may need to be packed in the right way. In a series of sermons or lessons you would not take each name and do a commentary-like listing of each one, but you could group names under topics—for instance, use the nine women as examples of the significant difference women can make in our churches (they are not meant only for the nursery or the hospitality ministry).

Or you could take this material and teach on the important place the poor can have in God's work, looking at the number of slaves and freedmen in ministerial positions in Rome. You could also teach on the place of wealthy Christians in the life of the church through those names here. Finally, many of those Paul names are described in detail, and it could be helpful to use those like Phoebe, Priscilla and Aquila, Andronicus and Junia, Rufus, Timothy, and others as models for our lives.

In the midst of this greeting, Paul inserts a warning against false teachers (vv. 17-20). Then and now countless Christians are being led astray by twisted teaching and preaching that promotes the preacher rather than God. These destructive movements are more numerous today than ever before, and we desperately need both teachers and ministries that draw people into God's word rather than use people to line the pockets of megastar preachers. Bible-based and Spirit-inspired wisdom is the need in our time as well as Paul's. In spite of the prevalence of false teachers, we can be filled with hope, for Paul promises ultimate victory over them and their demonically induced teaching. It is doomed, and our victory is sure.

Finally, the doxology (vv. 25-27) produces a wonderful closing with a perfect culmination to the truths we have encountered in this letter. We find strength to emerge from the battle victorious from the revealed truths of God. His hidden truths have been revealed, and his power has been made available to his people in the church. The goal of all this is for God's salvation to bring about faith and draw together a united church that lives entirely for Christ. The end result of all this is worship, and we exist to bring glory to God and enjoy his salvation every moment of our lives.

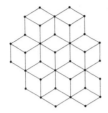

GLOSSARY

amanuensis A scribe or secretary hired to write letters in the ancient world.

chiasm (n.), chiastic (adj.) A stylistic device in which a passage is organized into two sections, with the contents of the statements in the first half repeated in reverse order in the second half (ABC:C′B′A′).

christological (adj.), Christology (n.) Refers to the New Testament's presentation of the person and work of Christ, especially his identity as Messiah.

eschatological (adj.), eschatology (n.) Refers to the last things or the end times. Within this broad category, biblical scholars and theologians have identified more specific concepts. For instance, "realized eschatology" emphasizes the present work of Christ in the world as he prepares for the end of history. In "inaugurated eschatology," the last days have already begun but have not yet been consummated at the return of Christ.

eschaton Greek for "end" or "last," referring to the return of Christ and the end of history.

Hellenism (n.), Hellenistic (adj.) Relates to the spread of Greek culture in the Mediterranean world after the conquests of Alexander the Great (356–323 BC).

inclusio A framing device in which the same word or phrase occurs at both the beginning and the end of a section of text.

lex talionis Latin for "law of retaliation." This is the principle that those who have done some wrong will be punished in a similar degree and kind.

parousia The event of Christ's second coming. The Greek word *parousia* means "arrival" or "presence."

Septuagint An ancient Greek translation of the Old Testament that was used extensively in the early church.

Shekinah A word derived from the Hebrew *shakan* (to dwell), used to describe God's personal presence taking the form of a cloud, often in the context of the tabernacle or temple (e.g., Exod 40:38; Num 9:15; 1 Kgs 8:10–11).

soteriological (adj.), soteriology (n.) Relating to the doctrine of salvation (Greek: *sōtēria*), including such subjects as atonement, justification, and sanctification.

typology A literary device in which Old Testament persons or events are the types that correspond to and are fulfilled in New Testament realities.

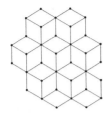

BIBLIOGRAPHY

Achtemeier, Paul J. *Romans*. Interpretation. Atlanta: John Knox, 1985.

Barrett, C. K. *The Epistle to the Romans*. Black's New Testament Commentary. London: Continuum, 1991.

Black, Matthew. *Romans*. New Century Commentary. London: Oliphants, 1973.

Bruce, F. F. *The Epistle of Paul to the Romans*. Tyndale New Testament Commentaries. Grand Rapids: Eerdmans, 1985.

Calvin, John. *Commentary on the Epistle of Paul to the Romans*. Grand Rapids: Baker, 1979 (originally 1540).

Fitzmyer, Joseph A. *Romans*. Anchor Bible. New York: Doubleday, 1993.

Hughes, R. Kent. *Romans: Righteousness from Heaven*. Preaching the Word. Wheaton, IL: Crossway, 1991.

Jewett, Robert. *Romans*. Hermeneia. Minneapolis: Fortress, 2007.

————. *Romans: A Shorter Commentary*. Minneapolis: Fortress, 2013.

Longenecker, Richard. *The Epistle to the Romans*. New International Greek Testament Commentary. Grand Rapids: Eerdmans, 2016.

Moo, Douglas J. *The Epistle to the Romans*. New International Commentary on the New Testament. Grand Rapids: Eerdmans, 1996.

Morris, Leon. *The Epistle to the Romans.* Pillar New Testament Commentary. Grand Rapids: Eerdmans, 1988.

Murray, John. *The Epistle to the Romans.* New International Commentary on the New Testament. Grand Rapids: Eerdmans, 1968.

Sanday, William, and Arthur C. Headlam. *A Critical and Exegetical Commentary on the Epistle of the Romans.* 3rd ed. International Critical Commentary. New York: Scribner's Sons, 1897.

Schreiner, Thomas R. *Romans.* Baker Exegetical Commentary on the New Testament. Grand Rapids: Baker Academic, 1998.

Stott, John R. W. *Romans: God's Good News for the World.* Downers Grove, IL: InterVarsity Press, 1994.

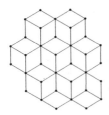

SUBJECT AND AUTHOR INDEX

Jews as, 366
love of, 397–98
enthronement, of Jesus, 22
envy, 48
Ephaphroditus, 496
Ephesus
Paul in, 2, 264, 485–86, 500–02
and Romans, 9
Timothy in, 512–13
epignōsis, 306
Epinetus, 500–01
equality, of Jews and Gentiles, 76
Erastus, 513–14
eritheia, 60
Esau, 287
vs. Jacob, 282–85
eschatology, inaugurated. *See*
already/not yet
ethics, biblical, 57–58
euchomai, 273
eudokia, 304
euschēmonōs, 421–22
evangelism, 35–36
and discipleship, 23–24, 29–30
Eve, 40–42, 202
everyone, and the gospel, 316–17
evil
for evil, 400–03
and God's sovereignty, 329
hatred for, 392–93
law of, 214–15
overcoming, 404–05
evildoers, and government,
411–12
exaltation, of Christ, 262, 313–14
example, of Adam, 148
exchanges, of depraved
humankind, 41–51
excommunication, 508
excuse, without, 40–41, 54, 326
exhortation, 378–79, 387–88, 507

exodus, the, and God's power,
288–89
exomologeō, 439
expectation
of believers, 245
of creation, 240–43
expiation, 101–02
expulsion, of the Jews, 5, 408,
427, 499
eyes, darkening of, 339–40

F
failure
of Israel, 272–74, 339
moral, 211
of the weak, 456–57
fairness
of God's judgment, 58–61
of Roman justice, 413
faith
alone, 111–32
and atonement, 102
and "calling on" the Lord, 320
in Christ, 98–99
and hope, 469
and justification, 100,
105–09, 254–55
and the law, 107–09
measure of, 383–84
and obedience, 23, 478
and peace, 135–36
and prayer, 247
and prophecy, 386
and righteousness,
33–35, 300–03
of the Roman church, 25, 28–29
salvation by, 32, 313–18
standing by, 355–56
strong vs. weak, 428–29, 452–53
testing of, 137
word of, 312–13
vs. works, 59, 75, 309–12

genre, of Romans, 8–9
Gentiles
  accountability of, 92–93
  blasphemy of, 73
  and circumcision, 118–19
  depravity of, 41–51
  faith of, 302–03, 517
  forgiveness of, 117
  God as turning to,
      327–28, 344–47
  guilt of, 37–38, 53–54
  as grafted in, 349–57
  and Jews, 5–8, 32, 70–71,
      315–17, 464–68
  vs. Jews, 56, 60–61,
      106–07, 427–28
  and the law, 62–65,
      75–76, 190–91
  mission to, 23–24, 30, 325–26
  in the new community, 294–98
  salvation of, 362–64
gift
  eternal life as, 186–88
  justification as, 100
  of salvation, 113–14, 124, 152–54,
      260, 337
gifts
  covenant, 367
  spiritual, 28–29, 384–89
ginōskō, 326
giving, 388
glorification, of God, 462
glory
  future, 239–44, 293–94
  of God, 42–43, 86, 99, 136–37,
      174, 276–77, 351, 374–75
  as a reward, 59–61
  sharing in, 236
  and suffering, 245, 261
God
  Christ as, 278
  doctrine of, 14

and government, 409–13,
    416, 425
of hope, 469
of peace, 492, 511
God-fearers, 5, 71
God-haters, 49
godlessness, 89
gold, testing of, 138
golden chain, 251–55
good, the, 212–13, 392–93
  working together for, 249–51
goodness
  of the law, 203–04, 208, 211–13
  of the Roman Christians, 475
gospel
  as the core idea, 7–8,
      14–16, 20–23
  and human depravity, 51–52
  and Paul's mission, 19–20,
      27–28, 476–80, 515–16
  preaching of, 320–24, 366
  rejection of, 350–51,
gossip, 49
government, 408–16, 425
grace, 102–03, 152–54, 159–60, 281,
    357–58, 370–71
  common, 184
  as a greeting, 25
  irresistible, 16, 254
  vs. law, 175–76, 179
  prayer-wish for, 512
  realm of, 136
  and the remnant, 336–37
  salvation by, 100, 124
  vs. sin, 156–63
grace-gift, 100, 113, 119, 124,
    151–55, 260, 385
grafting, of the Gentiles, 350–57,
    363–66
graves, open, 89
greed, 48
Greeks, vs, non-Greeks, 30

of Paul, 19-20, 23-24, 29-30
universal, 325-26
model
Abraham as, 111-32
Christ as, 471
David as, 115-16
money, 400
monotheism, 107
Moo, Douglas, 1
Moses, 276, 287-88, 338
and Abraham, 112, 122, 132
and Adam, 159
intercession by, 274
and the Jews, 67
and obedience, 310-11
as a prophet, 20
and sin, 149-50
mother, of Rufus, 505
mourning, with those who
mourn, 398-99
mouth, confession with, 313-14
mystērion, 361, 516
mystery, 347, 361-62, 368, 371-72,
516-17

N
naïveté, 510
Narcissus, household of, 504
nations
faith of, 517
many, 124-27
as worshiping God, 467-68
"natural," 45
nature, divine, 40
neighbor
love for, 418
pleasing, 457-58
Nereus, 505
Nero, 3, 407, 416
and Narcissus, 504
and Paul, 261, 264
persecution by, 398

new perspective, 93-94, 307
night, and behavior, 421-22, 426
Noah, 276
"no way," 83-86. See also *mē*
genoito

O
oath, of Paul, 26
obedience, 180
of Christ, 155-56, 160
and faith, 23, 478
and hearing, 320, 323-24
vs. knowledge, 69
to the law, 63-64, 74-78, 309-10
obligation, to the Spirit, 230
obstinacy, of Israel, 328
offering
Christ as, 223-25
of oneself, 173-78
officials, in the church, 514
oiketēs, 432
oikonomos, 513
Old Testament, 459-60
and the gospel, 20, 34
value of, 81
and worship, 466-68
olives, in the Mediterranean,
349-50
Olympus, 505
omission, sins of, 59
ōphelei, 74
oracles, of God, 81
Origen, 192, 197
orthodoxy, of Paul, 6, 13
overcomers, 405

P
parabasei, 73
parakaleō, 28, 378
paraptōma, 151
paredōken, 43
parents, disobeying, 49

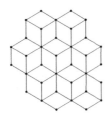

INDEX OF SCRIPTURE AND OTHER ANCIENT LITERATURE

Old Testament

Deuterocanonical Works

Printed and bound by CPI Group (UK) Ltd, Croydon, CR0 4YY

09/06/2025

14685748-0003